THE GOOD LIFE AND OTHER FICTIONS

The Good Life and Other Fictions

DAVID DWAN

PRINCETON UNIVERSITY PRESS
PRINCETON & OXFORD

Published by Princeton University Press
41 William Street, Princeton, New Jersey 08540
99 Banbury Road, Oxford OX2 6JX

press.princeton.edu

GPSR Authorized Representative: Easy Access System Europe - Mustamäe tee 50, 10621 Tallinn, Estonia, gpsr.requests@easproject.com

ISBN 978-0-691-26128-7
ISBN (epub) 978-0-691-29520-6
ISBN (PDF) 978-0-691-29440-7

British Library Cataloging-in-Publication Data is available

Editorial: Ben Tate and Josh Drake
Production Editorial: Jill Harris
Jacket Design: Emily Bluedorn
Production: Danielle Capurso
Publicity: Natalie Zander and Charlotte Coyne
Copyeditor: Leah Caldwell

This book has been composed in Arno

Printed in the United States of America

10 9 8 7 6 5 4 3 2 1

MIX
Paper
FSC FSC® C183721

For Chris, Matt, and Theo

'I *am* real!' said Alice, and began to cry.

—LEWIS CARROLL

CONTENTS

ACKNOWLEDGEMENTS

THE COMPLETION of this book sometimes felt like one of its more improbable fictions. I'm grateful to many friends for helping it into a more factual state. Richard Bourke, Peter Boxall, Stephen Donovan, Renata Dwan, Nick Gaskill, Marina Mackay, Patrick Mackie, Katie Murphy, Adrian Poole, Emma Smith, and Wendy Xin all read chapters and provided insightful comments. Discussions with Charlotte Brewer, Stefano Evangelista, and Jo Kavenna were also fortifying and much appreciated. I'll be forever grateful to Chris Insole and David Russell for reading through the entire manuscript with their characteristic subtlety and imagination, and to Matt Bevis for reading, re-reading, and brilliantly mulling over its vital parts. I owe a significant debt to the readers from Princeton University Press and to all those who helped with the book's production: Jesse Astley, Leah Caldwell, Susan Clark, Jill Harris, and Josh Drake. I am particularly grateful to my editor, Ben Tate, for his encouragement and trust. Huge thanks, too, to Aida Edemariam for her rigorous attention to all aspects of the book and to Rahel Edemariam Dwan for her wise advice about titles. Without these two people around—and the general support of the Dwans and Edemariams—my sense of the good life would feel very unlived. Four of the book's chapters draw on previously published essays, and I'm grateful for the permission to redeploy them here:

'Unlucky Jim: Conrad, Chance, Ethics,' *Journal of Modern Literature* 46, no. 1 (2022): 1–17.

'Woolf, Scepticism and Manners,' *Textual Practice* 22, no. 2 (2008): 249–68.

'The Problem of Romanticism in Wyndham Lewis,' *Essays in Criticism* 65, no. 2 (2015): 163–86.
'Philosophy and the Novel: Iris Murdoch,' in *The British Novel of Ideas*, eds. Rachel Potter and Matthew Taunton (Cambridge University Press, 2024).

THE GOOD LIFE AND OTHER FICTIONS

Introduction

LIVING AS IF

Let's Assume

Let's assume for a moment that we know what a fiction is and turn to the more practical question: How does it help us live? This book focuses on *literary* fiction and the ways it might be approached as a resource for living well or at least better.[1] It also draws on this richly self-reflexive form of madeupness to examine the wider role of fictiveness in our lives: the storied character we give experience, the illusions this can produce, and the benefits and pitfalls of such make-believe.[2] In an age of bad fiction—disinformation, fake news, and fake anti-fakery—we need some respect for fact, but we also need a more differentiated sense of the fictive, its many forms and its heterogenous uses. Fiction is not necessarily fraud, nor is it simply error and unreality.[3] Indeed, it is often the

1. The tradition is too long to list in detail, but, broadly speaking, I am interested in a very self-conscious form of ethical criticism unfolding from the work of Martha Nussbaum and Wayne Booth in the 1980s and 1990s and the polemics surrounding them. See, for instance, Siebers, *The Ethics of Criticism* and *Morals and Stories*; Palmer, *Literature and Moral Understanding*; Goldberg, *Agents and Lives*; Parker, *Ethics, Theory, and the Novel*; Newton, *Narrative Ethics*. More recent contributions to this tradition are mentioned downstream.

2. By calling literary fiction self-referential I am not suggesting it is exclusively self-referential. For a critique of this position, see Miller, 'Is Literature Self-Referential?'

3. This seems to be the position taken by Bertrand Russell about all literary fictions when he declared that all the propositions of *Hamlet* 'are false because there was no such man.' Russell, *An Inquiry into Meaning and Truth*, 277.

source of what's best about us—the space in which the good life is imagined and talked into being.

Fiction has many faces and the aim here is not to reduce it to a common essence, single definition or unitary function.[4] While I show that fictions can help us to tell the truth, I also dwell on a number of practices where truth might seem to take second place to other kinds of value, from certain kinds of aesthetic experience to the little fictions we call politeness to more deceptive fictions such as lies and self-delusions. I am equally interested in those situations in which the truth of something seems to be assumed or disbelief at least suspended, or where the normal entailments of believing and disbelieving are put aside.[5] I also examine situations in which this fictive attitude breaks down and the not-so-ness of our stories and practices loom large. This may make it impossible to proceed 'as if,' or it may, in fact, embolden us to do so. As Lytton Strachey once declared to Virginia Woolf: 'We can only live if we see through illusion.'[6] Much of this book hinges on the different meanings we might give to the word 'through.'

The everyday experience of reading fiction provides us with some lived evidence that we can simultaneously commit to two sides of 'seeing through' at once. We know little Nell is made up, but this may not stop our tears when she goes to that storied place in the sky.[7] Many have wondered about the seeming paradox of fiction and have tried to account for the affective force of illusions.[8] These may be mere pseudo-feelings or 'quasi-feelings,' but it's hard not to feel or quasi-feel that much of everyday life involves feeling quasi (to invoke the Latin for 'as if')—say, when we wonder, speculate, or populate gaps in our

4. On what she calls the 'pluri-significance' of the word 'fiction,' see Cohn, *The Distinction of Fiction*, 1–17.

5. My discussion of this 'as-if-ness' is deeply indebted to Vaihinger, *The Philosophy of 'As If.'* Also, Appiah, *As If*.

6. Woolf, *Diary*, 3.233.

7. On the oddities of such tears, see Radford, 'Tears and Fiction.'

8. Radford and Weston, 'How Can We Be Moved by the Fate of Anna Karenina?'; Walton, 'Fearing Fictions'; Lamarque, 'How Can We Fear and Pity Fictions?'; Yanal, *Paradoxes of Emotion and Fiction*.

knowledge with fictions that we half-believe or provisionally assent to.[9] 'Do tell me everything that has, or hasn't, happened,' Henry James wrote to a friend, knowing that key parts of our lives are spent on things that don't occur.[10] Or as Wilde noted: 'To most of us the real life is the life we do not lead.'[11] Many of our most intense moments take place in the 'imagined "otherwise."'[12] This counterfactuality is built into sentiments like hope or regret. 'What queer speculations,' Thackeray mused, 'the "might have beens" are!'[13] Yet there is some counterfactual queerness to all desire. After all, desire desires the world to be different so that its designs can be met—even when it yearns for the world to stay the same. The sense that life could be otherwise or that we could do otherwise is clearly foundational to our sense of freedom. Moral reality demands imagination—a fecund sense of 'what if' and an ability to think and act 'as if.'

Though the book considers the moral significance of fictiveness, I also keep in mind that morality in general has often been declared a fiction.[14] If literature sometimes invites us to think this unsettling thought, it should be admitted, nonetheless, that the thought is a vague one and may not lead to any revision of our practices. To emphasise the fictiveness of something may not say or do very much. Property is a fiction but only after the revolution will we truly think so. The same may be said about money. We can readily concede that ethical norms are artificial—say, historical and human-made—but this does not stop

9. On the role of quasi-emotions in art, see, in particular, Walton, *Mimesis as Make-Believe*. On why the distinction between 'real-world feelings' and fiction-inspired feelings has no real purchase, see Cohen, *Thinking of Others*, 29–51.

10. James, *Letters*, 3.174. For accounts of this would-be living, see Philips, *Missing Out*; Miller, *On Not Being Someone Else*.

11. Wilde, 'The English Renaissance of Art,' in *Essays and Lectures*, 128.

12. Eliot, *Middlemarch*, 440.

13. Thackeray to Mrs. Carmichael Smyth, 17–19 April 1852. See *The Letters and Private Papers of William Makepeace Thackeray*, 3.39. Cited in Williams, *The Art of Uncertainty*, 109.

14. This moral fictionalism is often traced back to Nietzsche. But for more systematic defences of the position, see Mackie, *Ethics*; Joyce, *The Myth of Morality*; Kalderon, *Moral Fictionalism*.

them from becoming real or acquiring objectivity among ourselves.[15] Of course, a very thick or ontologically committed sense of the objective can make us doubt our moral experiences. All moral interpretation, in certain eyes, is misinterpretation, while all moral judgement is error.[16] Others dispute such views—not because moral judgements are true, but because they are deemed to state nothing and are therefore neither true nor false. The aim here is not to settle these meta-ethical questions, though I do want to stress literature's stubborn power to raise them.

One of the grounding assumptions of the book is that there is an irreducible as-if-ness in moral life.[17] This, in a sense, is simply to acknowledge the limits of justification. We must all take certain things on trust if ethical experience is going to get off the ground. So, we behave *as if* we are free even though we may lack exhaustive grounds to conclude so. Or we often bring a certain as-if-ness to moral obligation: We operate as if certain rules are absolute and universally binding, though we may simultaneously feel that all rules must allow for exceptions. Many of us, it seems, are conditional norm-followers, choosing to assent to a rule when enough people do so—and some of us do so with our fingers crossed.[18] As Kant urbanely observed in 1798, much of social life is a form of moral theatre:

> On the whole, the more civilized human beings are, the more they are actors. They adopt the illusion of affection, of respect for others, of modesty, and of unselfishness without deceiving anyone at all, because it is understood by everyone that nothing is meant sincerely by this. And it is also very good that this happens in the world. For

15. As John Searle has argued, things may be observer-relative and ontologically subjective, but this should not lead us to surrender all notions of epistemic objectivity or truth and falsehood. Searle, *The Construction of Social Reality*.

16. Nietzsche, *Twilight of the Idols and the Anti-Christ*, 66.

17. Some might feel that moral seeing and, indeed, fictive seeing, involve a simple seeing-as rather than something more conditional or optional. When it comes to fiction, for instance, Hamburger emphasises its 'as structure' not its 'as-if structure.' See Hamburger, *The Logic of Literature*, 58. My position is that fiction allows for both forms of seeing.

18. On conditional norm-following, see Bicchieri, *The Grammar of Society*.

> when human beings play these roles, eventually the virtues, whose illusion they have merely affected for a considerable length of time, will gradually really be aroused and merge into the disposition.[19]

Not all of morality is mere pretence here: Our moral fictions are parasitic on 'real virtue.' However, pretence is also constitutive: When enough of it goes on, the distinction between real and affected states becomes quite happily blurred. As if becomes just so. If literary fictions often pretend to see through pretence, they also suggest that it may be a mistake to get too wound up about the authenticity of moral appearances. As Kant noted, 'If semblance indeed fell away, very likely nothing would remain for us at all.'[20]

Nevertheless, there are times in moral life when our performances dip and we begin to fluff our lines. I consider those moments of moral turbulence when key elements of our ethics—say, our confidence in freedom or the dignity we feel it enshrines—begin to seem hollow or we struggle to align our sense of ourselves as moral agents with the idea of our own thinghood within a material universe. The root of the comic, according to Wyndham Lewis, derives from the fundamental absurdity of witnessing a thing behaving as if it were a person—as if, in other words, it were a free and self-legislating being.[21] Lewis never quite got over the joke or ceased to disparage those who were taken in by it. And yet he never entirely relinquished his own need to be taken in or to regard humans as persons.

Here we might seek refuge in a certain kind of fictionalism—the conditions and limits of which I examine throughout the book. This is the Janus-faced knack of seeing through illusion—an ability, which in its baldest form involves committing to the utility of fictions that we simultaneously know to be untrue.[22] As Wallace Stevens put it, 'The final

19. Kant, 'Anthropology from a Pragmatic Point of View,' in *Anthropology, History, and Education*, 263.

20. Kant, *Lectures on Anthropology*, 380.

21. Lewis, *The Wild Body*, 159.

22. As Vaihinger maintained: 'Fictions are never verifiable, for they are hypotheses which are known to be false, but which are employed because of their utility.' Vaihinger, *The Philosophy of 'As If*,' xlii.

belief is to believe in a fiction, . . . to know that it is a fiction and that you believe in it willingly.'[23] Few of the writers who I consider in detail—Charles Dickens, George Eliot, Henry James, Joseph Conrad, Virginia Woolf, Wyndham Lewis, and Iris Murdoch—openly embrace this fictionalism, but they all advertise the difficulty, even undesirability, of living without illusions. As Woolf put it, rather self-referentially, in *Orlando*, 'Illusions are the most necessary and valuable things.'[24] No enthusiast of Woolf, Wyndham Lewis aspired to an entirely disenchanted condition. However, he ultimately drew on Kant to arrive at the paradoxical conclusion that 'illusion must in short be our "real."'[25]

Underlying the endorsement of illusion in and through modern literature we find significant doubt.[26] I dwell on the ways our fictions—literary and nonliterary—allow us to express and mitigate our scepticism at one and the same time, allowing us to see through things in a double sense. Of course, the logical and psychological viability of such doubleness is open to question. Belief implies a conviction that something is true, not just a pretence that it is.[27] There may be cases, as William James insisted, where a certain '*faith in a fact can help create the fact*'—where, say, a conviction of the value of life can create a valuable life—but he also noted that these occasions were quite circumscribed.[28] The acrobatics of the White Queen are certainly impressive—'sometimes I've believed as many as six impossible things before breakfast'—but this isn't quite enough to squash Alice ('one *can't*

23. Stevens, *Opus Posthumous*, 159.

24. Woolf, *Orlando: A Biography*, 139.

25. Lewis, *Time and Western Man*, 378. This included the notion of freedom as well as the illusion of a self—'the arch-illusion, the ground and condition of all others' (394).

26. As Zadie Smith recently put it: 'Fiction—at least the kind that was any good—was full of doubt, self-doubt above all.' Smith, 'Fascinated to Presume,' 73.

27. My sense of the grammar of belief is partly drawn from Bernard Williams, 'Deciding to Believe,' in *Problems of the Self*, 136–51.

28. See James, 'The Will to Believe,' in *The Will to Believe and Other Essays*, 29. As James noted, 'The freedom to believe can only cover living options which the intellect of the individual cannot by itself resolve' (32).

believe impossible things').[29] Even in Wonderland there may be logical and grammatical constraints on what we can believe.

But believing may not be the right word when it comes to fiction—not least if we doubt whether fictions truly state anything. When we entertain or are entertained by a fiction we commit to a broad spectrum of attitudes—from receptive openness to ironic toleration to muzzled doubt—many of which fall well short of full belief. Moreover, our literary fictions repeatedly suggest that much of life is spent in this epistemic twilight. Hence the protracted as-if-ness and conditional metaphors of writers like Dickens, James, Conrad or Woolf.[30] The 144 instances of 'as if' in *To the Lighthouse*, for instance, can make all life feel provisional, 'as if solidity had vanished altogether.'[31] Which is not to say that nothing is captured or affirmed by Woolf's many as ifs:

> So fine was the morning except for a streak of wind here and there that the sea and sky looked all one fabric, as if sails were stuck high up in the sky, or the clouds had dropped down into the sea. A steamer far out at sea had drawn in the air a great scroll of smoke which stayed there curving and circling decoratively, as if the air were a fine gauze which held things and kept them softly in its mesh, only gently swaying them this way and that. And as happens sometimes when the weather is very fine, the cliffs looked as if they were conscious of the ships, and the ships looked as if they were conscious of the cliffs, as if they signalled to each other some secret message of their own.[32]

These adventures in as-if-ness exhibit the epistemic virtues of a certain kind of fictionalism—the value of descriptions that are literally false. There are no sails in the sky, but operating as if there are helps us to appreciate the peculiar blueness of that fine day. The air is not made of gauze, but the simile successfully snags the inertness of the sky's contents. Of course, the repeated as ifs concede to the not-so-ness of

29. Carroll, *Alice's Adventures in Wonderland*, 177.

30. For a discussion of Dickens's addiction to 'as if' expressions, see Farina, '"Dickens's As If": Analogy and Victorian Virtual Reality.'

31. Woolf, *To the Lighthouse*, 80.

32. Woolf, *To the Lighthouse*, 197–98.

analogy or simile, and as the similes accumulate, it can feel like we venture ever further into the improbable if not the unhelpfully false—not least when we are invited to treat the cliffs as if they are conscious. Behind such anthropomorphism in Woolf, we find a longing for metaphysical integration, a consonance between the ways of the world and human practices and modes of understanding—as if values nestled in facts, as if everything were purposive, as if the world participated in the human need for meaning. But harmony in the passage above is notably incomplete: If ship and cliff communicate, they do so in a language that remains unintelligible to human ears. 'As if' contains as much alienation as it does conviction in Woolf.

The 'as ifs' of metaphor express a need for meaning in the world. But since it is often unclear whether this meaning is invented or found, description lends itself to different kinds of fictionalism. This fictive attitude is most self-consciously expressed in Woolf's conviction that 'the whole world is a work of art'—a position that is presented as an empirical statement but equally operates as a rule or formula for living as if.[33] Woolf was neither the first nor the last to suggest that the world is best approached and vindicated when conceived as an aesthetic phenomenon.[34] In the chapters ahead I examine various attempts to treat life in the spirit of art, alongside the risks of doing so.[35] This fictionalism is not just aired in novels; the novel has also been cast as the paradigm for fictive living.[36] Henry James wondered in 1902 if we were not 'pretty well all novelists now?'[37] Daniel Dennett in the 1980s had much the same

33. Woolf, *Moments of Being*, 85. This, of course, is an old fantasy. As Schelling put it: 'The universe . . . is also to be viewed as an absolute work of art in which infinite intention mutually interpenetrates with infinite necessity.' Schelling, *The Philosophy of Art*, 31.

34. Nietzsche, *Birth of Tragedy and Other Writings*, 33. Martha Nussbaum would also declare that the 'well-lived life is a work of literary art.' See Nussbaum, *Love's Knowledge*, 148. Collingwood put the matter a little more subtly: 'All life is art, but no single moment of life is mere art.' Collingwood, *Speculum Mentis*, 83.

35. The phrasing is drawn from Pater, *Appreciations*, 62.

36. 'We live in a colossal novel,' Novalis declared, though he also insisted that this novel should be made by us, not simply given to us. Novalis, *Philosophical Writings*, 134, 66.

37. James, *Literary Criticism*, 2.346.

feeling: We are all 'virtuoso novelists,' he insisted, busily writing ourselves up as heroes of our own plots.[38]

But not all of our literary fictions are willing to indulge this story of our story-telling selves—not least because some of them believe that the task of living a life and narrating one involve very different requirements.[39] Moreover, the difference between real life and novelistic life is internal to the novel itself. The comedy of one of the first novels, *Don Quixote,* depends on the difference, and readers are invited to laugh at those who can't manage the distinction (though this may also be a safe way of laughing at ourselves). Flaubert derives more tragic results from those who live novelistically.[40] This may be a classic gambit of fiction—illusions exposing illusions to boost their reality-effect—but clearly most novels proceed as if there is a reality independent of the stories we tell about it. Despite these 'realist' commitments, some writers and thinkers continue to cultivate a romantic or putatively postmodern picture of the world—namely the view that life is one 'enormous novel.'[41] This pan-fictionalism might capture the lived experience of a hypermediated or so-called post-truth world, yet it also overextends fictiveness until the category disappears. A basic condition of fictional experience, I argue, is that there are limits to this experience even if these limits are not easily drawn. Which is not to say that we haven't a lot to learn by thinking analogically—as if novels were life, though there are evident restrictions to how much the analogy can be reversed.

So, this is a book about the novel's metafictional powers and what it reveals about life's many as ifs. I draw on philosophy to help say what fiction shows us about fictiveness, and I invoke fiction to expose the limits of what philosophy can say (not least about the ways in which the world might resist our conceptual schemes, or how perception and persuasion often exceed the power of argument). This may be to combine one minority sport with another in a fond address to the converted—the

38. Dennett, 'Why Everyone Is a Novelist.'

39. According to Sartre's Roquentin, we must choose either 'to live or to recount.' Sartre, *Nausea,* 61.

40. See Flaubert, *Madame Bovary.*

41. J. G. Ballard, 'Introduction,' in *Crash,* 5.

diminishing band who believe in fiction or at least the value of the dense, self-reflexive fictions that I examine in this book.[42] The very 'literary' novel may not have the prestige in our culture it once had.[43] Nonetheless, it is worth spelling out why people might continue to stick with this antiquated progenitor of virtual experience—and why such experience is nontrivial, even vital. As I argue, belief in the value of the novel or the general value of the virtual is easily undermined by certain fictions about fictiveness—not least that it is always and simply false—as well as balder fictions about fact (what Sellars called 'the myth of the given': namely, that facts are directly available and self-interpreting and demand no mediation or construction-work).[44] Both myths breed dogmatism and dismissiveness. A fictive stance, however, usually demands a more subtle set of attitudes, shades of assent and dissent, and quasi-feelings. Fiction knows that most of life is spent between polar extremes of reality and unreality, actuality and wishfulness, arctic certainty and antarctic doubt, and that any mean we strike up will never be golden or endure for very long.

In what follows, then, I show how the novel expresses and conditions a kind of double vision: an epistemic doubleness where we can doubt and assent at one and the same time combined with an ontological unsteadiness where things feel real and don't.[45] Within these states, moreover, we can strike a range of attitudes between a spectator's distance and a participant's absorption.[46] These fictive experiences, I argue, help

42. Zadie Smith suggests that we now 'hardly see the point' of this kind of fiction. 'Why,' she rhetorically asks, 'have a silent dialogue with an invisible person about imaginary things?' Smith, 'Fascinated to Presume,' 85.

43. Back in 1938 Collingwood was already issuing *ubi sunts*: 'The novel, once an important literary form, has all but disappeared, except as an amusement for the semi-literate.' Collingwood, *The Principles of Art*, 331. On the ways in which we may have lost our faith in the novel and why we may need it more than ever, see Boxall, *The Value of the Novel.*

44. See Sellars, *Empiricism and the Philosophy of Mind.*

45. As Mann put it, 'Authorship itself has always seemed to me to be a witness to and an expression of ambivalence, of here and there, of yes and no, of two souls in one breast, of an annoying richness in inner conflicts, antitheses and contradictions.' Mann, *Reflections of a Non-Political Man*, 9.

46. According to Walton: 'The dual standpoint which appreciators take is . . . one of the most fundamental and important features of the human institution of fiction.' Walton, 'How Remote Are Fictional Worlds from the Real World?,' 21.

us to live more amphibiously or at least to come to terms with our own doubleness, our inwardness and outwardness, our social and antisocial natures (as we read about others alone),[47] our subjective and more objective sense of things.[48] Consistency demands, perhaps, that we remain in two minds about this two-mindedness—not least for the way it might seem to connive against certainty or what Harry Frankfurt called 'wholeheartedness'—and there are situations in which a fictive attitude might seem unhelpful, even vicious.[49] Nonetheless, within the precincts of the novel and a good bit beyond it, we can experiment with the 'ifs' we live with and are often forced to repress. Doubt, as Charles Peirce remarked, is often 'an uneasy and dissatisfied state,' yet fiction allows us to savour our uncertainty as a form of pleasure.[50] Here we learn to appreciate that a life without 'if,' and the perhapsness it conditions, would be no life at all.

Fictive Thinking

How exactly do novels think? Perhaps they don't think at all, and we are drawn to them because they provide a reprieve from the burdens of reflection. They were once disparaged, let us remember, as a kind of mental opium.[51] Coleridge—who knew something about opiates—felt they led over time to 'the entire destruction of the powers of mind.'[52] Nonetheless, I want to focus here on how the mind might benefit from

47. This is a very broad-brush account of reading, and I don't want to diminish the importance of Dickens's public performances of his work. On this point see Gettelman, *Imagining Otherwise*, 56.

48. Cohen identifies another doubleness: the way we do and don't want to court the possibility of death—and are partly drawn to tragedy for this reason. See Cohen, *Thinking of Others*, 48.

49. See Frankfurt, 'Identification and Wholeheartedness,' in *The Importance of What We Care About*, 159–76.

50. Peirce, 'The Fixation of Belief,' in *The Essential Peirce*, 1.114.

51. One Victorian commentator produced an ambiguous commendation: 'The slightest novels are a blessing to those in distress, not chloroform itself a greater.' See 'The Morality of the Profession of Letters,' reprinted in Stevenson, *Essays in the Art of Writing*, 69.

52. Coleridge, *Lectures on Shakespeare*, 6.

the novel's 'as ifs'—as if events had a narrative aspect, as if someone were at hand to narrate, as if human beings are characters, as if these creatures think in sentences, as if we have intimate access to these sentence-like thoughts. The tall tales get even taller when they use a determinate plot. 'Men can do nothing without the make-believe of a beginning,' Eliot announced at the start of one of her last beginnings.[53] The same might be said about our sense of an ending. Though philosophers have queried the hallowed status that has been given to narrative in recent decades, many still insist that our 'lives are somehow only comprehensible through a narrative explanatory structure.'[54] Novels explain reality partly by simplifying it, trimming out its complexity to reveal some pattern.[55] Woolf felt that they falsified life, but they also make sense of it through their useful falsehoods.[56] We see through them in a double sense.

But even enthusiasts of the novel might feel that they lack the cognitive dignity to be false. This is because fiction in general has often been regarded as nonreferential and nonassertoric. Defenders of the nonassertoric theory admit that novels *do* seem to assert things, say, about the past being a foreign country or about all happy families being alike, but they contend that these are just pretend-assertions or pseudo-statements.[57] However, this makes fiction pretend too much and rests on an over-rigorous conception of the really real statement. As Kendall Walton noted, there are different ways of asserting—declaring something to be the case in a lecture, raising a flag, honking a horn, wearing

53. Eliot, *Daniel Deronda*, 3.

54. Goldie, *The Mess Inside*, 1. See also Rudd, *Self, Value, and Narrative*. For scepticism about the centrality of narrative to our lives, see Galen Strawson, 'Against Narrativity.' On both the value and limits of understanding ourselves in narrative terms, see Hutto, *Narrative and Understanding Persons*.

55. As James put it in a letter to Robert Louis Stevenson in 1884: 'All art is a simplification.' See James, *A Life in Letters*, 167; James was essentially agreeing with Stevenson's own view that novelists necessarily simplified. See Stevenson, 'A Humble Remonstrance.'

56. As she put it in 1915: 'Its a bad habit writing novels—it falsifies life, I think.' Woolf, *Diary*, 1.28. Rudd, nonetheless, maintains that we can tell shapely stories about life 'without *necessarily* falsifying it.' Rudd, *Self, Value, and Narrative*, 182.

57. Searle, *Expression and Meaning*.

a particular kind of rose—and there is no good reason to think that literature is incapable of making statements, however indeterminate or indirect.[58] Fictions like *Animal Farm* owe their being to such confidence, though presumably part of the power of this book derives from its pretence to assert nothing about any specific historical world.[59] Some novels could pretend a little harder not to assert and are spoiled by their need to tell us things. Fortunately, novels do more than describe or make statements—they express, solicit, play, and fool about, often leaving the paler game of factual description to others. As we are bluntly told in *Daniel Deronda*: 'Attempts at description are stupid.'[60]

Novels clearly convene experiences as much as they enlist descriptions, aspiring to a kind of experiential knowledge that is different from forms of 'knowing that.' They aim, we might say, for a 'knowledge by acquaintance' over and above mere 'knowledge by description.'[61] This is a kind of knowledge that normally attends the mere having of an experience—for instance, the knowledge of eating chocolate ice cream that comes with eating chocolate ice cream.[62] We can easily doubt, of course, that fictions acquaint us with anything in this direct sense. Indeed, we may query the very notion of 'knowledge by acquaintance,' regarding it as yet another myth of the given.[63] If the concept is little more than a fiction of knowledge, it nonetheless underscores the distinctiveness of novelistic thinking. Literary fiction repeatedly strives to

58. Walton, *Mimesis as Make-Believe*, 78.

59. *Animal Farm* embodies a power that Catherine Gallagher attributes to all fiction—'a nonreferentiality that could be seen as a greater referentiality.' See Gallagher, 'The Rise of Fictionality,' in *The Novel*, 342.

60. Eliot, *Daniel Deronda*, 91.

61. See Murdoch, *Existentialists and Mystics*, 414; Zhang, *Strange Likeness*, 146–53. Collingwood makes a related distinction between 'expression' and 'description.' See Collingwood, *The Principles of Art*, 105–24.

62. As William James explained, 'I know the color blue when I see it, and the flavor of a pear when I taste it'—to know these things is indistinguishable from experiencing them. James, *Principles of Psychology*, 1.217.

63. According to Monroe Beardsley, for instance, 'Acquaintance . . . does not become knowledge in the strict sense until the data are combined and connected by reasoning.' Beardsley, *Aesthetics*, 383. I treat Wittgenstein's doubts about this kind of knowledge in chap. 7.

understand what it's like *to be* an 'x' or what it's like *to be* in situation 'y.'[64] One of its foundational 'as ifs' is the attempt to know from the inside—to summon up the what's-it-likeness of certain tastes, moods or emotions through the voodoo of words.[65] Again, this is not a creditable epistemic task for some—arguably, it invests knowledge with mystical objectives, a search for the holy qualia of consciousness or some inwardness which can't in principle be known[66]—but an investment in the inner-thisness of beings, I would argue, remains one of fiction's key regulative ideals and is one of the reasons why it exceeds (for better or worse) philosophical or propositional forms of knowledge.[67]

The difficulty of capturing this inner-thisness is acknowledged by the analogical way the epistemic quest is conceived: 'What's it *like*?'[68] The search for likeness concedes in advance to the as-if-ness or near-miss quality of descriptions in pursuit of experience. 'It seemed as if an electric stream went through Dorothea, thrilling her from despair into expectation': This gives us some sense of another person, but the narrator and even Dorothea struggle to identify fully what's it like to be Dorothea.[69] Conrad's Marlow is deeply sceptical of ever being able to recover these inner states even for their erstwhile experiencer ('No, it is impossible; it is impossible to convey the life-sensation of any given epoch of

64. 'Facts about what it is like to be an X,' Nagel admits, 'are very peculiar, so peculiar that some may be inclined to doubt their reality, or the significance of claims about them.' But he mounts a famous defence of these facts nonetheless. See Nagel, 'What's It Like to Be a Bat?' My position on literature's commitment to what's-it-like states is similar to the one adopted by Catherine Wilson in 'Literature and Knowledge.' See also Day, *Novel Sensations*.

65. Day rightly notes that the literary search for these inner states intensifies under modernism. See Day, *Novel Sensations*.

66. On why this desire for knowledge from inside is usually misplaced, see Hacker, 'Is There Anything It Is like to Be a Bat?' See also Dennett, *Consciousness Explained*.

67. Of course, there are exceptions that confirm the rule. Take, for instance, Wyndham Lewis's 'externalist' method and his insistence that 'good art must have no inside.' See Lewis, *Tarr*, 267.

68. Hence the centrality of metaphor to fictive experience. On this see Gass, *Fiction and the Figures of Life*, 64–65, where he argues that metaphors attempt to acquaint and not just describe.

69. Eliot, *Middlemarch*, 35.

one's existence').[70] Novels, nonetheless, continue to bend language into new shapes to create what's-it-like feelings—what it's like to be Marlow or Mrs. Dalloway, what it's like to murder someone or to have an affair. Thomas Nagel thinks this curiosity has its limits—we can't quite fathom what it's like to be a bat—though the characters of some novels have found Nagel too defeatist on this point.[71]

One may well wonder whether inwardness is invented or represented through novels, but throughout the book I consider the various arguments that are often made to defend this fictional thinking: the way it can condition a respect for persons by giving us a sense of their complexity and distinctiveness; the way we might extend our own minds by imagining the lives of others and so forth.[72] Indeed, the great 'as if' of free indirect discourse—as if we live within a character's head, though we abide in the third person—is arguably a cognitive and moral achievement.[73] It remains an achievement despite and because it is an idealisation, giving us access to a mind that its ostensible owner might never seem to possess.[74]

Novels, however, do not just lean into characters, they also lean out and capture experience through a wider lens. One of the most famous of these perspectival shifts occurs in the transition between the first and second sections of Woolf's *To the Lighthouse*. Figures who had loomed so large in the inward-leaning first section are despatched in a series of cold parentheses in the second, more distanced account of human affairs. Life lived from the inside, the novel intimates, is an important business,

70. Conrad, *Heart of Darkness*, 30.

71. Nagel, *Mortal Questions*, 168–69. Our lack of epistemic access to bats is challenged by Coetzee's protagonist in *Elizabeth Costello*, 75–80.

72. According to Iris Murdoch, novels embody the principle of tolerance and respect for the sovereignty of individuals. Murdoch, *Existentialists and Mystics*, 472. On the novel as a school for sympathy or a form of attunement to others, see chap. 3.

73. On its epistemic and ethical significance, see Cohn, *Transparent Minds*.

74. For D. A. Miller this is an 'impossible identification,' for it affords the reader 'at one and the same time the experience of a character's inner life as she herself lives it, and the same experience of an inner life as she never could.' See Miller, *Jane Austen*, 61. For a recent attempt to present this free indirectness as a foundational feature of the novelistic, see Bewes, *Free Indirect*.

but watched from without—or from some notional point of view of the cosmos—this conceit can seem absurd.[75] Novels repeatedly oscillate between these immanent and transcendent perspectives—or what Lukács called their 'subjective' and 'objective' poles.[76] From an immersive inwardness we move to a very different 'as if'—a fictive standpoint in which the world is viewed from nowhere within it. The aim here may be to arrive at a *total* or, indeed, perspectiveless perspective—yielding, in Woolf's words, a 'world seen without a self' or without the usual limitations of an empirical seer.[77] This may be a mere fiction of omniscience—incompletely realised, say, by the narrative voice in a novel or occurring in the gaps between characters and awaiting completion by the reader. But the friction between the subjective and objective 'as if' is a rich source of irony, making values, commitments, and attachments flicker in and out of life.[78]

In the chapters that follow, I treat the novel as a fundamentally ironic structure—a source of double consciousness of various kinds.[79] This is partly a product of the doubleness that I've suggested all readers bring to all fictional experience, the way we treat a thing as true while knowing that it isn't.[80] But it is also a function of the novel's perspectival character. This perspectivism is not an invitation to conceive of everything as relative or subjective.[81] The belief that we see from a perspective, I argue, is entirely compatible with a strong commitment to objectivity in practical and theoretical life. One reason why we read is to expose ourselves to different and rival outlooks—arguably in the name of a

75. I draw here on Nagel's ideas of the absurd in *Mortal Questions*, 11–23.

76. See Lukács, *The Theory of the Novel*.

77. This is the world 'seen without a self.' Woolf, *The Waves*, 221.

78. Lukács, *The Theory of the Novel*, 75–76, 84.

79. The ironic aspect of not only the novel but literature in general has long been emphasised. As Northrop Frye proposed, 'The literary structure is always ironic because "what it says" is always different to "what it means."' Frye, *The Anatomy of Criticism*, 81. See also Booth, *A Rhetoric of Irony*.

80. As Newsom put it: 'The essence of entertaining fictions is to inhabit a dual standpoint while denying that there is more than one frame at all.' See Newsom, *A Likely Story*, 103.

81. Here I am indebted to Simon Blackburn's essay 'Perspectives, Fictions, Errors, Play.'

greater objectivity.[82] Yet, as I show, novels also force us to experience the painful gap between perspectives—not just the rifts between characters but the chasms within character, the fractiousness of any one person's vision of anything. The disjunctions lend themselves to different kinds of description—the distance between the personal and impersonal, immanent and transcendent, engaged and disengaged viewpoints—but they have long shaped the house of fiction, not least because they structure the palace of thought itself.[83]

When we think 'as if' through fiction, of course, it can feel as if we have overcome the limits of thought or as if the chasms between perspectives have been finally bridged. So, we get the impression that we can know another from the inside, allowing self and other, or first-person and third-person knowledge, to merge in the fictional 'as if.' David Copperfield feels he *is* Tom Jones when he reads Fielding and maybe we feel like David when we read David.[84] Novels allow us to escape into other lives, but we also discover that those fictional lives are characterised by many of the epistemic constraints that we endure in our own. The difficulty of aligning a personal and impersonal perspective is writ large in the novel—shaping its characters' experiences and the rudiments of its form—and it informs other kinds of duality. 'I'm not an observer. I'm a hater,' somebody says in *The Awkward Age*.[85] The contrast is starkly drawn, but it shows how difficult it is to be an impartial spectator and a committed agent at one and the same time (though again readers are often tantalised by the fantasy of being both). We are both things and persons, yet, as Lewis noted, it is hard to subscribe to both of these thoughts at once.

This splitness reveals why fictional thinking is a source of ironic understanding—or a self-consciously incomplete form of knowledge. Fiction helps us to think more than we know, but it also shows that we know a lot less than we think. Or it reveals the incorrigible plurality of

82. Nietzsche, *On the Genealogy of Morality*, 92.

83. Nagel, *Mortal Questions*, 196–213; Peter Strawson, *Freedom and Resentment*, 10. See also McGinn, *The Subjective View*, 127.

84. Dickens, *David Copperfield*, 53.

85. James, *Novels, 1896–1899*, 733.

knowing. If we know from different perspectives, we have different perspectives on knowing—as lived acquaintance, say, or as description—and not all of these can be reconciled. Because fiction aspires to an experiential knowledge exceeding mere description, it can be notoriously difficult to describe what our fictional experiences say or what this lived knowledge knows.[86] One of the more plausible theories of the aesthetic is that it is a pleasurable form of unknowing, pre-knowing, or would-be knowing. As Kant suggested, the intellectual faculties are aroused by the attempt to identify what our aesthetic feelings might say, but these quests never reach the promised land of knowledge or at least conceptual knowledge—though they repeatedly urge us to seek this knowledge out.[87] So, we respond to a first-order set of as-if-experiences with a second-order 'as if'—namely, criticism. In the criticism practiced in these chapters, I consider different ways that fictions curate complex events that can never be fully cashed in for propositional knowledge or final beliefs—though I repeatedly reach for propositions and philosophical discourse to account for what these experiences might mean.[88]

The speculative character of these 'as ifs' may seem futile—arguably as cognitively fruitless as fiction itself. But in the chapters that follow I intend to tease out the intellectual and moral value of fictional thinking: its readiness to venture into what's-it-like states; its openness to wonder mixed with a certain refusal to be fully taken in; its awareness of its own incompleteness as a form of knowledge, but also as a version of doubt, its deeply interested disinterestedness, its gift of double vision. Novels also turn their own doubleness on themselves and find themselves wanting. 'As if there could possibly be true stories,' scoffs Sartre's Roquentin. Narrative rigs our explanations in advance and predetermines

86. For the sense that the inner is a 'delusion' and that attempts to know it violate the basic grammar of knowing, see Wittgenstein, *Last Writings on the Philosophy of Psychology*, 2.84.

87. See Kant, *Critique of the Power of Judgment*. Collingwood would present art as a 'question which expects no answer.' Collingwood, *Speculum Mentis*, 79.

88. So, while I accept the broad sweep of Lamarque and Olsen's critique of the 'propositional theory of literature,' I also think it is overstated, overlooking the way literature both makes statements and solicits statements, while triggering useful wonder about their truth. Lamarque and Olsen, *Truth, Fiction and Literature*. For a critique of Lamarque and Olsen, see Rowe, 'Lamarque and Olsen on Literature and Truth.'

the meaning of actions through the fatal teleology of plot. As Roquentin puts it: 'You appear to begin at the beginning . . . And in fact you have begun at the end.'[89] Novels, however, are not an endless series of Cretans, toothlessly declaring they're false. Their doubts about themselves are also doubts about the world and the fundamental concepts we bring to it—character, action, intention, agency, and value. As we shall see, suspicions about these properties in a novel can easily make us suspect the moral intelligibility of experience as such.

Moral Irony

'The good ended happily, and the bad ended unhappily. That is what Fiction means.'[90] Wilde liked to expose the moral wish-fulfilment that drives much of our fiction-making, and many novelists have followed suit with their own disillusioning tales. Nonetheless, critical discussion of the novel's powers can still breed wishfulness and metafiction. The tales we tell about its moral value, for instance, are sometimes too good to be true and overlook the downsides of its many virtues. So, while we can easily emphasise the novel's modal force—its ability to make us feel as if 'we have lived another life'—this itself is not an unmixed good.[91] We can emerge from these counterfactual worlds with a rich sense of possibility and even an enhanced feeling of freedom.[92] However, the what ifs of fiction also alert us to the frightening contingency of what is. Novels extend our sense of the possible—allowing us to experience this state as not quite actual and yet as something more than the wholly unreal—but visits to these elsewhere worlds can also distract us from our freedom.[93] This is the

89. Sartre, *Nausea*, 62.

90. Wilde, *The Importance of Being Earnest* in *Complete Works*, 376.

91. James, *Literary Criticism*, 2.242. Miller makes the nice point that in reading we also perform a commitment to being ourselves—remaining on the sofa independent of the narrative. See Miller, *On Not Being Somone Else*, 55.

92. Mandel, Hilton, and Catellani, *The Psychology of Counterfactual Thinking*. On fiction as emancipation, see Berman, *Fiction Sets You Free*.

93. This is to draw on James's sense of the possible in its fullest sense. James, *Pragmatism*, 88. According to Cora Diamond, fiction allows us to approach the world as a space of 'wonderful possibilities'—a claim I return to in the epilogue. See Diamond, *The Realistic Spirit*, 313.

romantic's mistake, in Hegel's eyes—someone who chooses to live in would-be, could-be or might-be worlds, never in the finite or actual world.[94] Freedom would appear to require proper exercise—the actual practice of deeds, not just the cultivation of options—if it is to stay in shape.[95] A recurrent fear of novels—and one often voiced within them—is that they are a bad distraction from the real business of doing and turn us into addicted spectators instead of committed agents.[96]

By considering the moral hazards as much as the benefits of fiction's 'as ifs,' I hope to make a contribution to what is broadly known as 'ethical criticism.' The phrase can sound both tautological and oxymoronic. Many have found the method too foresworn, instrumentalising, or beside the point when it comes to art. We can easily maintain, on the other hand, that criticism is always 'ethical' and is as old as reading itself.[97] However, the more circumscribed and philosophically self-conscious version that I have in mind came to life in the late 1980s and 1990s[98] and has thrived ever since—despite and because of the various waves of criticism it has drawn.[99] In recent years, the approach has met with some resistance even by those who concede to the practical or didactic value of art, with efforts to differentiate an aesthetic education from a

94. See, in particular, Hegel, *Elements of the Philosophy of Right*, 37–39.

95. As William James baldly noted, every deed involves the 'murder' of possibilities. See James, 'On Some Hegelisms,' in *The Will to Believe*, 200. On the necessary 'murder' of potential selves, see 'Great Men and Their Environment,' in *The Will to Believe*, 171.

96. James, *Principles of Psychology*, 1.129.

97. As we shall see in the chapter on James, the defence of art's independence from a marauding moralism has long roots. Many of these moves were rehearsed by Richard Posner over a hundred years later. See Posner, 'Against Ethical Criticism' and 'Against Ethical Criticism: Part 2.'

98. For histories of this 'ethical turn,' see Davis and Womack, *Mapping the Ethical Turn*; Garber, Hanssen, and Walkowitz, *The Turn to Ethics*; Altes, 'Ethical Turn,' in *Routledge Encyclopaedia of Narrative Theory*; Murphy, '"Let me look again."'

99. Recent works exemplify the good health and methodological diversity of the tradition. Jesse Rosenthal looks at the literary significance of moral sense theory in *Good Form*, while Matthew Sussman emphasises the virtues of virtue ethics in *Stylistic Virtue and Victorian Fiction*. Elsewhere Dorothy Hale has readvertised the ethical virtues of narrative in *The Novel and the New Ethics*, though the novelty of such ethics might well be queried at this point in the story.

moral one when it comes to the study of literature.[100] I try to have it both ways by offering a 'critique' of ethical criticism in the old sense of that term, providing an account of both its powers and its limitations.[101]

Ethical criticism has repeatedly shown how literature can join hands with philosophy to produce a sophisticated form of reflection on the good life. The two disciplines have proved complementary, precisely because of their differences. If literature strives to recover what's-it-like feelings, philosophy helps to clean up and organise the intuitions that are activated by these encounters.[102] A novel, in turn, can stress-test our more systematic theories and expose the limits of all abstract theorising.[103] 'Dense fictions,' as Bernard Williams called them, obviate the situational complexity of ethical deliberation and decision-making, the difficulty of applying and interpreting rules in specific settings.[104] They may even emphasise the ultimate irreducibility of moral life to rules. The temporal dimension of novels, moreover, reveals the trickiness—and often the unwisdom—of arriving at any principles that would see us through an entire life. Finally, the identifications and allegiances we often strike with characters—as we age, endure, and feel alongside them—can make us question the nature, possibility and value of impartial judgement. Fiction, then, can make us think more sensitively about ethics, but this subtlety is belied by too much boosterism about its

100. See Clune, *A Defense of Judgment*, 186. For a sophisticated sense of the moral elements and limits of aesthetic experience, see Bromwich, 'How Moral Is Taste?,' in *Skeptical Music*.

101. By old sense I mean Kantian sense—as opposed to the kind of 'critique' that is caricatured by Rita Felski in *The Limits of Critique*.

102. Daniel Dennett has also emphasised the importance of 'intuition pumps' within philosophy. Dennett, *Intuition Pumps*.

103. On the limits of our ethical theories and the ways literature attunes us to their inadequacies see, in particular, Diamond, 'Losing Your Concepts.' See also Diamond, *The Realistic Spirit*, 291–307, 367–81. For a broader discussion of the limits of moral theory in relation to literature, see Hämäläinen, *Literature and Moral Theory*.

104. Eliot put this particularism best: 'Moral judgements must remain false and hollow, unless they are checked and enlightened by a perpetual reference to the special circumstances that mark the individual lot.' Eliot, *The Mill on the Floss*, 498.

powers. Indeed, the moral case for literature has repeatedly been overstated in ways that do violence to a range of values, even perhaps to moral ones.[105] I remain convinced, nonetheless, that a reflective ethical criticism—one that attunes us to the complexity and weirdness of moral experience—remains crucially important in what can feel like crudely moralistic times. The historical conditions that call for a reappraisal of moral criticism are examined at the end of the book.

At this point I would merely suggest that any plausible criticism needs to acknowledge two kinds of limit. The first and rather obvious constraint is that morality does not exhaust normativity. 'Literature,' as Iris Murdoch noted, 'is soaked in the moral,' but it is also steeped in a wider language of import.[106] Our fictions house a range of goods—aesthetic, cognitive, political, and moral. Some of these values are potently mixed (and the various blends will be studied throughout), but they can also stand apart from each other and make very different calls on our respect and attention. The object of the 'good life' may be to integrate our interests and attachments as much as possible, a harmonisation that may require us to exceed narrow conceptions of the moral in the name of a more expansive kind of 'ethics'—and this is a kind of breadth that I consider and endorse throughout the book.[107] Yet unless things are made vanishingly broad, clashes between ethical commitments and other values will not go away and I shall explore a range of these conflicts in the chapters that follow. A second constraint on ethical

105. In Kant, for instance, the overriding of art's independence in the name of morality risks undermining the very freedom that allows art to function as a 'symbol of the good.' See Kant, *Critique of the Power of Judgment*, 225. I take this point up again in the epilogue.

106. Murdoch, *Existentialists and Mystics*, 254.

107. The pathway for such an expansion was set out by Bernard Williams in the 1980s, though Williams also suggested that this was merely a turn towards earlier habits of thinking about a decent life after the bad rigours of modern forms of moralising—its attachment to strict 'oughts' and universal prescriptions, its relentlessly other-regarding sense of virtuous action, its tendency to identify goodness with impartiality and so forth. Williams spoke up for something less pure and more plural, an approach that acknowledged the legitimacy of self-care and self-culture, values that are expressive of who we are as agents within a particular time and location in the world, as well as a range of lowercase virtues—goods that did not need to be converted into strict obligations for their value to be seen. See Williams, *Ethics and the Limits of Philosophy*.

criticism derives from the limits of moral thinking itself. This is not just the way our moral values and practices fail to internally cohere or to deliver final and definitive knowledge. It is also a function of the practical ironies of moral thought itself—the reflection that moral reflection may not always be very good for us.

'Nothing humanely great,' Conrad insisted, 'has come from reflection.'[108] This may be a self-indicting thought, but it is staged throughout his novels and the modern novel as a whole. The disease of self-consciousness is one of the novel's great themes and it might seem to resist in advance the Socratic presuppositions of much ethical criticism: the strong confidence that a reflective life is a good one.[109] Reflection may make us human, but it can also transform us into depraved animals: alienated from our natural intuitions and often no closer to the good.[110] Its moral hazards were emphasised by Bernard Williams: '*Reflection can destroy knowledge*.'[111] Williams overstated the case, but it is clear that reflection can erode confidence and leave us feeling lost in moral space. Faced with the impenetrable darkness of the world on the Congo River, Marlow intimates that the best course of action is to stop thinking and to attend to the engine. As he makes clear in *Chance*, 'to be busy with material affairs is the best preservative against reflection,' adding to this the mordant joke that a man contemplating suicide finds some sort of relief in the practical act of preparing the razor.[112] It is ultimately unclear what we should *do* with these thoughts. Should they generate more thought or less? And how should we appraise novel-reading itself: Is it a form of distraction from the razor, or an extended education in our need for one?

108. Conrad, *A Personal Record*, 11.

109. For a defence of this Socratic outlook and a critique of what she identifies as the Tolstoyan view—namely, that we should stay away from 'fundamental questions'—see Callard, *Open Socrates*. Callard notes fiction's ability to raise fundamental questions and its intrinsic limitations when it comes to answering them.

110. Rousseau, *The Discourses*, 138.

111. Williams, *Ethics and the Limits of Philosophy*, 148. The italics are in the original.

112. Conrad, *Chance*, 253.

If books are machines to think with, as I. A. Richards proposed, they can sometimes make us think too much.[113] The point, of course, is easily exaggerated. Virginia Woolf noted her capacity to read automatically, 'very much like a cow chewing cud.'[114] We often read to be absorbed—not necessarily to think—and yet novels can absorb us into compulsive forms of thinking.[115] In *The Sacred Fount*, for instance, Henry James seemed to parody the kind of obsessive inquiry that his own novels practiced and were liable to bring about. It is as if the narrator has taken James's advice too seriously—'to guess the unseen from the seen, to trace the implication of things, to judge the whole piece by the pattern'—and the process seems to drive him mad (at the end of the novel the reader, too, might need an ambulance).[116] He is fatally prone to the same over-seeing that Gilbert Osmond detected in Madame Merle: 'You always see too much in everything; you overdo it; you lose sight of the real.'[117] We may crave the simple real, but novels often fail to secure its location. This is partly because of the ironies of their form—a perspectivism in which 'everything is seen as many-sided'—and the kinds of doubleness they force us to endure.[118]

Novels, therefore, can provoke second thoughts about thought itself and can expose and arrest the vulnerable optimism of assuming that our next thought will be a better one. We may have no choice but to think on, but the activity doesn't necessarily end in a reflective equilibrium in which the poison finally acts as cure.[119] If novels disturb our confidence in the reflective life—while also forcing us to practice it—they equally test a Socratic faith in the unity of knowledge and virtue. This

113. Richards, *Principles of Literary Criticism*, vii. Some suggest that the fault lies not with books but with their oversophisticated readers. On the supposed dangers of reading too deeply, see Best and Marcus, 'Surface Reading'; Felski, *The Limits of Critique*; Moi, *Revolution of the Ordinary*, 175–95.

114. Woolf, *Diary*, 3.103.

115. On the ways in which fiction absorbs us, see Ong, *The Art of Being*, 11, 58, 74, 158–62.

116. James, *Literary Criticism*, 1.53.

117. James, *The Portrait of a Lady*, 517.

118. Lukács, *Theory of the Novel*, 75.

119. What Nussbaum calls 'perceptive equilibrium' is, in my view, equally elusive. Nussbaum, *Love's Knowledge*, 168.

presumption might seem to underpin some of the sunnier versions of ethical criticism, feeding the belief that novel-reading is doubly improving, that moral and epistemic progress are co-extensive, that good books make us good, if only by helping us to determine what goodness is.[120] One reason I begin with the Victorian novel is that it often lacks this confidence about itself or must make the case for its own moral value in the face of a more suspicious set of audiences.[121] These novels frequently confirm that Aristotle was right: that knowledge of the good is of supreme importance to our lives, that in the absence of such knowledge we are like archers without any clear sense of our target.[122] But novels can also make us doubt that there is any such target or that we can speak of *the* good as something unified, objective, or independent of the archer.[123] Henry and William James often suggest that the target is produced by the act of aiming: that the good or the meaningful is always in the process of being invented rather than found—and that novels might even partake in this moral creativity.

The thought that the good is a fiction need not be deflationary or devaluing and can inspire new experiments in living. Nor does it preclude knowledge or agreement about the many goods we have made up. Clearly, some people doubt a fiction's ability to know anything or to allow us to agree on anything, but this is not the approach I take here.[124] Our stories can at least supply us with a lived acquaintance with the practical and theoretical limits of knowing: the gap that appears between knowledge and virtue, or the knowledge that knowledge isn't

120. The connection between intellectual and moral virtue is extremely strong in Nussbaum's appraisal of novels. These artworks are 'moral achievements'—acts of perception that perform and train up our capacities 'to see and feel and judge . . . to miss less, to be responsible to more.' Nussbaum, *Love's Knowledge*, 164. Novels are not only morally educating, they are a key 'vehicle of citizenship.' Nussbaum, *Cultivating Humanity*, 94.

121. As one of the chief devotees of the novel's moral powers concedes: 'We are so accustomed to the novel that we tend to forget how morally controversial a form it has been in the eyes of various sorts of religious and secular moralisms.' Nussbaum, *Love's Knowledge*, 184.

122. Aristotle, *Nicomachean Ethics*, 4.

123. On these points see Wiggins, *Needs, Values, Truth*, 88–137.

124. As Kant argued, an aesthetic judgement 'does not belong to the faculty of cognition at all.' Kant, *Critique of the Power of Judgment*, 26.

always in our interests. The value of even this wisdom may be doubted though it may also indicate that we are inevitably drawn to knowledge as a value in-and-for-itself (a position I assume throughout this book). It simultaneously demonstrates that valuing is a plural affair and that not all goods can be reduced to the *morally* good or practically beneficial. Our fictions often record our devotion to truth even if it leads to heartache and moral nausea. Kafka's sadomasochistic sense of reading may not be for everyone: Books need not wound or stab us or affect us like a disaster.[125] Nonetheless, ethical criticism can deliver too safe an account of our reading encounters, making them fit with a preexisting moral framework or moral theory.[126] Or it subordinates the novel to an all too simple tale of self-improvement, often overlooking the heterogeneity of the better.[127] As we shall see, our fictions repeatedly disturb our basic intuitions about what is true or right or valuable and can leave us more confused than improved, or at least deeply uncertain about what improvement would look like. Some, of course, might embrace the paradox and deem this an improvement on the kind of certainty they set out with.

Novels clearly depend on a spirit of openness or what is sometimes talked up as a suspension of disbelief, but, as I show throughout the book, they also possess a sceptical energy that is in part a product of their form. This propensity for doubt is celebrated in James's 'The Middle Years' and generates a strange sense of commitment ('Our doubt is our passion, and our passion is our task').[128] One may well wonder, of course, how far doubt can or ought to go (as we've often been told: 'If you tried to doubt everything you would not get as far as doubting anything. The game of doubting itself presupposes

125. Franz Kafka to Oskar Pollak, letter, 27 January 1904, in *Letters to Friends, Family, and Editors*, 16.

126. In Nussbaum, for instance, novels repeatedly threaten to make Aristotelians of us all, so we learn that on essential ethical issues 'James's view is the Aristotelian view.' Nussbaum, *Love's Knowledge*, 201.

127. Some worry that a reality-cancelling fantasy of improvement has 'infected' the novel itself. See Cusk, *Outline*, 99.

128. James, *Collected Stories*, 2.123.

certainty').[129] If there are epistemic and psychological limits to how much doubting we can reasonably do—either in novels or outside of them—there may also be *moral* limits to our cultivation of doubt. I take seriously Raymond Gaita's contention that scepticism in ethics is either a frivolous or corrupt intellectual practice, for it questions what no one *really* doubts or it doubts what one really shouldn't.[130] There is much to be said for this position and it captures the kind of moral queasiness many of us are liable to feel when exposed to the novels of Wyndham Lewis—where rape is smilingly rendered as a cosmic jest and human beings are less moral agents than talkative machines.

Lewis's nihilistic comedies often bring us to the threshold of the palatable—to that limit-point noted by Hume—where moral discomfort or disapproval make it impossible to experience aesthetic pleasure.[131] Or, if we continue to experience pleasure, we might begin to worry about ourselves. But Lewis also shows how difficult it is for scepticism in ethics to be fully maintained. Nihilism, in Lewis, after all, is strikingly incomplete, at least on the question of freedom. He repeatedly sets out to doubt this fundamental value, but, as we shall see, he also struggles to sustain such scepticism.[132] His heroes often end up in a bad place: neither credulous enough to embrace their freedom nor sceptical enough to disavow it. They are thus locked into a toxic form of irony and approach all life with a sneer. If they make occasional raids into the land of sincere conviction and moral action, they often remain deeply compromised as agents.

Lewis helps us to appreciate that not all forms of irony are benign and that if we are to survive as moral agents, irony will have to practice some doubleness about itself. But it is important to stress that we do not necessarily embark on doubt or irony for corrupt or frivolous reasons.[133]

129. Wittgenstein, *On Certainty*, 18.

130. Gaita, *Good and Evil*, 314.

131. See Hume, 'On the Standard of Taste.'

132. As Peter Strawson noted, humans lack the capacity to fully disbelieve in their freedom, even if they lack sufficient grounds to believe it. Strawson, *Freedom and Resentment*, 1–28.

133. On irony as a form of '*committed* reflection,' see Lear, *A Case for Irony*. Lear draws this conviction from Kierkegaard or one of his pseudonyms: 'From the fact that irony is present it

Our questions may stem from a desire for wholeheartedness or a justified life—even though both goals are liable to retreat as we advance towards them. It may be a mistake, of course, to seek justifications for everything or to demand grounds where none are to be found—not least because the moral norms we set out to scrutinise might seem foundational to all proper scrutiny itself. But the mistake is not necessarily a moral error, nor is all scepticism about ethics embarked on in bad faith. As I argue throughout this book, the novel is very good at recovering the phenomenology of those moments where the world—and not just our will—makes us doubt the intelligibility and viability of our moral schemes.[134] Moreover, the wonder is frequently motivated by moral commitment, not by intellectual gamesmanship. Dorothea Brooke is no slouch on moral matters, but, as we shall see, her devotion to the good life frequently leads to bewilderment and muddle.

Bewilderment may be partly the point.[135] As George Eliot put it to Charles Bray in 1859: 'I only wish I could write something that would contribute to heighten men's reverence before the secrets of each other's souls, that there might be less assumption of entire knowingness.'[136] Though she was sometimes regarded as a woman of 'no doubts,'[137] Eliot brought her dislike of such knowingness remarkably far, even querying the basic 'line between the virtuous and the vicious.' That line, she argued, was not a safeguard to morality but was, in fact, an 'immoral fiction.'[138] Fiction was too true to be good in any simple sense for Eliot because goodness was a blurry and complex matter. Of course, it is one

---

does not follow that earnestness is excluded.' Climacus [Kierkegaard], *Concluding Unscientific Postscript to Philosophical Fragments*, 277n.

134. According to Diamond, literature can sensitise us to those moments where we feel 'shouldered out' from our moral schemes. Diamond, 'The Difficulty of Reality and the Difficulty of Philosophy,' 58.

135. As James put it in his preface to *The Princess Casamassima*: 'If we were never bewildered there would never be a story to tell.' James, *Literary Criticism*, 2.1090. On these issues, see Armstrong, *The Challenge of Bewilderment*.

136. Eliot, *The George Eliot Letters*, 3.163.

137. James, *Literary Criticism*, 1.1009.

138. Eliot, *Essays*, 147. On moral agency and decision-making in the face of uncertainty, see Williams, *The Art of Uncertainty*, chap. 1.

thing to present vagueness or complexity as a moral fact; it is another to doubt moral fact altogether. I explore these different shades of doubt in the chapters ahead. We may continue to doubt the value of doubt, or we may feel that 'wonder-sickness' should not be part of these adventures in wonder.[139] The novel's irony may not be for everyone, but in a world of often militant certainty, there may be some virtue to these kinds of unknowingness. This, at least, is one of the book's final beliefs or animating fictions.

A theory of fiction is also a theory of life, and no single book can do remote justice to either. The discussions that follow are incomplete studies, a series of night raids into vast topics. Though reflections ranging across a century of fiction may seem too widely dispersed, I am aware that the book covers a fairly restricted length of time in the life of the novel. It also remains rather provincial in its focus on European-based writers all working in English. While provincialism is an inevitable fact of mental and moral life—or so I argue at various points in this book—I am aware that I might have made my provinces bigger. The novels I have chosen are simply the books I have thought about and thought with for several years and I believe there are advantages to the fact that they are old friends to many others: Some background can be assumed as we home in on specific moral questions. A final practical note: I have kept the chapters reasonably discrete and free-standing so that they may be read on their own or skipped out. I'd like the book to inform, not impede, the proper task of living as if.

139. The condition of 'wonder-sickness' is diagnosed by James in 'The Sentiment of Rationality.' See James, *Writings 1878–1899*, 150.

1

Imaginings—c. 1850

THIS IS A TALE about the imagination—or about how that faculty was once imagined—and it turns around three main figures. The first is a man who allegedly had little or no imagination (this, at least, was the portrait of Jeremy Bentham bequeathed by his most famous pupil, J. S. Mill).[1] The second is a man who was sometimes said to have too much (the 'imagination of Dickens,' Hippolyte Taine observed, 'is like that of monomaniacs').[2] Finally, I consider a woman who was deeply ambivalent about imagination's powers (Eliot would even cast her own imagination as an 'enemy'—though this may have been her particular way of toying with fancy).[3] The general aim is to get to the psychological root of the various fictions that animate this book. Not all imaginings are fictions—at least in the sense of being untrue or unreal—but imagination is usually deemed to be the source and ground of the fictive and is built into its definition and functional explanation. So, a fiction, we are told, is an invitation, even a *prescription*, to imagine.[4] Yet the fictions I

1. Mill conceded that Bentham had imaginative skills as a writer and rhetorician, but his inability 'to conceive the absent as if it were present, the imaginary as if were real' was, he intimated, an intellectual and moral disaster. J. S. Mill, 'Bentham,' *Collected Works*, 10.75–160.

2. Taine, *A History of English Literature*, 4.124. Rumours of Dickens's madness circulated in the press in 1840, and he moved publicly to squash them. Long, '"It Is Said That Dickens Is Insane."'

3. Eliot, *The George Eliot Letters*, 1.134. All further references are given in the text under the abbreviation 'L.'

4. See Walton, *Mimesis as Make-Believe*, 61. See also Friend, 'The Real Foundations of Fictional Worlds,' and Abell, *Fiction*, 52.

explore below invite us to meta-imagine and to investigate the source, texture and significance of an everyday yet mysterious power. Hume thought the imagination was a 'magical faculty' in that its operations could not be fully explained; if it conditions much of our thinking, the imagination is itself unthinkable—or at least unknowable.[5] In the Victorian novel, however, the mind's eye turns upon itself and tries to know what it must imagine or to imagine what it knows it cannot know.

Indeed, imagination in these novels often presents itself—in a very Humean light—as a kind of magical thinking. An amateur magician himself, Dickens repeatedly talked up this mental voodoo in himself and in others.[6] George Eliot, moreover, begins *Adam Bede* with a wry celebration of her sorcerer's skills:

> With a single drop of ink for a mirror, the Egyptian sorcerer undertakes to reveal to any chance comer far-reaching visions of the past. This is what I undertake to do for you, reader. With this drop of ink at the end of my pen, I will show you the roomy workshop of Mr Jonathan Burge, carpenter and builder in the village of Hayslope, as it appeared on the eighteenth of June, in the year of our Lord 1799.[7]

It is not clear if this mind magic is genuinely world-making or an elaborate sham—a problem that goes to the heart of what reality we should invest in fictions or the epistemic value we should accord to imagination. In Eliot's translation of Feuerbach, imagination appears as 'a divine power.'[8] This may be largely tautological praise, since imagination is also the fabricator of the divine in Feuerbach, but it's easy to understand how imagination might seem to possess almost God-like force. It can conjure something from nothing and transcend the limits of time and space, all from the mind's sofa. If it can bring us back to the year 1799 when it is 1859—or now—it can also whisk us to Hayslope in the wink of an eye. The imagination, as Eliot puts it later in *Adam Bede*, 'is a

5. Hume, *Treatise of Human Nature*, 21.

6. On this theme, see Peter Conrad, *Dickens the Enchanter*; see also Keable, *Charles Dickens Magician*.

7. Eliot, *Adam Bede*, 5. All further references are given in the text under the abbreviation 'AB.'

8. Evans, *The Essence of Christianity*, 75.

licensed trespasser: it has no fear of dogs, but may climb over walls and peep in at windows with impunity' (AB, 65).[9] Eliot clearly celebrates the mind's right to roam—though the assurances that this is licenced trespass may make us wonder if mental travel can take more licentious forms.

Imagination is not one thing but many in Eliot—as you can tell from her attempts to decide between its 'active,'[10] 'vivid' (MF, 282), 'susceptible' (MF, 199), 'constructive,'[11] 'glorifying,'[12] and 'silly' (AB, 61) incarnations. She will also distinguish the 'veracious imagination'[13] from its false and ill-disciplined forms—in ways that seem to emulate earlier attempts to distinguish imagination per se from her more disreputable sister, fancy.[14] The extent to which this Cinderella of the mind can ever be removed from her corrupt relations might well be questioned. Dickens did little to honour the terminological distinction and was happy to present fancy as the one thing needful in a utilitarian age ('A nation without fancy, without some romance, never did, never can, never will, hold a great place under the sun').[15] The excessive nature of Dickens's own imagination became a common complaint.[16] Eliot baulked at the 'transcendent . . . unreality' of Dickens's prose (E, 271), while G. H.

9. Henry James admired these powers of trespass in Eliot: 'She had an imagination which enabled her to sit at home with book and pen, and yet enter into the life of other generations; project herself into Warwickshire ale-houses and Florentine symposia, reconstitute conditions utterly different from her own.' James, 'The Life of George Eliot,' in *Literary Criticism*, 1.1007. That said, James had also suggested that she was 'deficient in imagination.' 'The Novels of George Eliot,' in *Literary Criticism*, 1.932.

10. Eliot, *Mill on the Floss*, 65. All further references are given in the text under the abbreviation 'MF.'

11. Eliot, *Daniel Deronda*, 252. All further references are given in the text under the abbreviation 'DD.'

12. Eliot, *Impressions of Theophrastus Such*, 234. All further references are given in the text under the abbreviation 'ITS.'

13. Eliot, *Essays of George Eliot*, 267. All further references are given in the text under the abbreviation 'E.'

14. For a committed defence of the distinction between fancy and imagination, see Coleridge, *Biographia Literaria*, 295–305.

15. Dickens, 'Frauds on the Fairies,' in *Selected Journalism*, 566.

16. As Orwell later noted: 'His imagination overwhelms everything, like a kind of weed.' Orwell, 'Charles Dickens,' in *Essays*, 70.

Lewes was both impressed and appalled by the way he allowed the wildest unrealities to feel almost physically sensed. Never before had he witnessed a 'vividness of imagination approaching so closely to hallucination.'[17]

Dickens came close to conceiving his own gift as a problem. As he put it in a letter in 1865: 'I think it is my infirmity to fancy or perceive relations in things that are not apparent generally.'[18] His uncertainty about the exact nature of the issue—whether the relations in question were merely fancied or in fact perceived—might seem like an enactment of the difficulty. But the compelling force of his own fancy also impressed him. As he wrote to his wife, Catherine, after reducing the actor William Macready to tears: 'If you had seen William Macready last night—undisguisedly sobbing and crying on the sofa, as I read—you would have felt (as I did) what a thing it is to have Power.'[19] Many readers have acknowledged this power, though they have also been puzzled by it, and have even resented it. Bagehot insisted that the unreality of Dickens's characters was entirely transparent—'You could no more fancy Sam Weller, or Mark Tapley, or the Artful Dodger really existing than you can fancy a talking duck or a writing bear'—yet he also acknowledged their strange magnetism.[20] Indeed, Esther Summerson articulates what she and the rest of his creatures frequently invite us to feel: how 'the unreal things were more substantial than the real.'[21] Dickens, nevertheless, admitted to not fully understanding his own conjuring—not least when it came to the invention of character. As his friend James T. Fields reported in 1870:

> The growing up of characters in his mind never lost for him a sense of the marvellous. 'What an unfathomable mystery there is in it all!' he said one day. Taking up a wineglass, he continued: 'Suppose

17. Lewes, 'Dickens in Relation to Criticism,' 144.

18. Dickens, *The Letters of Charles Dickens*, 11.113.

19. Dickens, *The Letters of Charles Dickens*, 4.235. Dickens never entertains the possibility that he was taken in by Macready and that the tearful scene reflects the actor's power.

20. Bagehot in Collins, *Charles Dickens*, 394.

21. Dickens, *Bleak House*, 913. All subsequent references are given in the text under the abbreviation 'BH.'

> I choose to call this a *character*, fancy it a man, endue it with certain qualities; and soon the fine filmy webs of thought, almost impalpable, coming from every direction, we know not whence, spin and weave about it, until it assumes form and beauty, and becomes instinct with life.'[22]

Again, fiction operates like some kind of magic show: We don't know quite how it works, but it gives life and value to inanimate things. The same animistic energies can be seen throughout Dickens's prose—a place where boots can have a mind of their own and where a man and his doorknocker have some degree of 'resemblance and sympathy.'[23]

These sympathetic encounters would also seem to confirm the mind's inexhaustible capacity for projection. In *A Treatise of Human Nature*, Hume had famously shown how 'the mind has a great propensity to spread itself on external objects, and to conjoin with them any internal impressions, which they occasion.'[24] Our projections might distort reality—and Hume presented our mental spreading as a recurrent source of error—but he also maintained that it was the basis of much of our sense of reality. It was the ground, too, of aesthetic and even moral value. In the case of taste, for instance, the mind gilds and stains all natural objects with colours borrowed from our inward life and raises before it 'a new creation.'[25] Like Hume, Eliot had mixed feelings about these powers of projection—their world-making and world-mistaking aspects. If imagination 'exalts the solid fact,' it can also alienate us from fact altogether—assuming, of course, we even know what fact is or where it lies.[26] After all, the ambitious doctor of *Middlemarch* may

22. Fields, 'Some Memories of Charles Dickens.'

23. Dickens, *Sketches by Boz*, 58.

24. Hume, *Treatise of Human Nature*, 112.

25. Hume, *An Enquiry Concerning the Principles of Morals*, 163.

26. Eliot, *Daniel Deronda*, 322. All further references are given in the text under the abbreviation 'DD.' In her translation of Spinoza, Eliot underlined the point that '*the mind does not err because it imagines*,' yet like Spinoza she often presented the imagination as a wayward power that produced an incomplete or distorted picture of things. As Spinoza put it: 'So far as the human mind *imagines* an external body, it has an inadequate cognition of that body.' See Eliot, *Spinoza's Ethics*, 132, 137.

search for the 'primitive tissue' underlying all our sensations—but even this must be accessed indirectly and requires the help of the imagination. If Lydgate distinguishes the scientific imagination from a vulgar inventiveness, this engine of the mind doesn't lead him to Reality with a capital 'R.' Instead, it brings him to 'an ideally illumined space' in which we observe actions that are 'inaccessible to any sort of lens' and can only be understood through fictions (M, 154). As Lewes maintained in research that Eliot would help to edit, science also requires imagination and fictiveness.[27] However, Lewes was as determined as Lydgate is to distinguish 'the fictions of the thinker' from 'the fictions of the poet.' The latter were mere caprice, but the thinker's fictions were 'constructed according to rigorous canons and moulded by the pressures of Reality.'[28] Eliot may be less hard on the poet, but central to her own enterprise is a devotion to rigorous fictions in which we come closer to the truth and learn to distinguish good imaginings from bad.

So, this is a story about the ambiguous powers of imagination and its moral significance. Few Victorians could match Shelley's confidence that imagination is '*the* great instrument of moral good,' but it was usually deemed a moral disaster to be without one.[29] Bentham would come to epitomise this deficiency in his detractors' eyes, even if there was something deeply imaginative about his attempts to reach the outer limits of the imagination. If it yielded fantasies of pure fact—or the thoroughly non-imagined—it also made him campaign against fiction in its many forms. Fiction struck back in books like *Hard Times*—an ostensible attack on Benthamania—but the dream of the totally real would also be pursued within fiction itself. This is arguably the goal of what was called 'realism'—a term that increasingly did the rounds in England

27. 'The truth is that Science mounts on the wings of Imagination into regions of the Invisible and Impalpable, peopling these regions with Fictions more remote from fact than the phantasies of the Arabian Nights are from the daily occurrences in Oxford Street.' Lewes, *Problems of Life and Mind*, 1.289.

28. Lewes, *Problems of Life and Mind*, 1.289.

29. Ruskin put it more bluntly than anyone: 'An unimaginative person can neither be reverent nor kind.' He went on to suggest how the reading of works of fiction might help to correct this deficiency in some people's minds. Ruskin, *The Works of John Ruskin*, 27.627–28.

in the 1850s. All realisms—metaphysical and literary—would seem to invest in a world independent of mind and put the mind to work in search of this mind-independent space.[30] The world given to us by realism may remain an 'ideally illumined space,' but the realist aspiration to reality could also foster suspicions of imagination and idealisation. The mistrust can be seen in the definition Eliot provided of realism in 1856: 'the doctrine that all truth and beauty are to be attained by a humble and faithful study of nature, and not by substituting vague forms, bred by imagination on the mists of feeling, in place of definite, substantial reality.'[31] This confident conclusion—produced a year before she published her first short stories and almost three years before the publication of her first novel—did scant justice to her subsequent literary practice. It also failed to capture how the mist of imagination is a condition of moral perception throughout her writing life.

How 'substantial,' 'definite,' or 'ideally illumined' reality ever is or could be remained an unresolved issue for Eliot.[32] She was clearly acquainted with a philosophical tradition that traced our entire sense of reality to imagination. As Hume had argued, the continuity of objects, cause and effect, and the basic connections between thoughts ultimately depended on its empire.[33] In Kant, too, imagination constructs much of what we take to be real and is a 'necessary ingredient of perception itself.'[34] Seeing also had an imaginative element in Eliot's eyes ('the most active perception,' she maintained, 'gives us rather a reflex of what we think and feel, than the real sum of objects before us' [E, 89]). Within this seeing, moreover, values repeatedly supervene upon facts—or exalt

30. According to Carolyn Williams: 'Realism—in whatever genre or medium it occurs—is the representation of the world (understood as "the world as it is," the world free of representation and independent of shaping human perception or desire) along with the clear indication that the representation itself is an artifice or construction, a mediated and therefore not a direct rendering of reality.' See Williams, 'Melodrama and the Realist Novel,' 209.

31. Eliot, 'Art and Belles Lettres,' April 1856, 343. Eliot attributed this idea of realism to Ruskin.

32. William Blackwood was impressed by the way the real presupposed the imagined in Eliot's theorising—'you could not have the former without the latter' (L, 3.427).

33. Hume, *Treatise of Human Nature*, 21.

34. Kant, *Critique of Pure Reason*, 239.

the solid fact—and perceptions always seem on their way to becoming committed value-judgements. If imagination supplies an evaluative dimension to the world in Eliot, it also exposes the fragility of what we esteem, for it can make value itself seem dangerously mind-dependent or observer-relative. As Wittgenstein noted: 'The human gaze has a power of conferring value on things; but it makes them cost more too'—not least, we might add, when people fail to see or refuse to acknowledge what we hold dear.[35] The dispassionate eye of others can be a humiliation and it can reveal a brutal, even nihilistic, side to objectivity—or at least to reductive versions of it. Under a certain gaze, all imaginings can look imaginary, and all fictions seem like errors. Even the greatest enthusiasts of fact, however, will struggle to live in such a disenchanted world. Bentham soon discovered this little fact about fiction—its epistemic and existential necessity—and it is to this bold imaginer that I first turn.

The Ubiquity of Fiction

Bentham often yearned for the disenchantment of reality. In his *Anarchical Fallacies*, for instance, he suggested that the simple invention of the newspaper would help rid the world of phantoms: 'Before this talisman, not only devils, but ghosts, vampires, witches, and all their kindred tribes, are driven out of the land, never to return again: the touch of holy water is not so intolerable to them as the bare smell of printers' ink.'[36] However, it would take more than ink and newspapers to exorcise superstition from his own private life. Terrified by ghosts and goblins as a child, he often fled to the fields to be free of them. He was unusually vulnerable, moreover, to the conjuring powers of art.[37] A visit to a Punch and Joan show—where he encountered the devil and his imp—would leave him haunted for many years. Far from being dead to imagination, as some of his contemporaries claimed, the faculty was

35. See Wittgenstein, *Culture and Value*, 1.

36. Bentham, *The Works of Jeremy Bentham*, 2.2.400. All further references are given in the text under the abbreviation 'Works.'

37. On his interest in novels, see Shanafelt, 'Jeremy Bentham and the Pleasures of Fiction.'

terrifyingly alive in Bentham, though he was often inclined to experience its actions as a form of unfreedom ('my judgement is wholly free, my imagination is not wholly so' [Works, 10.18]). It's hardly a surprise, then, that he worked hard throughout his life to defend the sovereignty of judgement from the encroachments of imagination. The battle would also lead to campaigns against fiction—'the parent of confusion and error in all its shapes' (Works, 3.1.81).

Bentham conceded that there were many different types of fiction—the logician's fictions differed from those of the poet, priest, and lawyer—and he ultimately recognised that some of them were unavoidable (Works, 8.199).[38] Yet he continued to emphasise the moral hazards of various fictions in public life: They debased the 'moral' constitution of their users and impeded the 'intellectual' development of their dupes (Works, 9.1.59). He was particularly critical of legal fictions—including the fiction that legal fictions were necessary ('Fiction,' as he put it, 'is no more necessary to justice than poison is to sustenance' [Works, 6.2.582]). He castigated the law's deployment of fictitious persons, fictitious jurisdictions, and fictitious needs—not least the need for legal jargon that lined the pockets of lawyers and prohibited ordinary Joes from understanding the law. Here he would at least find an ally in Dickens.[39] Indeed, when it came to the obfuscatory fog of legal fiction—'the mountains of costly nonsense,' 'the pretence of equity' (BH, 14), the 'trickery, evasion, procrastination, spoilation, botheration, under false pretences of all sorts' (BH, 17)—Bentham and Dickens were largely on the same page.[40] But even Dickens would struggle to match Bentham's vehemence when it came to legal make-believe: 'In English law, fiction is a syphilis, which runs in every vein, and carries into every part of the system the principle of rottenness' (Works, 5.92). Bentham was an equally ferocious critic of political fictions—the sophistries of natural law and natural rights. The idea of an original contract for the state was

38. One of the first to discuss the importance of fiction for Bentham was Charles Ogden. See Ogden, *Bentham's Theory of Fictions*.

39. As Dickens put it in 1853: 'The one great principle of the English law is to make business for itself' (BH, 621).

40. Stone, 'Dickens, Bentham, and the Fictions of the Law.'

'a pure fiction; or in other words, a falsehood' (Works, 2.501). Such fables, he conceded, may have once had their uses, but in the auspicious year of 1789, he confidently announced that 'the season of *Fiction* is now over' (Works, 1.269).

This post-fictitious dawn would never quite commence. Fictions, after all, were embedded in the language and could not be easily excised. It was a natural tendency for the users of words to assume the real existence of the entities or properties to which they referred. But this was where language repeatedly led us into error, committing us to a belief in 'fictitious entities' that had no foothold in the world. Bentham accepted that some of these entities were necessary constructions, but in several cases, he aimed to reduce these fictions to something more basic, through a combination of definition and 'paraphrasis.' These techniques allowed him to translate 'the language of fiction into the language of reality' (Works 3.189), substituting terms for fictitious entities in a sentence with terms for real ones until the proposition contained as few of these illusions as possible. However, the tenability and cognitive value of such reduction was questionable. It is hard to say whether Dickens had this periphrastic method in mind when he describes Gradgrind's absurd acts of definition and his confidence that no facts can be secured without them ('Girl number twenty unable to define a horse!' . . . Girl number twenty possessed of no facts, in reference to one of the commonest of animals!). Bitzer's definition of a horse—'Quadruped. Graminivorous. Forty teeth, namely twenty-four grinders, four eyeteeth, and twelve incisive'—doesn't seem to bring reality any closer to us.[41]

Bentham did not spend his days periphrasing horses, but his various proposals for substituting fictitious entities with real ones met with one obvious problem: the elusiveness of reality itself. True to his empiricist roots, Bentham defined a real entity as 'an object, the existence of which is made known to us by one or more of our five senses' (Works, 8.325). However, this confident empiricism was troubled by the theory of

41. Dickens, *Hard Times*, 7. All subsequent references are given in the text under the abbreviation 'HT.'

perception on which it relied. According to Bentham: 'It is only by the evidence afforded by perceptions that the reality of a body of any kind can be established' (Works, 8.196). But perceptions, he conceded, do not secure a direct acquaintance with reality.[42] We have immediate access to impressions and ideas, not their ostensible object. This led Bentham to the very Humean thought that we are not entitled to conclude that perceptions capture or are the product of real entities. Far from providing evidence of external bodies, our experience indicated that 'a body is an aggregate of fictitious entities.'[43] Our ideas of matter, form, quantity, and space are first-order fictions, and they are often conjoined with second-order qualities: colour, taste, beauty, and so forth. Indeed, Bentham's conception of fiction was so broad that it risked subsuming all facts under its mantle. All qualities outside of brute substance, all relational properties, even matter itself were acknowledged to be fictitious. Time was a 'still more fictitious fiction' (Works, 8.200). In fact, any object with a temporal or spatial location, any entity in a state of rest or motion, is in part a fabrication: 'Of nothing, therefore, that has place, or passes in our mind, can we speak, or as much as think, otherwise than in the way of fiction' (Works, 8.199).

So much for the worshipper of fact. Bentham continued to sponsor a periphrastic method where he attempted to recover the physical object or raw fact underlying a thicket of fictions, but, as we have seen, much of what we might ordinarily regard as a physical object was itself fictitious. The fugitive nature of reality was ultimately acknowledged in one of Bentham's other definitions of a 'real entity'—if he sometimes defined it as an object that was accessible to the senses, he also presented it in a much more attitudinal or semantic light: It was 'an entity, to which, on the occasion and for the purpose of discourse, existence is really meant to be ascribed' (Works, 8.196). Here—more promisingly—reality is a way of speaking or a largely pragmatic affair. Fiction, too, we might add, is a mode of speech or attitude—a particular stance that we

42. On these points see Stolzenberg, 'Bentham's Theory of Fictions.'

43. Bentham Manuscripts, University College London, 135.69, quoted in Takashima, 'Bentham's Theory of Language,' 3.

adopt when we talk about devils, imps, or entities from which we withhold full assent even though this nonbelief may take considerable mental discipline.[44] Fiction may be a form of language or a distinctive attitude in which we renege on belief or disbelief, but considered in the more metaphysical light that Bentham often reverts to, much of experience carries the gild of fiction. Though he set out to purge the world of ghosts, he discovered that key aspects of life are phantoms of the mind. Indeed, the mind, as such, was another spectre.[45] If he bowed to the necessity of such illusions, he also remained in thrall to a certain dream of reality—the pure fact that underlies all our fictions.

This is a dream he would be remembered for. As Gradgrind declares in *Hard Times*: 'Facts alone are wanted in life' (HT, 5). Dickens's portrait of Gradgrind clearly owes much to romantic critiques of a utilitarian worldview. Wordsworth's criticisms of utilitarians, for instance, were accompanied by dark prophecies of an age 'When fact with heartless search explored / Shall be Imagination's Lord.'[46] The fact-worship of *Hard Times* builds on this and on Mill's portrait of a myopic fact-gatherer. As Mill maintained, Bentham's approach to knowledge was 'wholly empirical'—but it was the empiricism of a man who was deficient in experience of both an inward and outward kind.[47] The same solipsistic scientism can be seen in Gradgrind: 'As if an astronomical observatory should be made without any windows' (HT, 75). This image of a solipsist captures—inadvertently, perhaps—the strange reality-dissolving power of Bentham's empiricism. As we have seen, the method could leave little of our everyday sense of the world intact, showing how much we live in our minds, or within the magic castle of fiction. And while he repeatedly sought escape from that castle, we have

44. As Bentham put it: 'A fictional entity is an entity to which though by the grammatical form of the discourse employed in speaking of it, existence be ascribed, yet in truth and reality existence is not meant to be ascribed' (Works, 8.195).

45. Reflecting the materialist assumptions behind much of his philosophising, Bentham declared that 'all language which has *mind* for its subject, is unavoidably fictitious, speaking of *mind* as if it were *matter*' (Works, 8.73).

46. Wordsworth, *The Poetical Works of William Wordsworth*, 8.299.

47. Wordsworth, *The Poetical Works of William Wordsworth*, 92.

seen him frequently admit to the necessity of fiction and fictitious entities.

Bentham's ultimate position, in fact, was similar to the view taken in 'The Spirit of Fiction,' an essay published in Dickens's own magazine *Household Words* in 1867. The essay—once presumed to be by Dickens but now thought to have been penned by Henry Morley—pays homage to the constructive imagination, apprising readers of 'the philosophical fact that we are all partly creators of the objects we receive.' Since the spirit of fiction haunts everything, it is impossible to cast fictions aside. Fictions are necessary and find their vindication in 'the utility of the result.'[48] The striking thing about Bentham's thought, however, was not just its exhausting attention to fictions and fictiveness, but also its attempts to make 'utility' a rigorous master-principle that might allow us to decide between good fictions and bad, indeed between good and bad anythings.[49] However, this also raised a number of self-referential questions. To what extent is 'utility' itself a fiction—either false or ontologically subjective—and can it nonetheless function as an epistemically objective or mutually binding criterion of value? Is it a fantasy to think that utility can be accurately measured, and do attempts to either measure or maximise utilities lead to perverse results? These questions lead us into the heart of Bentham's utilitarianism and to Dickens's attack on this system in *Hard Times*. They also raise questions about fictionalism—or the ways we might seek to justify a life lived 'as if.'

The Uses of Fancy

The brilliant rules—'Never wonder' (HT, 41), or 'You are never to fancy' (HT, 9)—are bound to produce what they set out to prohibit. Indeed, they might make us wonder about their adequacy as a portrait of Benthamism. In *Chrestomathia*, Bentham certainly worried

48. Dickens, 'The Spirit of Fiction,' in *All the Year Round*, 119.

49. According to Bentham: 'Fiction may be applied to a good purpose, as well as to a bad one: in giving support to a useful rule or institution, as well as to a pernicious one' (Works, 7.1.287).

about the mischief that springs from 'curiosity' and the dangerous 'pleasure of the imagination' (Works, 8.10). But he remained an active imaginer and mental pleasure-seeker throughout his life. His indefatigable verbal inventiveness ('maximize' and 'minimize' took off; 'morphoscopic posology' somehow didn't [Works, 8.85]) point to his imaginative fecundity. His utilitarianism, moreover, was a virtual science of imagination (or its critics might say an imaginary science). For all of Mill's conviction that Bentham lacked the power to make absent things present to the mind, this is precisely what his felicific calculus set out do, at least when envisioning prospective states: It was a calculus that gave imagined pleasures a determinate form and weighting. However, the criteria that Bentham supplied to give substance and value to imagined feelings—the intensity, duration, certainty or uncertainty, propinquity or remoteness of would-be pleasures—can seem naive, a doomed arithmetic of the counterfactual. Such confidence in quantification is clearly lampooned in *Hard Times*, where it can sometimes seem to reflect an impoverished theory of value.

Not all goods can be counted or compared under the master-value of utility. *Hard Times* repeatedly tests the limits of this utility principle, revealing it to be either too broad or too narrow. Moreover, to invoke one of Bentham's more helpful coinages, the principle repeatedly leads to 'paradoxicality' (Works, 8.484). Bentham's confidence in a common metric for all values would also help to secure his reputation as an 'arch-philistine.'[50] His iconoclastic remarks on the value of poetry—no better than pushpin and potentially worse since it was enjoyed by so few—did little to detract from that impression. And though he accepted that literature usually traded in nondeceptive fictions, he also berated it for its falsehood ('between poetry and truth there is a natural opposition'). Poetry was a dangerous progenitor of 'false morals' (Works, 2.253) and he condemned the mischiefs caused by this 'magic art' in public life (Works, 2.254). And yet it is easily forgotten that Bentham defended the utility of poetry and the fine arts in general. In fact, 'there is nothing the

50. Marx, *Capital*, 758.

utility of which is more incontestable' (Works, 2.253). His sense of this utility can seem a little begrudging or satirical at points—the arts weaned us from violent and vicious pursuits and were 'excellent substitutes for drunkenness, slander, and the love of gaming' (Works, 2.254). But since the useful, for Bentham, is ultimately what gives pleasure, he was forced to concede that the arts supplied generous amounts of this commodity. This is why Sleary's dictum in *Hard Times*—'People mutht be amuthed' (HT, 35)—is less a refutation of utilitarianism than a simple reiteration of one of its fundamental commitments—namely, its hedonistic conception of value.[51]

Dickens scores many points against utilitarianism in its Benthamite form—its quantitative ambitions; its seemingly egotistical moral psychology (life is 'not all Thelf-interetht after all' [HT, 218]); its lack of respect for the integrity of persons in the pooling of pleasure or happiness (can the well-being of 'a million million' really sanction the starvation of five-and-twenty? [HT, 47]); its insensitivity to the agent-relativity of moral reasoning (as if people were utility-machines 'wi'out loves and likeins, wi'out memories and inclinations' [HT, 116]); its lack of respect for moral sentiments or 'the wisdom of the Heart' (HT, 168). Still, the imputation that the Benthamite is an ardent pleasure-killer is hard to credit. Indeed, it was with a view to defending pleasure that Bentham condemned aesthetic purists and connoisseurs—those snobbish 'interrupters of pleasure' who looked down their noses at certain amusements in the name of good taste. 'There is no taste which deserves the epithet *good*' (Works, 3.254), Bentham insisted, unless it operates in the service of some broader utility; conversely, none was bad unless it culminated in some palpable form of mischief. This was not a call to take down the credulous wallpaper or to cancel the circus.

Bentham's refusal to subscribe to a standard of taste (outside of utility itself), was, of course, one of the more controversial aspects of his outlook. To draw on a Gradgrindeanism, 'What is called Taste, is only another name for Fact,' namely, the fact of pleasure, and there is no criterion outside of quantity itself to distinguish between better and

51. The point is well made in Blake, *The Pleasures of Benthamism*.

worse forms of it (HT, 9). Even Bentham's disciples were inclined to feel that there was a philistine, even immoral, aspect to such permissiveness. The same might be said about Dickens's very catholic sense of fun: Take his enlistment of the circus as the supreme playground of the imagination, or indeed his sponsorship of 'fancy'—much less respectable than imagination—as the epitome of the mind's freedom. Critics like F. R. Leavis sometimes worried about Dickens's taste and wondered if such a low form of pleasure as the circus—so replete with 'squalor, grossness and vulgarity'—could carry its symbolic burden or claim any cousinship with higher forms of art.[52] After leaving the matter hanging for a bit, Leavis did conclude that Dickens managed to pull off the symbolic investment.

Operating on the margins of the system it rejects, Sleary's circus demonstrates the utility of seemingly useless things (certainly, his happy children show a 'special inaptitude for any sharp kind of practice' [HT, 31]). The therapy provided by the circus might imply that this playground is in cahoots with the reality from which it provides a reprieve—that play is the way we are restored to work, that the palace of imagination is built on the despotism of fact, that fancy's freedoms are mental candyfloss. Providing an outlet for pent-up energies, the circus may even sustain a bread-and-circuses model of social control (while allowing the authorities to skimp on the bread). But whatever its ultimate social function or the weighting we give it, the circus's useful uselessness exposes the limits of utility as a criterion of value. It also draws out a sister issue: the disutility of making everything an object of utilitarian action.

Hard Times gets us to reflect on utility's limits, but the issues also rebound on the novel itself. By asserting the practical and therapeutic value of 'idle imagination,' the novel risks instrumentalising its core principle in the service of some broader end (HT, 18). The novel is never quite idle enough. The programmatic aspects of the text have long been noted, and it generates related kinds of paradox: It is too systematic in

52. Leavis, *The Great Tradition*, 265. As Bagehot also observed, 'There has been much controversy about Mr. Dickens's taste. A great many cultivated people will scarcely concede that he has any taste at all.' Bagehot felt, at least, that Dickens had 'creative taste.' See Bagehot, 'Charles Dickens,' in *Charles Dickens*, 399.

its criticisms of moral systems, too pious about pleasure, a little too serious about the need for play. The aim may be to instruct and delight, but extended instruction on the importance of delight can vitiate pleasure.[53] In short, '*Hard Times* is boring' or so it has been uncompromisingly said.[54] Perhaps an anti-Benthamite point is at work here—the reader is forced to endure the lesson that pleasure isn't the only value. People mustn't be amused, at least for significant stretches of the novel. The novel, therefore, is aesthetically perverse, undermining the gospel of amusement by preaching it so wholeheartedly. *Hard Times* activates several problems of self-reference that will also haunt the utilitarian. As Mill painfully discovered for himself: Too systematic a pursuit of happiness can undermine happiness and the same might be said for the happiness of a text. Core aesthetic principles like play or pleasure are liable to be destroyed by their overzealous defence or by their hypostatisation as value or doctrine.

But not all forms of self-reference in *Hard Times* are unhappy. The novel, after all, is also an insightful piece of metafiction that considers how we live fictitiously or conjure much of what we take to be real. Here Dickens restages Bentham's dream of a world shorn of fictions while making the Benthamite point that a life without fiction would be unliveable or even unthinkable. Conversely, the demand for pure fact is unsayable. 'Teach these boys and girls nothing but Facts. . . . Plant nothing else, and root out everything else' (HT, 5): The prescription violates its own rule by being an imperative, not a factual statement. It is also embarrassingly figurative, even if the metaphor of planting is hackneyed or half-dead. Of course, the philosophical stakes of metaphor come into view when one recalls Bentham's profound mistrust of figurativeness or, to draw on his own figure, his fear of its obfuscating 'mist' (Works, 2.307). The kinds of ambivalence he brought to fiction reappear in his comments on figurativeness: It was unavoidable, useful, and often

53. As Bentham noted himself: 'Happiness is a very pretty thing to feel, but very dry to talk about' (Works, 4.1.64).

54. Durnan, 'Getting Bored with *Hard Times*,' 403.

profoundly misleading.[55] He insisted that metaphors should be used sparingly or else paraphrased out of existence, never pausing to consider whether the method of paraphrasis itself was a mere metaphorical practice—a means of describing one thing in terms of something else. *Hard Times* delightedly enacts the revenge of metaphor on those who would do without it.[56] Take the opening description of the great evangel of fact:

> The scene was a plain, bare, monotonous vault of a schoolroom, and the speaker's square forefinger emphasised his observations by underscoring every sentence with a line on the schoolmaster's sleeve. The emphasis was helped by the speaker's square wall of a forehead, which had his eyebrows for its base, while his eyes found commodious cellarage in two dark caves, overshadowed by the wall. The emphasis was helped by the speaker's mouth, which was wide, thin, and hard set. The emphasis was helped by the speaker's voice, which was inflexible, dry, and dictatorial. The emphasis was helped by the speaker's hair, which bristled on the skirts of his bald head, a plantation of firs to keep the wind from its shining surface, all covered with knobs, like the crust of a plum pie, as if the head had scarcely warehouse-room for the hard facts stored inside. (HT, 5)

The language—initially bare, monotonous, and ascetic—may attempt to cling to facts and remain fancy-free, but it soon succumbs to the dazzle of figurativeness. There is, perhaps, a certain vindictiveness in the narrator's recourse to imagery, in the surreal humour of planting firs on a man's head or converting it into a plum pie. It is easy to see why Sartre

55. As Bentham put it: 'Figurative language is very useful for facilitating conception, when it follows in the train of simple language: it is mischievous when it occupies its place. It accustoms us to reason on the most false analogies, and gathers round the truth, a mist which the most enlightened minds are scarcely able to penetrate' (Works, 2.307). In a self-referential moment, Bentham invoked the figure of 'rags' to denounce figurativeness and then immediately proceeded to acknowledge its necessity: 'But away with these figures of speech: they are troublesome to manage; and have been worn to rags. Unhappily, there is no such thing as speaking—nor even as thinking—without such figures' (Works, 4.446).

56. See, in particular, Dahmane, '"A Mere Question of Figures."'

would associate the imagination with negativity and the image with 'the negation of the world.'[57] There are pleasures to be had, it seems, in making a meal of a pleasure-killer. Metaphor here is a kind of murder or cannibal reckoning.[58] This may only be pretend-murder—figurativeness as a rough kind of fun. Nonetheless, fancy seems to assert its freedom through the denial of the actual. The reader is invited to counter-imagine what is the case—hair becomes a forest, a head becomes a pie—but in ways that disturb our sense of what the real case is. The metaphors, after all, face in two directions: towards facts and away from them, superimposing themselves on Gradgrind, but also telling us something about him through the positing of likeness. His head, we are made to feel, *is* like a pie: bald, knobbled, even a little beige perhaps, if not exactly delicious.

It is sometimes claimed—quite controversially—that metaphors don't say anything outside their literal content and that that content is usually patently false (firs, we will observe, don't grow on people's heads).[59] However, Dickens, it is worth noting, often plays with similes, not just metaphor in a restricted sense. If metaphors are false at a literal level, similes, according to Donald Davidson, are always true. For Davidson 'everything is like everything' in the end, and similes posit a likeness so open-ended that they can never really be false.[60] Gradgrind's pie-likeness therefore cannot be entirely refuted. Yet many of Dickens's similes are prepared to acknowledge their own tendentiousness or counterfactuality through the use of 'as if' ('as if,' for example, 'the head had scarcely warehouse-room for the hard facts stored inside' [HT, 5]). They tell the truth about not quite hitting the mark and in doing so complicate the identification Bentham often made between fiction and falsehood. Moreover, if Bentham hoped to speak the 'language of reality' (Works 3.189), then Dickens both delivers and parodies this dream in the passage above. It is as if physical reality is given a language or a

57. Sartre, *The Imaginary*, 185.

58. Ortega y Gasset describes poetic metaphor as a kind of weapon that 'turns against natural things and wounds or murders them.' See Ortega y Gasset, *Dehumanization of Art*, 35.

59. See Davidson, 'What Metaphors Mean.'

60. Davidson, 'What Metaphors Mean,' 39.

type of rhetoric. For instance, we get four helpings of the 'emphasis was helped' though it is physical facts themselves that seem to do all the emphasising: forehead, mouth, voice, and even hair conspire in the anaphora of the actual. The world, it seems, is always already 'rhetorical' and arrives with a particular inflection or evaluative colour.

Bentham repeatedly longed for neutrality—even if scientific neutrality was ultimately subordinate to utility or the happiness of humankind.[61] It made him yearn for a more continent set of vocabularies—with less moral prejudice built in and where 'passion-kindling' associations could be removed (Works, 2.438). However, Dickens often intimates that this neutrality is an illusion. Seemingly innocuous terms develop a strange significance in *Hard Times*. The word 'square' above, for instance, thickens in meaning through repetition: 'the square forefinger' and 'square wall of a forehead' are soon joined by other squares: a 'square coat, square legs, square shoulders' (HT, 5). These are metaphorical squares—literally false—and they query the dream of a purely factual description entertained by Gradgrind. The squareness that the world is made to yield in *Hard Times* also draws attention to the Benthamite investment in a kind of moral geometry—a confidence that ethical life lends itself to the same kind of calculability, certainty and precision that the mathematical sciences enjoy. But this fantasy does violence to moral facts just as the squareness that the world is forced to deliver is a distortion of physical facts. Indeed, 'fact' is one of those words that is made uncanny through repetition ('"Fact, fact, fact!" said the gentleman. And "Fact, fact, fact!" repeated Thomas Gradgrind' [HT, 9]). A noun, an imperative, a mantra, and a purely phatic utterance, fact acquires so many different senses that it risks losing all sense.

Ruskin derided Dickens's lack of interest in the 'pure fact,' but Dickens repeatedly makes us wonder whether the pure fact is the ultimate fiction—at least when it insists on purities shorn from value, interest,

61. 'Neutral expressions can scarcely be found,' he complained, 'to designate the motives which determine human actions' (Works, 2.255).

metaphor, or concept.[62] Indeed, one might well conceive of Dickens as an epistemic and moral fictionalist. This is a position that concedes to the 'as-if-ness' of all knowledge, and pretty much all virtue, as well as to the 'real' virtues of proceeding 'as if.'[63] Despite Dickens's concerns about utilitarianism and the paradoxes and perversions it could breed, this fictionalism might seem to prioritise utility over truth as the best means of getting on in the world. Like Silas Wegg's 'timber fiction' in *Our Mutual Friend,* fictions have practical value and help us to get about.[64] So, we may decide to believe—or pretend to believe—what is convenient to credit. The novels, after all, are full of characters who manage to live within worlds of their own making. The fiction of 'Happy Cottage' in *Little Dorrit*—a mere picture of a thatched house daubed onto a shop wall—may be an illusion, but it does seem to constitute a certain happiness for the Plornishes. As Wemmick or Dick Swiveller confirm, fiction in Dickens is something we can quite happily live in.

Things in this fictionalist scheme may not be as simple as Little Dorrit hopes—'we can always go back to the plain truth'—and Dorrit herself, to pause for a moment on the novel that followed *Hard Times,* remains a devoted deceiver.[65] She colludes in the genteel fictions of her father—wishing to 'conceal all his faults until she dies'—and hides unpleasant facts from her lover right to the novel's final page (LD, 461). As she candidly admits, sounding a little like her own inventor: 'I could never have been of any use, if I had not pretended a little' (LD, 143). Nonetheless, *Little Dorrit*—like all of Dickens's fictions—revolves around the exposure of shams and 'false pretences' (LD, 668). The financial fictions of Mr. Merdle; the duplicity of Mr. Casby

62. 'John Ruskin on Dickens' in Collins, *Charles Dickens,* 444.

63. For a study of the role of useful, indeed necessary, falsehood in *Little Dorrit,* see Carlisle, '*Little Dorrit*: Necessary Fictions.' On the role of pious fraud in *Our Mutual Friend,* see Tsutsui, 'The Morality of Fiction-Making in *Our Mutual Friend.*' On Dickens's extensive use of the term 'as if' see Farina, '"Dickens's As If."' Also see Mullan, *Artful Dickens,* chap. 2.

64. Dickens, *Our Mutual Friend,* 303. All subsequent references are given in the text under the abbreviation 'OMF.'

65. Dickens, *Little Dorrit,* 416. All subsequent references are given in the text under the abbreviation 'LD.'

('a philanthropic sneak' and 'shabby deceiver' [LD, 667]); the polite frauds of Mrs. General (where all is 'show without substance' [LD, 422]); the deceptions and self-deceptions of Mrs. Clennam ('you cheat yourself,' Flintwinch finally announces [LD, 652]) are gradually flushed out. The most industrious self-cheater in the novel is Mr. Dorrit himself. For the most part, the costs of his 'castle-building' are borne by others as he forces his supporters to bend to his pretensions. Fiction, we see, is not without its tyrannies, though in the end reality can only be bullied so much.

Dorrit's eventual breakdown may reveal the psychological limits of a certain kind of fictionalism—a mark of the resistance of the real within oneself. If Dorrit is too taken in by his own fancies, it is worth noting that Dickens also satirises those who are not taken in enough or only *pretend* to believe what it is advantageous to believe. The fact that there are virtuous hypocrites like Little Dorrit certainly complicates the issue. The crucial difference may lie in the fact that her virtuous pretence—like Mr. Boffin's 'pious fraud' in *Our Mutual Friend*—is conducted for other-regarding reasons, though it may be a fiction to think we may be able to tell the difference (OMF, 771). The 'as ifs' of Josiah Bounderby would certainly appear to be entirely self-regarding. He is a man of elastic beliefs or, rather, pseudo-beliefs. As he proudly admits: 'I am quite as much attached to it as if I believed it. I am quite ready to go in for it, to the same extent as if I believed it' (HT, 100). If the good, in Dickens, are often gullible, Bounderby is not good enough to be properly credulous. Even fiction requires immersion for its charms to fully work, and the same might be said for the general theatre of moral life—hence Dickens's delight in 'a child's trustfulness' and his hope that it can be retained or rekindled in an adult state. But Bounderby lives at a cynical remove from everything.[66] If he attests to a lack of principle within utilitarianism—an ethos where nothing has intrinsic value outside of pleasure itself—he also exposes the moral hazards of a fictionalism in which the usefulness of an attitude presides over its truth. Whether the

66. Dickens, 'A Christmas Tree,' *Selected Journalism*, 16. This cynical distance can also be observed in Harold Skimpole in *Bleak House*—a figure who repeatedly pretends to be a child.

distinction between a self-regarding and other-regarding fiction is enough to manage the moral pitfalls of pretence is unclear. But there is a sense in Dickens that too much pretending is bad for even self-regarding reasons.

So, while *Hard Times* seems to give a thumbs-up to certain fictions—the pleasures of De Foe, the splendours of the circus, or the mixed joys of *Hard Times* itself—the novel also suggests that we should not sentimentalize story or fancy. Pure fiction is not really pure. This is made clear by the various 'fictions of Coketown' (HT, 91)—the fiction of equal opportunity and just reward, the fiction that any worker is free to make their fortune, the fiction that every worker is a happy one. The grounding fiction of political economy—that rational self-interest is the principle we are steered by—is also constitutive. It produces Bitzer, the utilitarian Frankenstein brought up on the scripture of the new social sciences ('What you must always appeal to is a person's self-interest' [HT, 214]). Gradgrind may campaign against imagination, but he clearly reveals its darker sides, not least in his fanciful vision of a purely factual world. The world-negating powers of fancy are all too evident in these revolutionists of the moral world. The wilder metaphors of *Hard Times*—factories like fairy palaces, engines operating as mad, sad elephants—reveal how a certain dream of a world has negated the actual and installed a grotesque alternative. The satirical imagery may be a negation of a negation, but it reveals the ambiguous power of imagination: its role as creator and destroyer.

When certain phantasms of fact have become the fact—as they do in Dickens's 'Cacotopia' (Bentham's word for the very worst of all worlds [Works, 3.493])—the 'pure fact' may feel further away than ever. But the fiction of the pure fiction—either total in scope or supremely good—must also be relinquished. Everything depends, we might say, on how a fiction is used. 'We know that it's a base pretension,' Frederick Dorrit proclaims, 'by its having that effect'—namely, a bad one (LD, 405). This might emphasise the importance of consequences and utility as their ultimate measure, but *Hard Times* also reveals the moral disaster—and evaluative incoherence—of making 'utility' the only kind of importance. At the very least, the novel would seem to call for a more sophisticated fictionalism in which we operate *as if* some things are true independently of being useful and some things are worth doing entirely for their own sake. Dickens hated the cynical gospel 'that you were to do good not because it *was* good, but because you were to make a good thing of it' (OMF, 215). Or at least he made a good show of hating it. In the end, it can be hard to tell a sophisticated fictionalism—one that *pretends* that fiction has its limits (moral and epistemic)—from a position that really *believes* in those limits. Of course, what believing *really* amounts to is also queered by Dickens's fiction—not least when we find ourselves shedding tears for those who don't exist.

Seeing-As

In his celebrated study of Dickens, Chesterton outlined the kind of fictionalism that the writer permitted us to see from both within and without: 'Our solid houses and square meals are in the strict sense fiction. They are things made up to typify our thoughts.'[67] Chesterton clearly set a low bar for what counted as fiction—it is virtually anything that is expressive of mind—but he was convinced that Dickens allowed us to appreciate how the most basic aspects of our world are mind-dependent or observer-relative. Indeed, the pantomimes of Christmas might seem to confirm a general Dickensian law: 'Nothing is, but thinking makes it so.'[68] Not that we are necessarily free to think whatever we like. In this last section, I want to consider in more detail the moral significance of this mind-dependence and the way it might animate a sense of value. This is to give a Hamlet-like spin to life's pantomime—'There is nothing either good or bad but thinking makes it so.'[69] However, the moral fictions that I wish to examine—namely, values or a very basic set of attachments—often precede the will. Indeed, they condition and even bind it, making it undesirable, if not impossible, to resist the force of our

67. Chesterton, *Charles Dickens*, 16–17.

68. Dickens, 'A Christmas Tree,' in *Selected Journalism*, 9.

69. Shakespeare, *Hamlet*, 2.2.48–49, 53. For these links between Christmas pantomime and *Hamlet*, see Conrad, *Dickens the Enchanter*, 130.

own imaginings.[70] These fancies, moreover, precede assessments of use and have a quasi-perceptual and nondeliberative character. Let us consider, then, the phenomenology of this way of seeing in Dickens and Eliot. Both writers are clearly very different—if Dickens was an avowedly fond father of the imagination, Eliot was a much stricter parent[71]—yet they each remain devoted to an imaginative vision that reveals 'the romantic side of familiar things' (BH, 7). Here the world is awash with normativity—facts carry a halo of value and values seem to have a factual presence in the world.

We have noted, after all, how the differences between a fact and an evaluation are often hard to parse in Dickens. Sights and sounds almost overcommunicate, and perception is often indistinguishable from judgement. Take the sound of Jenny Wren's drink-addled father: 'The very breathing of the figure was contemptible, as it laboured and rattled in that operation, like a blundering clock' (OMF, 241). Or consider the delectably disgusting Mr. Casby, beaming at the hob in *Little Dorrit:* 'with his benevolent knobs shining as if the warm butter of the toast were exuding through the patriarchal skull, and with his face as ruddy as if the colouring matter of the anchovy paste were mantling in the patriarchal visage' (LD, 570). Here we see how we view the world interpretatively in images that communicate but don't quite assert. It may be hard to make out what exactly the anchovy paste is saying, but we can probably guess it's not anything particularly nice. This may be a very subjective way of seeing, but part of the 'hypnotism of Dickens,' as Chesterton called it, is to make us feel how value is 'out there' and part of the furniture of the world.[72] Of course, the furniture in Dickens is always liable to develop a 'shrivelled human face' in ways that make us look again at this business of looking.[73]

70. These imaginings become what Harry Frankfurt called 'a volitional need.' See Frankurt, 'Necessity and Desire,' in *The Importance of What We Care About*, 104–16.

71. As Dickens put it in the preface to *David Copperfield*: 'I am a fond parent to every child of my fancy.' See Dickens, 'Preface,' *David Copperfield*, 870.

72. Chesterton, *Charles Dickens*, 16.

73. This is to describe Tom Smart's encounter with a chair. Dickens, *The Pickwick Papers*, 167.

Dickens clearly delighted in a wild border-country between perception and imagination, between a sensory and a more interpretative experience, between seeing the object as it is and seeing it as it isn't. We can also find Eliot in the same place, looking, perhaps, a little nervous. 'Falsehood,' after all, 'is so easy, truth so difficult' (AB, 160), and Eliot is often disturbed by the banditry of imagination. So, while Eliot celebrated its powers of trespass, she also stressed its responsibilities, often wondering how our fancies might be controlled by the rational and moral will. Imagination, in this context, might also present itself as something very different to perception: We can't quite decide what to see, but we often believe that we have some control over what we imagine.[74] And this, in turn, alerts us to other differences between perceiving and imagining: their different phenomenological textures; their contrasting directions of fit with the world, one imposing on the object while the other receives (though the basic science of sight might also put pressure on this distinction); as well as the varying levels of credulity they each elicit (if seeing is usually believing—or at least accepting—we don't necessarily commit to what we imagine).[75] Yet, for all of these differences, the distinction between perception and imagination in Dickens and Eliot remains troubled by an ambiguous seeing-as.

There are many occasions in life, after all, when we *both* imagine and see. As Wittgenstein showed, for instance, it takes some imagination to see a pattern on a page *as* a rabbit or a duck.[76] Paul Dombey similarly imagines as he perceives, though he populates the wallpaper with a more exotic set of animals: 'He was intimate with all the paper-hanging in the house; saw things that no one else saw in the patterns; found out miniature tigers and lions running up the bedroom walls, and squinting faces leering in the squares and diamonds of the floorcloth.'[77] It is, of

74. Wittgenstein, for instance, insists that imagining is 'subject to the will.' Wittgenstein, *Philosophical Investigations*, 182; see also Scruton, *Art and Imagination*, 95.

75. On the differences between both, see Sartre's *The Imaginary* as well as McGinn's *Mindsight*.

76. Wittgenstein, *Philosophical Investigations*, 165–69.

77. Dickens, *Dombey and Son*, 179.

course, a short road in Dickens from perception to hallucination. Take his ruminations on a train in 1851: 'Now a wood, now a bridge, now a landscape, now a cutting, now a—Bang! a single-barrelled Station—there was a cricket-match somewhere with two white tents, and then four flying cows, then turnips.'[78] The flying cows casually float by in a series of seemingly ordinary impressions and noticings. By the time the turnips arrive, it is hard to tell if we are in the land of vision or imagination or whether objects so ordinary, yet so de-worlded, are imagined or perceived. It is difficult to tell, too, whether willpower is in operation here. The viewer seems to be deeply stuck—a passenger on a train and a passenger to his own thought—and so, in turn, is the reader. Dickens, of course, may be delightedly driving both trains with his will, but, as Emerson noted, Dickens was also a prisoner to his own unstoppable genius ('it is a fearful locomotive to which he is bound and can never be free').[79]

Eliot may have aspired to a more sober and controlled vision. Yet sight itself is a fiction-maker in Eliot's philosophical eye. As she put it in 1856: 'Each man sees things not as they are, but as they appear through his peculiar mental media.'[80] How peculiar each man's medium is might be debated, but it is clear that there is an imaginative element to all vision in Eliot just as there is for Dickens. Conversely, she also conceives of imagination as a kind of mental seeing or imagistic thinking. As she puts it in *Middlemarch*, 'Our moods bring with them images which succeed each other like the magic-lantern pictures of a doze' (M, 181–82). This was to exploit the simple etymology of the word 'imagination'—its roots in the term 'imago' or image—but also draws on a philosophical commonplace to be found in Hobbes, Spinoza, Kant, Feuerbach, or, indeed, in her partner G. H. Lewes (as Lewes put it in the book that Eliot would help to edit: 'Imagination is the production of images').[81]

78. Dickens, 'A Flight,' in *Selected Journalism*, 139.

79. Annie Fields, *Memories of a Hostess*, 174.

80. Eliot, 'Belles Lettres and Art,' July 1856, 272. She also makes this claim about herself ('I only try to exhibit some things as they have been or are, seen through such a medium as my own nature gives me' [L, 2.362]).

81. Lewes, *Problems of Life and Mind*, 3.451.

'We are all of us imaginative in some form or other,' we are told in *Middlemarch*, 'for images are the brood of desire' (M, 304). This makes their direction of fit with the world ambiguous: Images express our wishes, yet they underwrite our strongest beliefs about the world. 'Our most intimate convictions,' Eliot declares, 'are simply images added to more or less of sensation' (E, 445).[82]

Imagination, of course, does not necessarily require us to think in images or pictures.[83] In literature we imagine through words, not directly through visual images (even though Eliot's contemporaries and indeed Eliot herself often maintained that we make sense of words by generating internal representations).[84] *Middlemarch* contains an interesting conversation about the relative superiority of language over pictures—partly because of the former's productive vagueness—and yet Eliot also troubled the distinction by casting literature as a kind of 'picture-writing of the mind' (E, 267).[85] Indeed, the nonpropositional character of the picture remains central to her own 'aesthetic teaching' (L, 4.300) and it was an aspect of her work noted by her contemporaries.[86] A picture may viscerally affect us, though we can't always determine what it *says*, and the world acts upon the retina in similar ways. Key to Eliot's sense of lived experience is the conviction that we see through a haze of images—'half real, half fantastic'—that communicate but don't assert (DD, 299). If we can't quite know what we imagine in

82. Nietzsche also connected thought and sensation, presenting the former as a diminished trace of the latter: 'Thoughts are the shadows of our sensations—always darker, emptier, simpler.' Nietzsche, *The Gay Science*, 137.

83. Wittgenstein, *Philosophical Investigations*, 149–50, 155, 167; see also Ryle, *The Concept of Mind*, 235–42.

84. Comte, for instance, insisted that 'each word should recall as far as possible an Image, and each Image a Feeling,' allowing the subjective to merge with the quasi-objective or publicness of signs. Comte, *System of Positive Polity*, 2.202. Eliot will also speculate about the different images triggered by different words in different people in her essays (E, 267).

85. The tendency to regard language in imagistic terms remains in place here. As Will puts it: 'Language gives a fuller image, which is all the better for being vague' (M, 179).

86. As James Sully put it, 'George Eliot gives us a life-like picture of the moral struggle, and not a theory of it.' Sully, 'George Eliot's Art,' 391. Henry James seemed to disagree. The novel, in her hands, was 'not primarily a picture of life, . . . but a moralised fable, the last word of a philosophy endeavouring to teach by example.' James, *Literary Criticism*, 1.1002.

Eliot, we must repeatedly imagine what we cannot know. So, the future 'comes inevitably in the form of images' (DD, 78) and our lives are shadowed by 'rapid images of what might be' (DD, 176). The visceral nature of these projections again seems to blur the boundary between imagination and perception. Thus, Romola finds images pressing upon her 'almost with the imperious force of sensations' (R, 332), while the hunted Bulstrode discovers that he cannot shake off 'images with their hateful kindred of sensations' (M, 647). Precisely because imagination is so embodied, it can feel as involuntary as the circulation of the blood.[87]

Imagination, then, is a dangerous trespasser in Eliot, blurring the boundaries between seeing and inventing, thinking and feeling, perceiving and wishing. If it brings the world to our minds, it also risks devouring the world. Images may be the brood of desire; yet we also feel that our images should remain responsible to the world. This is why the imagination leads to epistemic and even moral disaster: It reverses the proper direction of fit between representations and their objects. Humans are bold projectors in her work, gilding and staining the world in their own sentimental colours. Eliot is clearly ambivalent about this psychological industry and the way it allows us 'to imagine more than the fact' (M, 188). Her hesitation, moreover, is partly bound up with an associative psychology—in which objects generate the most random set of connections in our minds ('give me a three-legged stool,' she announces in a letter, 'and it will call up associations moral, poetical, mathematical' [L1, 139]). Locke, however, had decried the association of ideas—in which a contingent or arbitrary relation between two discrete ideas is experienced as a necessary or natural connection—as an irrational mode of apprehension; indeed, it was a type of 'madness.'[88] Eliot could also view these contingent associations as a kind of folly or, as we hear in *Middlemarch*, a

87. There may be a Spinozan basis to the embodied nature of imagination. As we hear in the *Ethics*: 'When the human mind contemplates external bodies through ideas of the affections of its own body, we say that it imagines.' Spinoza, *Ethics*, 137.

88. Locke, *An Essay Concerning Human Understanding*, 354. Eliot may also have been influenced by Spinoza's discussion of the association or 'concatenation' of ideas—the way 'each man passes from one thought to another, according to the order which habit has given to the things in his body.' See Spinoza, *Ethics*, 133.

'disease of the retina' (M, 182). Yet she also observed how the same disease gives pattern and significance to our world. Theophrastus Such is a severe judge of folly, but he also speaks warmly of the nimbus of 'ideal association which informs every material object, every incidental fact with far-reaching memories and stored residues of passion' (ITS, 238).

Our values, then, reflect our lived histories of imaginative association. In the *Mill and the Floss*, for instance, Eliot traces the origins of normativity to our childhood imaginings. Here the associations and projections of youth constitute the basic grammar of esteem. The flora and fauna of childhood experience teach us how to care about things and make seeing itself a kind of valuing:

> These familiar flowers, these well-remembered bird-notes, this sky, with its fitful brightness, these furrowed and grassy fields, each with a sort of personality given to it by the capricious hedgerows—such things as these are the mother-tongue of our imagination, the language that is laden with all the subtle, inextricable associations the fleeting hours of our childhood left behind them. (MF, 41–42)

This youthful seeing-as is of vital importance—indeed it grounds all future sense of import—though it is notable, too, that Eliot's prose stands at some remove from what she celebrates. Dickens might have dwelt a bit longer on the personality of those capricious hedgerows giving us an inside view of the child's vision, but Eliot's narrator remains a little outside the experiences she exalts. The deictic expressions—'*these* familiar flowers, *these* well-remembered bird-notes, *this* sky'—certainly conjure up the nowness, particularity, or thisness of certain experiences, making them imaginatively present or well remembered. Nonetheless, these states are also transcended by the generalisation they service. There is certainly 'thought' here—to invoke what Lewes and Bagehot found so absent in Dickens's imagination—but arguably one thought too many for visceral particulars to retain their full empire over the mind.[89]

89. James praised the 'constant presence of thought, of generalizing instinct, of *brain*, in a word, behind her observation,' but he also complained about its lack of immediacy ('Instead of feeling life itself, it is "views" upon life that she tries to feel'). James, *Literary Criticism*, 1.965, 1.986.

This distance may be an epistemic and moral necessity in Eliot. Maggie's efforts in *The Mill on the Floss* might be a model for us all: to learn how to live without romance and to leave behind its 'enchanted land' (MF, 441). A life without enchantment, however, is often a grim one in Eliot. For this very reason, Maggie tries to resist the despotism of fact and to refashion 'the world afresh in her own thoughts' (MF, 235). These negations and recreations, however, fail to satisfy:

> She could make dream-worlds of her own—but no dream-world would satisfy her now. She wanted some explanation of this hard, real life: the unhappy-looking father, seated at the dull breakfast-table; the childish, bewildered mother; the little sordid tasks that filled the hours, or the more oppressive emptiness of weary, joyless leisure. (MF, 286)

This may be the task of all realism: to confront the hardness of reality and not look away. Here Eliot seems to provide a counter-list to the pastoral delights that were listed earlier. No flowers or grassy fields, just the bric-a-brac of depression—'the unhappy-looking father, the dull breakfast-table; the childish, bewildered mother.' We are invited to feel for a moment that this is seeing-as-it-is: vision without the false comforts of mist, gild, or stain of significance. The definite articles are strangely de-specifying in this case: as if individuals have ceased to matter and have dissolved into their types. The glum father and bewildered mother are as flat and as de-individuated as the dull table. Of course, projection and evaluation continue to do their work: Dullness and sordidness still supervene on things. But it can seem as if the imagination has reached its outer limits and has encountered the brute resistance of the actual.

Eliot's work repeatedly returns to these moments of disillusionment where life loses its colour—even its moral colour—and familiar objects are 'for ever robbed of their charm' (AB, 358).[90] But these moments of

90. See Hardy, 'The Moment of Disenchantment in George Eliot's Novels.' In *Middlemarch*, it can seem as if the moment of disenchantment—where the world discloses itself without value—is less real than when it is full of normative colour. Here Dorothea experiences 'a pale fantastic world that seemed to be vanishing from the daylight' (M, 258).

despair might only seem to emphasise the practical value of romantic seeing or imaginative vision—the perceptual idiom through which we initially learned to care about things. Eliot may want us to put aside childish things, but she doesn't want us to outgrow the associations that connect us to the world and bind the self to itself. To invoke the celebrated line: 'Our delight in the sunshine on the deep-bladed grass to-day, might be no more than the faint perception of wearied souls, if it were not for the sunshine and the grass in the far-off years which still live in us, and transform perception into love' (MF, 42). Again, we might wonder about this loving vision. Is love a condition of moral perception—a 'seeing-as' that requires commitment, not neutrality, for moral objectivity to be possible—or is it the fond result of habits of projection, association, and error? In *Middlemarch*, Eliot suggests there is a circular quality to all love. For Dorothea, it begins 'by showering kisses on the hard pate of her bald doll, creating a happy soul within that woodenness from the wealth of her own love' (M, 186). And Dorothea remains a generous projector, making value out of the dead wood of the world.[91] The same talent, of course, can also make her appear a little too fond throughout the course of the novel. The bald doll, perhaps, is her first Casaubon.

'The first condition of human goodness,' we are told in 'Janet's Repentance,' is 'something to love; the second something to reverence.'[92] Maybe so, but we have also seen how love and reverence—and consequently goodness—depend for better or worse on fiction and fancy. Eliot may have desired to see the world as it is without the obscuring mist of imagination. But she repeatedly suggests that mist is a condition of seeing—or at least of moral seeing. Tom Tulliver, after all, has 'very clear prosaic eyes, not apt to be dimmed by mists of feeling or imagination' (MF, 276). Such clear-sightedness, however, is a form of moral impoverishment. While Eliot may ultimately approve of mist, she also remains wedded to metaphors which suggest that values are a

91. Love—'that gossamer web!'—is similarly both circular and binding for Lydgate and Rosmond (M, 325).

92. Eliot, *Scenes of Clerical Life*, 228.

projection, a superimposition, or even a distortion of the world. When she speaks of 'the superadded moral life' in her letters, she seems to imply that all moral value supervenes upon a more brute state of affairs (L, 1.315). This may have preserved the substantial and definite reality that underpins her realism, but it also risked making reality nonmoral and all values seem unreal or at least ontologically subjective. As Hume bluntly stated about moral value: 'It lies in yourself, not in the object,'[93] and this might sound like a precarious source of the good for so committed a moral thinker as Eliot (though, as she admitted in 1872, 'the division between within and without . . . seems to become every year a more subtle and bewildering problem' [L, 5.280]). She may have believed with Hume that morality 'depends on some internal sense or feeling which nature has made universal in the whole species,' yet we have also noted how sympathies are shaped through highly contingent and individuated associations across her moral universe.[94] Maggie Tulliver clearly thinks that some humans are wired very differently. As she tells her brother Tom: 'You can't quite judge for me—our natures are very different. You don't know how differently things affect me from what they do you' (MF, 393). The moral boorishness of Tom only confirms her point, though the fact that readers are at hand to sympathise with Maggie also indicates that she is less alone or unusual in her values than she might think.

There will aways be Tom Tullivers in circulation to make the misty-eyed look ridiculous. Eliot acknowledges, moreover, 'that hard rind of truth which is discerned by unimaginative, unsympathetic minds' (MF, 393). Indeed, objectivity might seem to lie with the naysayers, allowing the imagined to be dismissed as the imaginary, and the subjective to be dispatched as unreal. Unless, of course, we're prepared to acknowledge that the subjective *is* an objective feature of reality. This is something we co-experience with others and is the condition of much of what we call real. 'Art is the nearest thing to life,' Eliot maintains, not least because it shows us in a very lived and visceral way just how much of life is made

93. Hume, *Treatise of Human Nature*, 301.

94. Hume, *An Enquiry Concerning the Principles of Morals*, 75.

up (E, 271). She drew on Saint-Beuve in her final work to make the same point: '*la vie est une chose apprise et inventée*' (ITS, 184)—or life is a learned and invented thing.[95] The good life, too, is a fiction—or, to use Eliot's fine phrase, it is a 'fellowship of illusion' (M, 304)—but that doesn't make it any less important, or, in most lights, any less real.[96]

95. For the broader context, see Saint-Beuve, *Les Cahiers de Saint-Beuve*, 99.

96. Eliot's doubleness about mists—an impediment to perception and a condition of it—may imply that she is a 'realist' in her metaphysics but an 'anti-realist' in her ethics. Some might prefer to call her a 'quasi-realist' in her ethics, for once inside a moral viewpoint—and Eliot rarely stepped outside such a position—she feels fully justified in regarding values as real; perhaps she finds it impossible not to do so (on quasi-realism, see Blackburn, *Essays in Quasi-Realism*). Or she may remain a fictionalist, always aware of the iffyness of what she nonetheless accepts or pretends to accept. Ultimately, there is no stable basis to decide between these views in and of her work.

2

Perspectives—Eliot

NIETZSCHE WAS FAMOUSLY rude about her—not that this really sets her apart—but Eliot was as obsessed as Nietzsche was with the way our grasp of truth is determined by perspective.[1] To take the homely philosophising of Adam Bede: 'Some 's got one way o' looking at things and some 's got another' (AB, 10). The epistemic and ethical implications of this banal fact would dominate her writing life. The range of perspectives to be found in the world and of the world could lead philosophers like Nietzsche to an extreme form of relativism or even nihilism about truth. As he put it in 1885: 'There are many kinds of eyes . . . and consequently there are many kinds of "truths," and consequently there is no "truth."'[2] But the philosopher took a different perspective on perspectivism a year later: 'There is *only* a perspective seeing, *only* a perspective "knowing,"' but this was no basis, he intimated, for giving up on knowledge or objectivity altogether.[3] After all, perspectives can be pooled, compared, and integrated until something that might count as knowledge is produced.[4] As Nietzsche put it, 'The *more* affects we allow to speak about a thing, the *more* eyes, various eyes we are able to use for the same thing, the more complete will be our "concept" of the thing,

1. Nietzsche, *Twilight of the Idols*, 45.

2. Nietzsche, *The Will to Power*, 291–92.

3. Nietzsche, *On the Genealogy of Morality*, 92.

4. As David Wiggins put it: 'Perspective is not a form of illusion, distortion, or delusion.' Wiggins, *Needs, Values, Truth*, 108.

our "objectivity."'[5] Nietzsche may have baulked at the idea of being linked with the moral fanatic he so disparaged, but this sounds like the kind of 'objectivity' to which the novel in Eliot's hands aspires.[6] Her novels see with many eyes and expose the relative limits of each, allowing the reader, at least, to aspire to a more comprehensive wisdom.

'It is a narrow mind which cannot look at a subject form various points of view,' Mr. Brooke volunteers, and Eliot's novels offer themselves as a corrective to all kinds of mental narrowness.[7] *Middlemarch,* for instance, allows us to see through many eyes and to regard many eyes—Dorothea's 'large' and 'unusual' eyes (M, 9); Casaubon's 'blinking eyes,' hurt, we are told, from too much reading (M, 261, 38); Lydgate's 'steady eyes,' though occasionally as 'blind and unconcerned as a jellyfish' (M, 85, 255). Mary Garth has a fine, discerning set: eyes that were 'nothing more than clear windows where observation sat laughingly' (M, 130). Dorothea, on the other hand, is 'short-sighted' (M, 28)—'she does not see things,' Celia proclaims (M, 52)—though this may simply emphasise Dorothea's attentiveness to the 'higher inward life' (M, 21). This, of course, can make her see too much, taking Casaubon's grey hair and deep eye-sockets, for instance, as signs of his resemblance to Locke. As her sister naughtily asks: 'Had Locke those two white moles with hairs on them?' Dorothea's response is sharp: 'Oh I dare say! when people of a certain sort looked at him' (M, 19). So, eyes adjudicate other eyes, and we see the limits of all ocular instruments: 'Even with a microscope directed on a water-drop we find ourselves making interpretations which turn out to be rather coarse' (M, 55). The novel also looks at its own looking and sometimes finds it wanting. Take the famous self-correction in chapter 29—'Why always Dorothea? Was her point of view the only one possible with regard to this marriage?' Casaubon, we are reminded, has an 'intense consciousness within him' that deserves our attention—despite the blinking eyes and the moles that Celia

5. Nietzsche, *On the Genealogy of Morality,* 92.

6. Nietzsche, *Twilight of the Idols,* 45.

7. Eliot, *Middlemarch,* 61. All further references are given in the text under the abbreviation 'M.'

finds so objectionable (M, 261). Yet Dorothea is initially as oblivious to Casaubon's inward troubles as he is to hers.

There is, as William James noted, a tragic blindness in human beings and part of it stems from life's perspectival gaps. In particular, James outlined the differences between a spectator's knowledge and a participant's or a third-person and first-person viewpoint:

> The spectator's judgment is sure to miss the root of the matter and to possess no truth. The subject judged knows a part of the world of reality which the judging spectator fails to see, knows more whilst the spectator knows less; and, wherever there is conflict of opinion and difference of vision, we are bound to believe that the truer side is the side that feels the more, and not the side that feels the less.[8]

Eliot often tries to overcome these perspectival differences by cultivating a capacious sympathy, a double vision that might seem to straddle the gap between a participant's and a spectator's knowledge. This straddling is arguably performed in the narrative voice in the third-person-cum-first-person magic act of free indirect discourse and in readers' vicarious participation ('one feels almost uncomfortably in the thick of it,' John Blackwood observed to Eliot [L.5, 293]). There is also a diachronic dimension to this perspectivism, revealing how 'time changes the proportion of things' (M, 339–40). So, we grow a bit older alongside Dorothea and see her in various lights (it's not always Dorothea, but very often it is). We visit her many times in her bow-windowed room at Lowick and observe its ghostly contents through the different prisms of her moods.

We also encounter her in Rome not quite seeing things in the Vatican Museum: 'She was not looking at the sculpture, probably not thinking of it: her large eyes were fixed dreamily on a streak of sunlight which fell across the floor' (M, 177). She, in turn, is seen and unseen through the relentlessly symbolic eyes of the artist Naumann. Dorothea is a Christian Antigone—Naumann will later make her a Santa Clara—but she is not allowed to be herself. Will Ladislaw takes issue with Naumann's

8. James, 'On a Certain Blindness in Human Beings,' in *Talks to Teachers on Psychology*, 133.

sublimations and objectifications. The 'true seeing,' Will insists, 'is within' (M, 179). Taking Will's cue, the novel duly switches, moving away from external spectatorship, to give us the inside view of the morning Dorothea has endured. We follow each step of her painful quarrel with Casaubon, the harsh words, the mortifying breakfast, the woman's shock and moral solitude. All this is filled in so that when we return to the Hall of Statues in the Vatican to reencounter Dorothea and to resee what she doesn't see, we do so with a much wiser eye: 'She did not really see the streak of sunlight on the floor more than she saw the statues: she was inwardly seeing the light of years to come in her own home and over the English fields and elms and hedge-bordered highroads; and feeling that the way in which they might be filled with joyful devotedness was not so clear to her as it had been' (M, 190).

This is essentially how *Middlemarch* builds its vision, perspectives qualifying perspectives to give us a completer picture. It is significant that the subsequent picture is 'not so clear as it had been' and the growth of wisdom is often an acknowledgement of uncertainty and ignorance. Nonetheless the moral and epistemic task presented to us by *Middlemarch* is a little like its protagonist's: to combine thought and feeling across a range of perspectives, bringing 'the whole consciousness towards the fullest truth, the least partial good' (M, 190). We might call this, *pace* Nietzsche, a more perfect 'objectivity'—and perhaps it is, but it is an objectivity that must accept that the subjective, namely the 'inward life,' is a real and irreducible feature of the universe. In the pursuit of the fullest truth, therefore, the novel must see both from within and from without, aspiring, perhaps, to a kind of absolute knowledge, in which the lamb sits down with the lion, the participant joins hands with the spectator, and the subjective and objective merge.

Eliot makes it easy to see why Lukács regarded the novel as the epic of a world that has been abandoned by God—while also being, in some small way, a compensation for such abandonment.[9] For her novels sometimes allow us to entertain a certain fantasy of omniscience. As one of Eliot's contemporary readers, Edith Simcox, noted: 'It is not

9. Lukács, *The Theory of the Novel*, 88.

natural to most men to know so much of their fellow creatures as George Eliot shows them.'[10] Nietzsche may have disparaged Eliot and the English for clinging to God or at least 'the good' long after the metaphysical foundations for this attachment had been dismantled.[11] But it is the ostensible aspiration to a God-like knowledge—or a *total* view of the world—that is one of the remarkable features of the novel under Eliot. It is also an aspiration that is repeatedly disappointed in and through her writing. So, even though Simcox noted how her novels allowed one to feel like a divine watcher of all things, she also believed that this transcendent vision—even with Eliot's assistance—was not sustainable for very long. Indeed, the watching inevitably yielded to 'painful bewilderment' when confronted by the sheer complexity of what we encounter in her miniworlds.[12] The aim here is to explore this double action in Eliot: the longing for a total vision of things, twinned with the perspective that an absolute perspective of the world is neither possible nor desirable.

For obvious reasons, it is hard to know—even in theory—what God was supposed to know. If he knew everything, then this achievement lends itself to the paradox that he couldn't know ignorance, making him in a sense stupidly clever. John Searle has claimed that there are many things a wholly transcendent God would not see. From his station in the sky, he would not see screwdrivers, cars, bathtubs, and so forth because for all their material content, these entities are not intrinsic elements of the world but social fictions. Such fictions are observer-relative facts—or so Searle maintains—and owe their reality to human observers and human perspectives.[13] A wholly transcendent God, therefore, is liable to come across as transcendentally blind: oblivious to many of the goods that are traditionally assigned to him—love, beauty, or goodness—at least if these values are understood as properties that exist in and through the eyes of humans. One reason for Jesus in the Christian story is that he provides a necessary supplement to or

10. Carroll, *The Critical Heritage*, 324.

11. Nietzsche, *Twilight of the Idols*, 45.

12. Carroll, *The Critical Heritage*, 324.

13. Searle, *The Construction of Social Reality*, 12.

compensation for this bad transcendence: He allows God to assume human limitation and look through human eyes. Jesus helps God to feel foolish or at least humanly knowing. In Hegel and, indeed, Feuerbach (whose *Essence of Christianity* Eliot translated in 1854), the Christian story is also an epistemic one: It is a tale of how a transcendent and impersonal perspective of the world merges with a situated and personal one. If God paradoxically extends himself by taking on the limitations of the subjective, human beings return to God, or complete him, by learning what it is to be objective.[14] The merger of these subjective and objective paths is what Hegel called absolute knowledge.

This epistemic paradise is not exactly where we end up in Eliot—indeed, the impossibility of ever exceeding our limits and arriving at this neverland of knowledge is the theme we relive over and again in her books. The lesson can only be experienced, however, by some initiation into the hope that it dashes, some seduction into a fiction of omniscience in which the subjective and objective are finally merged to deliver some unified or total perspective. One of the reasons why Eliot is so exalted or why *Middlemarch* can feel like a minor miracle is the way it can conjure up the fiction of all-seeing-ness, as if we hold a piece of Feuerbachian divinity or human-made omniscience in our hands—until, of course, we properly read the title page. The idea of a total vision of the world is already dashed in the novel's unsexy subtitle—'A Study of Provincial Life.' The 'of' here is ambiguous and it soon becomes clear that *Middlemarch* is as much an enactment of provincialism as it is an examination of it. Its narrator is equally bound to a particular piece of the jigsaw or 'web' and must resist 'that tempting range of relevancies called the universe' (M, 132). Some provinces, we learn, cannot be transcended—nor should they be if one's identity as a moral agent, a citizen of here not an ambassador of nowhere, is to be preserved.

Like Hegel, Eliot wanted us to resist both the provincialism of the subjective and the unsituatedness of the objective by getting us to think both perspectives at once or alongside each other. But the clash

14. As Feuerbach summed it up: 'The raising of man to God is made a consequence of the humiliation or descent of God to man.' Evans, *The Essence of Christianity*, 78.

between these outlooks can be seen throughout her novels. It appears in the dialectic between the would-be objectivity of her narrators and the inwardness and mental provincialism of her characters; in the din between individuals as they strive to come to terms with the objectivity of 'another myself'; we see the ruptures within each of these characters themselves.[15] Many of them are 'unhappy'—to invoke Hegel's description of a consciousness that is painfully torn between first-person thoughts and feelings and a more impersonal sense of the world.[16] This 'double consciousness' is lived out in different ways in Eliot, but it is a continual source of upset and irony as people alternate from seeing themselves as giants and specks. The task for many of her people—and the task of realism itself—is how to establish a more integrated picture—how to align our sense of ourselves as agents and experiencers with a realistic appraisal of how the world is. Even the pursuit of alignment may make us a little less foolish—and as Eliot repeatedly proposes—a little less self-absorbed. But, as we shall see, the process of convergence repeatedly encounters practical and theoretical limits.[17]

There is in the end no unified picture, however her characters or her readers may hope for one. This is not to say that perspectives are entirely discrete and cannot be integrated. Indeed, perspectives are mutually constitutive across Eliot's fictions, just as they are in life. The look of others affects our outlook upon ourselves: 'Even our own persons in the glass are apt to change their aspect for us after we have heard some frank remark on their less admirable points' (M, 369). Lydgate, Rosamond, and Will grow bigger under Dorothea's charitable gaze ('Full souls,' after all, 'are double mirrors' [M, 691]).[18] Confronted by the same moral force, Casaubon feels smaller. The way we incorporate other people's

15. This is to invoke the phrase that Stanley Cavell gives to Aristotle's notion of a friend. See Cavell, *Conditions Handsome and Unhandsome*, 59.

16. Hegel, *The Phenomenology of Spirit*.

17. Eliot, for this reason, can seem more Nagelian than Hegelian. As Nagel has frequently maintained: 'A unified world view' is impossible—partly because of the irreconcilability of subjective and objective outlooks. Nagel, *The View from Nowhere*, 4.

18. This line is drawn from the epigraph of chap. 72 in *Middlemarch* and is a self-quotation of one of Eliot's own poems.

assessments into our own is therefore a key feature of Eliot's world-making. Much of a man's inward life, she maintains, 'is made up of the thoughts he believes other men to have about them' (M, 647). If this leads to vanity and self-alienation, it is also a condition of self-expansion and moral growth. But the extent to which we can genuinely see how others see remains a key problem in Eliot. It affects not only our relations to other people but also the way we relate to ourselves as we move through time, recalling our once-lived emotions from a more distanced or third-person perspective. As Eliot puts it in *Daniel Deronda*: 'What passion seems more absurd, when we have got outside it and looked at calamity as a collective risk, than this amazed anguish that I and not Thou, He or She, should be just the smitten one?' (DD, 245). If Eliot often celebrates this self-transcendence and our safe deliverance from the maws of an emotion, she also defends the need to look at the world feelingly from within a particular here and now. How we integrate our lived passions with our cooler or more disengaged reflections is no easy science and it indicates that perspectives may be as hard to unite within a life as they are hard to stitch together across various lives.

A perspective that incorporates all perspectives may forever elude us, but this does not necessarily stop Eliot from trying. Her many-eyed novels issue the same kind of handoff as William James later delivers, while also striving to transcend some of its implications: 'Hands off: neither the whole of truth, nor the whole of good, is revealed to any single observer, although each observer gains a partial superiority of insight from the peculiar position in which he stands.'[19] Eliot's novels may strain for the whole truth and the whole good—or at least the fullest truth and least partial good—but they are also an extended education in our need for epistemic humility. If they advertise the limits of all perspectives, they emphasise the irreducible importance of any one perspective, what James calls the 'partial superiority of insight' of any one person's take on the world. And yet Eliot is deeply concerned by the way our first-person perspectives are all too partial—incomplete, biased, even stupid—and it often generates an austere and

19. James, 'On a Certain Blindness in Human Beings,' 149.

self-punishing conception of objectivity across her work. More promisingly, perhaps, it also leads to a more intersubjective form of understanding that Eliot calls sympathy—though this virtuous seeing has also its moral and epistemic limits. I want to explore how Eliot leads us through each of these forms of seeing, often making a noble stab at omniseeing even when, or precisely when, she notes her own limitations. She may have been 'the first great godless writer of fiction'—as one of her contemporaries maintained—but Will Ladislaw is surely right in thinking that 'we mortals have our divine moments' (M, 341).[20]

The View from Here

The view from here may be the only real viewpoint—or so we can often feel—but it is often a poor one. A mere speck, after all, can blot out the glory of the world, and for Eliot at least, there is 'no speck so troublesome as self' (M, 392). In this section I want to explore how egoism is both a moral and epistemic problem in her work. 'We are all of us born in moral stupidity,' we are famously told, 'taking the world as an udder to feed our supreme selves.' This stupidity is a problem in Eliot precisely because it obscures our epistemic access to other selves—other islands of ego in which 'the lights and shadows must always fall with a certain difference' (M, 198). This brings us to a familiar doubleness about the ego in Eliot's writing—if it must be recovered from others, it must be transcended in ourselves or at least subjected to a rigorous kind of discipline.

If Victorians were often preoccupied by the question of selfishness, Eliot brought the question to the point of obsession.[21] Selfishness is everywhere in her novels and in her letters and often risks becoming 'The Key to all Psychologies' (L5, 291)—to adapt Lewes's joke about his

20. David Carroll, *Critical Heritage*, 453. The opinion is W. H. Mallock's—published in *The Edinburgh Review* in 1879.

21. As Stefan Collini has argued, 'Victorian moralists exhibited an obsessive antipathy to selfishness.' Collini, *Public Moralists*, 65.

own interminable labours during the writing of *Middlemarch*.[22] Eliot's narrators practice an elaborate moral botany, introducing us to various subtypes of the vice—'a conscious selfishness'[23] (FH, 96), a 'scheming selfishness,'[24] a 'dishonest selfishness' (FH, 115), an 'idle selfishness' (FH, 183), an 'industrious selfishness' (FH, 183). Stories like *The Lifted Veil* expose the grim ubiquity of the condition while also introducing us to new variants. Latimer, the jaded narrator of this tale, has an uncanny ability to see the inner thoughts and motivations of others and is dismayed by what it reveals: 'all the suppressed egoism . . . from which human words and deeds emerge like leaflets covering a fermenting heap' (LV, 14). The only thing that mitigates Latimer's contempt for others is the sense that he himself is just as bad. Indeed, he may be worse: Instead of practicing the complacent and happy egoism of his brother, for instance, he has simply opted for a brand of 'suffering selfishness' (LV, 25).

The Lifted Veil also reveals what a blunt instrument the charge of selfishness can be. Ultimately, any desire that inheres in a self might be construed as selfish—just as any interest it expresses can be called self-interested. Eliot indulged in the same insinuating vacuity when she observed in a letter: 'The martyr at the stake seeks its gratification as much as the court sycophant' (L1, 194). This can make various unveilings of universal selfishness in her work both boring and empty—or, if not empty, then obtusely untrue. Precisely because egoism is so all-encompassing in Eliot and incorporates both moral and epistemic failings, its descriptive and critical powers can disappear. Hence the numerous adjectival qualifications of the condition—an 'arrogant egoism' (ITS, 148), 'a dissatisfied egoism' (ITS, 15), 'an irritable form of . . . egoism' (ITS, 146) to take from the stock of Theophrastus—though this might suggest that the issues of real moral substance are to be found

22. For Lewes's remark, see Eliot, *The George Eliot Letters*, 5.291. All further references to Eliot's letters are given in the text under the abbreviation 'L.'

23. Eliot, *Felix Holt*, 96. All further references are given in the text under the abbreviation 'FH.'

24. Eliot, *The Lifted Veil*, 32. All further references are given in the text under the abbreviation 'LV.'

more in the qualifying properties (arrogance, dissatisfaction, irritability) than in the thin shell of egoism itself. Or we may feel that the ubiquity of selfishness in her work ultimately stops it from operating as a vice altogether.

Eliot never quite goes to these permissive lengths. Nonetheless, she had clearly read her Spinoza—a philosopher for whom egoism in some form was fundamental and necessary. All human beings, he maintained, were characterised by *conatus*—a striving for self-preservation and self-empowerment—and it was perfectly natural and even virtuous for each person to pursue these ends. This self-regard did not preclude a concern for other people and may even seem to require it, but Spinoza remained convinced that 'men will be most useful to each other when each most seeks his own good.'[25] Eliot was too enamoured with a direct and transparent altruism—to invoke the term that her partner G. H. Lewes had helped to introduce into the language—to travel all the way with Spinoza on this point.[26] Think of the aptly named Farebrother in *Middlemarch* or of Maggie Tulliver—a woman who sacrifices her life out of love for her brother. Yet this same action also invites us to consider the limits of altruism. At what point does it represent a harmful assault on our own *conatus*? If *Middlemarch* has been commended as 'a brilliant study of being-for-others,' it is also, perhaps, an initiation into the Spinozan limits to other-regarding action.[27] In the end, Dorothea seems to settle for a life of small goodnesses—including her own happiness—instead of a more capacious and self-immolating form of charity.

'Forsake thyself': The command of Thomas à Kempis has its seductions in Eliot, where it insistently presents itself as a condition of truth and goodness, but its contradictions and perversities are also kept in view (MF, 209). Indeed, this self-forsaking is repeatedly called out as a type of fanaticism, or a way of 'mutilating one's nature' (MF, 413). Even a deluded self-love, Eliot suggests, is better than no love of self. In the

25. Spinoza, *Spinoza's Ethics*, 250.

26. Lewes, *Comte's Philosophy of the Sciences*, 217. On the emergence of altruism as a concept, see Collini, *Public Moralists*, chap. 2; Dixon, *The Invention of Altruism*.

27. Murdoch, *Sartre: Romantic Rationalist*, 88.

'The Sad Fortunes of the Reverend Amos Barton,' for instance, we learn that vanity often works in the service of the good:

> Thank heaven . . . that a little illusion is left to us, to enable us to be useful and agreeable—that we don't know exactly what our friends think of us—that the world is not made of looking-glass, to show us just the figure we are making, and just what is going on behind our backs! By the help of dear friendly illusion, we are able to dream that we are charming—and our faces wear a becoming air of self-possession; we are able to dream that other men admire our talents—and our benignity is undisturbed; we are able to dream that we are doing much good—and we do a little. (SCL, 14)

Adam Smith had speculated that we would all be forced to reform if we were exposed to what other people really thought of us, but Eliot suggests that such an exposure to truth might make us even worse.[28] Narcissism of some form is a condition of moral agency—our 'very capacity for good would go out of us,' if we were bled of our self-conceit (SCL, 13). And yet our own conceit is left a little bruised by the passage above. Eliot tells us that it would be unbearable to live in a world made of looking-glass where we would have to confront our moral blemishes and bald spots at every turn. Nonetheless, through her cheerfully inclusive 'we' she invites us to contemplate our own narcissism in the light of her cruel mirror. If illusions are necessary, one wonders how many Eliot allows us to keep. 'We are poor plants,' she maintains, 'buoyed up by the air-vessels of our own conceit: alas for us, if we get a few pinches that empty us of that windy self-subsistence!' (SCL, 13). Eliot, however, likes to pinch, convinced that the sharp edges of objectivity may do us good. But if her narrator is right—and an assault on our self-love is also an assault on our capacity for good—she might even do us a moral harm. Behind the moral teacher in Eliot, we might even detect a sadist grinning.

28. 'If we saw ourselves in the light in which others see us, or in which they would see us if they knew all, a reformation would generally be unavoidable.' Adam Smith, *Theory of Moral Sentiments*, 184.

Other people's egoism can be fun to watch, and Eliot repeatedly invites us to savour its many ironies, the different ways that selfish actions tend to be self-sabotaging over time. This moral irony can be seen in all her novels, but it is most systematically developed in the figure of Tito in *Romola*. Problems arise not just from Tito's self-regard, but from his impoverished sense of value: Nothing has intrinsic value in Tito's world outside of his own pleasure.[29] But this proves to be a disastrously unstable criterion to live by and yields several kinds of paradox. Tito destroys his own pleasure by thinking only in terms of pleasure and giving a purely instrumental value to everything else. This instrumentalism operates like a 'virulent acid' eating away at his connections to others and to his own moral intuitions (R, 116). Methodical attempts to optimise pleasure yield further ironies ('even in the pursuit of what was agreeable, this paradoxical life forced upon him the desire for what was disagreeable' [R, 496]). It also generates suboptimal results: When he realises that much of his happiness depends on other people's good opinion of him it is already too late—he has forfeited this in the pursuit of narrowly conceived interests. In the end, his attempts to maximise his interests are baffled by the complexity of the world. There is, he discovers, a disastrous fecundity to actions, yielding unpredicted results that often conspire against one's ultimate ends.[30] The arch-strategist is outfoxed by his own desire and ends up feeling lonely and lost.

So, it is not in our interests to be too self-interested, and life is clearly tough for committed narcissists in Eliot's work. As she notes in *Daniel Deronda*, it 'is possible to have a strong self-love without any self-satisfaction, rather with a self-discontent which is the more intense because one's own little core of egoistic sensibility is a supreme care' (DD, 13). Despite their differences, Gwendolen, Casaubon, and Rosamond all bear this psychology out. A keen reader of Rousseau, Eliot is alert to the ironies of *amour propre*.[31] If it dangerously extends the

29. 'What, looked at closely,' he asks, 'was the end of all life, but to extract the utmost sum of pleasure?' Eliot, *Romola*, 115. All further references are given in the text under the abbreviation 'R.'

30. On this issue, see Fessenbecker, 'The Fragility of Rationality.'

31. Eliot noted early on 'a desire insatiable for the esteem of [her] fellow creatures' (L1, 19). On the distinction between *amour propre* and *amour pour soi*, see Rousseau, *The Discourses*, 152.

boundaries of our self-love—mediating it through the world's regard—it also exiles us from ourselves, forcing us to live through the eyes of others. Those afflicted by vanity often live at a tragic distance from themselves: For these riven souls, the view from here is always an attempt to figure out the view from there. This is certainly Rosamond's plight. She is, we are told, a thorough-going actress: 'She even acted her own character, and so well, that she did not know it to be precisely her own' (M, 109). The narrator's tone here is tart—as it often is when the pretty blonde is around—but we see, too, that there is something deeply forlorn about all this moral theatre.[32] Rosamond is a social ideal of femininity masquerading as a person or she is a person lost to an ideation of what a woman should be.

The irony of vanity, perhaps, is that it is never self-centred enough. Indeed, for this reason, there is something potentially redemptive about *amour propre*: As Rousseau and Hegel noted, something good might emerge from our unappeasable need for recognition from others.[33] It is in pursuit of this recognition from Daniel Deronda, moreover, that Gwendolen begins her attempts at self-reform. This is merely to build on what she has always done: to live through the eyes of others. But she has, it seems, chosen a good set of eyes—a morally reliable external perspective to think her way into. The advice that Daniel doles out may be little more than a commonplace—'Try to care about something in this vast world besides the gratification of small selfish desires' (DD, 383)—but it can yield its own set of contradictions. It is hard to become genuinely concerned about others or the world when they are so nakedly forms of self-concern. Self-help is no help if it is too direct and transparent. Gwendolen, for instance, repeatedly plays host to the old hedonic paradox—a mindset in which a self-consciousness about

For a good discussion of the influence of Rousseau on Eliot, though it avoids the question of *amour propre*, see Hertz, *George Eliot's Pulse*, 42–62.

32. Incidentally, Eliot herself would also be proclaimed a vain performer. As Eliza Lynn Linton quipped: 'I have never known anyone who seemed to me so purely artificial as George Eliot.' Linton, *My Literary Life*, 104.

33. This is arguably the theme of *The Social Contract* (1762). On recognition in Hegel, see, in particular, *The Phenomenology of Spirit*.

happiness routs its very possibility. However, the egotistical root of her cultivated concern for others is not easily eluded. 'You must let me make you happy now at last,' she tells her mother. But this wilful benevolence is succeeded by a sad and self-preoccupied question: 'Else what shall I do?' (DD, 646).

So, again we find tensions between third-person wisdom and first-person attitudes. Giving up selfishness may be good for you, but knowing this can also be unhelpful, allowing the boomerang of self-love to land in our faces. Eliot may want us to curb—if not to relinquish—our selfishness, but one of the problems with this is it is hard-wired into the way we see the world. Egoism, in other words, is an epistemic problem, not just our moral condition. The point is most vividly made through the metaphor of the pier-glass in *Middlemarch*—a passage so familiar that its ambiguities can be passed by:

> An eminent philosopher among my friends, who can dignify even your ugly furniture by lifting it into the serene light of science, has shown me this pregnant little fact. Your pier-glass or extensive surface of polished steel made to be rubbed by a housemaid, will be minutely and multitudinously scratched in all directions; but place now against it a lighted candle as a centre of illumination, and lo! the scratches will seem to arrange themselves in a fine series of concentric circles round that little sun. It is demonstrable that the scratches are going everywhere impartially, and it is only your candle which produces the flattering illusion of a concentric arrangement, its light falling with an exclusive optical selection. These things are a parable. The scratches are events, and the candle is the egoism of any person now absent. (M, 248)

The weight we should give to this celebrated parable is difficult to decipher—not least because it raises questions of epistemic authority from the outset: It begins in the first person but ends with a challenge to this perspective; it references a fact which has been only given on hearsay; it champions a scientific experiment only to service a vague analogy; it extols the serene light of science, yet metaphors of illumination soon become sources of illusion (from distorting candles to little suns); indeed, as her narrator has already proclaimed in *The Mill on the Floss*, there is always something potentially distorting about metaphor in the way it invites us to take one thing for another.[34] The epistemic unreliability of such devices is also noted in *Middlemarch*: 'All of us get our thoughts entangled in metaphors, and act fatally on the strength of them' [M, 79]). Perhaps we should pause a little, then, before we act on the strength of Eliot's.

Metaphors, of course, are useful fictions—as G. H. Lewes would point out in work that was written alongside the writing of *Middlemarch*. Lewes may not be the eminent philosopher inhabiting Eliot's own work of fiction, but he did insist that much of the order that the mind finds in the world is in fact fictitious or ideal. As Lewes put it: 'Out of the manifold irregularities presented to Sense it abstracts an ideal regularity; out of the chaos, order.'[35] This was to reiterate a broadly Kantian point about the ideal nature of phenomena, but if this ideal order is a form of subjectivism, then it is worth recalling how circumscribed and regulated the subjective is in Kant. The phenomenal world may be ontologically subjective or quasi-fictitious in Kantland, but this does not preclude some notion of universality and epistemic objectivity across our mind-dependent experiences. The world, after all, appears to Kantian observers in fairly regular and uniform ways. It is not clear whether the parable of the pier-glass expresses the same epistemic confidence or whether it gestures towards a more extreme and erratic subjectivism. What philosophical candle we should bring to Eliot's metaphor is, therefore, far from clear.

The moral spoor that hangs around perceptual 'egoism' in Eliot should nonetheless give us pause.[36] Adam Smith might have declared

34. 'O Aristotle! if you had had the advantage of being "the freshest modern" instead of the greatest ancient, would you not have mingled your praise of metaphorical speech, as a sign of high intelligence, with a lamentation that intelligence so rarely shows itself in speech without metaphor,—that we can so seldom declare what a thing is, except by saying it is something else?' (MF, 140).

35. Lewes, *Problems of Life and Mind*, 1.432.

36. What we recurrently see in Eliot, though the position survives in people like Iris Murdoch, is what Lorraine Dalston calls the 'moralization of objectivity.' See Dalston, *Objectivity*, 81.

that 'every thing appears magnified and misrepresented by self-love,' but he would also recognise the practical value of self-interest.[37] It may even have an epistemic value ('there is *no* "truth" without *some* interest,' William James maintained).[38] So, when the narrator in *Adam Bede* suggests that 'we look at the face of our mother earth, and see all sorts of answers to our own yearnings' (AB, 188), this doesn't necessarily mean that all the answers are wrong (though it may confirm that all answers are in part circular). Nonetheless, Eliot wants us to see how vices of the head and those of the heart repeatedly join hands: how a preoccupation with ourselves can distract us from reality; how impatience for what we wish for preempts proper reflection on what our desires entail; how wishfulness blurs the world. Half of what Fred Vincy sees in his uncle, for instance, 'is no more than the reflex of his own inclinations' (M, 111)—and many of these bold projectors can be found throughout Eliot. Since these epistemic vices often prevent people from flourishing, their removal or correction might seem to be a more sustainable form of self-love or self-interest. But the discipline of the self is often quite extreme in Eliot and feeds a highly demanding ideal of objectivity.

Views from the Mountain

In a letter to a friend in 1870, Eliot outlined one of her spiritual exercises: 'I try to delight in the sunshine that will be when I shall never see it any more' (L5, 107). The aim here is to experience the world without the distorting presence of its experiencer. 'I think it is possible,' she proclaims, 'for this sort of impersonal life to attain great intensity—possible for us to gain much more independence, than is usually believed, of the small bundle of facts that make our own personality' (L5, 107). This longing for impartial vision continues into Eliot's last work. Theophrastus Such builds his hopes on the science of optics:

> In certain branches of science we can ascertain our personal equation, the measure of difference between our own judgments and an

37. Smith, *Theory of Moral Sentiments*, 182.

38. James, *Selected Letters*, 240.

> average standard: may there not be some corresponding correction of our personal partialities in moral theorising? If a squint or other ocular defect disturbs my vision, I can get instructed in the fact, be made aware that my condition is abnormal, and either through spectacles or diligent imagination I can learn the average appearance of things: is there no remedy or corrective for that inward squint which consists in a dissatisfied egoism or other want of mental balance? In my conscience I saw that the bias of personal discontent was just as misleading and odious as the bias of self-satisfaction. Whether we look through the rose-coloured glass or the indigo, we are equally far from the hues which the healthy human eye beholds in heaven above and earth below. . . . The standing-ground worth striving after seemed to be some Delectable Mountain, whence I could see things in proportions as little as possible determined by that self-partiality which certainly plays a necessary part in our bodily sustenance, but has a starving effect on the mind. (ITS, 14–16)

This is not quite an attempt to see the world without a seer, but it is an effort to approximate a sense of the world as it is or as it might appear to all human spectators if personal idiosyncrasies were removed. Science may allow us to identify and correct myopia with reference to an 'average standard,' but one may well ask how far moral theorising should submit to averageness. Conscience often dictates otherwise, or at least Dorothea's does (as she confidently declares, 'I still think that the greater part of the world is mistaken about many things' [M, 505]).[39] We might equally wonder if mountaintops furnish the best views of moral life. Eliot, after all, will repeatedly dwell on the bad transcendence afforded by aerial views. 'Perspective,' she ironically remarks, 'is a beautiful thing,' often securing for the spectator a picturesque distance from what is ugly and awful to the participant (DD, 131). The call to see things in perspective is often a disguised command to disregard them altogether.

39. Caleb Garth also insists that the voice of conscience trumps the opinions of others: 'That signifies nothing—what other men would think. I've got a clear feeling inside me, and that I shall follow' (M, 531).

Eliot clearly struggles to identify what objectivity looks like or how it should be conceived. Is it derived from an empirical average or some ideal consensus (what 'the healthy human eye beholds in heaven' [ITS, 15])? Are its criteria in physical science different from those that we should adopt in moral life? What is the best metaphor for this elusive knowledge: Is it a view from a mountaintop, a view from nowhere, a view without a viewer? As her spiritual exercises reveal, Eliot's aspirations to objectivity push against the basic grammar of viewing. This may expose the limits of the visual metaphor or the limits of the objectivity that is being envisioned. It is as if Eliot yearns for a perspectiveless perspective—a view that suffers from none of the constraints that normally attend a viewpoint. But the only 'perspectiveless conception of life' that we really get in Eliot is that owned by a child—someone who is too innocent or yet too undifferentiated from their environment to appreciate that their view is a point of view (MF, 66). Built into most people's perspective, of course, is the idea that there are better and worse perspectives, even, perhaps, an ideal one. It is entirely understandable, then, that Dorothea yearns for 'a standing-ground from which all truth could be seen more truly' (M, 59). Yet the question remains where this is to be found. The view from nowhere may lie precisely there—nowhere. It can equally seem like a view from no one. If Dorothea yearns for 'consciousness of life beyond self' (M, 3), this can sound like a desire for a consciousness beyond consciousness.

The Delectable Mountain may be a fiction, then, and the same might be said for views from nowhere or sights without a seer. Nonetheless, these dreams of seeing may be useful idealisations. Eliot certainly dwells on the moral and epistemic advantages of taking a wide perspective on things. Views from the mountaintop reveal the bigness of the world and the enormity of our own littleness within it. She often does this in a gently mediated way, allowing her readers to feel big for a bit, by looking down on the pettiness of others. Take this *de haut en bas* view of Gwendolen, for instance:

> Could there be a slenderer, more insignificant thread in human history than this consciousness of a girl, busy with her small inferences

> of the way in which she could make her life pleasant?—in a time, too, when ideas were with fresh vigour making armies of themselves, and the universal kinship was declaring itself fiercely: when women on the other side of the world would not mourn for the husbands and sons who died bravely in a common cause, and men stinted of bread on our side of the world heard of that willing loss and were patient: a time when the soul of man was walking to pulses which had for centuries been beating in him unheard, until their full sum made a new life of terror or of joy. (DD, 102–3)

The passage has a self-referential quality and celebrates the historical emergence of its own perspective—a global viewpoint based on a sense of universal kinship. This is a moral and epistemic achievement, though we may also worry a little about some of the initial results of this capacious vision: a stoicism, for instance, where one refuses to mourn death in a good cause, or one remains 'patient' in the face of bread shortages when one hears of these sacrifices from afar. So wide a lens risks making us too patient about everything. Or it may make us all too impatient with the sufferings of spoiled young women.

The cynicism that may emanate from global views is noted and performed throughout Eliot. If a cosmic perspective checks the hubris of the ego, it can also succeed too well, making the speck of the self look like so much anxious dirt. The narrator of *The Lifted Veil* reveals the dangers of life seen *sub specie aeternitatis*: It exposes the mental and moral littleness of every panting ego. Latimer, of course, may not be adopting the absolute viewpoint correctly—and perhaps this position could never be captured in terrestrial prose.[40] But if the absolute perspective is a source of delight in Spinoza, it is a cause for despair in *The Lifted Veil*. The true Spinozan seer is struck by the rightness of everything—the recognition that everything is at it must be—but this happy acceptance seems to elude the all-seeing, all-complaining Latimer. The same notes of sourness and contempt can be seen in Theophrastus. Here the search for an impersonal viewpoint yields a cranky

40. On the morally paralyzing effects of omniscience, see Greiner, *Sympathetic Realism*, 122–39.

misanthropy. Theophrastus even questions the value of consciousness itself and wonders if it is not 'an idle parasite on the grand sequence of things' (ITS, 304). He envisions a future where humans have been superseded by a species that has no need of consciousness to navigate the world.

But until these machines arrive (which may be sooner than Theophrastus or Eliot imagined), consciousness remains a fact of the world and the place that humans live in. This sets limits to the objectivity to which they can or should aspire while also setting a target for what any objective account must meet: It will have to accommodate the fact that mind or subjectivity is a real feature of the universe. It was in order to experience this fact from the inside—which is the necessary place to experience it—that the Christian God sent his son into the world. It is also the reason why Eliot might seem to eschew the bad transcendence of the Father or wonder about a non-human view of the world (however Theophrastus may court it). The note that she transcribed from Comte in her notebooks puts the matter clearly: 'The only point of view from which the facts of nature can be regarded as a whole is their relation to Humanity.'[41] She often invites us to exceed our limits and to think our way into other viewpoints within nature—to consider how 'a truly respectable and amiable hen' might talk its way out of execution (MF, 245); how Brazilian monkeys might perceive us (AB, 185); to empathise with the egotistical thoughts of a 'humble mollusc' (ITS, 84). But the jocose tone and unbudging anthropomorphism of these thought experiments also betray their limits. The human prejudice cannot be entirely transcended—nor should it be if we want the world and each other to remain morally intelligible.[42]

Though repeatedly drawn to scientific metaphors—and to meta-ethical reflections about microscopes and telescopes—Eliot often suggests that objectivity in ethics should be conceived differently than it is in much of science. This is because the moral point view is *irreducibly* mind-dependent or observer-relative. As we noted in the last chapter,

41. Eliot, *Some George Eliot Diaries*, 1.169.

42. On this general philosophical point, see Williams, 'The Human Prejudice.'

we see the world though mist—the mist of value, attachment, and feeling—and it is through the sharing of these superadditions that we build up a moral world. From a disengaged or transcendent position our moral community may be little more than a 'fellowship of illusion,' but this is why aerial views are dangerous—it risks removing us from moral space altogether (M, 304). It can be unhelpful, therefore, to view the world from 'a telescopic distance' (E, 370). Moreover, there is often something unreasonable about 'bird's-eye reasonableness' in moral affairs (DD, 638). This is not to say that Eliot eschews the idea of objectivity in moral life—this remains a key goal. But her point is that it is not to be discovered on a mountaintop by a spectator or lonely mountaineer; it is found through our involvements in the world and our interactions with other people. Nor, incidentally, is it to be derived from an ostensibly omniscient narrator, but it is to be discovered in the space between this fallible creature and her own erring creations. As we read in Eliot's translation of Feuerbach: 'Only through his fellow man does man become clear to himself' (EC, 82). By exposing ourselves to other minds, we strengthen and extend our own. Gradually, these interpersonal relationships allow us to construct an impersonal sense of ourselves—a viewpoint not owned by any empirical someone but that might apply to anyone.

In a sense, universality is a fiction that we construct out of our interactions with others, and Eliot is often nervous about how it is invoked. In a review of the work of Otto Friedrich Gruppe in 1856 she noted how the languages of all nations soon arrive at general expressions—concepts like '*all, universal, necessary*,'—but, true to her empiricist roots, she maintains that the terms have their origin and ground 'purely in the observations of the senses' (E, 151). Her point, moreover, is to insist that these universalising terms have only a pragmatic use within a particular and limited context. It is a dangerous error, she insists, to make a fetish of such vocabularies:

> To isolate such expressions, to operate with them apart from experience, to exalt their relative value into an absolute value, to deduce knowledge from them alone, and to make them a standing point higher than all experience—this, which is what Parmenides and all

> speculative philosophers since him have done, is an attempt to poise the universe on one's head, and no wonder if dizziness and delusion are the consequence. (E, 151)

She is also aware of how manipulating and manipulated these abstractions can be. Take, for instance, the 'anybody' that Gwendolen constructs to justify her own selfish choices. In a kind of parodic application and violation of the categorical imperative, Gwendolen uses the all-permissive 'verdict of "anybody"' to override her own moral intuitions about the wrongness of marrying Grandcourt (DD, 253). It is certainly not a perspective that incorporates the perspective of Mrs. Glasher. But in her real collisions with others even Gwendolen begins to see the partiality of this anybody, noting her 'hard, unfair exclusion of others' from the circle of her concern (DD, 283).

The journey to a wider vision of things in Eliot is often brutal. Moral objectivity in her work is built on conflict, opposition, and negation—just as it is in Hegel and Feuerbach. Through the friction of others, the ego discovers both the distinctiveness and boundedness of its own point of view—often a painful experience—but it also learns to transcend those limits by incorporating other perspectives into its own. This process, for Feuerbach, is evident in the very act of looking at another's look: 'The *ego* first steels its glance in the eye of a *thou* before it endures the contemplation of a being which does not reflect its own image' (EC, 82). This check to solipsistic ways of seeing is the first step towards a more objective sense of self and of others. The chastening effect of another's look, for instance, is evident in the first scene of *Daniel Deronda*. Gwendolen at the roulette table is 'unpleasantly conscious' of Daniel's gaze (DD, 5). Unsurprisingly so: His gaze, after all, is both objectifying and reductive and risks seducing us into the same judgmentalism ('Was she beautiful or not beautiful?'). His own outlook on her looking is also crassly moralistic: 'Was the good or evil genius dominant in those beams?' (DD, 3). No wonder Gwendolen finds the inspection humiliating and resents its condescension. And, yet, for all of its crudities, Deronda's gaze seems to provide Gwendolen with a new perspective of herself. Readers may wish for the learning process to be a bit more dialectical or equitable in *Daniel Deronda*. Nonetheless, the 'exasperating irony' of Deronda's gaze emphasises the ironising potential of any look we might notice: It forces us to do a double-take on ourselves (DD, 12). Seeing ourselves as others see us, moreover, may give us a little more objectivity on ourselves. But it is also mortifying. As Feuerbach once put it, 'The consciousness of the world is a humiliating consciousness'—not least because it arrests the ego's pretensions to unlimitedness (EC, 82).[43] Gwendolen is eventually jolted out of her own narcissism, namely, from the entrenched impression that 'whatever surrounded her was somehow specially for her' (DD, 689). However, her enlarged sense of the world is also a 'self-humiliation' (DD, 689)—a process that may generate both approval and some vengeful delight in onlookers.

Destiny is 'sarcastic' in Eliot, and humiliation is one of her preferred sports (M, 88). As the narrator tells us in *Middlemarch*, doing some of destiny's work: 'We are all humiliated by the sudden discovery of a fact which has existed very comfortably and perhaps been staring at us in private while we have been making up our world entirely without it' (M, 312). Virtually every major character is humiliated in Eliot's novels and finds the limits of their imagination exposed by the resistance of others and the friction of the world. Readers, too, are humiliated—why always Dorothea, you fool?—and the presumption of lady readers comes in for some particularly tough treatment (SCL, 36). Perhaps Eliot enjoys the humiliation a little too much—some of her contemporary readers, and not just the lady ones, felt she was 'needlessly sarcastic, with her own erring children'—but debasement is repeatedly cast as a condition of moral and epistemic growth in her work.[44] Some naughty children resist the bitter pill and 'can only sustain humiliation so long as they can refuse to believe in it' (MF, 197). So, we find Mr. Tulliver still acting the lord in his own imagination despite reality's best efforts to reveal his littleness and absurdity. He departs the novel with 'half his humiliation unlearned' (MF, 224). His daughter is a better learner. Maggie 'is not fond of humiliation,' but experiences it

43. This is noted in Albrecht, *The Ethical Vision of George Eliot*, 22.

44. Colvin and Morley, 'Daniel Deronda,' 603–4.

again and again, even choosing to reside for a time in its 'narrow valley' (MF, 325).

The humiliations of *Middlemarch* are generally reciprocal. Lydgate's complacent assumptions about love and women are tested by Rosamond's 'negations' (M, 550), while she has her own phantasms of marriage checked in turn.[45] Casaubon introduces Dorothea to the limits of her own idealism, but he ultimately shrinks from correction himself. Instead, he forces his wife to serve his own uneasy egoism. There are, of course, Hegelian ironies to this supremacy.[46] The master achieves his mastery at the expense of a proper sense of others and of himself. The subjugated Dorothea, on the other hand, learns to transcend the limits of her own ego, partly by recognising both the independence and alterity of another's outlook. The acquisition of objectivity is a fitful business for Dorothea—and remains forever incomplete—but its golden dawn can be seen in a celebrated moment where she looks out of a window having travelled through her own valley of humiliation:

> She opened her curtains, and looked out towards the bit of road that lay in view, with fields beyond, outside the entrance-gates. On the road there was a man with a bundle on his back and a woman carrying her baby; in the field she could see figures moving—perhaps the shepherd with his dog. Far off in the bending sky was the pearly light; and she felt the largeness of the world and the manifold wakings of men to labour and endurance. She was a part of that involuntary, palpitating life, and could neither look out on it from her luxurious shelter as a mere spectator, nor hide her eyes in selfish complaining. (M, 741)

Casaubon's house is 'small-windowed' (M, 67), while his own outlook—or rather inlook—reflects an entire 'absence of windows' (M, 185). But Dorothea demonstrates the advantages of opening the curtains and looking out. It allows her to wake up to other people's wakings and to a more objective sense of things. She is a little closer, perhaps, to her ultimate goal of acquiring 'the fullest truth, the least partial good' (M, 190).

45 On the broader issue of marriage in Eliot, see Carlisle, *The Marriage Question*.

46. See, in particular, Armstrong, 'George Eliot, Hegel, and *Middlemarch*.'

Dorothea may aim for the least partial perspective, but it must also be admitted that her outlook still remains distinctly partial. It is still confined to a room, still seen through glass, still incomplete (only a bit of road), and still rather vague (is that really a shepherd and his dog?). She continues to entertain a view from somewhere rather than nowhere. Indeed, viewing may no longer be the relevant metaphor here. Dorothea wants to be no 'mere spectator' of the world but an agent within it.[47] This cannot be achieved from a Delectable Mountain or even from a window. At some point the task must be to change the world not just to understand it. Dorothea will leave her home to do just that. But she will also take up a position as mere part of the world—and a very partial part: drawn to some people over others, and in the end confined to a quite limited circle of concern. Eliot wants us to think large thoughts, but not so large that we disappear.

Seeing Double

'You see I have two minds, and both are foolish,' Fedalma declares in *The Spanish Gypsy*.[48] She or they are not alone; several of Eliot's people play host to a 'double consciousness.'[49] The doubleness stems from many things—a dissonance issuing from the memory of who one was and the feeling of who one is, the impression that we are living the experience of others alongside our own (a feeling brought to Gothic heights in *The Lifted Veil*), or it is the beside-oneself feeling that one gets from approaching life as a performance requiring lots of 'sincere acting' (DD, 539). Tito's 'double consciousness' is a simple manifestation of a common bind: the conflict between duty and desire in his life (R, 352). Tito may try to resolve this conflict by making desire his duty, but it's not clear that he persuades himself of this or indeed anyone else. So, the would-be hedonist ends up sad and put out. The reasons for an unhappy unconsciousness in Hegel are not dissimilar: It stems from an inability to

47. However, on the difficulties of acting, see Markovits, 'George Eliot's Problem with Action.'

48. Eliot, *The Spanish Gypsy*, 110.

49. On aspects of doubleness in Eliot, see Tate, *The Poet's Mind*, 125–52.

integrate the personal and impersonal outlook within oneself. The unhappy consciousness flits between contempt for the world and contempt for itself in a doomed effort to escape its torn nature. The only medicine in the end is for philosophy to unify these outlooks and to show that the subjective and objective perspective are different facets of each other.

Eliot's novels might represent a similar search for fusion albeit in a very different mode and with a very different outcome. The attempt to unite first-person and third-person perspectives is arguably evident in the very form of her novels—as she dips into the mind of her creations all the while remaining in the third person. We see it in her related efforts in her prose to conjoin knowledge by acquaintance—the what's-it-likeness of experiential states—with an external or more distanced form of knowledge by description. Yet, even as she attempts these mergers, we also see her insist on the irreducibility of first-person and third-person accounts. The issue is beautifully presented in *Middlemarch* in Casaubon's imminent sense of his own death:

> Here was a man who now for the first time found himself looking into the eyes of death—who was passing through one of those rare moments of experience when we feel the truth of a commonplace, which is as different from what we call knowing it, as the vision of waters upon the earth is different from the delirious vision of the water which cannot be had to cool the burning tongue. When the commonplace "We must all die" transforms itself suddenly into the acute consciousness "I must die—and soon," then death grapples us, and his fingers are cruel; afterwards, he may come to fold us in his arms as our mother did, and our last moment of dim earthly discerning may be like the first. To Mr. Casaubon now, it was as if he suddenly found himself on the dark river-brink and heard the plash of the oncoming oar, not discerning the forms, but expecting the summons. (M, 397–98)

We can easily do the syllogism: All men are mortal. Casaubon is a man. Therefore, Casaubon is mortal. But Eliot points to a distinctive kind of first-person awareness, which she prefers to call feeling rather than knowledge (which, presumably, is more respectably third person). Nonetheless, Eliot's prose goes some way to trigger these what's-it-like-to-be-Casaubon feelings in us. The opening 'Here was a man'—with its sad tension between the nowness of 'here' and the then-ness of 'was'—might sound like it is already giving up on Casaubon and relinquishing him to the barge. But the indexical 'here' also yanks us into the scene and the later 'now' thrusts us into Casaubon.[50] The sensory impressions—the onomatopoeic 'plash' of Charon's oar—also put us on the river-brink, awaiting the 'summons' that ends the hypotactic sentence that we endure alongside Casaubon. The prose makes the phenomenological point that the view from here is always different from the view from there—that there is something irreducible about the first-person standpoint, not least when it comes to death. The illocutionary and perlocutionary force of the statement 'I must die' is different to the effect of 'They must die' or even the marginally more anxiety-inducing statement 'We must die.'

The irony of this powerful account of dying in the first person is that it is largely written in the third. The very technique of the passage suggests that the distinction between internal and external perspectives is easily overdrawn. Or it emphasises the epistemic achievement that is free indirect discourse: It straddles the gap between third-person and first-person reports, knowledge by description and knowledge by acquaintance. The technique may also be a moral victory and gets to the heart of what Eliot meant by sympathy—to invoke the famous ground and apology for her art—a way of understanding another's experience in a way that might blur or even overcome spatial metaphors of inside and out. Nonetheless, I want to dwell a little on some of the limitations of this seeming eraser of limits. In other words, some doubleness about sympathy allows us to see that the cure for doubleness and division can never be total.

Like egotism, its ostensible foe, sympathy, for Eliot, is both an epistemic and moral tool, incorporating 'our best insight and our best love'

50. As Colin McGinn maintains, albeit somewhat circularly, 'the egocentric character of indexical thought makes it peculiarly subjective.' McGinn, *The Subjective View*, 140.

(AB, 436). Its mechanics, however, are not straightforward.[51] How does sympathy allow us to understand 'another myself' or overcome the gap between third-person and first-person viewpoints? Stephen Darwall suggests it doesn't and has distinguished 'sympathy' from a much more immersive 'empathy': Sympathy, he suggests, demands attentiveness and solicitude for another, but it remains a third-person emotional response; empathy, on the other hand, involves putting oneself in another's shoes and reconstituting in oneself the feelings of another.[52] Of course, this terminological distinction was unavailable to Eliot or to earlier moralists and the word 'sympathy' could include both a distanced concern and a more intimate participation in the feelings of another. All of these positions were entertained by the great theorist of sympathy Adam Smith: Sometimes it demanded putting oneself in the situation of another; sometimes it entailed reconceiving oneself as that other person so that 'we enter as it were into his body and become in some measure him.'[53] This spiritual substitution is impressive though it's always liable to fall prey to projection and false identification—a problem to which Eliot is deeply alert.

Even Dorothea—the great sympathiser-in-chief of *Middlemarch*—tends to sympathise in a circle. The solipsistic quality to her initial interest in Casaubon is clearly noted: She looks deep into his mind and finds 'reflected there in vague labyrinthine extension every quality she herself brought' (M, 22). While she makes clear efforts to emerge from his moral stupidity, there is some evidence to suggest that Dorothea continues to see in circles right to the novel's end. In her triumphant moments of sympathising with Lydgate and with Rosamond, for instance, she continues to act and speak from 'the heart of her own trial' and 'out of her own sorrow' (M, 747). Her confidence in Rosamond's good nature, moreover, stems from her 'usual tendency to over-estimate the

51. The literature on sympathy in Eliot is too extensive to list, but I have benefited in particular from the following: Fessenbecker, 'Sympathy, Vocation, and Moral Deliberation in George Eliot,' and the three essays: Gatens, 'A Roar of Sound'; Albrecht, 'Sympathy and Alterity'; and Donlin, 'The Grounds of Exception,' in Harris and Sussman, *Antipodean George Eliot*.

52. Darwall, *The Second-Person Standpoint*, 45.

53. Smith, *Theory of Moral Sentiments*, 12.

good in others' (M, 750). But this moral trust is also strangely constitutive.[54] If there often seems to be a friction in Eliot between a descriptive 'rationality' and a projective 'generosity'—embodied, say, in Caleb Garth or Dorothea (M, 531), not all circularity, we learn, is vicious. For there are people who 'bind us over to rectitude and purity by their pure belief about us' (M, 726).[55] This is what we might call a 'constituting sympathy' to invoke a suggestive phrase from Eliot's notebooks.[56] Dorothea's 'believing conception' of others is a fertile *as if*—one that conceives in a double sense, allowing thoughts to become flesh (M, 726). This moral creativity, moreover, builds productively on *amour propre*: Rosamond sees reflected in Dorothea's eyes the image of the good person she is believed to be and now wants to be. The downcast Lydgate, on the other hand, feels he is restored to 'his old self in consciousness that he was with one who believed in it.' This is the effect of 'generous sympathy,' and Lydgate gives himself up to it completely (M, 717–18).

Sympathy may be benign even when it is mistaken, but there are moments where we think it may be at fault even when it is right in its convictions about others. As the narrator of *The Lifted Veil* recognises, a knowledge of other minds is an intrusive power and not without its responsibilities ('The horror I had of again breaking in on the privacy of another soul' [LV, 38]). Perhaps some of Eliot's characters should dwell on this horror a little more. After all, the knowledge of others that sympathy may communicate is sometimes experienced as a violation—an infringement of another's autonomy or private world. Dorothea knows that in certain cases 'sympathy might make a wound' (M, 721). A declared sympathy with Lydgate, for instance, over his marital woes would—initially at least—be a painful assault on his *amour propre*. It would be a painful violation of his privacy, not least by revealing how little of it is in fact private. Such sympathy would also be coercive: It would force Lydgate to acknowledge things he may not want to know

54. On this point, see also Fessenbecker, 'Sympathy, Vocation, and Moral Deliberation in George Eliot.'

55. This circularity can also be seen in Mordecai in *Daniel Deronda*. He plays host to 'that passionate belief which determines the consequences it believes in' (DD, 438).

56. Eliot, 'Notes on *The Spanish Gypsy* and Tragedy,' in Pinion, *A George Eliot Miscellany*, 128.

or know that they are known. In this context, Dorothea regulates her compassion well, but the same moral tact is not always extended to her husband. Here sympathy *does* wound. Within Dorothea's solicitude Casaubon discovers a terrifying perceptiveness and a cruel judgmentalism. He had expected her to perch on his life like an ornamental and uncritical canary-bird; instead, she takes up position as 'a spy watching everything with a malign power of inference' (M, 188).[57]

Casaubon, admittedly, is a sad case: 'His experience was of that pitiable kind which shrinks from pity, and fears most of all that it should be known' (M, 262). Other people's pity is a humiliation—an exposure of his own limitations both to himself and to others—and he recoils from this double consciousness in terror. Casaubon's vision of his wife—'a cruel outward accuser' (M, 188)—is, of course, cruel and accusing, but his feeling that there is often a deep judgmentalism within sympathy is not wrong. In Smith's eyes, approbation was a condition of sympathy while disapprobation was its limit, though in Dorothea's case the value-judgements are more subtly mixed. Dorothea is convinced that if her husband had been more generously open, she would never have assumed the role of judge: 'If he had drawn her towards him, she would never have surveyed him—never have said, "Is he worth living for?" but would have felt him simply a part of her own life' (M, 399). Her sympathy, she believes, would be fully immersive, not just a third-person solicitude for a separate person but a full identification with another, allowing him to become part of herself. Here the gap between first-person and third-person perspectives would be transcended—at some cost, perhaps, to the independence of persons.

But the narrative voice shows just how difficult it is to close that gap. The narrator certainly tries to practice the sympathy she preaches and to immerse herself in the outlook of her characters—as we have seen,

57. The options men extend to women in marriage in *Middlemarch* are often disastrously reductive. Lydgate, for instance, had hoped for a wife who 'would reverence her husband's mind after the fashion of an accomplished mermaid, using her comb and looking-glass and singing her song for the relaxation of his adored wisdom alone' (M, 547). Like Casaubon, Lydgate, it would seem, deserves his humiliations.

free indirect discourse is its discursive effect—yet the voice can remain tartly judgemental and external. This is evident in her avowed attempts to sympathise with figures like Casaubon:

> For my part I am very sorry for him. It is an uneasy lot at best, to be what we call highly taught and yet not to enjoy: to be present at this great spectacle of life and never to be liberated from a small hungry shivering self—never to be fully possessed by the glory we behold, never to have our consciousness rapturously transformed into the vividness of a thought, the ardour of a passion, the energy of an action, but always to be scholarly and uninspired, ambitious and timid, scrupulous and dim-sighted. (M, 263)

How sorry are people really when they say they are sorry for us—not least when they proceed to litanise our vices? We sympathise sometimes to cause a wound. For all the professed sympathy of Eliot's narrator, there is a severity of judgement in the passage above. The use of the first-person plural may dilute the charges against Casaubon by implicating us all. But the language remains categorical—a series of 'nevers' succeeded by an absolute 'always'—and the repetitive syntax communicates a prosecuting zeal. Balance is affected in the final clause in a dialectic of approbation and disapprobation 'scholarly and uninspired, ambitious and timid, scrupulous and dim-sighted.' This may read like the systole and diastole of sympathy or at least the mechanics of fairness, but each couplet ends on a negative note, as does the sentence as a whole. If sympathy relies on approbation, as Smith had suggested, then Eliot's prose easily shows how it is also arrested by disapproval and moral judgement. But this doesn't mean that we should necessarily retire our judgement; rather, it might imply that we must often stand aside from our sympathy in art and in moral life. After all, moral perspective and critical independence might be lost in our attempts to fully identify with the perspective of another.[58]

58. It was precisely because our identifications could be so undiscerning that Smith suggested we should regulate our sympathy with reference to an impartial spectator.

These problems are clearly lived out in another born-again sympathiser: Daniel Deronda. In some respects, Daniel's sympathy is too immersive and leads to a surrender of moral distance and discrimination. On the other hand, it is all too distanced, because Daniel seems to practice an 'impartial sympathy' (DD, 638)—a sympathy for everyone that is almost indistinguishable from sympathy for no one. This is a sympathy that soars above preference: 'His imagination had so wrought itself to the habit of seeing things as they probably appeared to others, that a strong partisanship, unless it were against an immediate oppression, had become an insincerity for him' (DD, 307). Daniel's seeming concern for everyone makes advocacy for anyone feel insincere and arbitrary. He is, it would seem, another unhappy consciousness, someone who struggles to integrate a particular point of view with a universal point of view. But the will-to-universality risks jeopardising his moral sense. 'A too reflective and diffusive sympathy,' we are told, 'was in danger of paralysing in him that indignation against wrong and that selectness of fellowship which are the conditions of moral force' (DD, 308).

Eliot again makes the point that partisanship and selectivity are conditions of moral life; indeed, 'partiality . . . is man's best strength' and 'makes sympathy practical' (DD, 638). An 'impartial sympathy,' on the other hand, is self-undermining and violates the basic grammar of our affections. As Hume had noted there was an irreducible partiality—even a chauvinism—built into sympathy ('We sympathize more with persons contiguous to us, than with persons remote from us: With our acquaintance, than with strangers: With our countrymen, than with foreigners').[59] Eliot, in some senses, is deeply hostile to this moral confinement. Indeed, her whole sense of the moral vocation of art reflects a desire to widen our circle of concern and make us a little less provincial ('If art does not enlarge men's sympathies, it does nothing morally' [L9, 220]). This sympathetic enlargement clearly continues in *Daniel Deronda*—where even the smallest minds are pierced by a sense of 'universal kinship' (DD, 102). It is a novel, moreover, that also aims to

59. Hume, *Treatise of Human Nature*, 371.

extend this sense of kinship to victimised groups such as Jews.[60] So, it can feel a little ironic if not self-undermining to find its narrator championing selectness of fellowship over universal kinship at a key juncture in the novel. This may be the only option, but it can make sympathy look like an enlarged narcissism. As Hume had pointed out, we tend to sympathise with those who resemble us, and Daniel certainly chooses to do just that. 'I consider it my duty—it is the impulse of my feeling,' he declares, 'to identify myself, as far as possible, with my hereditary people' (DD, 566). Daniel's Judaism represents a certain cure for doubleness. If he has operated as an unhappy consciousness for much of the novel—riven between over-general sympathies and more personal needs—then he leaves it in a happier condition. By discovering a nation, he has discovered himself and vice versa; personal and public concerns now conjoin in a lived concern for his people.

How far we should sympathise with this sympathy—or rely on some other moral resource—is far from clear. Daniel's partial sympathies might be defensible on universal grounds ('selectness of fellowship,' in other words, should be an option for everyone), but it is hard to see how his particular form of fellow-feeling could be a choice for all—not least when the terms of his identification are so 'hereditary' and exclusive.[61] The point is made through Leonora. Daniel's mother restores the novel to doubleness by rejecting her son's sentimental view of maternal, familial, and ethnic bonds. These, she reveals, are often forms of bondage—not least for a woman. Leonora doesn't do sympathy or doesn't want to ('I am not a loving woman' [DD, 571]) and we can sympathise with this. She isn't the first to suggest that our sympathies are frequently pathological and compel rather than persuade. If they are experienced inside as unfreedom, they can also make us assent to our fetters. Leonora

60. As she put it in a letter: 'There is nothing I should care more to do, if it were possible, than to rouse the imagination of men and women to a vision of human claims in those races of their fellow-man who most differ from them in custom and beliefs' (L6, 301).

61. Anderson argues that Daniel tries to supplement this ethnic idea of community with 'civic' principles, but she also admits that Eliot's account of collective identity in *Daniel Deronda* 'is ultimately raced-based.' Anderson, *The Powers of Distance*, 133.

resists this sentimental subjection. She may not succeed fully—and cares about Daniel in spite of herself—but this failure may also be to her credit. We, too, it seems, feel double about the value of sympathy. If it helps us to pass into others, we know that it can make us trespass against ourselves. It may also stop us from trespassing—always returning us to the inner parishes of the self under the pretence of roaming abroad.

Impossible Vastnesses

Art, we are often told, can help us to think eternal thoughts. As Wittgenstein put it in 1916, sounding very much like Spinoza: 'The work of art is the object seen *sub specie aeternitatis* and the good life is the world seen *sub specie aeternitatis*.'[62] Eliot could do a good impression of this all-seeingness. Through her novels, third-person and first-person-knowledge—or God the Father and God the Son—are combined within a capacious sympathy, a total view of things that is nonetheless inwardly lived. Amen to all this. And yet, in the little lapses from godliness within her form, in the failures of sympathy and the little sneers of judgement, in the gap between an austere transcendence and the questionable immanence of fellow-feeling, in the dubious partialities of focalisation itself, we see the difficulty of absolute knowledge performed. Why always Dorothea or why anyone or anything in particular? Yearn as we might for that Delectable Mountain, objectivity in Eliot must always remain incomplete or can never quite join eyeballs with an inward view. As one of the most celebrated passages in *Middlemarch* makes clear, there are limits beyond which the mind cannot trespass:

> If we had a keen vision and feeling of all ordinary human life, it would be like hearing the grass grow and the squirrel's heart beat, and we should die of that roar which lies on the other side of silence. As it is, the quickest of us walk about well wadded with stupidity. (M, 182)

62. Wittgenstein, *Notebooks 1914–16*, 83. This also summed up, for Wittgenstein, 'the connection between art and ethics' (83).

We may end this novel a little less wadded, even, perhaps, slightly wiser and better, but we also realise how exhausting it must have been to be God—an entity that experiences the what's-it-likeness of everything, while remaining magnificently transcendent of everything.[63] Even the attempt to arrive at this all-seeing, all-hearing, all-participating knowledge is liable to drive us insane.[64]

An infinite sympathy is not for us—as our efforts to think our way into animals or blades of grass soon reveal—and it may be some comfort to us that we only hear our own heartbeat, not the squirrel's. Eliot forces us to reflect, nonetheless, on the proper extent of our solicitude. 'We must look all over the globe,' Mr. Brooke chirrups (M, 474), and Eliot repeatedly invites us to do so. But she also remains concerned about the moral dangers of global travel. As she memorably put it in *The Mill on the Floss*: 'Our instructed vagrancy, which has hardly time to linger by the hedgerows, but runs away early to the tropics, and is at home with palms and banyans . . . is nourished on books of travel, and stretches the theatre of its imagination to the Zambesi' (MF, 262). Here Eliot expresses an ambivalence about the kind of mind-journeys that her own books condition. If imagination, like charity, begins at home, and extends outwards, Eliot does not want it to forget its humble origins and old attachments. But once the mind has travelled the world, it is hard for it to return to familiar parishes. Similarly, when we have done as Eliot has asked, and extended our moral horizons, it may be impossible to rejoin our little platoons with happiness or confidence. As she intimated in *Adam Bede*, after we have gained a more capacious sense of the good, 'we can no more wish to return to a narrower sympathy, than a painter or a musician can wish to return to his cruder manner, or a philosopher to his less complete formula' (AB, 473). Imagination, therefore, is liable to make unhappy consciousnesses of us all, dividing our attention between local and universal standpoints—not that they always present themselves as crudely opposed. Doubleness may be a

63. As Cavell notes: 'Only God could bear to be God.' Cavell, *The Claim of Reason*, 429.

64. On the Lockean background to these cognitive limits, see Yousef, *The Aesthetic Commonplace*, chap. 2.

basic fact of mind—as Lydgate observes, 'a man's mind must be continually expanding and shrinking between the whole human horizon and the horizon of an object-glass' (M, 602)—but it isn't always easy to endure. The task may be to alight upon a golden mean, but, like many a march to the middle in Eliot, this success can also feel like everyday failure.

3

Lies—James

WHY SO MANY LIES? In fact, lying or a more oblique deceptiveness is so ubiquitous in James's fiction that it almost loses its disreputable character.[1] Consider the ceremonies of 'high hypocrisy,' the strange draw of 'fine dishonesty,' duplicity both 'beautiful' and 'happy.'[2] 'How they do lie,' a mother observes to her daughter in *The Awkward Age*. The daughter's response is at least honest: 'Yes, but we lie so to *them*.'[3] The untruths and half-truths come in many forms: from 'conscious perjury' (GB, 482) to 'successful vagueness' (GB, 479), from culpable silence to falsehoods in which none is really deceived, and all seem complicit in the charade. There are those who believe they 'lie badly' and feel lucky in their ineptitude, and there are others who exult in their own talent for deceit ('*I* lie well, thank God').[4] James is fascinated by actors who can make 'the fictive true' wherever they go and is wryly aware of those who lack such charisma: the unfortunates who make 'even the true seem fictive.'[5] Short stories like 'The Liar' (1888) deliver studies of

1. Some of the permutations of deceit have been explored. See, in particular, Bersani, 'The Jamesian Lie.' Also Miller, *Literature as Conduct*, chaps. 4 and 5. See, too, Tredy, Dupperay, and Harding, *Henry James and the Poetics of Duplicity*.

2. James, *The Golden Bowl*, 492. All further references are given in the text under the abbreviation 'GB.' James, *The Sacred Fount*, in *Novels, 1901–1902*, 148, 85, 149.

3. James, *The Awkward Age*, in *Novels, 1896–1899*, 858. All further references are given in the text under the abbreviation 'AA.'

4. James, *The Wings of the Dove*, 324. All further references are given in the text under the abbreviation 'WD.'

5. James, *The Tragic Muse*, 144.

wild deceivers—their motivations, their objectives, their various enablers, and the strange virtues and dedication they bring to their craft.

There is an obvious self-referential element to all this duplicity. James played with the ancient calumny—fondly embraced by Wilde—that all artists are liars.[6] 'The Liar,' for instance, both invites and rejects this charge. The ostensible liar at its centre—Captain Capadose—is more a Platonic bullshitter, perhaps, than a 'liar platonic' (CS, 1.936).[7] If he occasionally 'lapses into flat veracity' (CS, 1.937), he remains sublimely indifferent to the truth in a way that liars can never quite afford to be.[8] But the salient point is that there is a strange connection between this bullshit-artist and the real artist in this tale. As its painter-hero notes of Capadose: 'He paints, as it were, and so do I!' (CS, 1.937). Classic defences of art are duly reassigned to the bullshitter: Capadose's talk is pursued for no personal gain or desire to injure, it is perfectly disinterested and is a virtual end in itself. If his falsehoods make any contact with a world, it is a nobly counterfactual world: life as it might have been, or as it could and should be, never as it is. This may dignify bullshit, but it also undermines art. As the very name of the painter ('Lyon') insinuates, artists can seem to misrepresent for a living. Or if the story refutes Plato's charge that artists are liars, it arguably does so by intimating that they are bullshitters instead—they don't deceive people about the truth, because they never aim to tell it in the first place.

Yet the story's desire to reveal even this fact about itself complicates the picture. 'The Liar,' after all, is deeply invested in the idea that art tells the truth. It is ultimately left to a painting—an unfinished portrait of Capadose—to reveal to a fantasist and his unsettlingly 'faithful' wife the full extent of his falseness. If truth is like a lion, then 'Lyon' may be this truth-revealing animal (as the aghast Mrs. Capadose proclaims: '*He* knows—he has seen. Every one will know—every one will see' [CS, 1.953]). The truth, however, can be hard to bear, even for someone so

6. 'Lying,' Wilde proclaimed, 'the telling of beautiful untrue things, is the proper aim of Art.' Wilde, 'The Decay of Lying,' in *Complete Works*, 1091–92.

7. James, *Collected Stories*, 1.936. All further references are given in the text under the abbreviation 'CS.'

8. On the differences between lies and bullshit, see Frankfurt, 'On Bullshit.'

inured to its value as Capadose, and he duly destroys the portrait—a piece so life-like that the act is described as akin to murder (the narrator may stretch the truth a little when he proclaims 'the Colonel literally had hacked it to death' [CS, 1.954]). James, however, leaves little ambiguities in place about the motive and meaning of this crime. Whether Capadose kills the painting because of his sense of its unbearable truth or its terrible falsehood—or merely because it has upset his wife—is never made clear.[9] His wife's own sense of the 'painted betrayal' (of whom or of what?) leaves us none the wiser (CS, 1.953).

'The Liar' could easily be pulling our leg about the truth-revealing properties of painting and, by extension, literature itself. The epistemic powers it describes are, it would seem, too good to be true. A painting, after all, doesn't *say* anything. Being nonlinguistic, it doesn't propose or assert and can't therefore be true or false. James liked to analogise between literature and the visual arts, precisely because it allowed him to resist the pressure of the propositional and the demand for a 'moral' from art. This was the move he made in 1884 when rejecting Walter Besant's attempts to saddle the novel with a 'moral purpose.' A novel, he insisted, is essentially a picture, and it makes as little sense to ask for a 'moral picture' as it does to demand 'a moral statue.'[10] But 'The Liar' conjures up for us an extraordinary moral picture—an X-ray of the soul that seemingly reveals to a man the full extent of his moral squalor. Someone at some point seems to have been bullshitting.

'The Liar,' then, may function a little like a Cretan liar, telling lies about its truth and truth about its lies. But the paradox should not detain us too long, for the story is arguably more interested in the functional significance of truth than its own performative contradictions: the reasons why we tell the truth, what our revelations *do* to others, how we change the world by adding our descriptions of the world to the

9. The object of the Colonel's curses remains opaque: '"Damn him, damn him, damn him!"' (CS, 1.952). When the curses are repeated Lyon, too, is confused: 'It was not clear to Lyon whether this malediction had for its object the original or the painter of the portrait' (CS, 1.953). The Colonel's destruction of the portrait is also cast as a 'figurative suicide' (CS, 1.954).

10. James, *Literary Criticism*, 1.62. All further references are given in the text under the abbreviation 'LC.'

world. After all, we often tell the truth for the wrong reasons. Lyon may not be lying, but his art seems to be oriented towards other ends than truth alone. If we know from the start that the artist has loved Mrs. Capadose in the past, the painting may be an attempt to destroy a competitor and to revive an old suit. The painting, he believes, is 'a tremendous hit' and the violence of the metaphor tells its own truth (CS, 1.952). Accuracy and malice are entirely compatible—though this fact may be not acknowledged or 'known' by the painter himself. Our capacity for self-deception—as agents and as readers—is also one of James's great themes, and, as we shall see, it may be an irreducible feature of what James calls at one point 'the illusion of life' (LC, 1.53).

My aim here is to probe what lies and more ambiguous deceptions say about James's ideas of the good life and the different—even rival—normativities that fall under that concept. What does deceit reveal, for instance, about the value of truth in his ethical universe?[11] Moreover, if we have good reasons to lie, might our lies also reveal that we have reasons not to be too good? James, after all, often seems to be a bemused critic of a narrow and zealous moralism, choosing to defend instead a more capacious, plural, and less resolved notion of virtue. This can make him seem like a fairly forgiving type of moralist, at least where lies and other peccadillos are concerned. The task life sets us, as Chad Newsome might say, is not to be morally perfect but to be 'all right'—a condition that can tolerate, at least in Chad's case, a significant amount of deception.[12] Of course, as Maggie Verver observes in *The Golden Bowl*, '*all* right's a good deal to say' (GB, 454). Maggie lays the emphasis on the comprehensiveness of 'all,' but we might stress the difficult fecundity of the word 'right'—the way it might seem to combine different standards of rightness, both moral and epistemic. Partly because the colloquialism pretends to so much, its use and reuse in James can begin to feel fishy,

11. Bernard Williams believes that to speak of 'the value of truth' is, in a very strict sense, a category mistake (since truth is a property of sentences and can't in this context have a value). I follow Williams, however, in taking the 'value of truth' as a 'shorthand for the value of various states and activities associated with the truth.' See Williams, *Truth and Truthfulness*, 6–7.

12. James, *The Ambassadors*, 114. All further references are given in the text under the abbreviation 'A.'

so much so that 'all right' can begin to sound 'all wrong' (AA, 885)—yet another one of the casual falsehoods that are tossed out in his work. In an effort to clarify the kind of normativity that is brought to deceit in James—the kinds of rightness it violates and the rightness it may honour—I want to first explore the value of truth and truthfulness in his work. I'll then consider how these values sit alongside other moral goods. This should leave us with some normative criteria with which to navigate the long vistas of deceit that we encounter in the late work—namely, 'The Beast in the Jungle,' *The Ambassadors, The Wings of the Dove,* and *The Golden Bowl.* By the time we reach these tales we may be in a better position to judge—in so far as such judgements are ever possible—whether acts of deception can ever be all right.

Looking for Truth

Truth-seeking in James is a tough business, for characters and readers alike. Sometimes a fundamentalism about truth in his work seems to preclude any possibility of knowledge, generating a scepticism that flies in the face of James's own conviction that there are 'things we cannot possibly *not* know sooner or later, in one way or other' (LC, 2.1063). If truth is the name we give to the expedient in our thinking—or so his brother William sometimes said—Henry himself can seem demandingly absolutist.[13] His characters, at least, often go to deeply inexpedient lengths to find 'Truth with a big T.'[14] If big T is rarely if ever reached—in ways that might begin to demonstrate in Williamish ways that the ideal itself is a delusion—the process has left some readers feeling cheated. 'He doesn't even seem to want to find things out,' H. G. Wells complained.[15] A fundamentalism about truth, after all, can soon look like a contempt for all ordinary forms of it. It is a short road, perhaps, from idealism to scepticism to cynicism to bullshit. Where James sits on this spectrum is not easy to say.

13. James, *Pragmatism,* 106.
14. James, *Pragmatism,* 111.
15. Edel and Ray, *Henry James and H. G. Wells,* 245.

If vagueness is sometimes a virtue in James, he is also prepared to give accuracy or 'truth of detail' its due (LC, 1.53). His narrators share with characters a passion for exactness and seem fastidiously devoted to *le mot juste*.[16] Epistemic virtues such as perceptiveness repeatedly shade into moral qualities in James, which is not to say that 'fine attention' exhausts what it is to be good (CS, 2.957). James may sympathise with his creation Fanny Assingham ('what is morality but high intelligence?'), but he is not in thrall to her. Nor does he necessarily feel that 'stupidity pushed to a certain point *is* . . . immorality' (GB, 66). Stupidity, after all, has its consolations and protections, and is perhaps the closest we get to innocence in James.[17] Conversely, those who have chomped on the apple are often cruel and use their cleverness to deceive.

James's willingness to describe or even to expose deception may reflect a strong commitment to truth—but he also voiced doubts about the basic attractiveness of this value. Reviewing the memoirs of Madame de Sabran in 1875, his eye was drawn to her melancholy sense of truth:

> I believe that illusion is useful in all things, and for myself all that I fear in this world is the truth. The truth is almost always sad and she leaves almost no consolation behind her. Happily every individual has a common interest in being cheated, and the human race in this respect doesn't spare itself. What is most to be desired is to be *well* cheated, till one's last day. (LC, 2.656–57)

We often find a similarly disillusioned illusionism in the fiction. Take the view of the life fantastic in 'The Middle Years' (1893): 'It was the abyss of human illusion that was the real, the tideless deep' (CS, 2.103). If there are deceivers throughout his work, there are also people who are 'determined to be deceived' (CS, 2.12).

These statements clearly bend back on James and on us. How much does he indulge our determination to be deceived? Again, it may be

16. As William Gass maintained, 'Henry James's sentences are continuous qualifications, nuance is the core and not the skin.' See Gass, *Fictions and the Figures of Life*, 15.

17. Take the likeable Bob Assingham, for instance, a 'dear, fond, stupid, uneasy man' (GB, 391).

itself deceiving to say that fiction deceives or, indeed, informs. Fiction, it is often said, is neither true nor false, because it states nothing; at best it only *pretends* to state things.[18] I have shown how this theory of pretence rests on an overly constrained conception of the really real statement, yet it does help us to foreground James's particular resistance to categorical assertion. 'It is a great temptation,' as Wittgenstein noted, 'to try to make the spirit explicit,' but James generally managed to resist that temptation.[19] He was the great master of 'roundabout arts' (LL, 501) and preferred to intimate than to declare. Throughout his work people think in metaphors, even organise their lives around them, but what 'The Beast in the Jungle' really means even when it finally springs upon a life is not perhaps fully clear. Terms like 'The Real Right Thing' (CS, 2.543) or 'The Great Good Place' (CS, 2.557) shimmer with meaningfulness but lack reference. Of course, some readers have deplored the hazy portentousness of it all. His brother William found the method perverse in an age of hurry, and he was convinced that it antagonised ordinary punters: '"Say it *out*, for God's sake," they cry, "and have done with it."'[20]

But Henry liked to play with the possibility that his tales have nothing substantive to say. As he intimates in 'The Figure in the Carpet' (1896), there may be no actual figure, or it may simply stand as the image of an illusion—an unmeetable hope for a final truth in art—or perhaps in anything. This can make art sound a like a classy form of bullshit, but it also advances a very Kantian notion of the aesthetic. The mind, in other words, is aroused when confronted by the beautiful and seeks a concept adequate to its experience. Yet no such concept is to be found.[21] If this makes the aesthetic a pointless exercise, pointlessness may be partly the point, allowing art to be its own end and its contemplation a form of play. James is seriously committed to open-ended play and to intellectual pleasures that yield no definitive cognitive

18. Searle, *Expression and Meaning.*

19. Wittgenstein, *Culture and Value,* 8.

20. James, *Selected Letters,* 234. Collin Burrow has recently reiterated the impatience: see Burrow, 'Just Say It, Henry.'

21. As Kant suggests, the beautiful 'pleases universally without a concept.' See Kant, *Critique of the Power of Judgment,* 104.

result.[22] To find the figure in the carpet and arrive at some 'final knowledge' would only spoil the fun (CS, 2.327).

Not everyone, of course, finds bafflement so amusing. Wells despaired of the way James's tales seemed to culminate in 'nothingness.'[23] The bathos arising from the severe demands of reading these works and their cognitive returns was, in Wells's eyes, immense: It was as if a sacred temple had been erected around 'a dead kitten, an egg-shell, a bit of string.'[24] Even James recognised that the game could exhaust its players—the narrator of 'The Figure in the Carpet' loses his joy in all the sleuth-work. Here and elsewhere (say, 'The Aspern Papers' or *The Sacred Fount*) the obsessive search for some ultimate big 'T' can seem deranged. The search confirms that uncertainty is often a deeply painful state—for characters and readers alike—and it can make thinking through or reading James feel like a sadomasochistic experience.[25] James's hedonistic sense of the aesthetic—'It all comes back to that, to my and your "fun"' (LC, 2.1338)—was, therefore, a risky apology for difficult books.[26] It could also downplay James's own sense of the novel's cognitive vocation. He put it a little sententiously in an early unpublished review: 'When once a work of fiction may be classed as a novel, its foremost claim to merit, and indeed the measure of its merit, is its *truth*' (LC, 1.607). He presented things in more Platonic terms in 1884—'the novel, the picture, the statue partake of the substance of beauty and truth' (LC, 1.64). The idea of participating in truth allowed James to resist the idea of merely telling it. Moreover, he often argues that art partakes in the search for truth by remaining confused. As he put it in

22. T. S. Eliot famously noted this dimension of James: He had 'a mind so fine that no idea could violate it.' Eliot, *Complete Prose*, 1.650. Clearly, James permitted his mind and his works to be penetrated by ideas, but in the face of Shaw's predictable demands for conclusions from art, James defended the imagination's right 'to *play* with an idea—an idea of life—under a happy obsession' (LL, 474).

23. Edel and Ray, *Henry James and H. G. Wells*, 249.

24. Edel and Ray, *Henry James and H. G. Wells*, 248.

25. On the pain of uncertainty and doubt, see Peirce, 'The Fixation of Belief,' in *The Essential Peirce*, 1.109–23.

26. He was on equally vulnerable ground when he defended the 'good old fashion of "liking" a work of art or not liking it' (LC, 1.57).

the preface to *What Maisie Knew*: 'The muddled state . . . is one of the very sharpest of the realities' (LC, 2.1164). His novels may win some transcendence from the muddle—and invite us to savour our uncertainty as pleasure. But James also maintains that art must remain accountable to the muddle and has a duty to keep our perplexity in sight.

This perplexity is as remote from total ignorance as it is from final knowledge. James isn't a thorough-going sceptic about knowledge, though he doubts its completeness and repeatedly queries its value.[27] 'I find it very pleasant not to know,' Isabel Archer declares, and the Countess Gemini takes a similar view: 'The more you know the more unhappy you are.'[28] But ignorance in James can never be pure or infinitely sustained and it remains impossible *not* to know some things sooner or later, though this knowledge frequently arrives too late or is experienced as bathos.[29] The beast in the jungle in the end is not exactly a dead kitten, but it is not far off. This is not just a mean trick of a truth-indifferent art—as Wells might have us believe—but James often implies that this disenchantment is our basic epistemic condition. In the sad miaow of the beast, we hear that the truth is trivial and has lain on the surface all along. Bathos, of course, is also the result of putting even this knowledge into words. The gap between what our experiences *show* and what we can *say* is basic to life itself and to these artworks.

Knowledge in James, then, is not always very good for us, or even in the end all that interesting, but we can't simply retire 'the insurmountable desire to *know*'—despite some of his characters' best efforts (LC, 2.297). We are, it seems, truth-seeking animals even if this commits us to lives of disappointment. To add to the epistemic complexities, we are also truth-makers. As his brother William declared: 'In our cognitive as well as in our active life we are creative. We *add*, both to the subject and

27. As he put it in a review of Flaubert's letters, 'We pay more for some kinds of knowledge than those particular kinds are worth' (LC, 2.297). On his ambivalence about knowledge, see Wood, 'What Henry Knew.'

28. James, *The Portrait of a Lady*, 174, 260.

29. As he brilliantly put it in a review of Turgenev: 'But the world as it stands is no illusion, no phantasm, no evil dream of a night; we wake up to it for ever and ever' (LC, 2.998).

to the predicate part of reality. . . . Man *engenders* truths upon it.'[30] This, in a sense, was to reiterate the long-observed powers of mind to spread itself on the world and to thicken itself through its interactions with its own fictions. Henry described this projection in a more dismissive vein in *The American Scene*: 'We capture verily, I think, nothing; we merely project a little, from one room and from one mild aspect of the void to another, our old habit of suppositions.'[31] Here James can sound like a sceptic about truth or a stalwart believer in the 'big T' version—making everything else mere projection and supposition—but he remains fascinated by the ways these projections shape our lives and win our assent. Of course, the way we attribute reality to what we simultaneously make up can feel like an elaborate form of self-deception.

As Henry notes, usually our world-making happens unreflectively behind our backs through the force of habit and the steer of others (another great theme of William's). However, both James brothers were interested in the way truth—or at least a conviction of truth—might be conjured through a more deliberate will to believe. The scope for such credulity, William insisted, was highly circumscribed: Many of our convictions are not a product of choice but seem to be imposed on us by the fabric of the world.[32] Nonetheless, on some specific matters, faith in a fact could help to create a fact. Henry himself drew attention to the particular situations that William had in mind when he selected a passage from his brother's works for an anthology—or manual of wartime self-help—published by Robert Bridges in January 1916 (a month before Henry's own death): 'These then are my last words to you. . . . Believe that life *is* worth living, and your belief will help create the fact.'[33]

The will to believe, as William noted, was often mocked as a 'will to deceive' or a 'will to make-believe,' and Henry himself often ironised

30. James, *Pragmatism*, 123.

31. James, *The American Scene*, in *Travel Writings*, 625.

32. Or he suggested that the will to believe was only feasible when things were undecidable ('the freedom to believe can only cover living options which the intellect of the individual cannot by itself resolve'). See 'The Will to Believe,' in *Pragmatism*, 217.

33. Bridges, *The Spirit of Man*, 295. The excerpt is drawn from the essay 'Is Life Worth Living.'

this kind of wishfulness.[34] In an essay on life after death (written six years before his own) he distanced himself from 'those shallow minds who are happily and foolishly able to believe what they prefer.' Nonetheless, in the same essay, he conceded that wishful thinking could carry us quite far. As Henry explained: 'It isn't really a question of belief . . . it is on the other hand a question of desire, but of desire so confirmed, so thoroughly established and nourished, as to leave belief a comparative irrelevant affair.' Here Henry seems to acknowledge that a desire has a very different direction of fit with the world than a belief, but if a 'confirmed' desire begins to sound remarkably like a belief (or something stronger than a simple knowledge of our own desire), then he ultimately seems to cede the relevance of the distinction: 'If one acts from desire quite as one would from belief, it signifies little what name one gives to one's motive.'[35] The difference between conviction and desire in his fiction is often hard to parse. Tales like 'The Altar of the Dead' or 'The Beast in the Jungle' feature people who organise their lives around elaborate ceremonies of desire and supposition—secret devotions to the dead or private eschatologies in which some supreme good or truth-event is anticipated. Again, James stands within and without these rituals of conviction, noting both their fanaticism and their strange constitutive power—the way faith in a fact can create a fact, at least for the committed believer. Here the dividing lines between making it, faking it, and mistaking it are impressively unstable, and we often find rich combinations of all three conditions.

The will to believe or even self-deceive is hard to sustain on one's own.[36] Every Jack needs a Jill, William noted, in the house of conviction: 'Jill, who knows her inner life, knows that Jack's way of taking it—so importantly—is the true and serious way; and she responds to the

34. See James, *Pragmatism*, 124.

35. James, 'Is There a Life After Death?,' 614. On the role of mutual recognition in James see also Pippin, *Henry James & Modern Moral Life*.

36. As Amelie Rorty argued, 'Like other epistemic attitudes, successful self-deception typically requires the collusion of contributory agents. . . . It is extremely difficult to sustain self-deception without a little help from our friends, often rendered by observant, but tactful silence.' Rorty, 'User-Friendly Self-Deception,' 224.

truth in him by taking him truly and seriously too.'[37] In 'The Beast in the Jungle' John Marcher plays Jack to May Bertram's Jill. Marcher's faith in a momentous truth-event that awaits is sustained by May's 'beautifully believing him' (CS, 2.751). Faith in some fantastical creature of supreme meaning helps to create that animal. But if people engender truths together, their content, for James, usually exceeds what they predict or intend. This is true of Marcher's beast: Making it and mistaking it travel hand in hand. With the help of another, Marcher has organised his life around a myth of significance, and this *really* makes his life significant or at least deeply unusual—powerfully wasted, richly missed, and eventually recognised as such.

Value-creation and self-deception, then, are painfully close cousins in James. Clearly, there is something solipsistic about Marcher's will to believe and something enigmatic in Bertram's willingness to assent to it ('May' is well named, capturing the way she provides her friend with permission to live in a purely modal state). The story provides a fatally one-sided version of the way our subjective life is made real to ourselves through the recognition of another, if not the—equally requisite—resistance of another. But Marcher is too egotistical to recognise the other person in his life and can only reach the outer precincts of his own solipsism at the end of the tale when he gains a third-person perspective of another man's first-person experience of disinterested love: 'He had seen *outside* his life, not learned it within, the way a woman was mourned when she had been loved for herself' (CS, 2.781). Loving someone for themselves is a complex moral and epistemic achievement in James and one can debate whether it ever really happens. But it certainly doesn't happen for John Marcher.

None of James's stories traces a more delicate path between tragedy and farce, irony and compassion than 'The Beast in the Jungle.' There is something laughable about Marcher's self-conceit and the kind of assent it receives ('"It's heroic?" "Certainly—call it that"' [CS, 2.756]). It is hard to know if May is generous or cruel in her collusion with these

37. James, 'What Makes Life Significant?,' in *Talks to Teachers on Psychology*, 151.

fictions; nor can we fully gauge how much she sees through him while pretending to see with him. Focalised as the tale is through the mind of a solipsist, every sense of May is a vulnerable maybe. 'She had deceived him to save him,' we are told, but this, too, may be a delusion (CS, 2.770). 'The Beast in the Jungle' reveals the grim fecundity and ferocity of our will to believe. If it can lead to moral and epistemic disaster, it also declares James's interest in the complex ontology of fiction. Every reader is a little like May, willing to say 'Yes, I believe you' or 'I pretend to believe you' or 'I'll provisionally believe you,' as a condition of their amusement. Every author, perhaps, is a little like Marcher, desperate for another to vouchsafe their significance. But this economy of need and belief is not so unusual. Much of social life, James suggests, is organised like this.

'To live *in* the world of creation—to get into it and stay in it—to frequent it and haunt it'—this may be a writer's fantasy, but it is also a state of mind we daily live out.[38] James's novels expose how we collaborate to build a world and constitute its truth through shared make-believe. Perhaps truth is the wrong word here, for these social fictions resemble and rely on performative utterances: language that is neither true nor untrue but is, as Austin suggested, 'happy' or 'unhappy.'[39] Marcher and Bertram may be an infelicitous pair, but they talk themselves into feelings of rightness: 'We're just right as it is,' Marcher observes. Bertram's response: 'Oh, I am, . . . if you are!' (CS, 2.744). These collaborations can be seen throughout James. 'I depend upon you now to make me right!' Kate Croy ambiguously proclaims to her lover in *The Wings of the Dove* (WD, 290). In *The Golden Bowl,* Charlotte Stant exposes the mutual make-believe at the heart of all relationships—in this case Amerigo and Maggie's ('The reality of his belief will depend in such a case on the reality of hers' [GB, 173]). This love might even seem to

38. James, *The Complete Notebooks of Henry James.* All further references are given in the text under the abbreviation 'N.'

39. This is what Austin calls 'the doctrine of the *Infelicities.*' See Austin, *How to Do Things With Words,* 14.

come true in the end through their reciprocal confidence in its existence in the other and in themselves.[40]

James is fascinated by this performative voodoo—the way new facts and values are summoned into life by interpretation and belief—and he both applauds and worries about its strange success. He is intrigued by the conditions that make it successful or not, the dividing line between 'happy' and 'unhappy' performances, whether people simply lie to themselves or constitute the truth with the help of others. How much aid do we need before a fiction becomes real or something broader than a solipsism à deux? James is also interested in the ethics of this world-making—not least when people set out to overrule the existing facts through the force of deliberate and clear-eyed deception. Having teased out some of the ambiguities of truth—the thin divide between tracking it, distorting it, and inventing it—I want to see how these epistemic practices might fit into James's broader notion of the good life. This will help us to consider the dense normativity that he and his characters will bring to the 'virtuous, heroic lie' (N, 135).

The Good-Enough Life

'Morality' was a 'good old word,' James admitted, but he also shows how it can preside over a sadly restricted notion of the good life.[41] In his search for a more capacious version, he often suggests that morality might take its coordinates from art. As he put it to H. G. Wells in 1915: 'It is art that *makes* life, makes interest, makes importance.'[42] This may not have been the main headline issuing from Gallipoli or Ypres that year, but it reveals how important art was to James (as he admitted in his notebook, life would be a 'howling desert' without it [N, 31]). James

40. James, however, tests all comic wishfulness by supplying a notoriously ambiguous ending that combines notes of blinding and self-burial within the one embrace: '"See? I see nothing but *you*." And the truth of it had, with this force, after a moment, so strangely lighted his eyes that, as for pity and dread of them, she buried her own in his breast' (GB, 567). I am grateful to Adrian Poole to opening my eyes to this passage.

41. James to Mrs. Alfred Sutro, letter, 25 June 1913, in *The Letters of Henry James*, 2.319.

42. Edel and Ray, *Henry James & H. G. Wells*, 267. Also, James, *Henry James: Letters*, 3.770.

may have overstated the case to Wells—he recognised that art suffers (alongside human beings) if it is made the sole ground or form of value—but it captured, perhaps, James's own sense of the artfulness of everyday life itself, the way we conspire to invent the good, not simply to describe it, the importance of a fictive attitude in practical matters, a willingness to proceed 'as if' and the ways this becomes dangerously close to lying to oneself in order to lie to and with others.[43]

James clearly shows that moralists have a lot to learn from the aesthetic—its virtues and its pleasures, not least the 'disinterestedness' of its pleasure, its strong sense of value, its epistemic humility about what it esteems, its seeming willingness to remain uncertain.[44] Aesthetic excellence may be admired, but it isn't codifiable, and the same might be said about moral goodness. Indeed, ethical discernment operates like aesthetic judgement in James—so much so that it is often hard to tell whether 'good taste' is a moral or aesthetic attribute (LC, 2.484). Not everything hinges on taste, but to be without it is clearly a disaster. As he put it in an essay on Zola: 'There is simply no limit, in fine, to the misfortune of being tasteless; it does not merely disfigure the surface and the fringe of your performance—it eats back into the very heart and enfeebles the source of life' (LC, 2.888). These strictures about taste might seem to epitomise a priggishness that William disliked in his brother's work, but they also attest to the austere side of what Henry called 'the conscience of taste' (LC, 2.888).[45] This ambiguous formula may illustrate how the moral and the aesthetic merge in his work, or it may simply indicate that morality does not exhaust normativity: that art has its standards, obligations, and discipline too even if these are liable to be passed over by some of its chief celebrants.

43. This sense of the 'made' quality of the good was also shared by his brother. As William put it in 'The Moral Philosopher and Moral Life': 'Moral relations now have their *status*, in that being's consciousness. So far as he feels anything to be good, he *makes* it good.' William James, 'The Moral Philosopher and the Moral Life,' in *The Will to Believe and Other Essays*, 145–46.

44. This chimes with William James's demand for an ethical literature 'which is confessedly tentative and suggestive rather than dogmatic.' James, 'The Moral Philosopher and the Moral Life,' in *The Will to Believe and Other Essays*, 159.

45. See William James, *Selected Letters*, 91.

James's defence of the conscience of taste certainly helped to correct contemporary caricatures of 'aestheticism'—'a horrible insidious foreign disease . . . eating the healthy core out of English life,' as Gabriel Nash winkingly puts it in *The Tragic Muse*.[46] Even devotees of this disease had sometimes identified aestheticism with an unfettered hedonism, but as every rational hedonist knows, pleasure has its duties as much as its joys. Moreover, as Nash points out, aesthetic excellence requires a host of virtues—courage, diligence, independence, perceptiveness, openness—allowing life to be lived in a 'free brave personal way.'[47] Art, he maintains, teaches us how to care in a pure form—how to value things as ends in themselves and not as means to some extrinsic goal, interest, or use. This is a vital evaluative skill for James, and it is not certain that anyone ever fully masters it—but it explains why Gilbert Osmond is such a phony: His approach to beauty (and, indeed, other people) is purely instrumental, an extension of his vanity and longing for prestige.[48]

In his pursuit of a sufficiently broad conception of the good life, James usually tries to navigate between two overspecialized conceptions of value: an aesthetic fundamentalism, on the one hand, and a philistine moralism on the other.[49] As Mrs. Gereth ably demonstrates in *The Spoils of Poynton*, devotees of beauty can bleed themselves of 'humanity.'[50] Moralists, on the other hand, often fail on both moral and aesthetic grounds. In 'The Author of Beltraffio' a 'tremendously moral' mother effectively kills her child in her attempts to secure him from the corrosive effects of her husband's seemingly louche art (CS, 1.752). Elsewhere, James suggests that moralistic interference with art violates the 'priceless freedom' that is the animating condition of aesthetic

46. James, *The Tragic Muse*, 361.

47. James, *The Tragic Muse*, 121.

48. This is something Ralph spots well before Isabel: 'Ralph was a clever man; but Ralph had never—to his own sense—been so clever as when he observed, *in petto*, that under the guise of caring only for intrinsic values Osmond lived exclusively for the world.' James, *The Portrait of a Lady*, 391.

49. Flaubert, in particular, was accused of being an aesthetic fundamentalist or 'monomaniac' (LC, 2.308). This also accounts for the 'unhuman' side of his work (LC, 2.340).

50. James, *The Spoils of Poynton*, 24.

play—and arguably moral life as a whole: the mind's right to think its own thoughts for itself (LL, 197). When defending that freedom, James was sometimes drawn to the conviction that 'art and morality are two perfectly different things, and that the former has no more to do with the latter than it has with astronomy or embryology' (LC, 2.1014).[51] Yet his works supply a much more complicated picture. Here we find gaps and conflicts between aesthetic and moral values, but there is also a rich commerce between them. Their relationship can even feed a Platonic confidence that 'there is an ideal *beauty* of goodness' (LC, 2.1306).

Throughout his fiction, therefore, we encounter people 'beautifully existing,'[52] 'beautifully behaving' (GB, 203), doing 'everything beautifully' (PL, 184). Perhaps it is all 'too beautiful' (PL, 554) or at least too vague, though again vagueness may be partly the point. Underlying the affinity between the beautiful and the good, in other words, is their indefiniteness and conceptual indeterminacy: the way they seem to communicate something vital and universal, while resisting full conceptualisation. It also suggests that we might lack exhaustive grounds for our judgements about these values. As William James once put it, 'The nobler thing *tastes* better.'[53] This was to emphasise the limits as much as the conditions of moral judgement, and it clearly concedes to the fact that at some point we will run out of explanations for why we deem something estimable or worth doing. This doesn't make moral judgement any less important, but it does make the business more fraught. It also underscores the huge importance of tact for James—an aesthetic and moral virtue that respects the limits of the sayable in our lives.[54]

By invoking a very 'aesthetic' sense of what morality entails, James also tried to defend a more inclusive sense of the good than many purists would allow. To invoke the distinction that Bernard Williams later

51. This is a view he attributed to Ivan Turgenev—a writer he very clearly admired.

52. James, *The Portrait of a Lady*, 227. Further references are given in the text under the abbreviation 'PL.'

53. James, 'The Moral Philosopher and the Moral Life,' in *The Will to Believe and Other Essays*, 143.

54. Not everything, it seems, should be subject to 'the grossness of discussion' (GB, 327). On the importance of tact in this period and beyond see Russell, *Tact*.

promoted, James backed the capaciousness of 'ethics' over the tighter restrictions of 'morality,' despite his fondness for the good old word. Morality, according to Williams, was a peculiar institution wedded to a very specific kind of normativity: (a) it aspired to rules or prescriptions that could be universally valid and binding; (b) it focussed on strict 'oughts'—notions of duty and obligation—at the expense of other, less obligatory virtues—say, heroism or bravery; (c) morality tended to be demandingly other-regarding, while ethics can be legitimately self-regarding—seeing goals like self-realisation or self-perfection as equally worthwhile or more important than certain other-regarding actions.[55] These are bald contrasts, and James did not necessarily feel the need to choose between them. But we can see how he searched for a normativity that brought him to the outer fringes of the moral and beyond strict obligations, allowing him to focus on modest or lowercase virtues like attentiveness, patience, discretion, delicacy, and his beloved tact. He also liked to dwell on what might seem like venial sins: coarseness, vulgarity, or a lack of imagination. 'Whether or no being hopelessly vulgar is being "bad" is a question for the metaphysicians,' we are told in *Daisy Miller*.[56] Nonetheless, if it is bad to be bad in James, it is sometimes worse to be vulgar. This is not to say that he simply collapsed ethics into etiquette. *Daisy Miller* is all about the cruelties perpetrated by various defences of good manners and good taste. Breaking with these restrictions, James shows, is essential to moral freedom. Many of his heroines—not least when it comes to lying—appear to be in agreement with the novelist's brother: Moral life 'consists at all times in the breaking of rules which have grown too narrow for the actual case.'[57]

So, the riddle of life cannot be solved by mere adherence to universal rules or social codes. As James put it in a celebrated letter to Grace Norton: 'Remember every life is a special problem which is not yours but

55. See Williams, *Ethics and the Limits of Philosophy*.

56. James, *Daisy Miller*, 33.

57. James, 'The Moral Philosopher and the Moral Life,' in *The Will to Believe and Other Essays*, 158.

another's, and content yourself with the terrible algebra of your own.'[58] This also generates some resistance to the other-regarding demands of 'morality'—at least as someone like Williams understood that institution. James clearly endorses—even exalts—caring for others, but he also knows that it can betray our responsibilities to ourselves. 'I seem to have a life only for other people,' Lambert Strether observes (A, 191). This is not a boast but a critique of the way he has dodged the problem of who he is or should be.[59] An eternal ambassador for others, he has failed to represent himself.[60]

Strether seems to convert this remorse into a simple precept: 'Live all you can; it's a mistake not to' (A, 153). This might seem to be the closest James came to issuing a general prescription or rule of conduct. He certainly gave this advice to others in his own personal affairs, though, like Strether, he felt that he had failed to live it out or live it up. The sense of failure says a lot about James—not least his sense of his own temerity as well as his immense appetite for the might-have-been—but it also exposes frailties in the principle itself: not least the unworkable breadth of its basic demand. Of course, the open-endedness of living as one can may be one of its attractions. As Strether makes clear, the precept is largely agnostic about the content of the good life—'It doesn't matter what you do in particular, so long as you have your life' (A, 153). The stress may fall on the pronoun 'your,' emphasising the importance of self-determination in any scheme of the good. Nonetheless, it can seem as if a quantitative sense of 'life' or living it all has shirked the question about the qualities a life must have: 'Can,' in the end, is a large step away from 'ought.'

58. James to Grace Norton, 28 July 1883, in *Henry James: Letters*, 2.424.

59. Self-realisation, of course, is a high-risk operation in James: Often embarked on in bad faith, forever contingent on others, and never fully achieved, it remains, nonetheless, a key ideal in his fiction. As Nanda observes in *The Awkward Age*: 'It's rather intoxicating to be oneself' (AA, 863). Not everyone, of course, agrees: 'Be somebody else—that's your only chance' (AA, 769).

60. Significantly, the flip-side of self-alienation might be an impressive disinterestedness. James seemed to praise both in his conception of the critic: 'His life . . . is heroic, for it is immensely vicarious' (LC, 1.99).

According to William James, there are two essential moral styles that tend to distinguish people: the 'easy-going and the strenuous mood.'[61] His younger brother often appears to be one of the more easy-going sort, although Henry's criticisms of moral murderers, moral dogmatists, and people who are 'all moral pressure' can seem strenuous enough (A, 346). Moreover, the conscience of taste can make fairly onerous demands. The same might be said of living all you can, particularly if one takes to heart the maximising ambitions of the little word 'all.' In practice, living as you can may be hard to distinguish from merely doing as you like, but even this louche programme involves its own terrible algebra. For it forces us to take responsibility for our 'likes,' or more respectably, our 'values'—to determine what they are and how they can be optimally combined. No easy task. Even for the committed pleasure-seeker life remains a predicament. The predicament, moreover, might involve more than a little deceit—a practice that involves some difficult diplomacy between contrasting values across *The Ambassadors*.

Let us focus, then, on one thicket of deceit in particular. At a key juncture in the novel Strether learns that he has been deceived by Chad Newsome and Madame de Vionnet about their friendship. A chance meeting with the pair by a river in a country town finally reveals to Strether that the two are, in fact, lovers. Looking back on the scenario in his hotel room shortly afterwards, Strether is forced to contemplate the '*lie* in the charming affair' (A, 393). It is a lie, moreover, that has contaminated his own sense of integrity, for when he meets the pair emerging from their boat trip, he fails or refuses to call out their deception and even partakes in a little make-believe himself. Everyone professes to be overjoyed by the serendipitous encounter, in a general attempt to save appearances. Mutual comfort, it seems, takes priority over truth. Alone in his hotel room later that night, Strether experiences some nausea at the whole charade—'It was the quantity of make-believe involved and so vividly exemplified that most disagreed with his spiritual stomach' (A, 396)—but he also manages to admire what the lie

61. James, 'The Moral Philosopher and the Moral Life,' in *The Will to Believe and Other Essays*, 159.

ostensibly defends: the precious 'intimacy' of two lovers alone together on a boat. Moreover, when he meets Madame de Vionnet the next day, he is struck by the virtues she brings to deceit and to its seeming exposure. Her ability to neither confirm nor deny what has happened but to continue with the fiction of a faultless relationship—abetted by sympathetic witnesses like Strether himself—is a virtuosic exhibition of tact. The performance is so smooth that it convinces Strether of the virtue of the general deceit:

> [I]t herewith pressed upon him that their eminent 'lie', Chad's and hers, was simply after all such an inevitable tribute to good taste as he couldn't have wished them not to render. Away from them, during his vigil, he had seemed to wince at the amount of comedy involved; whereas in his present posture he could only ask himself how he should enjoy any attempt from her to take the comedy back. He shouldn't enjoy it at all; but, once more and yet once more, he could trust her. That is he could trust her to make deception right. As she presented things the ugliness—goodness knew why—went out of them; none the less too that she could present them, with an art of her own, by not so much as touching them. She let the matter, at all events, lie where it was—where the previous twenty-four hours had placed it; appearing merely to circle about it respectfully, tenderly, almost piously, while she took up another question. (A, 403)

The episode may again suggest that Strether has lost his moral bearings, allowing his ethical intelligence to be entirely routed by charm.[62] One of the most striking things about the passage is the way a moral vocabulary has almost entirely acceded to an aesthetic idiom—assuming we can still tell the difference. Justification has been reduced to enjoyment, 'lies' have become a matter of good taste, and 'ugliness' has been successfully banished from the scene. Earlier moral qualms return as minor aesthetic objections to generic conventions (the 'comic' elements of the

62. We are told earlier in the novel that this middle-aged man 'didn't know what is bad' (A, 114)—though again this ignorance may do him credit.

previous day's charade). It all conspires to produce the extraordinary confidence that Madame de Vionnet makes 'deception right.'

Assuming that 'right' here is an ethical concept, it shows how truth or general rules against lying take second place to other virtues. So, if privacy is a good, many of James's characters often protect that good with deception.[63] Or they lie for other-regarding reasons: to save people from humiliation and embarrassment. They even, at times, tell falsehoods in defence of a broader truth. The 'technical lie' (A, 419) that Little Bilham tells Strether, for instance—namely that the relationship in question is a 'virtuous attachment'—is perhaps a quasi-truth, though it initially misleads Strether (A, 128). For the affair *has* made Chad a 'better' or at least smoother person—a fact Strether gleans even by the way he now enters an opera box. Admittedly, this grace of manner is not easily described or vindicated and is liable to appear all too easy-going for the strenuously minded.

The theory of moral behaviour that informs these ideas of the defensible lie might seem to be broadly consequentialist: a form of justification that depends on what our deeds effect. To the interpretation of the consequences, moreover, James brings a wide and plural sense of value. The values of privacy and intimacy, as we have seen, loom particularly large. Strether seems to feel that it is permissible to defend these goods with lies well told or deceptions that are beautifully unspoken—not least if the deceitfulness generates few harms outside of a mild moral discomfort to those in the know. But consequences are often hard to assess or predict: the fact that 'relations stop nowhere,' as James famously put it, is as much a moral problem as it is an artistic one (LC, 2.1041). It is a particular issue in *The Wings of the Dove*. Here the unforeseen results of a lie—starting from the banal fact that it is found out—lead to disaster. But who the agent or even victim of this catastrophe might be is much harder to assess.

63. 'Just as each man is thought to have a natural right to personal security,' Henry Sidgwick maintained, 'it seems strange if we may not lie, if lying will defend us better against a palpable invasion of our rights.' Sidgwick, *The Methods of Ethics*, 315.

Fatal Deceit

Towards the end of *The Wings of the Dove* Kate Croy talks to her lover Merton Densher about a woman they have both in different ways deceived—the dying Milly Theale.

> 'She never wanted the truth'—Kate had a high headshake. 'She wanted *you*. She would have taken from you what you could give her and been glad of it, even if she had known it false. You might have lied to her from pity, and she have seen you and felt you lie, and yet—since it was all for tenderness—she would have thanked you and blessed you and clung to you but the more.' (WD, 477)

Here we find several of James's recurrent themes: the questionable value of truth or the subordinate role it plays next to other ends, the consequent willingness to deceive and to be deceived, the sustained confidence in the benevolent lie. Nothing can be right, Kant suggests, that others cannot in principle assent to and this may partly explain why he so deplored a lie: By definition, lying precludes this freedom of agreement—at least from those it wishes to dupe.[64] But Kate tries to face down these objections, arguing that Milly would gladly assent to being lied to. This can easily seem like wishful thinking—an attempt to deceive herself or at least her lover about the stakes of deception itself, and it's not clear that the speculation convinces Densher or even Kate. Kate's very name—drawn from *croyer* 'to believe'—seems to make a bid for our assent. 'Dear man, . . . only believe in me, and it will be beautiful' she proclaims to her fretful lover, but the novel exposes the moral hazards of such an investment (WD, 254). Densher's own name suggests that he, too, wears a false smile.

The wrong these two do to Milly Theale by concealing the fact of their own relationship is both palpable and opaque. The intentions they bring to the deception shift in different lights and are repeatedly re-spun

64. Or as Williams put it in reference to even the kindly misled, 'I do not give her a chance . . . to form her own reactions to the facts.' Williams, *Truth and Truthfulness*, 118.

in reaction to events.[65] Moreover, consequentialist assessments of the initial deceit are hard to arrive at as relations end nowhere and results keep unfurling till the tale's bleak end. Moreover, the results are partly constituted by competing interpretations of how wrong deceit is perceived to be—in the eyes of its apparent victim and its executors—and these deliberations never yield to a final one. Kate and Densher can't quite agree on what they have done, who really did the deceiving or is the more culpable, whether a sense of culpability is the right response, what amends need to be made or whether anything can be amended. The intimacy that the couple have enjoyed in and through the concealment of their relationship—their strong belief in each other while 'making believe everywhere else' (WD, 70)—slowly collapses under the pressure of the lie. They may struggle to confront the moral reality of their actions—but they refuse to tolerate the deceptions of the other: Densher will not submit to Kate's declarations that they've 'succeeded' or at least 'not failed' (WD, 480), and she will not believe Densher's reassurances that they can be as they once were. Kate clearly knows how to end a romance and a novel: 'We shall never be again as we were!' (WD, 533).

They have harmed Milly Theale—perhaps even killed her—but they also seem to have damaged each other. Again, the nature and source of that harm can seem undecidable: whether it stems from a moral response to deceit—shame, remorse, or some loss of confidence in each other (after all, a particular deceit, as Mill noted, can strike a more general blow at human trustworthiness).[66] Or perhaps the trouble stems from some other factor—the inconvenient truth, for instance, that Densher is now in love with a dead woman, though again this love may be little more than a sublimated remorse. Kant may have laid it on a bit thick when he declared that the liar 'annihilates his dignity as a human being,' commits a crime 'against his own person,' or 'generates a worthlessness that must make him contemptible in his own eyes.'[67] Kate is

65. On the opacity and social character of intention in James, see Pippin, *Henry James and Modern Moral Life*, 71–77.

66. Mill, *Utilitarianism*, 69.

67. Kant, *The Metaphysics of Morals*, in *Practical Philosophy*, 553.

certainly no Kantian—if she *ought* to feel self-contempt, it's far from evident that she does—yet she is not without her qualms. These misgivings may be more prudential or strategic than moral, but they produce the blunt admission: 'We've told too many lies' (WD, 385).

Densher's response is Jesuitical: 'I, my dear, have told none!' (WD, 385). This may be a belated attempt to salvage his moral dignity from the fact of his deceit: If he has uttered few literal falsehoods, he has clearly misled others. Besides, he soon agrees to telling outright lies—'I'll tell any lie you want' (WD, 386)—and the fact that he doesn't get to tell these may simply be moral luck. If Kate brings a certain bravery and chutzpah to the art of the lie, Densher brings sustained bad faith, repeatedly downplaying his own role in the game of deception. His conviction that he is 'acting for Kate' activates every permutation of the word 'acting' and suggests that his attempts to dodge the fact that he is also acting for himself are, in fact, a sham. Densher takes refuge in passivity—'it was his pure passivity that had to represent his dignity and his honour'—but he also intuits that often non-actions speak louder than words (WD, 389). Or he sees that silence is a kind of practice—'that everything was acting that was not speaking the particular word' (WD, 296). Again, the word 'acting' implies both agency and deceit and it makes the problem of negative responsibility impossible to dodge. The obdurate fact is he has failed to disabuse 'the successfully deceived' (WD, 290).

But perhaps he has simply failed to see the deceit through to the end. Densher, as we've seen, places a high price on his moral dignity, and it accounts for his initial refusal to tell an outright lie to Milly—one that would flatly contradict Lord Mark's exposure of the fact that Kate and Densher are lovers. However, the dividing line between a good conscience and moral narcissism can be hard to parse—not least when Kate insists that a lie might actually save Milly's life. Densher, in this context, can seem to love his moral dignity too much: Horror at the crime he would commit against his own person by lying seems to outweigh the benefits he would do to another—though, to be fair, he also dismisses the notion that a further lie would have these therapeutic results. When he finally decides to commit the crime of an outright lie, he does so for self-regarding reasons: namely, as part of a grubby barter for sex ('I'll tell any lie you want . . . if you'll only come to me' [WD, 386]).

Densher will hugely rue his deceit of Milly (if not his trade in indignities with Kate). He almost seems to think that his extreme regret will reconfigure the moral structure of what he has done, making everything seem a little less deceitful or vicious. Similarly, the desire for a kind of retrospective vindication of his behaviour makes him misbehave a little more: to court Milly's disfavour in Venice—and the world's disapproval of a would-be adventurer—to prove to himself that he never really sought her favour. His willingness to accept a loss of moral status is, he believes, 'a proof' of his moral substance, a sign that he had never sought any prize for himself (WD, 435). His final repudiation of Milly's fortune follows the same logic: It is a belated attempt to reconstrue the moral meaning of his action and to recover a disinterestedness from his role in the affair. Densher, in other words, adds self-deception to deception. One of his most questionable convictions is that he can dictate the meaning of his own deeds either to the world or to himself. He recognises the tendentiousness of his desire to override the public or outward meaning of his deeds and to install a purer and more private motive. As he ruefully admits: 'It was his own fault if the vulgar view, the view that might have been taken of an inferior man, happened so incorrigibly to fit him' (WD, 428). If he accepts his punishment here, he still finds it hard to accept that he *is* this inferior man. He rightfully believes that his own inwardness or intentions have a bearing on what his actions mean and yet he is never quite clear of what his intentions are or whether he fully believes them—that he is, for instance, acting *for* Kate, whatever this precisely means.

Perhaps deceivers always deceive themselves by overlooking the intrinsic wrongness of their lying acts. Kate might add one form of deceit to another when she claims that they are doing their 'best' for Milly ('We're making her want to live' [WD, 400]). Nonetheless, the idea of the benevolent lie remains in place throughout *The Wings of the Dove*. The lies that may be permissibly told to an invalid to secure her life are an ancient philosophical theme and its complexities are brilliantly played out in the novel.[68] Even Milly's doctor practices a 'beautiful beneficent dishonesty,' choosing to withhold from Milly, it would seem, an explicit diagnosis of her condition—though the reticence may also stem from the opacity of the illness itself (WD, 204). Densher is clearly taken aback by all the moral theatre that surrounds Milly:

> He hadn't only never been near the facts of her condition—which counted so as a blessing for him; he hadn't only, with all the world, hovered outside an impenetrable ring fence, within which there reigned a kind of expensive vagueness made up of smiles and silences and beautiful fictions and priceless arrangements, all strained to breaking; but he had also, with every one else, as he now felt, actively fostered suppressions which were in the direct interest of every one's good manner, every one's pity, every one's really quite generous ideal. It was a conspiracy of silence, as the *cliché* went, to which no one had made an exception, the great smudge of mortality across the picture, the shadow of pain and horror, finding in no quarter a surface of spirit or of speech that consented to reflect it. 'The mere aesthetic instinct of mankind—!' our young man had more than once, in the connexion, said to himself; letting the rest of the proposition drop, but touching again thus sufficiently on the outrage even to taste involved in one's having to *see*. (WD, 456)

This is not exactly lying en masse or even collective deception—since there is little sense that Milly is deceived about the severity of her condition or that people are deluded into thinking that she is—but it is a festival of euphemism, vagueness, and silence, 'a general conscious fool's paradise, from which the specified had been chased like a dangerous animal' (WD, 456). Perhaps not all of this theatre is benign—and people coo and smile in order to cash in—but Densher is also moved

68. Augustine felt that lies in this case were still impermissible. Augustine, 'Lying,' in *Treatises on Various Subjects*. 16.171–72. Mill, however, believed it was entirely acceptable to withhold 'bad news from a person dangerously ill.' Mill, *Utilitarianism*, 69. Sidgwick also concluded that 'most persons would not hesitate to speak falsely to an invalid'—for the purposes of sparing them a shock. Sidgwick, *The Methods of Ethics*, 316.

by the moral tact of the performance. If it is a generous fiction, it shows in a very Jamesian way, how noble ideals are created and sustained by the aesthetic impulse: It is the art of value in operation.

Milly, of course, is the consummate moral artist—a deceiver who repeatedly misleads others about her condition 'with no consciousness of fraud' (WD, 209). The deception may again stem from a kindness to others or from the deceptiveness of her condition itself. To state one of the balder possibilities: Her illness is a fiction. This isn't to deny its reality, but it does expose the strangeness of its ontology and the opacity of its source. Her health problems are as odd, perhaps, as William James's (neurasthenia? depression? a dangerous clarity about life and its abysses?), or those of the brilliant Alice James, whose ultimate diagnosis with cancer after being bed-ridden for years was experienced as almost a relief to her and those who loved her. Henry clearly began with a very physical interpretation of Milly's ills—she is 'a woman condemned to death by consumption, heart disease, or whatever,' but the 'whatever' clearly grew with the writing, creating some sense that her troubles are psychosomatic or profoundly mind-dependent (N, 102). 'So you don't think I'm out of my mind?' Milly asks Dr. Strett at the end of their first interview. 'Perhaps that *is*,' the doctor rejoins, 'all that's the matter' (WD, 200).

Milly's talent for life is only matched by her ambivalence about having one. This is what her doctor seems to diagnose and strives to address: '"My dear young lady," said her distinguished friend, "isn't to 'live' exactly what I'm trying to persuade you to take the trouble to do?"' (WD, 200). So, Sir Luke seems to offer some very Williamish advice to very Williamish problems: the need to believe in life, confident that faith in the fact will help to create the fact. But if this involves a certain will to believe, how does one believe in the 'will' or its engendering powers? In both James brothers, as we have seen, we gain faith in ourselves through the faith of another and by our believing in that other. Unfortunately, in Milly's case that other happens to be the *faux* smiler Merton Densher or—indirectly—the *incroyable* Kate Croy. When Milly learns that they are false she famously turns her face to the wall. But perhaps she has always been looking at the wall or veering that way—nobody's dupe, least of all life's, and deeply hesitant to pretend to herself that the whole affair *is* worth living. If she has been identified with death from the start, she has also identified with it—not least in her intimate moment with Bronzino's 'dead, dead, dead' girl (WD, 183). Though she does decide to live on, it is in the form of a 'dove' or what some might call a holy spirit. This is as much a death wish as it is a new vocation.

Milly's 'dovelike' role is an ironic confirmation of Kate's belief in her and it reveals the darker sides of mutual recognition and misrecognition in James. Kate's declaration—'you're a dove'—is not exactly a lie, for it may have never been offered as an accurate or factual description (WD, 226). It reveals instead the legislative force of metaphor: more a prescription of how Milly should behave (peaceable and other-regarding, let's say) than a description of how she is. This is one way of turning someone's face to the wall: by converting them into a holy ghost, a two-dimensional emblem of peace or saintliness, not a carnal, desiring being. Praise here is a form of abuse. If Kate's remark is partly a performative utterance, it is also grimly 'happy'—and not just in the technical sense that it succeeds or effects something. Milly is thrilled with the 'name so given to her.' It backlights her past and the dusk of the present ('*That* was what was the matter with her. She was a dove' [WD, 226]) and provides rich intimations of how the future might be ('the measure of the success she could have as a dove'). Her criteria for moral life are now set: 'She should have to be clear as to how a dove *would* act' (WD, 227).

But this is not a one-way story of linguistic entrapment—a tale of an innocent dove who gets caged in a metaphor. Milly is not a passive victim and the wilfulness of the will to believe can be seen on both sides. Indeed, Milly's hyper-fidelity to the dove metaphor invests it with almost monstrous powers: If the image inspires an early death, commencing her career as a holy spirit, it also extends her life, rendering her an unkillable ghost. Milly will haunt the duplicitous pair, smothering their happiness with her love (as Kate notes at the end, her wings 'cover us' [WD, 532]). The deceivers, it seems, have become the dupes—though it is also hard to tell whether these were ever stable or clear positions in the novel. It can be hard to know who is telling the truth in *The Wings of the Dove* or what this really means since it is often made in the saying, and there is, we have found, a very thin divide between making it and faking it. The novel, in part, is about the power of make-believe—a power, perhaps, that is neither true nor false but can feel distinctly suspect. As if faith in a fact could really make a fact. Yet it somehow does, at least some of the time, and not quite as we had envisioned.

The Cage of Deception

In *The Golden Bowl*, art seems to make life, make interest, make importance in very self-referential ways. It offers not just a fiction about the world but reflects on fiction's role within the world, inviting us to consider the fictitiousness of moral life itself: how values are created not found, how they are ontologically subjective or observer-relative, how they nonetheless gain general assent or yield shared feelings of something real and meaningful. Like many of James's best tales, the novel is an exercise in meta-symbolism, outlining how entities like a bowl—its identity, function, and value—acquire reality within a shared economy of belief, so much so that virtually 'all depends on the bowl' (GB, 421). Its meaning remains unstable and contested throughout the novel, but it shapes real attitudes and events—indeed, when it is finally smashed on a floor it can almost feel like we've witnessed a murder (albeit an overdue one). The bowl's flaw—the element that makes it a 'treacherous, cracked thing' (GB, 263)—again advertises the ambiguity of normativity in James—and the degree to which aesthetic and moral vocabularies merge or live to deceive each other. But the flaw also raises metaphysical questions about the ontology of observer-relative facts and values: How much or how widely do things have to be seen in order for them to exist? The seller of the bowl is also its philosopher: 'But if it's something you can't find out, isn't it as good as if it were nothing?' (GB, 86).

This is a key epistemic issue in James, but it is also a moral question—not least in the context of deceit. Do lies really harm if they are never discovered, or do they hurt even when unnoticed? This question pervades *The Golden Bowl*—though many of the lies are found out—and it allows us to consider some final thoughts on the potential wrongness of lying. Not that James's characters allow themselves to be detained for very long by the potential harms as they plunge headlong into deception. The novel is a veritable jamboree of deceit: Prince Amerigo and Charlotte Stant deceive Maggie Verver about the longevity of their relationship and the renewal of their affair; Maggie deceives them about being deceived; she simultaneously conceals her knowledge and its object from her father while also lying to her friends; meanwhile, her friends do their best to lie to her. Now a virtuoso in the game of deception, Maggie lies to Charlotte about her knowledge of the affair and sends her packing in a state of agonised uncertainty. Living all you can seems to have morphed into lying all you can. But the most arresting thing about this endless game of deception is the shared confidence all its players have in the moral probity of the lie.

The moral conviction that Maggie brings to deceit—'The right, the right—yes, it took this extraordinary form of her humbugging, as she had called it, to the end' (GB, 481)—can seem both heroic and psychotic, but it is widely shared. Take the following exchange between Fanny Assingham and her sluggish husband:

> 'We shall have, as I've again and again told you, to lie for her—to lie till we're black in the face.'
>
> 'To lie "for" her?' The Colonel often, at these hours, as from a vague vision of old chivalry in a new form, wandered into apparent lapses from lucidity.
>
> 'To lie *to* her, up and down, and in and out—it comes to the same thing. It will consist just as much of lying to the others too: to the Prince about one's belief in *him*; to Charlotte about one's belief in *her*; to Mr. Verver, dear sweet man, about one's belief in everyone. So we've work cut out—with the biggest lie, on top of all, being that we *like* to be there for such a purpose.' (GB, 389)

Fanny professes to dislike lying, even to hate it, but her belief in its moral necessity seems unshakable. Her confidence in benevolent deceit—that lying *to* someone is also lying *for* someone—is partly sustained by Maggie herself. In an extraordinary scene between the two women, Maggie pretends to believe that all is correct between Amerigo and Charlotte. Fanny pretends the same and both pretend to believe in the other's pretending. Indeed, the practice of this mutual deceit (if falsehood so transparent can be called deceit) breeds a perverse trust in each other: as if each can count on the efforts of the other to sustain appearances, whatever the moral or psychological cost. If Fanny admires the 'heroic' features of Maggie's deception—its apparent magnanimity, moral tact, and supreme self-control—the Prince will also fall in love with the same qualities (GB, 290). Maggie's lies reveal her to be a woman of moral depth.

The lies also expose her talent for cruelty. Maggie's refusal to inform her old friend that she knows about the affair may save everyone's blushes, but it keeps Charlotte in a pained state of unknowingness ('having gropingly to go on, always not knowing and not knowing!'—even the phrase itself gropingly goes on [GB, 448]). Ignorance in this case is a cage:

> The cage was the deluded condition, and Maggie, as having known delusion—rather!—understood the nature of cages. She walked round Charlotte's—cautiously and in a very wide circle; and when, inevitably, they had to communicate she felt herself, comparatively, outside, on the breast of nature, and saw her companion's face as that of a prisoner looking through bars. (GB, 466)

Perhaps this is all just deserts: Charlotte has relinquished all rights to the truth, assuming we ever possess these rights. But if Maggie's actions are a just retaliation or punishment, the retribution itself captures the harm that is internal to a lie: It deprives another of freedom by restricting their access to reality. As Maggie explains to Fanny, Charlotte is trapped by her 'ignorance' and the condition is experienced as a 'torment' (GB, 542). The image of Charlotte as a prisoner or a figure trapped in glass—'frantically, tapping, from within, by way of supreme, irrepressible entreaty'—provides a chilling sense of this distress (GB, 538). It also reveals the sadistic side of 'astonishing little Maggie' (GB, 204). With a merry confidence, Maggie sets out the logic of this sadism in her reflections on Charlotte to her restored husband ('It's as if her unhappiness had been necessary to us' [GB550]). Love here—even happiness—can sound like a zero-sum game. One of its constituent facts is that it is exclusionary and can't be equally extended to all. Moreover, lies can play a role in maintaining these exclusions and the vigour of this love. To develop a point that was also present in *The Ambassadors*: Not only do lies protect our intimacies, they seem to constitute these bonds, inspiring a confidence between conspirators that affection and the truth are now exclusive goods.

But the violence this does to others should not be downplayed. It deprives the duped of easy access to reality and makes them into mere instruments for the liar's own ends. As Kant repeatedly maintained, lies are a clear violation of the categorial imperative, a fact best seen in the imperative's second formulation: *'Act that you use humanity, whether in your own person or in the person of any other, always at the same time as an end, never merely as a means.'*[69] Kant's demand might again put huge pressure on the word 'act'—showing how moral rectitude comes very close to pretence. It is at least debateable that we ever do or can treat others as ends in themselves, assuming we even know what this means. Perhaps it is to people's credit in *The Golden Bowl* that they so openly and honestly instrumentalise or objectify each other since there are so few other options.

The basic symbolism of the novel—so overtly worked through by the protagonists themselves—seems complicit with this objectification ('Oh, if I'm a crystal, I'm delighted that I'm a perfect one, for I believe they sometimes have cracks and flaws' [GB, 103]). Here people have 'value' in an economy of mutual use. The prince wonders about his own value and knows he has 'cost a lot of money' (GB, 10). The novel ends with an assessment of 'Charlotte's *value*' (GB, 564)—a last appraisal of her charms that is also a final act of condescension. After all, these attributions of value can read like a denial of a person's intrinsic worth. *The Golden Bowl* often reads like a sustained assault on Kant's conviction

69. Kant, *Groundwork of the Metaphysics of Morals*, in *Practical Philosophy*, 4.429, 80. Gass rightly claims that much of James's morality hinges on this precept ('He is concerned with all of the ways in which men may be reduced to the status of objects'). Gass, *Fiction and the Figures of Life*, 181–82.

that human beings have a dignity—'an unconditional, incomparable worth'—not a 'price' or merely relative worth.[70] Anyone with Kantian intuitions is likely to feel that there is something monstrous about Adam Verver: 'Nothing perhaps might affect us as queerer . . . than this application of the same measure of value to such different pieces of property as old Persian carpets, say, and new human acquisitions' (GB, 145). Yet the tendency to reduce people to property or tools is widely shared in the novel, and characters let themselves down from the start by failing to remember that human beings are not for sale. It is easy to see why those who have been bought might want to sell a lie or cheat on their purchasers—it is a brittle attempt to recoup some freedom by reducing one's reducer, diminishing their power and freedom, by weakening their hold on the world. It is hard to know if Charlotte or the Prince *do* feel this way—so foresworn as they are to the make-believe of benevolent or conscientious deception.[71]

Deceit in James, therefore, often takes place in a world of mutual instrumentalisation and objectification, while also functioning as a particular form of it. Of course, human beings *are* objects as well as agents. Moreover, the uses we make of each other are heterogeneous and often innocuous enough.[72] As Amerigo points out to his wife apropos of Charlotte: 'You "use" her, and I use her . . . yes; but we use her ever so differently and separately—not all in the same way or degree' (GB, 354). Some, like Amerigo, buy into being bought, which at least complicates the charge of instrumentalisation. Nonetheless, when people are sold a lie, they often seem to feel cruelly used and not just in *The Golden Bowl*. Deceit, for Isabel Archer, for instance, is a humiliation—an assault on her moral personhood: 'She saw . . . the dry staring fact that she had

70. Kant, *Groundwork*, in *Practical Philosophy*, 4.436, 85.

71. The way this benevolence connives against Maggie's freedom is nonetheless clear: 'Baths of benevolence were very well, but, at least, unless one were a patient of some sort, a nervous eccentric or a lost child, one was usually not so immersed save by one's request. It wasn't in the least what *she* had requested' (GB, 330).

72. On the need for a more variegated sense of what 'objectification' involves, see Nussbaum, 'Objectification.' For a feminist deployment of the concept's Kantian heritage, see Langton, *Sexual Solipsism*.

been an applied handled hung-up tool, as senseless and convenient as mere shaped wood and iron' (PL, 545). Things are often treated very nicely in James—indeed, in some of James's works (*The Spoils of Poynton*, for instance) they are treated like persons or even better than persons.[73] But a key though often tacit moral task in James is how to treat persons as more than mere things or useful things—as priceless agents endowed with something more than instrumental value.[74] Whether this is a psychologically feasible or ever-realised demand is another question. Perhaps, for James, the best course is to proceed *as if* we could operate so in the hope that this is neither deception nor self-deception. Or is it dangerous make-believe to think we can successfully behave like doves? Lies and deceit are frequently bad things in James. However, to think we can live without them may be its own form of falsehood. Life may allow for a little doubleness or even require it, although on these points it may be better not to be too candid with ourselves. What is most desired, perhaps, is to be well cheated, till one's last day—not least when it comes to our own duplicity and need for self-deception. Too much knowledge about our devotion to illusion is likely to scare the good life away.

73. Take Fleda Vetch's assessment of the restored art works of Poynton Hall—items with a dignity, not a price, exceeding all notions of property or possession ('They were nobody's at all—too proud, unlike base animals and humans, to be reducible to anything so narrow'). James, *The Spoils of Poynton*, 163.

74. In works like *The Spoils of Poynton* James suggests that aesthetic appreciation is an initiation into this disinterestedness or pure attentiveness to an object's intrinsic worth—though, as Ms. Gereth shows, it's far from sufficient as an attitude to humans.

4

What Ifs—Conrad

HOW MUCH OF LIFE should be lived in the shadows of 'what if'? And how might such reflection attune us to our luck—the good or bad fortune of where we are or who we are now? These were very much Conrad's questions. As the mere titles of tales such as 'The Smile of Fortune' or *Chance* make clear, he was a writer intrigued by the machinations of what we broadly call luck—those events that exceed our control but shape how we appear to others and to ourselves. The hap within happiness, moreover, is one of his constant themes. Throughout his novels and his letters Conrad entertained metaphysical theories that limit the dominion we have over our lives, sometimes courting the possibility of an entirely determined universe.[1] This is life conceived as one vast knitting machine—'it knits us in and knits us out'—and the mechanism itself is the result of some 'tragic accident.'[2] Some form of freedom *may* be compatible with this determinism—a question that is probably undecidable in Conrad—but our actions are never invulnerable to luck: improbable events that we struggle to foresee and forestall. Such luck mediates our performance as moral agents—luring us into contexts that we have not chosen, producing outcomes that we do not intend, exposing fissures in ourselves that are themselves the legacy of luck. Yet all of this happenstance seems to affect how we are judged, making

1. On these metaphysical questions, see Schnauder, *Free Will and Determinism*.

2. Conrad, *The Letters of Joseph Conrad*, 1.425. All further references are given in the text under the abbreviation 'L.'

it difficult to distinguish the good from the lucky and the bad from the hapless.

The question of moral luck—and the degree to which moral agency, responsibility, and judgement are subject to the vagaries of chance—became a key topic of philosophical debate after Bernard Williams and Thomas Nagel published two celebrated papers on the issue in 1976.[3] Of course, the problem of moral luck is also an ancient literary theme. The putative pity and terror of classical tragedy stem in part from the genre's sensitivity to luck.[4] Few modern writers, however, have pursued the ethical ramifications of chance as exhaustively or intelligently as Conrad.[5] Much of his work is a compulsive rewriting of 'the chapter of accidents which counts for so much in the book of success'—particularly moral success.[6] He is even more fascinated, as we'll see, by the luck governing failure.[7]

Conrad's fiction anticipates many of the questions raised by the philosophical literature on luck, though it also contains more structural ambiguity and situational complication than philosophical argument can usually accommodate.[8] Moreover, unlike many philosophical accounts of the problem, Conrad shows how a self-consciousness about luck may harm us as ethical agents.[9] The differences between literary and philosophical

3. Bernard Williams, 'Moral Luck,' in *Moral Luck*, 20–39. Nagel, 'Moral Luck,' in *Mortal Questions*, 24–38. For more recent defences of moral luck upon which I draw, see Hanna, 'Moral Luck Defended'; Hartman, *In Defense of Moral Luck*.

4. On the links between tragedy and luck, see Nussbaum, *The Fragility of Goodness*, 378–94.

5. The issue of moral luck is suggestively raised but never systematically pursued in Simmons, *Joseph Conrad*; O'Hara, *Joseph Conrad Today*; and Schnauder, *Free Will and Determinism*.

6. Conrad, 'The Secret Sharer,' in *'Twixt Land and Sea*, 105. All further references are given in the text under the abbreviation 'SS.'

7. As Moser rightly recognised, Conrad is obsessed by 'moral failure,' but he places no emphasis on the way luck bears on the question. Moser, *Joseph Conrad*, 29.

8. On literature's ability to reveal the 'situational complexity' of moral judgement, see Nussbaum, *Love's Knowledge*, 180–82.

9. The self-referential problem is largely absent in recent discussions, most notably: Hanna, 'Moral Luck Defended'; Church and Hartman, *The Routledge Handbook of the Philosophy and Psychology of Luck*.

approaches, however, should not be overstated: After all, philosophers have repeatedly called upon fictions to think about luck. Nagel summoned up a mortified parent who forgot about their child in a bath, a truck driver who accidentally ran over a kid (children seem to fare badly in this famous essay), and a would-be Nazi who happened to leave Germany before the worst outrages took place. Williams wondered about Anna Karenina's luck and based much of his argument around a 'fictional Gauguin' (declaring it an 'uninteresting' objection that this was not the real Gaugin).[10] Here fictions help philosophy think—particularly about luck. After all, a sense of the counterfactual—an awareness that things could have happened otherwise—grounds the feeling of being in luck or out of it.

But novels such as *Lord Jim* raise troubling questions about counterfactual thinking itself. Jim, after all, over-relies on fictions for his sense of the world and his own luck within it. If a course of light holiday literature fuels his passion for the sea, it also feeds 'his avidity for adventure.'[11] The same greed for experience can leave him feeling short-changed by the world. Of course, we are often encouraged to approach life as an adventure, and fiction has been praised for helping us to do just that.[12] *Lord Jim*, however, removes some of the romance from this outlook by reminding us that some adventures end in disaster. The modal power of fiction is rightly celebrated by many—the way it sensitises us to possibility, even improbable possibilities. The thought that so much is possible—or so much could be otherwise—can nourish our sense of freedom, but it can also emphasise the limits of our powers by impressing upon us just how much of life is conditioned by chance. Too many what ifs, of course, can also distract us from what is. Jim's focus on what he might do or would have done is a deflection from the moral implications of what he has done.[13] 'I

10. Williams, 'Postscript,' in *Moral Luck*, 244.

11. Conrad, *Lord Jim*, 52. All further references are given in the text under the abbreviation 'LJ.'

12. On adventure, see Diamond, 'Missing the Adventure,' in *The Realistic Spirit*. For Nussbaum's sense of adventure, see *Love's Knowledge*, 142–43, 179–81. On the way adventure is overegged in Nussbaum and Diamond, see Maher, 'Making Good on Henry James,' chap. 3.

13. Hampson makes the interesting point that an investment in luck may lead to recklessness and extreme risk-taking, as exemplified by, say, Lingard in 'The Rescuer.' Hampson, *Joseph Conrad*, 80.

do what *happens*,' as Anscombe says. However, Jim struggles to align what happens with his sense of himself.[14]

We might justifiably wonder, of course, whether the plot of our lives ever does justice to who we are. As Henry James suggests, we tend to see these things as co-dependent both in life and in fiction: 'What is character but the determination of incident? What is incident but the illustration of character?' (LC, 1.55). We avoid purely behaviouristic accounts of action by bringing ideas of character, inwardness, and intention to its interpretation, while also treating our deeds as expressive of who we are.[15] But we may also feel that there remains an abysmal gap between the two. Jim certainly struggles to match his romantic sense of himself with the uglier actions of his life. As this sad sailor shows, we do more than we intend and intend more than we do, and we can easily feel that it is simply luck that is responsible for the differences between them. These differences can make it hard to tell our own story or to feel that the plot of our lives provides a fair indication of who we are. Or it may make us embrace the counterfactual in the conviction that a different plot would reveal a truer self.

Our what ifs, therefore, can distract us from our responsibilities, yet Conrad reveals how counterfactual thinking can also painfully distend our sense of responsibility by asking us to account for ourselves in alternative worlds. Faced with the example of others—even fictional others—we are sometimes liable to wonder: 'What would I do in this situation?' Conrad's characters often ask themselves this question and invite their readers to do the same.[16] The question can flatter our self-love, fuelling a confidence that we could do better, but it can also disturb our confidence in our own virtue. Indeed, for one of Conrad's characters,

14. Anscombe, *Intention*, 52. Anscombe is sympathetic to the difficulties of aligning a first-person sense of oneself as an agent and a third-person account of what's happened. 'In face of this how can I say: I *do* what *happens*? If there are two ways of knowing there must be two different things known' (53).

15. As E. M. Forster noted, characters in fiction often live in revolt from the plot and we can find ourselves in a similar state of mutiny in real life. Forster, *Aspects of the Novel*, 72.

16. As Acheraïou argues, *Lord Jim* is 'an odyssey of reading' in which several internal readers inform and complicate the external reader's task. Acheraïou, *Joseph Conrad and the Reader*, 132.

the question 'what would I do?' activates a kind of counterfactual guilt that ultimately leads to suicide. This may reflect a hyperbolical sense of responsibility, but it is a recognition of—as well as a protest against—the ways in which moral reputation hinges on luck.[17] If this contingency is unsettling, it points to a paradox that also haunts Nagel and Williams: a conviction that morality should be immune to luck, yet never is.[18] For Conrad, the paradox appears to be insurmountable,[19] and it feeds a scepticism about the coherence and viability of morality which even Williams would struggle to match.[20] In the chapter that follows I focus on *Lord Jim*—in my view, Conrad's most concentrated study of luck[21]—but I first want to put in place some of the conceptual infrastructure for the argument by considering how the dice may have fallen for Conrad himself.

Lucky Joe?

On one front, at least, Conrad was lucky. After a run of what might charitably be cast as bad luck in 1878—he had lost all his capital on a dubious smuggling scheme and had gambled away further funds that were borrowed in its stead—Conrad is reported to have shot himself in the chest.[22] The bullet missed the heart and every vital organ. The existence of all of Conrad's art depends on this piece of good fortune, but how should his subsequent career and its many glittering achievements frame our understanding of his suicidal episode?

17. For a provocative account of moral responsibility in spite of luck, see Zimmerman, 'Luck and Moral Responsibility.'

18. Nagel remains within the paradox, though Williams seeks to evade it by overruling the assumption that morality should remain immune to luck.

19. Many critics have pointed to moral paradox in Conrad's fiction—not, however, in the face of luck. See Gekoski, *Conrad*; Land, *Conrad and the Paradox of Plot*; Collits, *Postcolonial Conrad*.

20. Conrad's scepticism, both moral and epistemic, has often been noted. See, in particular, Wollaeger, *Joseph Conrad and the Fictions of Skepticism*.

21. Luck remains a leitmotif in Conrad's later fiction, but I share Gekoski's view that the ethical tensions of Conrad's writing gradually weaken in the later work. See Gekoski, *Conrad*.

22. See Najder, *Joseph Conrad*, 53.

The contention that our decisions might be legitimised or damned by events that occur afterwards is a leitmotif of Conrad's art. It was also a key feature of moral luck for Bernard Williams. Gauguin's decision to abandon his family to pursue his art, Williams argued, could only be vindicated by the subsequent success of that project—a type of success that is largely a matter of luck.[23] It is far from clear, of course, that justification properly operates in this retrospective fashion,[24] nor is it obvious that Gauguin's artistic success is an example of *moral* luck.[25] Yet it is easy to see how the complexion of our decisions is—intuitively at least—modified by what happens later. Conrad's success as a writer, after all, might make his suicide attempt appear particularly rash, shortsighted, or irrational. If it was a prelude to years of penury, starvation, and abandoned dreams of authorship, then his reasons for reaching for that pistol might seem more valid. As we shall see, suicide remains a radical solution to the problem of luck within Conrad's fiction.[26]

Before and after his attempted suicide Conrad was privy to several sermons about luck. Deeply aware of the ways in which luck might deplete responsibility, Conrad's long-suffering uncle warned him about attributing too much—indeed, anything—to it: 'You must not . . . believe in either good or bad luck.'[27] Uncle Tadeusz was clearly exasperated by Conrad's misadventures or at least his rationalisations of them ('Your misfortunes of the past year fill me with despair').[28] He urged his nephew to cultivate virtues—a stern work ethic and sense of perseverance, for instance—that might seem impervious to luck. His subsequent advice was a little less categorical: 'Certainly, your success depends to some extent on chance or luck, but your judgement plays an

23. As Williams puts it, 'The only thing that will justify his choice will be success itself.' See Williams, *Moral Luck*, 23.

24. To determine whether a decision is justified or not all we may need to recover, perhaps, is the information that agents have at their disposal at the time; what happens afterwards, we might conclude, is irrelevant.

25. See Nagel on this question. Nagel, *Mortal Questions*, 28.

26. On suicide, see also Cox, 'Joseph Conrad and the Question of Suicide.'

27. Cited in Najder, *Joseph Conrad*, 64.

28. Cited in Najder, *Joseph Conrad*, 74.

important part as well.'[29] Yet his nephew would remain fascinated by the ways in which judgement itself might be governed by luck—not least when human beings lack the time and relevant training to judge properly. It is certainly hard to say that Conrad took his uncle's advice. 'There are runs of bad luck,' he continued to insist years later, 'which no foresight and no incantation can turn away' (L, 3.267). Many of his characters feel the same way.

Artistic success, for Conrad, was primarily 'a matter of luck' and it was a fitting irony that he would secure popular success through the novel *Chance* (L, 4.157). Until that point, he had harboured mixed feelings about his own luck ('I had ten times the luck I deserved'; 'I haven't got any luck', etc. [L, 3.85; 4.311]). Even the writing process was luck-governed: 'For me it is a matter of chance, stupid chance,' he confided to H. G. Wells. The writer, it seemed, was simply the plaything of a nervous system over which he had little control ('when the nervous force is exhausted the phrases don't come:—and no tension of will can help' [L, 3.85]). Yet it was the ethical implications of luck which appeared to preoccupy Conrad the most, and they could render him deeply sceptical of traditional conceptions of responsibility and merit. As he put it in an author's note to *Youth* and *Gaspar Ruiz*: 'It can hardly be denied that it is not their own deserts that men are most proud of, but rather of their prodigious luck, of their marvellous fortune: of that in their lives for which thanks and sacrifices must be offered on the altars of the inscrutable gods.'[30]

By distinguishing between 'fortune' and 'deserts'—even as he shows how they are so often conflated in the world's eyes—Conrad confirms the intuition that luck is distinct from moral responsibility. The desire to keep these two things distinct has informed philosophers' attempts to isolate a person's will from anything that it might actually effect, since consequences lie within luck's empire. As Kant put it: 'A good will is not good because of what it effects or accomplishes . . . but only because of

29. Cited in Najder, *Joseph Conrad*, 74.

30. Conrad, *Youth, Heart of Darkness, The End of the Tether*, 6.

its volition, that is, it is good in itself.'[31] Even if fortune or nature made it impossible for this will to execute anything, Kant insisted that the good will would still shine out like 'a jewel,' resplendent in its own goodness. The actual fruits of that will have no bearing on its worth. Conrad often appears to be deeply sympathetic to this position. As he declared in the author's note to *Chance*: 'It is only for their intentions that men can be held responsible. The ultimate effects of whatever they do are far beyond their control.'[32] And yet Conrad was acutely sensitive to the fact that in everyday moral life, people are judged on results—results that may exceed or clash with their intentions.

The terror of moral life stemmed from precisely this fact. As he put it in a letter to Marguerite Poradowska in 1891: 'Each act of life is final, and inevitably produces its consequences despite all the weeping and gnashing of teeth, and the sorrow of feeble souls who suffer the terror that seizes them when confronted by the results of their own actions' (L, 1.95). This focus on what we end up doing—whatever we might think we intend—makes morality susceptible to luck and allows our mistakes to be seen as malign. As Marlow puts it in *Chance*, 'In our world of chances the luckless *must* be put in the wrong somehow' (C, 146). But how right is this sense of wrongdoing? This is a key question in *Chance*, but it is even more insistently posed, I will suggest, in *Lord Jim*—a story of a man who 'is very fine—and very unfortunate' (LJ, 178). The 'and' here may keep Jim's fineness discrete and unsullied, but even Jim's greatest admirers will hold 'his misfortune against him' (LJ, 232).

The Metaphysics of Chance

'Our captivity within the incomprehensible logic of accident,' Conrad once declared, 'is the only fact of the universe' (L, 1.303). *Lord Jim* bears witness to this intimidating fact on several levels. The *fabula* of the tale is a tissue of accidents, but so, too, is its *sjužet*. The story's various shifts

31. Kant, *Groundwork*, in *Practical Philosophy*, 50.

32. Conrad, *Chance*, 333. All further references are given in the text under the abbreviation 'C.'

in space, time, and point of view betray the series of lucky events that have made the tale a tellable one—from Marlow's random encounter with a French lieutenant in a café in Sydney to his improbable success in tracking down the villain of the tale on his deathbed in Bangkok.[33] As Conrad conceded, these various leaps could make the novel seem disorganised, making it feel like 'a patchwork,' 'a hash of episodes,' or a series of 'side shows' (L, 2.226). Yet this narrative happenstance yields its own kind of consistency in a novel preoccupied with chance. Almost everyone in *Lord Jim* shares this preoccupation. Conrad's sailors talk 'everlastingly of turns of luck' (LJ, 45) as does Jim himself. Marlow, too, is luck-obsessed. The sea in the novel is the great theatre of luck—as it so often is in Conrad. Those who make their living on it are engaged in a 'fool game, in which the sea wins every toss' (LJ, 72).

Luck raises a number of metaphysical questions in *Lord Jim*. It may point to an absence of causation in the universe, or to a simple ignorance of it; under both or either of these conditions, life can assume 'a vast and dismal aspect of disorder' (LJ, 288). The language of luck also concedes to the unpredictability of outcomes—a testament once again to the limits of human knowledge or to some real indeterminism in the world. Jim deeply resents the way the world takes him unawares. 'It is always the unexpected that happens,' Marlow ironically concludes (LJ, 113). The action of *Lord Jim* certainly hinges on a particularly chancy set of chances—events that might take place in the world but would not occur in other possible worlds with almost identical properties. If the spine of the story is supplied by a real crew's abandonment of their craft and its passengers off the Somali coast in 1880, Conrad's retelling of the tale talks up the role of chance.[34] Instead of encountering a storm, for instance, Conrad's boat hits a submerged object ('She went over whatever it was as easy as a snake crawling over a stick' [LJ, 58]). The incident emphasises the role of the improbable in our lives while simultaneously exposing our ignorance of causes. The identity of that mysterious object is never revealed.

33. On this point, see Paul Armstrong, *The Challenge of Bewilderment*, 120–22.

34. Watt, *Conrad in the Nineteenth Century*, 266, and Sherry, *Conrad's Eastern World*.

Our belief in efficient causality may survive the collision of the *Patna*—indeed, basic comprehension of the event may seem to require it—but luck in the novel often points to the absence of final causes.[35] Conrad's characters are still acclimatising to life after Darwin.[36] Of course, Darwin always tried to play down the role of chance in his system (the word itself was a 'wholly incorrect expression' that testified to a simple ignorance of physical causes[37]), but natural selection would be construed as the 'survival of the luckiest.'[38] The description was delivered as a form of disparagement, but it was a much more apposite shorthand than the 'survival of the fittest.'[39] Darwin, it appeared, had stripped the world of teleological structure or objective purposiveness, making any sense of existent order a simple matter of chance. Some of Conrad's characters would rather ascribe a malign design to the world than no purpose at all. Jim detects a 'fierce purpose' in a storm, for instance, and in a characteristic rush of self-importance, he believes that it is 'directed at him' (LJ, 40). Gentleman Brown even attempts to punish the world for his bad luck, aspiring to become 'the Scourge of God' (LJ, 336). His murderous rampage at the end of the book is 'not a vulgar and treacherous massacre; it was a lesson, a retribution' (LJ, 363). This may reflect a kind of insanity, but many of Conrad's characters struggle to adjust to a world that has no moral personality, design, or inherent justice. As Marlow maintains: 'It is not Justice, the servant of men, but accident, hazard, Fortune—the ally of patient Time—that holds an even and scrupulous balance' (LJ, 293).

'Fortune,' in this resonant aphorism, is distinct from 'Justice,' but it also masquerades as her noble sister (adopting her scruples, scales, and presumably her blindness). Marlow's main point is that justice is not an objective property of the universe but is internal to human practices.

35. On the ways in which narrative technique may undermine a reader's faith in even efficient causality, see Sheehan, *Modernism, Narrative and Humanism*, 77–78.

36. For more on the influence of Darwin, see Hunter, *Joseph Conrad and the Ethics of Darwinism*.

37. Darwin, *On the Origin of Species*, 125.

38. Butler, *Luck, or Cunning as the Main Means of Organic Modification*, 98.

39. Spencer, *The Principles of Biology*, 1.444.

Yet if justice is the 'servant of men,' human beings are also servants of the universe, subject to its accidents and events. When these events supervene upon moral agents, shaping what it is they end up doing, whatever they might intend, then the dividing line between fortune and justice is obscured. Jim often seems to blur the distinction—most obviously, perhaps, in his superb boast: 'I am equal to all my luck' (LJ, 281). The phrase may simply advertise that he can face up to his luck (indeed, Jim asserts that there's 'nothing he could not face' [LJ, 52]). But the declaration can also imply that he deserves his luck—that his luck or rewards are proportional to his merits. Marlow recognises that such confidence cuts both ways: If the hero was equal to his good fortune, he 'must have been equal to his misfortune' (LJ, 260). Readers might feel that the language of desert has little meaning here—that luck contaminates any genuine notion of merit from the outset—and yet this is not how Jim's luck plays itself out.

Varieties of Luck

If the basic concept of luck involves an ability to imagine possible worlds alongside the actual one, then Jim has a gift for this counterfactual thinking. It is at the heart of his 'romantic'—indeed, 'excessively romantic'—disposition (LJ, 372). Jim's romanticism dances merrily with his self-love, leading him to envision, with the help of 'light literature,' several situations in which he plays a starring role ('He saw himself saving people from sinking ships, cutting away masts in a hurricane, swimming through a surf with a line. . . . He confronted savages on tropical shores, quelled mutinies on the high seas, and in a small boat upon the ocean kept up the hearts of despairing men—always an example of devotion to duty, and as unflinching as a hero in a book' [LJ, 39–40]). The title of the novel smiles at this grandiosity, giving the banal 'Jim' the sheen of a 'Lord.' Jim's counterfactual existence has constituted 'the best parts of life, its secret truth, its hidden reality' (LJ, 52), but it also feeds his resentment. When bad things happen, he is acutely aware that things could easily have happened otherwise.

But Jim starts off rather lucky. Endowed with 'a steady head with an excellent physique' (LJ, 39), he has what some philosophers would call good 'constitutive luck'—a basic set of attributes that would seem to make a happy and virtuous life quite probable.[40] He is, we are told, 'the right sort' (LJ, 98). He has enjoyed a comfortable upbringing in a genteel parsonage, he has been nurtured and loved (remaining very much his father's darling), and has been initiated into an admittedly easy school of virtue. His education may have had its flaws, but all the rudiments seem to be in place for success in the moral world. Indeed, Jim's constitutive luck makes his various misdeeds very hard to accept: 'If this sort can go wrong like that' (LJ, 68), then what hope is there for the rest of us? But Jim does go wrong. Much of this wrongdoing, he believes, is attributable to luck, but the extent to which this serves as either a mitigation or a moral waiver remains to be seen.

Jim's assessment of his moral career anticipates much of what Thomas Nagel had to say about 'circumstantial luck.' As Nagel put it: 'It may be true of someone that in a dangerous situation he would behave in a cowardly or heroic fashion, but if the situation never arises, he will never have the chance to distinguish or disgrace himself in this way, and his moral record will be different.'[41] Jim is painfully alert to this fact. He is aware that for much of his career he has been the beneficiary of good fortune. He has risen to the position of chief mate 'without ever having been tested by those events of the sea that show in the light of day the inner worth of a man, the edge of his temper, and the fibre of his stuff' (LJ, 43). But Jim feels unlucky in his luck and craves a moral theatre that would allow him to display his worth to the world. At the same time, he remains deeply aware of the luck that conditions other people's heroism—so much so that he repeatedly doubts its substance. When his colleague saves someone from drowning in a storm, Jim feels the 'gale had ministered to a heroism as spurious as its own pretence of terror'

40. For a description of this luck, see Nagel, 'Moral Luck,' in *Mortal Questions*, 28. For the argument that constitutional luck is incoherent, since 'identity' precedes luck, see Rescher, 'Moral Luck.'

41. Nagel, 'Moral Luck,' in *Mortal Questions*, 33–34.

(LJ, 42). In the eyes of some, 'luck is better than courage'—or so a character declares in *Suspense*—but Jim is inclined to regard these two properties as the same thing, at least when other people are involved.[42]

Jim gets his test, of course, and he fails miserably. The moral ramifications of his awful leap from the *Patna*—when he abandons his ship and its passengers to their doom—will haunt him all his life. If, as Aristotle maintained, the good person is never overexercised by their luck—they will 'neither be excessively happy at good fortune nor excessively distressed at bad fortune'—then Jim is not good.[43] Having bemoaned his bad luck for never being tested, he now berates the fact that he has been tested ('Was ever there any one so shamefully tried!' [LJ, 121]). The cowardice the world has conjured out of him is, he suggests, a case of bad circumstantial luck. Again, Jim lives counterfactually, seduced by the person he would be if circumstances had been a little different. Jim may over-egg his luck to 'save from the fire his idea of what his moral identity should be' (LJ, 101), but, as Marlow concedes, he is on many levels unfortunate.

Such misfortune may reflect the 'villainy of circumstances' (LJ, 133), though it also hangs on results. Jim's 'resultant luck'—to use Nagel's phrase—might initially seem rather good. The *Patna*, after all, never sinks, and its passengers never drown. The fact that we continue to care about Jim or are moved by his plight may depend on such fortune. His leap might be viewed as cowardice or some serious dereliction, but he is not the monstrous enabler of some eight hundred deaths. Here plot would seem to affect the assessment of character in literature, as in life.[44] But Jim's luck is double-edged. The survival of the *Patna* greatly weakens the excuse that the sailors may have had for their abandonment of their craft: that their lives were in imminent danger and all were set to perish: 'The foreseen fact coming so swiftly had justified their haste' (LJ, 145). The sailors are desperate for the world to

42. Conrad, *Suspense*, 5.

43. Aristotle, *Nicomachean Ethics*, 69.

44. The resistance to plot in modern literature noted by Robert Caserio may reflect a broader resistance to the ways in which plot is often allowed to determine moral identity. Caserio, *Plot, Story, and the Novel.*

vindicate their actions by allowing the boat to go down ('Sink!—curse you! Sink!' [LJ, 118]). But the world does not oblige. This may feel like a bad case of epistemic luck, where the world reneges on a highly probable outcome and thus the most rational form of guess.[45] It is certainly a case of poor resultant luck—at least in the cynical scheme of saving moral appearances.

But the most dramatic example of resultant luck occurs at the end of the novel. This is the terrible consequence of Jim's decision to allow Brown and his crew free passage out of Patusan in full possession of their arms. The massacre that ensues again reveals how events can conspire to delegitimise our choices, at least in the world's eyes, turning an apparently generous action or decision into a moment of homicidal negligence. Adam Smith was rightly concerned by the terrible alchemy of results: 'That the world judges by the event, and not by the design, has been in all ages the complaint, and is the great discouragement of virtue.'[46] Yet a total overlooking of the event that occurs might seem equally wrongheaded. Jim's intentions may have been magnanimous and largely honourable, but judged in the light of what they lead to, his decision appears self-indulgent, reckless, and foolish—a disastrous bet on the well-being of the community he claims to protect.

There is, it would seem, real culpability here, but there is also considerable luck. Could Jim ever have predicted the extent of Brown's malice or the wider series of betrayals that made massacre possible? These are, perhaps, naive questions to ask about a fictitious character—an excessively earnest investment in the hidden life of metaphors—but our desire to get to the bottom of Jim's luck repeatedly invites this counterfactual speculation about a counterfactual world.[47] If the sense that things might have happened otherwise underpins our sense of luck, it also

45. On the differences between moral and epistemic luck, see Statman, 'Moral and Epistemic Luck,' and Pritchard, 'Moral and Epistemic Luck.' For the view that arguments for moral luck are often simply disguised cases of epistemic luck, see Latus, 'Moral and Epistemic Luck.'

46. Smith, *The Theory of Moral Sentiments*, 123.

47. Throughout the chapter I take Cavell's approach that a condition of intelligibility for literary characters is that we treat them *as if* they are real. Cavell, *Must We Mean What We Say?*, 246–49. On this approach see also Anderson, Moi, and Felski, *Character*.

informs our ideas of freedom. And with freedom comes responsibility—or so we often assume. This brings us to what Kipling identified as the central issue of *Lord Jim*: 'the question of whether a man is responsible for his actions.' As far as Kipling was concerned, Conrad had shown that responsibility 'almost ceases to exist' under certain conditions—a position that Kipling agreed with, though he counselled against propounding it in an English court of law.[48] But is Jim's responsibility routed by his bad luck? It is an issue that torments his internal interpreters—Marlow, Brierly, and the French lieutenant—and also puts real readers to the test.

Luck and the Blame Game

One of the striking things about Jim—at least initially—is his apparent lack of remorse. This may reflect the fact that he attributes his errors to luck, and he may have concluded that this leaves little room for responsibility. But even inadvertent or unlucky wrongdoers tend to show regret, and Marlow is troubled by its apparent absence in Jim: 'I asked myself, seeing him there apparently so much at ease—is he silly? is he callous? He seemed ready to start whistling a tune' (LJ, 68). Jim's emotions may be more complex than surfaces allow—Marlow sometimes feels he takes things too much to heart—yet the only regret he immediately relates during the *Patna* affair is a sense of an opportunity lost: He has scuppered his chance to display his heroism. Before, during, and after his terrible leap Jim remains a narcissist.[49] He consequently has great difficulties squaring his deeds with the romantic image he entertains of himself ('every time he shuts his eyes he sees himself as a very fine fellow—so fine as he can never be' [LJ, 208]). It is hard to know whether Jim's preoccupation with luck drives his narcissism or whether his narcissism drives his sense of luck, but it leaves him with the impression that his deeds are accidental to the person he really is ('some

48. Cited in Perlowski, 'On Conrad and Kipling,' 163.

49. On the way narcissism distorts Jim's judgement, see Brudney, 'Lord Jim and Moral Judgment.'

conviction of innate blamelessness . . . checked the truth writhing within him at every turn' [LJ, 99]). If he lays claim to the moral innocence of a child, the cost of this is a childish misconstruction of the world and his own responsibilities within it.

Jim may be an extreme case, but he expresses a difficulty we all share in aligning our sense of our own moral personality with its actual manifestations in the world.[50] As Jim's recollections of that night suggest, our conception of ourselves as agents—as the prime cause of our own actions—is so often disturbed by the basic mechanics of the world. The way luck conditions or completes our actions may make us wonder whether our deeds are ever really our own. We now stand the risk of dissolving as agents and becoming mere playthings of the world. Jim certainly undergoes some collapse on the *Patna*: He experiences 'a strange illusion of passiveness, as though he had not acted but had suffered himself to be handled by the infernal powers who had selected him for the victim of their practical joke' (LJ, 123). Significantly, Marlow presents Jim's passivity as an 'illusion'—a form of bad faith in which he actively disavows his own powers. Moreover, Marlow's judgement also implies that non-action is never inactive in a moral sense: It is only '*as though* he had not acted,' when in fact he had. Not doing anything in the face of injustice, Marlow implies, is itself a move in a moral game and we stand or fall by it.

But Jim does not feel like an owner of his own actions—an alienation heightened by the shift between third-person and first-person accounts of that terrible night on the *Patna*. Even as Jim narrates the events of that unfortunate night his movements are not quite his own (he rises slowly as he talks 'as if a steady hand from above had been pulling him out of the chair by his hair' [LJ, 125]). He denies basic awareness of his own jump ('I knew nothing about it till I looked up' [LJ, 126]) and can't quite make sense of how it happened: '"Didn't I get somehow into that boat? Into that boat—I . . ." The muscles round his lips contracted into an unconscious grimace' (LJ, 132). Jim's involuntary grimace repeats the lack

50. The role of alienation in Conrad has been observed by several critics: Watt, *Essays on Conrad*; Ghent, 'Lord Jim'; Hampson, *Joseph Conrad*.

of rational control that he possessed over his own actions on the *Patna* (indeed, Marlow casts the whole ordeal on the boat as a burlesque of 'funny grimaces' [LJ, 121]). Jim stumbles on the word 'I,' finding it impossible to locate his deed within the circle of himself (as Sartre recognised, the seeming clumsiness of Conrad's dialogue was part of its philosophical power [LJ, 22]).[51] When Jim jumps from the *Patna* it seems that he is not quite himself. The metaphysical comedy of this is brilliantly captured by the sailors' misidentification of him as 'George' ('"Jump, George! Jump! Oh, jump!"' [LJ, 125]). The name is peculiarly apposite: George is now a corpse and Jim feels dead to himself. As he bleakly concedes, '"Everything was gone and—all was over . . ." he fetched a deep sigh . . . "with me."' His leap precedes and conditions a kind of moral death (LJ, 128).

Thoroughly alienated from his moral personality—or the personality he would possess had not luck intervened—Jim even ceases to feel human: 'If I had opened my lips just then I would have simply howled like an animal' (LJ, 136). His beastly condition on the lifeboat returns us to one of the novel's most famous moments: his eloquent misapprehension that he has been called a 'wretched cur' during the official inquiry on the ship's abandonment (LJ, 92). The ground for Jim's mistake and its resolution is the actual presence of a 'yellow dog' in the courtroom. His discovery of the animal is a cruelly comic kind of *anagnorisis*:

> He appeared at first uncomprehending, then confounded, and at last amazed and scared as though a dog had been a monster and he had never seen a dog before. 'Nobody dreamt of insulting you,' I said.
>
> He contemplated the wretched animal, that moved no more than an effigy: it sat with ears pricked and its sharp muzzle pointed into the doorway, and suddenly snapped at a fly like a piece of mechanism. (LJ, 95)

Jim's protests have merely emphasised the kinship between himself and the dog—a canine 'effigy' of his moral state. He may discover his own

51. Sartre, *Literary Essays*, 22.

cowardice in the 'yellow dog,' or his humiliating passivity. The animal, moreover, functions 'like a piece of mechanism,' behaving more as a thing than as an agent—a little like Jim on the *Patna*. As Nagel pointed out, it often feels as if 'something in the idea of agency is incompatible with actions being events, or people being things.'[52] Jim cannot align his moral personality with the event of his jump, or the thing that landed in an awaiting lifeboat. It is why he sometimes prefers to describe his jump without a pronoun—'"Jumped," he corrected me incisively. "Jumped—mind."' (LJ, 141). Evidently, there has been very little mind in that jump.

Yet Jim is called to account for his actions in a court of law. Marlow proclaims that the ethical and existential issues at stake in Jim's case lie 'beyond the competency of a court' (LJ, 111) and he speaks dismissively of the inquiry as the 'yellow-dog thing' (LJ, 63)—an expression that emphasises the thingliness of the dog as much as it points to the absurdity of the court case. If there is something anomalous about a dog in a courthouse, there is, perhaps, something inappropriate about Jim's presence too. Neither are fitting objects of justice, for justice implies responsibility and this presupposes in turn both understanding and control. Jim possesses neither of these attributes—at least at some of the decisive moments of his life. The problem may be constitutional, a sad example of 'the perversions . . . of nerves' (LJ, 71), but it is also another instance of bad moral luck.

Jim, of course, may milk his luck in ways that reveal the 'subtle unsoundness of the man' (LJ, 108). His suggestion that his yapping companions—'"Yap! yap! Bow-ow-ow-ow-ow! Yap! yap!"' (LJ, 131)—are the real yellow dogs in this story seems like a dodge. His scapegoating of other crew members—'It was their doing as plainly as if they had reached up with a boat-hook and pulled me over' (LJ, 135)—is a grubby self-exculpation and certainly features a very over-burdened 'as if.' Jim downplays his own moral agency, but, significantly, he does not avoid all sense of culpability for his actions. His protests, after all, are intriguingly torn: 'Isn't it awful that a man should be driven to do a thing like

52. Nagel, 'Moral Luck,' in *Mortal Questions*, 37.

that—and be responsible?' (LJ, 132). Jim's use of the third person may be another form of self-distancing from his deed—he also claims that he was 'driven' to his leap rather than it being freely chosen—but he still concedes that he is accountable. Such responsibility may be 'awful,' but it appears to obtain nonetheless.

And so, Jim undergoes the humiliation of a public hearing. Jim's attendance at court is arguably an expression of shame rather than guilt—if we understand shame as a capitulation to a set of social standards or honour code (the importance of which is stressed throughout *Lord Jim*) and guilt as a more inward, private, or autonomous acknowledgement of culpability.[53] The distinction is a crude one and takes little account of the ways in which Jim may have *entirely* internalised the 'eye of others' (LJ, 154) in his perception of himself (I'll say more on this point later).[54] But it at least might begin to explain how Jim can hang on to a feeling of inner innocence while publicly owning up to a perceived injustice. Indeed, Marlow will wonder if Jim has not overdone the shame—making 'so much of his disgrace while it is the guilt alone that matters' (LJ, 178). Whether it's due to shame, guilt, or some combination of the two, Jim still feels that he has done wrong in a way that cannot be explained away by his luck.

'All the same, one is responsible,' Jim ruefully admits (LJ, 181). It is hard to know how fully Jim believes this about himself—or indeed how much the reader should. A lot hinges on whether or not Jim can be said to be in control of his actions and whether we believe responsibility requires this dominion. We may believe that our 'responsibilities outrun control,' as some philosophers insist.[55] The extent of Jim's control is certainly talked up in the novel: 'He had regulated so many things in Patusan! Things that would have appeared as much beyond his control as the motions of the moon and the stars' (LJ, 214). And yet the image

53. Hampson speaks of a larger rift between 'identity-for-self' and 'identity-for-the-other' in Jim. See Hampson, *Joseph Conrad*, 123.

54. On the reasons why the distinction may fail to do justice to shame, see Bernard Williams, *Shame and Necessity*, 81–85.

55. Walker, 'Moral Luck and the Virtues of Impure Agency.'

of Jim heading into the unknown with an 'unloaded revolver on his lap' (LJ, 234) is perhaps the more fitting emblem of the extent and limits of his power. The issue of control becomes particularly inflamed when we return to Jim's fatal decision to give Brown free passage. Jim may be at fault for a poor decision—a fault, moreover, that would seem to stem from narcissism as much as from a sense of honour, though honour for Jim has always been an 'idealised selfishness' (LJ, 178). Moreover, the magnanimous precept he applies to Brown—'Men act badly sometimes without being much worse than others' (LJ, 356)—is a charitable interpretation of his own moral history.[56] Jim's observation may largely be true, but unluckily in this particular case it proves to be disastrously misapplied. It sanctions a reckless charity in which the lives of others are sacrificed on the altar of his own self-love. And yet the homicidal result of his egotism is also terrible moral luck.

So how should we judge the unfortunate Jim? His own view on this question is at best ambiguous. On one level, it appears that he accepts all guilt for what has happened by offering himself up as a symbolic object of punishment. This, at least, is how some see his final actions: '"He hath taken it upon his own head," a voice said aloud.' Somehow it feels right that the source of this voice is unknown and its authority impossible to vouchsafe, though Jim casts it as the proper interpretation of his own act ('"Yes. Upon my head."' [LJ, 371]). Yet one might wonder whether Jim's presence in Doramin's court is a last attempt to persuade others—and himself—of his own 'innate blamelessness' (LJ, 99). The chief doesn't spend much time on these questions or on the broader issue of whether luck precludes responsibility. Or perhaps it is more accurate to say that he takes a very quick stand on the last question by shooting Jim through the chest. Luck, it seems, is no mitigation and Jim will die 'unforgiven' (LJ, 372).

56. This does not preclude the possibility that Jim's magnanimity is also a disastrous form of 'white solidarity.' Moore, 'Slavery and Racism in Joseph Conrad's Eastern World,' 23.

The Contagion of Example

Jim's fate is liable to prove humbling to a reader. We are repeatedly told that 'he is one of us' (LJ, 70, 98, 111, 122, 217, 297, 301, 329, 372)—a term that stands for the brotherhood of the sea while also operating as an ethnic category, securing Jim (and the ideal reader) from 'one of *them*' (LJ, 329),[57] but it is also an invitation to think of Jim in a general key and to include ourselves in his fate. He can be read as an exemplary moral agent and his failings are 'enough to affect mankind's conception of itself' (LJ, 111). If Jim 'is not good enough,' then this might indicate that 'nobody is good enough' (LJ, 292). Several of the novel's characters find themselves implicated in his fate and model its implications for the reader. Marlow is aware of the egotistical root of his own interest in Jim. The vindication he seeks for his friend—some 'profound and redeeming cause, some merciful explanation, some convincing shadow of an excuse' (LJ, 76)—is also an attempt to retain his sense of the world and his confidence in its moral intelligibility. But if Jim's case erodes Marlow's confidence, it has an even more disastrous impact on Captain Brierly. It is difficult to know what triggers Brierly's fatal leap into the sea, but he is clearly appalled by the moral ramifications of Jim's own leap. Faced with the same situation of a sinking ship, would Brierly do any better? His suicide may be a form of recognition that he would not.

Brierly models the ways in which reading might sensitise us to our own luck by luring us into possible worlds, encouraging us to compare ourselves with fictional figures and to test our mettle in counterfactual situations. He also advertises the dangers of doing so—presumably, it can be brought to fatal lengths—as does Jim himself. But if Jim's course of 'light literature' has fed his narcissism, his various misadventures are a deep disappointment to Brierly's own self-love, for they underline the instability of our claim to virtue. After all, Brierly is '*the* fortunate man of the earth' (LJ, 82) and has an impeccable moral record: 'He had never in his life made a mistake, never had an accident, never a mishap, never

57. On the ways in which Conrad enlists and troubles colonial distinctions between 'us' and 'them,' see White, *Joseph Conrad and the Adventure Tradition*.

a check in his steady rise, and he seemed to be one of these lucky fellows who know nothing of indecision, much less of self-mistrust' (LJ, 81). Brierly's self-satisfaction may stem from the fact that much of his luck is 'constitutive' and feels essential to who he is, but Jim's case disturbs his moral serenity, showing how even the constitutionally lucky may be undone by the villainy of circumstances or by the discovery of some 'infernal alloy' (LJ, 72) in their moral metal.

The key to virtue, Marlow maintains, is to retain a radical self-sufficiency—an immunity to 'the contagion of example,' to the destabilising influence of theories and even to the evidence of facts. Brierly appears to have attained this invulnerability—'The sting of life could do no more to his complacent soul than the scratch of a pin to the smooth face of a rock' (LJ, 82)—but he is undone by the contagion of Jim. Brierly's suicide may be a last attempt to win immunity from luck, and it is an option courted by Jim himself throughout the novel (death, after all, 'exorcises from the house of life the haunting shadow of fate' [LJ, 178]). His refusal to flee at the end of the novel and to turn himself in may represent a suicidal form of rectitude. So Brierly and Jim are fatal mirrors of each other. Both believe themselves equal to their luck; both believe themselves immune to it; both, ultimately, are deluded. 'I feel as if nothing could ever touch me,' Jim declares, and reiterates this sense of inviolability at the end of the novel (LJ, 180). '"Nothing can touch me," he said in a last flicker of superb egoism' (LJ, 369)—until, of course, he is touched by a bullet in the chest. Unluckily, not all shots miss the heart.

Surely Martha Nussbaum is right: 'Interference from the world leaves no self-sufficient kernel of the person safely intact.'[58] The search for independence has made Jim stand aloof from others: 'These men did not matter; he rubbed shoulders with them, but they could not touch him; he shared the air they breathed, but he was different' (LJ, 55). Yet Jim will soon find himself in the same boat with his fellows—most literally so after his leap from the *Patna,* although even on the lifeboat Jim will try to stand apart. Jim may clutch to a sense of inner difference—another

58. Nussbaum, *The Fragility of Goodness,* 381.

feature that makes him 'one of us'—but the public significance of his own leap cannot be avoided. As Marlow acknowledges, 'It is impossible to lay the ghost of a fact' (LJ, 194). And the fact is that Jim jumped. Facts, as Conrad demonstrates, are not self-interpreting, but the meaning that Jim attributes to the event of his leap is ultimately dependent on the meaning that is given to it by others. Total independence is unavailable when it comes to interpretation and self-interpretation. The most blunt acknowledgement of this condition is given in *Under Western Eyes*: 'A man's real life is that accorded to him in the thoughts of other men by reason of respect or natural love.'[59] Or as Razumov notes in the same novel: 'Life is a public thing.'[60] Our self-identity is partly derived from the recognition of others—which is what also makes it dependent on luck. The need for another's recognition, and consequently our vulnerability to luck, is acknowledged by Jim's desire for a hearing and by the epigraph from Novalis that prefaces the novel: 'It is certain my Conviction gains infinitely the moment another soul will believe in it' (LJ, 35). Yet it is not clear what we believe about Jim or what Jim ultimately believes about himself.[61] This is because he is one of us—a figure who nurses contradictory feelings about luck and morality itself.

Conrad often worried about the coherence of the moral point of view. As he declared in *A Personal Record*: 'The ethical view of the universe involves us . . . in so many cruel and absurd contradictions' (LJ, 86). The task of fiction, he suggested, was to explore these aporias: 'The only legitimate basis of creative work lies in the courageous recognition of all the irreconcilable antagonisms that make our life so enigmatic, so burdensome, so fascinating, so dangerous—so full of hope' (L, 2.348–49). As I have shown, one of the most dizzying contradictions, for Conrad, is in our moral attitude to luck: We believe that people are only responsible for what they control, yet they are repeatedly held accountable for actions and events that exceed their dominion. This is the contradiction that produces the 'unanswerable why of Jim's fate' (LJ, 258).

59. Conrad, *Under Western Eyes*, 11.

60. Conrad, *Under Western Eyes*, 40.

61. Here I depart from Greaney's judgement that *Lord Jim* 'reneges upon its own scepticism.' Greaney, *Conrad, Language, and Narrative*, 91.

Of course, we can attempt to defuse the contradiction by producing a more differentiated sense of control (no easy matter) or by relinquishing the notion altogether. Responsibility, in other words, may not require the control principle. However, this is liable to make morality itself seem like 'a beastly unfair thing' (LJ, 142).

The coherence of this last sentiment may be queried, but many of Conrad's characters wonder about the justice of justice itself. His secret sharer, for instance, admits to having killed someone, but he refuses to explain himself 'to an old fellow in a wig and twelve respectable tradesmen.' His guilt cannot be settled by them: 'What can they know whether I am guilty or not—or of *what* I am guilty either? That's my affair' (SS, 111). Jim is similarly dismissive of the theatre of justice to which he is subject, but he also seems to acknowledge that the question of his guilt is a valid one and cannot simply be settled by himself. He is, it would seem, no moral sceptic—'After all, one is responsible' (LJ, 181). Nonetheless, Jim's unlucky life may make us wonder how responsive to the world and to our experience of it the concept of responsibility really is.[62] We may depart from the novel with our faith in this concept weakened, but we may also find—like Brierly—that our responsibility has been horribly enlarged. The force of Jim's question—'but what would you have done?' (LJ, 110)—is certainly difficult to dodge. According to Conrad, readers bring to literature one basic imperative: 'Take me out of myself!'[63] But these counterfactual journeys also take us back to ourselves with dark and difficult questions.

62. For a philosophical account of how luck negates responsibility, see Levy, *Hard Luck*.

63. Conrad, *Notes on Life and Letters*, 16.

5

Doubts—Woolf

Snobs and Sceptics

'Am I a Snob?'[1] We might just as well ask: Are some questions rhetorical? When you consider Woolf's assessment of the 'underbred' *Ulysses* ('merely the scratching of pimples on the body of the bootboy at Claridges');[2] her queasiness over T. S. Eliot's tendency to run up stairs ('only the lower classes do that' [D, 3.129]); her frustration with Mary Hutchinson for behaving 'like a cook' (L, 3.328); or her more general views on 'servant psychology' (D, 3.327), there seems to be little doubt about the answer to Woolf's question.[3] 'Snob as I am' is at least an honest start to one of her sentences (D, 2.235). Woolf prided herself on the 'barbarous incivility' of Bloomsbury mores (L, 3.229),[4] but her disregard for established forms of decorum can present itself as a higher-order snobbery: Few, it might seem, were born to this kind of independence.[5] For

1. Woolf, *Moments of Being*, 62–77; cited hereafter in the text under the abbreviation 'MB.'

2. Woolf, *Diary*, 2.199. Further references to the diaries are given in the text under the abbreviation 'D.' Woolf, *Letters*, 2.551. Further references to the letters are given in the text under the abbreviation 'L.'

3. For an account of Woolf's dealings with servants, see Light, *Mrs. Woolf and the Servants*. For an interesting discussion of Woolf's snobbery in a broader social and cultural context, see Latham, *'Am I a Snob?'*.

4. Woolf did at least acknowledge that Bloomsbury mores involved their own snobbish values when she asked herself: 'Which is worse—Mayfair snobbery, or Bloomsbury?' (L, 3.241).

5. As Keynes put it about his gang, 'We repudiated entirely customary morals, conventions and traditional wisdom. We were, that is to say, in the strict sense of the term, immoralists.' Keynes, 'My Early Beliefs,' 446.

all of her desire to depart from conventions, Woolf's sense of good manners can seem strangely devoted. This may emphasise difficulties all of us face in escaping our conditioning, but manners play a more important role in Woolf than her casual *snobbisme* or her frustrations with 'second rate people' sometimes imply (D, 2.235). Drawing on David Hume and others, I want to emphasise the kind of philosophical significance manners have in Woolf, partly by remaining obdurately unphilosophical or unreflective—at least until they are thought about and made a little more mannered and deliberate. Manners are arbitrary norms that lack rational foundations, but Woolf shows that they add structure to our world. Moreover, they provide important relief from the various doubts that gnaw at the foundations of life across Woolf's writing.

The structuring power of manners can be glimpsed in *Moments of Being* when Woolf compares Victorian social life to a kind of game—a game in which one 'had to know the rules.' The rules constrain—and very clearly exclude—but they also supply people with some orientation in moral space. Woolf duly noted how she and her sister, Vanessa, had internalised those rules:

> We both learnt the rules of the game of Victorian society so thoroughly that we have never forgotten them. We still play the game. It is useful. It has also its beauty, for it is founded upon restraint, sympathy, unselfishness—all civilized qualities. It is helpful in making something seemly out of raw odds and ends. (MB, 152)

Though Virginia might often mock the conventions—and Vanessa also hatched ambitious plans 'to eradicate politeness'—Woolf repeatedly stresses the utility and moral substance of manners.[6] If we don't really think well of our neighbour, manners help us to pretend that we do. They enable us to make something 'seemly' out of unpromising materials—and the seemliness here communicates both their beauty and element of contrivance. Manners, moreover, curb the worst effects of uncertainty about the world and its Joneses. At the dinner table, at least, we can pretend to ourselves and to each other that life is

6. Vanessa Bell to Clive Bell, September 1905, in *Selected Letters*, 36.

rule-governed, that things have a certain predictability and pattern, that the world will behave well if we do, and we can try to make this contrived ease a basis for how we might live in general. Manners mitigate the worst effects of our doubts about order, value, and meaning while also confirming that these structures are simply made up. These social forms both express and help us to cope with what Wittgenstein called 'the groundlessness of our believing'—yielding a trust not built on a proposition or a verifiable truth, but on a way of acting.[7] It is perhaps understandable, therefore, that Woolf is reluctant to cast them aside.

Like their creator, many of Woolf's characters are deeply vulnerable to doubt: not just scepticism about the existence of God, the objective purposiveness of existence, or the reality of the good (suspicions of an increasingly conventional kind for Woolf's contemporaries), but doubts, too, about a substantive self, other minds, and an external world—or at least our cognitive access to each of these fabled things. 'No nothing is proved, nothing is known,' we are told in 'The Mark on the Wall' (1917).[8] Uncertainty is a condition of this short tale—activating its opening 'Perhaps' and its subsequent stream of 'ifs'—and the piece clearly shows that unknowingness can have its fun sides. 'The Mark on the Wall' reads, in fact, like a Cartesian meditation in which doubt operates as the engine of the imagination, inciting the mind to roam in the pleasant prairies of what if. Woolf's thinker is also beside a fire, and her doubt is as cultivated as Descartes's own: She duly withdraws her assent from virtually everything, even doubting what it is to know ('Knowledge? Matter for further speculation? . . . And what is knowledge?' [SF, 81]). Unknowingness is knowingly kept alive in the tale: After all, the speculator refuses to get off her chair to determine what the mark is, preferring to remain in a state of undecidedness. 'The

7. Wittgenstein, *On Certainty*, 24. According to Timothy Mackin, the sense that 'being is grounded is one of Woolf's most fervent beliefs'—but this is a bizarre claim in the context of his own argument—a case that rests on the redundancy of verifiable grounds for a feeling of certainty or ontological security. See Mackin, 'Private Worlds, Public Minds: Woolf, Russell, and Photographic Vision.'

8. Woolf, *A Haunted House*, 81. All further references are given in the text under the abbreviation 'SF.'

ignorance of humanity' is a cultivated good, allowing the mind to play (SF, 78).

Leonardo da Vinci once suggested that we could use spots and stains on a wall to conjure worlds—enabling landscapes, animals, battles, and heads of men to play themselves out on ordinary surfaces—and Woolf's mark is similarly suggestive.[9] But the game of imagination it elicits also invites us to see scepticism as a game. Here we may gently doubt the doubter—not least her conviction that certainty is not to be found ('I might get up, but if I got up and looked at it, ten to one I shouldn't be able to say for certain; because once a thing's done, no one ever knows how it happened' [SF, 77–78]). The goalposts clearly move in this game of uncertainty: First we were supposed to determine the identity of the mark; now we are trying to account for its origins. Woolf's speaker may well ask—'What is knowledge?'—but by the end of 'The Mark on the Wall' it is hard, if not impossible, to conclude that we don't know anything (at least in the ordinary sense of the word 'know'). The imaginative play comes to an end, after all, with the arrival of definitive knowledge: 'Ah, the mark on the wall! It was a snail' (SF, 83). We may regret the arrival of this game-spoiling knowledge and suspect its value, but it is difficult to see how we can dismiss its reality or its content. Scepticism, therefore, seems to be routed in this early short story. At best it is exposed as a form of intellectual sport—fun, perhaps, for a while, but soon terminated when someone else steps into a room or begins to speak (as Wittgenstein maintained, 'a language-game is only possible if one trusts something'—not least the words and intentions of speakers).[10] Nonetheless, for all this scepticism about scepticism, many of Woolf's characters—and it would seem their author—remain haunted by doubt. As Woolf put it in her diaries, 'I have a worm of uncertainty moving at the foundations of this pleasant life' (D, 2.126). Questions haunt minds across her fiction: 'Can I never know, share, be certain?'[11] One person

9. Da Vinci seemed to be invoking and rebutting Botticelli's apparent disparagement of landscapes—art that was as impressive as a sponge thrown against a wall. See da Vinci, *Notebooks*, 162.

10. Wittgenstein, *On Certainty*, 66.

11. Woolf, *Jacob's Room*, 80.

struggles to cross puddles because of a kind of doubt about the self; another queries 'the fixity of tables,' or 'the reality of here and now.'[12] 'To speak of knowledge,' we are told, 'is futile' (W, 88).

We may well take issue with this defeatism and its infinite doubt. As Wittgenstein maintained, 'A doubt without end is not even a doubt.'[13] The game of doubt presupposes certainty about something, and total doubt, he concludes, is impossible ('If you tried to doubt everything you would not get as far as doubting anything').[14] Wittgenstein's comments at the end of the *Tractatus* are typical of his general approach to scepticism: It is 'not irrefutable, but obviously nonsensical, when it tries to raise doubts where no questions can be asked.'[15] The sceptic's doubts about knowledge are unintelligible, in Wittgenstein's eyes, and rely on a distortion of what it ordinarily means to know something ('One is often bewitched by a word. For example the word "know"').[16] The view I adopt here is that the sceptic is not necessarily unintelligible—we can at least understand her questions and concerns—but we can see that her take on the world is a peculiar one.[17] Moreover, it is an outlook that involves its own presuppositions and investments—assumptions about knowledge, say, or about the nature of experience and perception, many of which are not doubted enough. However intuitive they may seem, Woolf's questions are animated by theoretically committed ideas of experience drawn from, or at least running alongside, a tradition of British empiricism that extends from John Locke to David Hume to

12. Woolf, *The Waves*, 47, 120, 221. Further references are given in the text under the abbreviation 'W.' Rhoda struggles with puddles, but so, too, it seems, did Woolf herself, see Woolf, *Diary*, 3.113; Woolf, *Moments of Being*, 90.

13. Wittgenstein, *On Certainty*, 83. Woolf was curious about Wittgenstein as a figure at Cambridge and there is some evidence to suggest they met, but it is hard to say how much she knew of his thought. See Monk, *Ludwig Wittgenstein*, 256–57. For a discussion of the parallels between Woolf and Wittgenstein (and Neo-Wittgensteinians like Cora Diamond), see Zumhagen-Yekplé, *A Different Order of Difficulty*, 106–63. See, too, Quigley, 'Reading Virginia Woolf Logically.'

14. Wittgenstein, *On Certainty*, 18.

15. Wittgenstein, *Tractatus Logico-Philosophicus*, 88.

16. Wittgenstein, *On Certainty*, 57.

17. This is to adopt an approach outlined by Michael Williams in *Unnatural Doubts*.

Bertrand Russell. Woolf's sense of how life is sensed—'the senses of sight, of sound, of touch—above all, the sense of the human being, his depth and the variety of his perceptions, his complexity, his confusion, his self, in short'—owes a significant amount to this tradition.[18]

She had access to the tradition on several levels. It was both written about and revered by her father—who felt it expressed key facets of British national character[19]—and it seems apt that the Leslie-Stephen-like Mr. Ramsay in *To the Lighthouse* is soon to lecture on Locke, Berkeley, and Hume. Stephen was not a writer for whom his daughter proclaimed to have a 'natural taste,' but she seemed to take his philosophical interests seriously enough to ironise them in her work (MB, 123).[20] The image of David Hume stuck in a bog—fondly remembered by Mr. Ramsay in *To the Lighthouse* and seemingly drawn from Stephen's own article on the philosopher in the *Dictionary of National Biography*[21]—may be a broader joke at philosophy's expense. It clearly emphasises the redundancy of highfalutin theory when one's in a fix.[22] However, the humbling of philosophy by life (the notorious sceptic is made to recite the Lord's Prayer by an old woman as a condition of his rescue) is also a theme of Hume's own work; here the natural rhythms of everyday existence are judged to take priority over our metaphysical qualms about its deeper structure. In the following discussion I want to suggest that Hume offers the best lens to study the problem of scepticism in

18. Woolf, *Collected Essays*, 3.358. Further references to the essays are given in the text under the abbreviation 'E.' Woolf in this essay ('How it Strikes a Contemporary') believes that moderns 'depend on their senses and emotions whose testimony is trustworthy, rather than on their intellects, whose message is obscure' (E, 359). But the limits of the testimony provided by the senses is evident throughout her work. For further background on Woolf and empiricism, see Alexander, *Conversation Pieces*.

19. See Stephen, *English Thought in the Eighteenth Century*, 1.34.

20. Indeed, the myopia of philosophy and philosophers is often one of Woolf's themes. On this strain in Woolf, see Lackey, 'Modernist Anti-Philosophicalism and Virginia Woolf's Critique of Philosophy.'

21. As Stephen had reported it, 'He had grown very fat, and was once rescued by an old woman from a bog into which he had fallen on condition of repeating the Creed and the Lord's Prayer.' Stephen, *Dictionary of National Biography*, 10.220.

22. Woolf, *To the Lighthouse*, 80. All references are given in the text under the abbreviation 'TL.'

Woolf.[23] Unlike many of the figures that are invoked as a heuristic for her work—Moore, Bergson, Russell, Wittgenstein, etc.—Hume is one of the few philosophers that she mentions both in her novels and in her diaries (where she prescribes for herself a proper dose of Hume's essays as a 'purge' for garbled thinking [D, 2.56]). She may have admired his clarity, but it is the way the philosopher helps us to understand her doubts that is my focus here. Hume permits us to see why experience—or rather a certain theory of experience—opens the door to uncertainty in Woolf. But he also shows how 'custom,' 'habit,' or 'manners' might allow us to close that door or to pretend to ourselves that it was never really open.[24]

What Do We Know?

According to Leslie Stephen's distinctly modern assessment of intellectual endeavour, the 'whole history of philosophical thought is but a history of attempts to separate the object and the subject, and each new attempt implies that the previous line of separation was erroneously drawn or partly "fictitious."'[25] Stephen would also struggle to say where exactly the line should be drawn, but it is fitting that Mr. Ramsay is to be found wrestling with the relationship between subject and object and related questions about the nature of reality. When Lily Briscoe labours to understand what this means she is asked to think 'of a kitchen table . . . when you're not there' (TL, 28). Leslie Stephen had used the same example of a table in his work to suggest that objects existed independently of our perception of them (though it should be said that tables were a fairly standard piece of philosophical equipment to be

23. On the importance of Hume for Woolf, see also Beer, 'Hume, Stephen, and Elegy in *To the Lighthouse*.' While Beer notes the ephemeral quality of experience in Hume and Woolf, she does not dwell on the mitigating effect of manners and custom for both authors.

24. Hume, of course, was neither the first nor the last to stress the anaesthetic value of habit or custom. Habit, according to William James, was society's 'most precious conservative agent,' while its individual constituents were mere 'bundles of habit.' James, *Principles of Psychology*, 1.125, 1.109.

25. Stephen, *English Thought in the Eighteenth Century*, 1.48.

found in Hume, Moore, Russell, and Wittgenstein).[26] A basic distinction between subjective and objective reality was, according to Stephen, a necessary constituent of an organised mind. But this did not mean that the distinction was easily drawn, and Stephen struggled to demonstrate—or even properly describe—what he assumed to be a basic condition of thought. Significantly, in *To the Lighthouse* Lily Briscoe suspects that Mr. Ramsay remains uncertain about his own conclusions: 'He must have had his doubts about that table, she supposed; whether the table was a real table; whether it was worth the time he gave to it; whether he was able after all to find it. He had his doubts, she felt' (TL, 170). The reasons why such doubt might not go away were well mapped out by Hume.

When it came to things like tables, Hume acknowledged that most people tended to subscribe to an uncomplicated realism. 'This very table which we see white, and which we feel hard,' he admitted, 'is believed to exist, independent of our perception, and to be something external of our mind which perceives it.' But Hume was also convinced that this opinion was soon overthrown by 'the slightest philosophy.'[27] We had no cognitive means, he suggested, of establishing the externality of objects or even their continued existence. The only thing of which we were certain, he argued, was the immediate contents of sense experience—that is, our perceptions. These perceptions were reducible to two kinds, namely 'ideas' and 'impressions.' On the whole, ideas were causally dependent on and were usually less vivacious than impressions.[28] Woolf also seemed to believe that perceptions were the only immediate facts to which we have access. She deployed a far broader

26. Stephen, *English Thought in the Eighteenth Century*, 1.46. Ann Banfield rightly regards the table as the 'paradigmatic object of philosophical thought.' Banfield, *The Phantom Table*. She notes, however, Woolf's particular debts to Russell when it comes to tables and much else. For the influence of Russell on Woolf, see also Hintikka, 'Virginia Woolf and Our Knowledge of the External World'; Joanne Wood, 'Lighthouse Bodies'; Quigley, *Modernist Philosophy and Vagueness*, 63–102. Erwin Steinberg suggests that Woolf's table is looted from Moore. See Steinberg, 'G. E. Moore's Table and Chair in *To the Lighthouse*.'

27. Hume, *An Enquiry Concerning Human Understanding*, 201.

28. Hume seemed to imply that some ideas could be produced that did not have impressions as their causal origin. For an account of this apparent anomaly, see Fogelin, 'Hume and the Missing Shade of Blue.'

range of metaphors to describe these sense-data, but they were always—as in Hume—multiple, discrete, and short-lived. 'The mind,' as she put it, 'receives a myriad impressions—trivial, fantastic, evanescent, or engraved with the sharpness of steel. From all sides they come, an incessant shower of innumerable atoms' (E, 4.160). Given all of this mind-stuff, both Hume and Woolf would wonder in their different ways if perceptions can ever yield justified belief or knowledge. There is no necessary reason, of course, for accepting this mind-model as one's starting point or to accept the kind of test it sets for knowledge. Moreover, if our tests go on to show that we don't know things, this perhaps is a good reason to discard the test, not our confidence in knowledge. However, wedded as they are to perceptions, both Hume and Woolf begin to wonder if they allow us to know anything.

Problems arise—as Hume had suggested—when one attempts to examine the cause of impressions, or to determine the nature of their relationship with their ostensible object. There was, he suggested, no independent criterion to test this relationship, and no noncircular means of testing things through the resources of perception itself. Here Hume adopted the representational model of perception of Descartes and Locke to produce profoundly sceptical results. Locke had set out to explain the origin and epistemic value of mental entities such as 'ideas'—none of which, he argued, could be treated as innate. Arguably—and any argument would have to treat at length the complex shifts in Locke's position—this resulted in a form of representational realism. The theory is realist in that it subscribes to a reality independent of mind; it is representational in that we have cognitive access to this reality only through perceptions or 'ideas.' Moreover, the model derives its epistemic status from a causal theory of perception: Simple ideas are caused by external entities which they often resemble.[29] The very paper on which Locke writes produces an idea through which means he affirms the existence and independence of such an object. But, as Hume

29. As Locke put it, 'External objects convey into the mind what produces there those perceptions.' Locke, *An Essay Concerning Human Understanding*, 110.

recognised, this position begs the question and presupposes the causal relationship it attempts to establish. 'The mind has never anything present to it but the perceptions,' Hume insists, 'and cannot possibly reach any experience of their connexion with objects.'[30] Hume, therefore, professes himself to be an agnostic about the ultimate origin and epistemic value of impressions.

The vulgar belief in an 'external world,' Hume concludes, has no rational foundation. Philosophical attempts to produce a more sophisticated realism are even less convincing, deprived as they are of the intuitive force of the vulgar view. The more philosophical position—he clearly has Locke in mind—acknowledges that we do not have direct access to an external world of objects; the latter is an inference we make on the basis of our perceptions. But this, for Hume, relies on a distinction between perceptions and their objects that has no foundation in experience. Such a model of representation leads, in fact, to the untenable notion of a 'double existence': When we perceive something, we are not aware of two things—a perception and the object it represents. The vulgar, on the other hand, simply identify their perceptions with objects and maintain that the latter have a continued existence distinct from the mind. But this, for Hume, ultimately produces the absurd conclusion that there are unperceived perceptions or sense experiences that continue independently of sense. The thought experiment Andrew Ramsay sets out for Lily Briscoe—'Think of a kitchen table . . . when you're not there'—captures the seeming oddness of this position (TL, 28). The demand for perceptions that are not themselves perceived seems impossible to execute. It was precisely because perceptions seemed to require a perceiving mind that Berkeley famously dismissed the idea of mind-independent objects as incoherent. 'Their esse,' he declared, 'is percipi.'[31] Here the belief in an external world is not simply false but is unintelligible. Hume came very close to this position, but he also resisted its attraction—at some initial expense to his own

30. Hume, *An Enquiry Concerning Human Understanding*, 202.
31. George Berkeley, *Principles of Human Knowledge*, 25.

argument.[32] One reason for this arises from the fact that human beings do happen to believe in an external world. This belief is not unintelligible; it is, for Hume, simply mistaken.[33]

Much of human life, however, depends on these mistakes. Ideas of space and time are for Hume salutary illusions: They do not possess rational foundations but are products of the imagination. When we have impressions we supply to them a spatial context even though we have no direct impression of space itself. The same largely holds for our notions of time. When we hear five notes on a flute we convert these five impressions into a temporal sequence, we do not receive a sixth impression of time itself—and ideas that cannot be ultimately cashed in for an impression are, for Hume, largely empty. If the imagination constitutes our ideas of space and time, it also forms the basis, Hume suggests, of all causal reasoning. The idea of a necessary cause may be real enough—it exists in our mind—but there is no basis for proving its operation in nature. We can never say, in other words, that event 'A' necessarily leads to the future event 'B.' To deny this is not self-contradictory. And to defend such a causal link on the basis of experience is to argue in a circle: It presupposes the very continuity between past and present that it sets out to prove. This, of course, is the problem of all induction. If the imagination, for Hume, underlies some of the basic connections we apply to experience, if it drives our belief in an external and enduring world, it also sustains our faith in an enduring self. This idea of personal identity is also an illusion: It asserts without grounds that we are a substance other than our perceptions and it does so by repressing the discontinuous and variable nature of our impressions. Human beings, according to Hume, are 'nothing but a bundle or collection of different perceptions, which

32. Hume may have objected to the complete identification of perceptions with objects in Berkeley, but he had engaged in this himself at points. It was a core strand of his attack on representational realism: 'Tis impossible for us distinctly to conceive, objects to be in their nature any thing but exactly the same with perceptions.' Hume, *Treatise of Human Nature*, 144. In general, Hume may have simply wished to suggest that the epistemological problem of separating perceptions from objects did not justify Berkeley's metaphysical idealism.

33. On this point see Fogelin, *Hume's Skepticism in the Treatise of Human Nature*, 6–12.

succeed each other with an inconceivable rapidity, and are in perpetual flux and movement.'[34] Since no simplicity or identity can be derived from this, the idea of an enduring self is also a fiction.

Woolf is haunted by these sceptical possibilities, and her doubts adopt a conceptual pattern similar to Hume's. Beginning with the 'myriad impressions' that constitute experience, Woolf can produce no adequate grounds for belief in external objects or enduring selves. She tracks the 'drip, drip of one impression after another' but can never trace their source to some underlying substance.[35] Moreover, these impressions lack continuity and seem to be 'disconnected and incoherent' (E, 4.161). Rhoda in *The Waves*, for instance, is troubled by the radically disjunctive quality of her perceptions: 'One moment does not lead to another. The door opens and the tiger leaps . . . I cannot make one moment merge in the next. To me they are all violent, all separate' (W, 97). Woolf seems to confirm Hume's opinion that human beings are nothing but bundles of impressions in perpetual flux. 'Arrows of sensation strike from my spine,' Bernard declares in *The Waves*, 'but without order' (W, 119). There is often something thrilling about this existential chaos, and Woolf frequently celebrates 'our enthralling confusion, our hotch-potch of impulses, our perpetual miracle' (E, 4.75). Such flux may be exciting, but it can also undermine all confidence in the idea of a substantive self. This lies at the bottom of much of Woolf's anxious self-questioning. 'Who am I, what am I, & so on: these questions are always floating about in me,' she complains in her diary (D, 3.62–63). If we attempt to find answers by studying our mental life, all we seem to experience is a sequence of impressions. We never witness the mind or self in which these perceptions supposedly inhere. 'I am hardly aware of myself,' Woolf noted of her own experience, 'but only of the sensation' (MB, 81). Here the notion of a substantive self comes under considerable pressure. Many of Woolf's characters continue to believe in an enduring

34. Hume, *Treatise of Human Nature*, 165

35. Woolf, *Mrs. Dalloway*, 166. All further references are given in the text under the abbreviation 'MD.'

self, but others have their doubts. Personal identity is a particular problem for Bernard in *The Waves* because he notices that he is 'not one and simple, but complex and many' (W, 56). By the end of the novel, he seems to have abandoned all faith in a discrete and enduring self. He is, he feels, a 'man without a self'—but one that is too discontinuous to remain resolved even on this (W, 219).

Woolf often contrasts the flux of personal experience to the apparent solidity and relative permanence of material objects. 'The tree alone,' we hear in *The Waves*, 'resisted our eternal flux' (W, 192). This solidity can be a source of support, providing us with some apparently stable coordinates in an otherwise chaotic existence. Woolf finds herself at times 'worshipping solidity, worshipping reality, worshipping the impersonal world which is proof of some existence other than ours' (SF, 82). Solid objects are also, however, testaments and measures of our own impermanence; they have a stability and 'sternness that our lives lack' (W, 193). There is a pathos in Woolf's fiction that originates from houses, rooms, armchairs, and boots that survive their owner.[36] Regardless of whether these descriptions yield sadness or comfort, Woolf in these instances seems to be a metaphysical realist: There is, she suggests, a reality independent of mind.[37] This leads her to believe in 'the thing that exists when we aren't there' (D, 3.114). But almost as soon as this realism is advanced, it raises sceptical questions. For a start, she is troubled by how we seem to lack direct access to these independent bits of reality: 'What is the thing that lies beneath the semblance of the thing?' she asks in *The Waves* (W, 123). Woolf's speakers often seem to retreat from a direct realism to at best a more representational account where objects are made available to

36. This is what James called 'the sadness of things'—those things that bear the spoor of 'old summers, dead people, people who will never come again.' James, *The Selected Letters of William James*, 155.

37. In a well-known article, Rosenbaum argued that Woolf was a realist. See S. P. Rosenbaum, 'The Philosophical Realism of Virginia Woolf.' My own position is that there is clearly a realist dimension or realist hope in Woolf's writing; however, the belief in a mind-independent reality almost invariably provokes doubts about our cognitive access to this realm. Moreover, there is no obvious road out of these doubts in Woolf.

us through the perceptions—or the semblances—they occasion. She has moved, as Hume might put it, from a 'vulgar' to a more philosophical position. But, as we have seen, this philosophical account won't stand up to scrutiny. There is no way we can test these perceptions against the reality they ostensibly represent and even the test itself seems to be question-begging.

All we seem to possess, therefore, are perceptions—'these dazzling, these dancing apparitions' (W, 168). In this context, the idea of an external object—or 'the thing that exists when we aren't here'—begins to seem unintelligible. Woolf sometimes brings us close to the Berkeleyan view that the being of objects is their perception.[38] Peter Walsh in *Mrs. Dalloway*, for instance, appears to court a complete metaphysical idealism. 'Nothing exists outside us,' he maintains, 'except a state of mind' (MD, 62). But, in general, Woolf's novels do not allow us to replace a metaphysical realism with a simple idealism in which all existence is ontologically dependent on mind. After all, she is highly sceptical of the notion of a substantive mind. Ultimately, what we are left with are reified perceptions whose point of origin or destination cannot be known. As Neville puts it in *The Waves*, there are 'no conclusions, only violent sensations, each separate' (W, 118). This account of matters seems to leave few elements of our ordinary world picture in place. It is hardly surprising, therefore, that many of Woolf's characters are plagued by radical uncertainty. 'There is no stability in this world,' Bernard declares in *The Waves* (W, 88), while Neville dismisses the 'illimitable chaos' and 'formless imbecility' of existence (W, 173). Mrs. Ramsay in *To the Lighthouse* believes there is neither reason nor order in the universe. 'Was there no safety? No learning by heart the ways of the world?' Lily Briscoe asks in a spirit of desperation (TL, 195). Here and elsewhere metaphors of water and fluidity emphasise the groundlessness of human affairs and suggest that we lack a solid basis for warranted belief. It is hardly a surprise, therefore, that 'our frail barks founder in darkness' (TL, 8).

38. Woolf read Berkeley and claimed to 'much admire' his thought (D, 2.33).

Therapies for Doubt

Hume's radical doubts bring him to a bad place in the *Treatise*, and he deploys the same nautical metaphors that Woolf would later use to outline his confusion: His 'leaky weather-beaten vessel' is no match for 'that boundless ocean, which runs out into immensity.' His doubts are so thoroughly alienating that he feels like 'some strange uncouth monster' who has been banished from all human society.[39] Hume's queries, nevertheless, continue to rain down from all sides. 'I am confounded with all these questions,' he admits, 'and begin to fancy myself in the most deplorable condition imaginable, inviron'd with the deepest darkness, and utterly depriv'd of the use of every member and faculty.'[40] Fortunately, for Hume, this miserable state of 'philosophical melancholy and delirium' does not last. Here nature seems to provide a solution where reason fails. He eats dinner, plays a game of backgammon, converses and is merry with friends, and gradually finds himself relieved of his former doubts. And while he might strive to return to his earlier speculations, they now strike him as dry, esoteric, and vaguely preposterous. Hume does not provide a theoretical refutation of scepticism—he believes no such refutation is possible. He simply maintains that nature does not allow us to remain in a condition of total doubt. Hume's naturalism, in other words, mitigates his theoretical scepticism: It is natural for human beings to believe—to believe in external objects and enduring selves despite their apparent lack of grounds.

Our habits and customs, Hume suggests, are built around these natural beliefs. Significantly, habit is not simply a result of our natural convictions, it helps to constitute these convictions. The force of habit underlies, for instance, all abstract ideas and all causal reasoning. The imagination attributes ideas of causal necessity to events that always occur in tandem, only because the force of habit makes it do so. Habit and custom, therefore, are the seemingly frivolous sources of many of our core beliefs:

39. Hume, *Treatise of Human Nature*, 172.
40. Hume, *Treatise of Human Nature*, 174.

> Custom, then, is the great guide of human life. It is that principle alone, which renders our experience useful to us, and makes us expect, for the future, a similar train of events with those which have appeared in the past. Without the influence of custom, we should be entirely ignorant of every matter of fact, beyond what is immediately present to the memory and senses. We should never know how to adjust means to ends, or to employ our natural powers in the production of any effect. There would be an end at once of all action, as well as of the chief part of speculation.[41]

Custom and habit, I want to argue, play an equally crucial role in Woolf's fictional worlds. In *Mrs. Dalloway*, for instance, the 'skeleton of habit alone upholds the human frame' (MD, 54). Or, as we are told in 'The Evening Party,' 'habit is everything' (SF, 93). On the most basic level, habit operates as a psychological defence against the worst effects of radical doubt. The great foil to the excessive principles of scepticism, Hume had maintained, was 'action, and employment, and the occupations of common life.'[42] Against a background of total uncertainty, Woolf often seeks refuge in 'the protective waves of the ordinary' (W, 70) or 'the quiet of ordinary things' (W, 109). Mrs. Ramsay may believe that there is 'no reason, order, justice' in the universe, but everyday practices help her to cope with this insight by making it impossible to sustain (TL, 71). Her husband's philosophical enquiries often bring him—and everyone else—to the edge of despair, but this is checked by mundane things: 'The ruin was veiled; domesticity triumphed; custom crooned its soothing rhythm' (TL, 36).

Scepticism frequently seems to have alienation as its method and further estrangement as its result. In other words, it demands a self-distancing from ordinary beliefs and attachments as a condition of impartial enquiry and the latter may leave us feeling thoroughly broken. Hume, as we have seen, emerged from his sceptical enquiries feeling like a 'strange uncouth monster.' Woolf, therefore, celebrates ordinary life-practices for the sense of integration they produce. 'We are all swept on

41. Hume, *An Enquiry Concerning Human Understanding*, 122–23.
42. Hume, *An Enquiry Concerning Human Understanding*, 206.

by the torrent of things grown so familiar that they cast no shade; we make no comparisons; think scarcely ever of I or of you; and in this unconsciousness attain the utmost freedom from friction and part the weeds that grow over the mouths of sunken channels' (W, 166). Habits and routines afford us some reprieve from the acute self-consciousness of scepticism. This, of course, is why the life of habit is so often disparaged—not everyone wants to live like a fish.

Woolf clearly acknowledges the deadening effects of habit and routine, and the complacency they appear to generate. Her characters frequently feel that 'the thick leaves of habit' obscure one's view of the world (W, 217). 'Custom blinds your eyes,' Neville believes (W, 163). He resents the 'usual order' with all its dullness and safety (W, 117). Neville wants 'no repetitions.' 'Each day is dangerous' because unique. (W, 163). There is no learning by heart the ways of the world, he feels, because there are no genuine regularities in experience. Indeed, there is a strand that runs throughout Woolf's work which relates genuine freedom or self-realisation to the rejection of habit, custom, and tradition. In the early novel *Night and Day*, for instance, Katherine Hilbery acknowledges the attractions of tradition but recognises that 'the traditional answer would be of no use to her individually.'[43] The novel—paradoxically, one of Woolf's most conventional works—tracks her search for an unorthodox solution to life's problems. Lily Briscoe in *To the Lighthouse* also resists the draw of traditional values in her search for autonomy. Woolf sometimes appears to have believed that her own life followed this trajectory, and it was reflected in her repeated criticisms of old mores from which she sometimes felt liberated. In 1925, she roundly dismissed habits and customs as 'a convenience devised for the support of timid natures who dare not allow their souls free play' (E, 4.74). This was actually presented as a sympathetic paraphrase of Montaigne, but it largely misconstrued his position. Montaigne had, in fact, resurrected the methods of ancient scepticism to argue that most of our epistemic judgements lacked rational grounds, but he ultimately used this position to provide a pragmatic defence of custom

43. Woolf, *Night and Day*, 299.

and tradition.[44] After all, no more rational foundations for social life, he believed, could be produced. This, as we shall see, is largely the view adopted by two of Woolf's most profoundly sceptical characters—Mrs. Dalloway and Mrs. Ramsay.[45]

Woolf's self-conscious iconoclasm clearly demonstrates that her approval of habit and custom was far from unqualified. The merit of scepticism, in her eyes, lay in its ability to disturb entrenched attitudes and to expose their arbitrary and nonrational character. This is why doubts are indulged in 'The Mark on the Wall':

> How shocking, and yet how wonderful it was to discover that these real things, Sunday luncheons, Sunday walks, country houses, and tablecloths were not entirely real, were indeed half phantoms, and the damnation which visited the disbeliever in them was only a sense of illegitimate freedom. (SF, 80)

Disbelief may be liberating, but Sunday rituals still have their uses. Scepticism, for Woolf, does not necessarily demand a comprehensive rejection of our commonsense views, assuming that this is possible. There are at least two basic reasons for this. The first is self-consciously therapeutic: Custom, as we have seen, immunises us from the worst effects of scepticism by distracting us from its truth. The second reason has a more theoretical character: If the sceptic is right, then the groundlessness of our customary views is not an argument against them, since all our beliefs suffer from this defect. Here an assent to custom may be an expression of our scepticism rather than its salutary limit. This insight, I want to argue, lies at the heart of Woolf's depiction of manners. Like the rest of our customs, manners lack a rational basis, but this is not a justification for their rejection. Lily Briscoe may worry that there are no solid foundations for belief—there is 'no guide, no shelter, but

44. 'Keep to the beaten track: it can hardly be good to be so subtle and so clever. . . . My advice to you is to cling to moderation and temperance, as much in your opinions and arguments as in your conduct, felling what is merely new or odd. All roads which wander from the norm displease me.' Montaigne, *An Apology for Raymond Sebond*, 137.

45. In Peter Walsh's eyes, Clarissa 'was one of the most thoroughgoing sceptics he had ever met' (MD, 85). Mr. Ramsay thinks something similar of his wife.

all was miracle, and leaping from the pinnacle of a tower into the air'—but no difficulties arise from this absence of grounds (TL, 195). We may, as Lily suggests, leap from towers into the air, but we don't necessarily fall. Our norms may be free-floating; they may be irrational or, as Lily suggests, miraculous, but they successfully coordinate action, nonetheless. This is the defence Mrs. Ramsay provides for manners in the famous dinner scene in *To the Lighthouse.* The case is made with reference to the French language:

> So, when there is a strife of tongues at some meeting, the chairman, to obtain unity, suggests that every one shall speak in French. Perhaps it is bad French; French may not contain the words that express the speaker's thoughts; nevertheless speaking French imposes some order, some uniformity. (TL, 98)

The French language has no natural connection to the world it describes and its obvious foreignness in this context suggests that it has no natural connection to its users. The decision of the chairman to select it above other available languages appears to be entirely random. However, despite the seeming arbitrariness of manners, they add pattern to life.

The pattern is in many respects false—that is, it is not an objective feature of the universe—but it is what Hume would call a 'fiction.' The dinner party, in other words, yields feelings of unity and coherence that have no foundation in fact; indeed, Woolf is at pains to emphasise their artificial basis:

> Now all the candles were lit, and the faces on both sides of the table were brought nearer by the candle-light, and composed, as they had not been in the twilight, into a party round a table, for the night was now shut off by panes of glass, which, far from giving any accurate view of the outside world, rippled it so strangely that here, inside the room, seemed to be order and dry land; there, outside, a reflection in which things wavered and vanished, waterily.
>
> Some change at once went through them all, as if this had really happened, and they were all conscious of making a party together in

> a hollow, on an island; had their common cause against that fluidity out there. (TL, 106)

The panes of glass, we are told, do not yield an 'accurate view of the outside world' and generate an illusory sense of coherence within the room. The watery aspect of the world is in this context a distortion; so, too, is the appearance of dry land. Of course, water metaphors appear throughout the novel as reliable indicators of our epistemic condition: They repeatedly point to the fact that our beliefs lack solid grounds. The whole point of the dinner party, it seems, is that it both affirms and mitigates this sceptical conclusion. The scene provides a therapeutic response to scepticism: Dinner distracts Mr. Ramsay from his radical doubts just as it did for Hume. But the rituals of dinner also bear out the truth of scepticism for the beliefs that constitute them are without foundation. On a basic level, these social gatherings implicitly depend on beliefs—say, in an external world or an enduring self—that are fictitious. Moreover, these rituals are in themselves second-order fictions and create the values that they ostensibly guarantee. Manners do not refer to the real properties of people or things, but their meaning is constituted by their practice. Dressing for dinner is only significant because people behave as if it is. This is something the young working-class academic, Charles Tansley, notes and attempts to override, at some cost to himself. For those dressed for dinner, the occasion may yield a sense of cohesion, but these feelings depend on fictions that have been intersubjectively shared and constituted. The company at dinner behave 'as if' they were a party on an island. This 'as if' is ambiguous: It is adjectival to the change that overcomes the group, but it is also constitutive of this change, so that real transformations are contingent on illusory identifications. Much of life depended for Woolf on this 'as if,' or on humanity's inexhaustible capacity for shared illusion-making. Charles Tansley clearly misses the point when he dismisses the dinner party for its 'insincerity' (TL, 98).

Woolf was understandably drawn to Lytton Strachey's remark that 'we can only live if we see through illusion' (D, 3.233). The doubleness of 'seeing through' here captures well the dual nature of the kind of scepticism that we see in Woolf's novels: It is a position that recognises the falsehood of everyday beliefs while also acknowledging their necessity. Woolf emphasised this point early on in her writing: 'If life were no longer circled by an illusion,' she declared, 'then it would be too dismal an affair to carry to an end' (ND, 469). She makes a similar point in *Orlando*: 'Illusions are to the soul what atmosphere is to the earth. Roll up that tender air and the plant dies, the colour fades.'[46] Social interaction, moreover, was a form of illusion-making. 'I must make human illusion,' she wrote in her diary, 'ask someone in tomorrow after dinner; & begin that astonishing adventure with the souls of others again' (D, 3.234). As Woolf's narrator explains in *Orlando*, a good hostess is a kind of sibyl or witch. She 'lays her guests under a spell,' allowing them to feel happy, witty, or profound.[47] But these feelings are 'all an illusion' (O, 139). Mrs. Ramsay is also an illusionist, conjuring fictions of order and well-being out of a chaotic world. This may explain the spiritual affinity that appears to exist between Mrs. Ramsay and the artist Lily Briscoe. Their activities, however different, are oriented towards similar ends: They aim to install a fictitious unity and coherence upon experience. Mrs. Dalloway has similar aspirations. Her parties are valiantly superficial exercises, an acknowledgement and repudiation of the world's formlessness. Clarissa's spiritual twin, after all, is Septimus Smith. If Septimus is clearly mad, he is not necessarily mistaken about the chaos he perceives. Septimus represents, as Woolf arrestingly put it, the 'insane truth.'[48] His difficulties are to a certain extent the modern sceptic's, which may, of course, raise questions about scepticism. His doctor encourages him to 'take an interest in things outside himself,' but his perceptions carry no reliable marks of an external world or indeed of a distinct internal one (MD, 23). Septimus's failure to distinguish between himself and his world—he often thinks he is the thing he perceives—may be a proof that he is insane, but it is not a

46. Woolf, *Orlando*, 142. All further references are given in the text under the abbreviation 'O.'

47. Woolf also records her ambivalence about this illusion-making, declaring that 'no real happiness, no real wit, no real profundity are tolerated where the illusion prevails' (O, 139).

48. Woolf, Reading Notebooks, 3.153.

proof that he is wrong.[49] If Wittgenstein had to remind himself at times that philosophers were not mad, he would have had extreme difficulties accepting that the mad were philosophers. But Clarissa Dalloway—and Woolf herself—come close to regarding Septimus as some sort of sage. If suicide is a valid response to a groundless existence, as Clarissa seems to suggest, so, too, she believes, are her parties.

But there are many who resist this illusion-making on the grounds of its untruth, in ways that force us to revisit the relationship between truth, scepticism, and ordinary life. 'By the truth we are undone,' we hear in *Orlando*, and it yields the following reflection: 'He who robs us of our dreams robs us of our life' (O, 142). There are a lot of these dream robbers about in Woolf. Moreover, their rudeness is one of their distinguishing features.[50] Mrs. Ramsay, for instance, finds that there is something barbaric in her husband's will to truth. 'To pursue truth with such astonishing lack of consideration for other people's feelings, to rend the thin veils of civilisation so wantonly, so brutally, was,' she feels, 'an outrage of human decency' (TL, 37). Mr. Ramsay, on the other hand, is driven to distraction by his wife's doting lies. This seems to point to a fundamental clash between the demands of truth and the values of common life. On a superficial level, the Ramsays seem to embody the two poles of the opposition. This contrast is sustained by their actual social roles, by the novel's use of cliché about masculine rationality and feminine emotion, and by the characters' own reflections on their position. His pursuit of knowledge renders him 'blind, deaf, and dumb, to the ordinary things' (TL, 77). Her concerns, we are told, lie with 'unity' not with 'knowledge' (TL, 57). Indeed, if a methodical self-distancing from ordinary beliefs and attachments is a basic requirement for objective enquiry, then Mrs. Ramsay seems to equate the very adoption of such

49. Other ostensibly sane characters in Woolf have difficulties distinguishing themselves from what they perceive. See, for instance, Louis's account of himself in *The Waves* ('I hold a stalk in my hand. I am the stalk' [W 7]) or Susan's experiences later in the novel ('I think I am the field, I am the barn, I am the trees' [W.72]).

50. The 'truth is . . . ill-mannered,' Bertrand Russell liked to observe, because it usually stands opposed to the irrational canons of decorum. Russell, *Sceptical Essays*, 5–6.

an attitude with egotism (TL, 42, 100). She repeatedly criticises both her husband and his pupil for this vice, and it seems to be structurally related to their will to truth—although Tansley's egotism is also an apparent sign of his underbred character. Both men elevate the role of the solitary enquirer over the shared values of everyday life and sanction this perspective on the grounds of its greater truthfulness.

But matters are more complicated than these simple oppositions suggest. For a start, Mrs. Ramsay's opposition to the self-abstraction of the philosophical attitude is far from absolute—after all, it lies at the heart of her own scepticism. She admires the courage and discipline of her husband's pursuit of truth and, if this demands self-abstraction, then she spends much of the novel in this disengaged state. Indeed, it pains her husband that she can 'look so distant.' In these moments Mrs. Ramsay resembles, we are told, a lighthouse, in its solitary, 'pitiless,' and 'remorseless' scrutiny of the world—an impartiality 'which was so much her, yet so little her' (TL, 72). This impartial attitude yields profoundly sceptical conclusions about the existence of God, about the possibility of order in the universe, about the idea of natural justice. Since Mrs. Ramsay's sceptical feelings strike her as true, Mrs. Ramsay's opposition to truth or truthfulness is not total. Mrs. Ramsay simply believes that the pursuit of truth reveals the necessity of its self-curtailment in ordinary life; similarly, the epistemological attitude is only questionable when it is unreflectively sustained. The differences between Mrs. Ramsay and her husband, therefore, are not as stark as we might initially think. After all, he, too, is a sceptic: Staring out upon the 'dark of human ignorance,' he concludes that 'we know nothing' (TL, 50). But it appears at times that Mr. Ramsay is not, in fact, sceptical enough. He is, after all, famously stuck on the letter R. His failure to get to Z may, of course, drive his scepticism; in other words, it is only because he is committed in advance to a totalising conception of knowledge—running from A to Z—that he can ultimately deem its pursuit a failure. A more modest conception of what knowledge demands would have yielded less damning conclusions and certainly less doubts about that table. The problem may lie less with Ramsay's scepticism—or the demanding view of knowledge that drives it—than with the way a sceptical attitude leads to the downgrading of ordinary life when it should in fact lead to its endorsement.

If Mr. Ramsay undergoes any kind of development, it appears to be on this point. He slowly comes to terms with the ordinary ways of the world. He initially tries to seek 'consolation in trifles,' but they fail to live up to his philosophical sense of truth and justice (TL, 50). He gradually seems to recognise, however, that if all belief is without foundation, then the groundlessness of everyday beliefs is not an argument against them. So, a capitulation to the demands of ordinary life may be an enactment of one's scepticism rather than its contradiction. Hume had argued precisely this and it is significant that Mr. Ramsay repeatedly invokes the image of the Scottish philosopher stuck in a bog.[51] Here the necessity of survival demanded the suspension of all of Hume's doubts about an enduring self, an external world—and given the religious zeal of his would-be rescuer—the existence of God.[52] Arguably, by the end of the novel, Mr. Ramsay has recognised that ordinary beliefs—however illusory—are a condition of human existence. He has begun to see ordinariness, as Cavell later would, as an 'achievement,' not as a tissue of deceit.[53] *To the Lighthouse* shows that there is a happiness to be found in familial expeditions and cheese sandwiches, even if, or precisely because, we are destined to perish alone.[54]

51. 'A true sceptic,' Hume had declared, 'will be diffident of his philosophical doubts, as well as of his philosophical conviction; and will never refuse any innocent satisfaction, which offers itself, upon account of either of them.' Hume, *Treatise of Human Nature*, 177.

52. Whatever its provenance, the story of Hume in the bog may show that he—and certainly his rescuer—is different from a Pyrrhonian sceptic. According to some reports, Pyrrho was so sceptical of the world of appearances that he refused to rescue his teacher Anaxarchus from a swamp into which he had fallen. See Diogenes Laertius, *Lives of Eminent Philosophers*, 2.477.

53. Cavell, *The Claim of Reason*, 463. Interestingly the type of reassurance that thinkers derive from the ordinary is also expressive of egotistical doubt for Cavell: 'Only the madness of their egotism, the monstrousness of it, requires such vaults of relief! Only sinners so crave sanctity!' (463).

54. Our metaphysical solitude often seems to be irreducible in Woolf, and solidarity has its limits ('Always to have sympathy, always to be accompanied, always to be understood, would be intolerable' [E, 4.320–21]).

Doubt and Dogmatism

'The greater part of mankind,' Hume observed, 'are naturally apt to be affirmative and dogmatical in their opinions.'[55] The tactic of sceptics from Pyrrho to Hume to Woolf is to reveal that many—if not all—of these opinions lack the foundations in reason that they often claim to possess. But this critical attitude can also become a dogmatism that expresses itself in its intolerance for ordinary life-practices. It yields the epistemic narcissist—all too sure of their own doubts and the gullibility of everyone else. So, as Bertrand Russell advised, 'we must be sceptical even of our scepticism.'[56] Woolf tries to live in this broken middle. She is arguably a sceptic in epistemology, but she is also critical of a prescriptive scepticism which holds that the groundlessness of ordinary beliefs is a sufficient basis for their rejection. Our continued assent to everyday attitudes may at least be accounted for on naturalistic or pragmatic grounds: It is natural to believe certain things and these beliefs serve a purpose. However arbitrary, our habitual beliefs and mores add pattern to our world.

Pattern, of course, may become a fetish and the basis for another form of dogmatism. William Bradshaw's divine 'Proportion' has, after all, a sister: 'Conversion is her name' (MD, 109). Here Woolf resists the dogmatism of commonsense ideas of proportion, exposing the arbitrary nature of positions that present themselves as indisputable facts. If proportion is sometimes coercive, this admittedly raises concerns about the structuring effect of manners throughout Woolf's work. Woolf repeatedly acknowledges that manners reflect and sustain structures of domination. She outlines, with some sympathy, Lily Briscoe's dislike of the patriarchal norms that govern polite conversation; with a little less sympathy, she tracks the difficulties of the working-class Tansley at an upper-class dinner table. This concern for the losers in a polite world was not always sustained. Manners may have mitigated her scepticism but not necessarily her snobbery. The essence of snobbery, Woolf once suggested, is a 'wish to impress other people' (MB, 64), but underlying

55. Hume, *Enquiry Concerning Human Understanding*, 207.

56. Russell, *Sceptical Essays*, 120.

the importance of manners and, perhaps, all culture in her work was a grain of misanthropy. As she frankly admitted in 1926: 'Really I don't like human nature unless candied over with art' (D, 3.85).

The candy of Woolf's art, however, also has its utopian elements. Written into the careful symmetry of its form we seem to find a social, even a metaphysical, hope—a unity-without-domination or freedom-within-lawfulness. If Woolf's art attempts to emulate the unifying effect of manners in its own aesthetic framework (a theme teased out by the extended parallels between Mrs. Ramsay and Lily Briscoe), it also makes us wonder whether art might be the source of pattern—not least in the conversations or sense of community it might inspire. Latent within our response to art, as Kant suggests, is a confidence that our aesthetic feelings are shareable and experienceable by others—feelings that might generate assent without the brutality of conversion.[57] Yet, as Woolf suggests, this confidence might be misplaced: The problem with much modern art, she proposes, is that writers and readers lack 'a code of manners'—both internal to art and perhaps external to it too—that would allow aesthetic matters to be meaningfully shared and discussed (E, 3.434). After all, Lily Briscoe's art is destined for an attic—and she has few delusions about its public powers. Moreover, in the dictatorial figure of Miss La Trobe in *Between the Acts*, Woolf concedes that there is a coercive potential in the social unity that art might condition (remember, again, Proportion's domineering sister). Yet she never quite relinquished her desire for pattern—aesthetic, social, metaphysical. In her diaries, at least, she outlines what she is tempted to call a 'philosophy': 'that behind the cotton wool is hidden a pattern' or that there is 'some real thing behind appearances.' Underlying this kind of metaphysical realism is the sense, perhaps, that the universe itself is well behaved and well mannered. The odd thing about this ostensible realism is that it often sits side by side with a kind of fictionalism—a sense that the pattern is a fiction that is written into being by the artist herself. As Woolf admits, 'I make it real by putting it into words.' 'It is only by

57. On Woolf's very Kantian investment in a sensis communis of taste, see Greer, *Fiction, Philosophy and the Ideal of Conversation*, 113–18.

putting it into words,' she adds, 'that I make it whole' (MB, 85). Only then can she persuade herself that the world will not hurt her or spit in her face. Woolf, in other words, might seek a fictionalist solution to the problem of doubt or an even deeper ontological insecurity in her life. 'How can I proceed . . . without illusion?' a figure asks towards the end of *The Waves* (W, 219). 'Why should one try?' another part of Woolf seems to answer. Seeing through illusion in a double sense may be our only option.

6

Ironies—Lewis

IN THE 1930S Wyndham Lewis asked a bald and self-referential question: 'Is the naked truth exactly what we require as human beings?'[1] His answer was a firm 'no' though this too might have been a bluff. He certainly liked to dismantle other people's dreams and to confiscate their comfort blankets—all those 'illusions hugged and lived in.'[2] If Woolf clung to the beautiful illusions of manners, Lewis preferred, if not quite the naked truth, then at least the ancient art of being rude. He had no time for 'Bloomsbury pantomime.'[3] He also devoted himself to disparaging romantics of all sorts—figures who were incapable, he believed, of distinguishing between fact and fiction. Lewis's own desire to keep boundary lines in place was recorded in a series of strong oppositions between life and art, reality and fiction,[4] distinctions which he insisted should never be blurred.[5] So, Novalis's romantic proposal to treat life as one giant novel was not a game that Lewis openly liked to

1. Lewis, *Men Without Art*, 157. All further references are given in the text under the abbreviation 'MWA.'

2. Lewis, 'Inferior Religions,' in *The Wild Body*, 151. All further references are given in the text under the abbreviation 'WB.'

3. Lewis, *Apes of God*, 81.

4. As we hear in *Tarr*: 'Life is art's rival and vice versa.' Lewis, *Tarr*, 293. All further references are to the 1918 edition—unless clearly shown otherwise—and are given in the text under the abbreviation 'T.' Zageus puts it less antagonistically, if no less emphatically, in *The Apes of God*: 'The real should not compete with creations of Fiction. There should be two worlds not one' (258).

5. Lewis, *Blast*, 1, 147. All further references are given in the text under the abbreviation 'B1.'

play.[6] Here was a man who wanted to keep things real—or at least pretended to do so.

But even pretending wasn't easy. Lewis's arduous self-education in philosophy—conducted very publicly in books like *Time and Western Man* (1927)—confirmed what he intimated throughout his novels: that the 'real' is not directly given to us, that it is mediated by concepts and ideas, and that the ontological status or terms of reference of this mind-stuff were not clear-cut. He emerged from a few rounds with Kant convinced, for instance, that 'illusion must be our "real."'[7] If Kant had denied our knowledge of things-in-themselves, he had at least insisted on our knowledge of appearances, and this is the position that Lewis often retreats to in *Time and Western Man*. He invites us to call off the search for ultimates and to accept the superficial truth:

> But we are surface-creatures only, and by nature are meant to be only that, if there is any meaning in nature. No metaphysician goes the whole length of departure from the surface-condition of mind—that fact is not generally noticed. For such departures result in self-destruction, just as though we hurled ourself into space—into 'mental-space,' if you like, in this case. We are surface-creatures, and the 'truths' from beneath the surface contradict our values. It is among the flowers and leaves that our lot is cast, and the roots, however 'interesting,' are not so ultimate for us. For us the ultimate thing is the surface, the last-comer, and that is committed to a plurality of being. (TWM, 377)

This investment in appearances was certainly pragmatic, but it could sound very much like the fictionalism that he so often disparaged—a romantic invitation to live 'as if' despite our intuitions that all is not quite so. Lewis's devotion to surfaces remained consistent with the 'externalist' method he advocated for much of his artistic life—a method that accepts the hard edges of our world and resists the metaphysical lure of '*The Great Within*' (MWA, 123). Lewis appeared to have picked

6. Novalis, *Philosophical Writings*, 66.

7. Lewis, *Time and Western Man*, 378. All further references are given in the text under the abbreviation 'TWM.'

his side—'I am for the Great Without'—and he used this as a basis to distance himself from the moral and metaphysical claptrap of personhood: a tabernacle of inwardness that vouchsafed the dignity and freedom of 'persons' and the real meaning of their deeds (MWA, 128). Truth may be on the surface, but problems always arise for would-be surface-lovers—post-metaphysical Nietzscheans, neo-Wittgensteinians, or today's critics of the hermeneutics of depth—when the surfaces themselves have pretentions to profundity: when texts gesture at their deeper meaning, when humans claim to be free or declare the reality of their own inwardness, etc. What should we do with these unruly surfaces and their stubborn dreams?

Lewis often found himself in two minds on this question. Two-mindedness, of course, was close to being a virtue for Lewis—insofar as virtues existed in his dark universe. As Lewis announced in *Blast* in 1915: 'You must talk with two tongues.'[8] The first edition of the magazine had already provided a rationale for this two-tongued talk: 'We start from opposite statements of a chosen world. Set up violent structure of adolescent clearness between two extremes' (B1, 30). The extremes were traced out further in the blast-and-bless method of his manifestoes, though the contrariness continued for much of his career. The political thought of *The Art of Being Ruled* (1926), for instance, was allegedly 'inspired by the Hegelian dialectic, with its thesis and anti-thesis—to state, here and there, both sides of the question to be debated and allow those opposites to struggle in the reader's mind for the ascendancy and there to find their synthesis.'[9] It was a strangely democratic or readerly outlook in a book devoted to the inadequacies of much of what we call democracy.

If Hegel's dialectic was propelled by a dichotomising between subject and object—between a personal viewpoint and an impersonal one—much of Lewis's own writing is organised around a similar schism. The division is clearly apparent in his distinction between an 'internal' and an 'external' approach (MWA, 127), in the gaps between a third-person

8. Lewis, *Blast 2*, 91. All further references to this edition will be given in the text under the abbreviation 'B2.'

9. Lewis, *Rude Assignment*, 183. All further references are given in the text under the abbreviation 'RA.'

viewpoint and a first-person perspective ('the seeing-of-ourselves-as-others-see-us, and the self-picture' [MWA, 122]), alongside the rift he discovered between an agent's outlook and a spectator's ('it is impossible to be an observer and a participant at once' [RA, 76]). Lewis was a man who liked to spectate—as he confided to Pound in a Nietzschean vein: 'Life, as you know, is only justifiable as a spectacle.'[10] He also liked to watch from a position of extreme detachment. Naturally, he wondered at times how detached it was possible or desirable to be, but he gave the method a good go, seeing it as the only route to objectivity (MWA, 121). From Lewis's space station in 'the Great Without' human affairs could look trivial indeed. He clearly exulted in the deflationary effect of a detached perspective and was even prepared to wax moral about its significance: It weaned us from 'our soft conceit' (MWA, 121). Good satire may be 'non-ethical' and 'non-moral' (MWA, 107), but this also explained why 'Satire is *good*!' (MWA, 121).

The perversities of this appraisal indicate how hard it might be to sustain a detached, 'non-personal,' 'non-human' outlook (MWA, 121). It can get lonely in the space station, and even Lewis acknowledged the dangers of a 'transcendental viewpoint' (MWA, 288). Much of life, after all, is lived *in* the world, not above it. As Lewis pointed out to a young correspondent in 1949, we are participants in life, not just amused spectators, and 'can't reasonably despise *all* the people who do something.'[11] Moreover, as agents in and of the world humans find it difficult not to care about things and even Lewis found himself in the vulnerable position of caring from time to time. We care, moreover, in the first person, however we may extend it across a third, and we tend to experience ourselves as subjects as much as we remain objects. Lewis acknowledged the draw,

10. Lewis, *The Correspondence of Ezra Pound and Wyndham Lewis*, 86.

11. See Wyndham Lewis to David Kahma, 3 September 1949, in *The Letters of Wyndham Lewis*, 506. While noting the tension between the 'participant attitude' and the 'objective attitude,' Peter Strawson plausibly maintains: 'A sustained objectivity . . . and the human isolation which that would entail, does not seem to be something of which human beings would be capable, even if some general truth were a theoretical ground for it.' See Strawson, *Freedom and Resentment*, 10, 12.

even the reality, of this situated, agential, and personal perspective, however he may have tried to write it off from an external, quasi-objective viewpoint. So, he often seemed to submit to the world ironically, nursing a self-conscious doubleness within himself. 'Why try and give the impression of a consistent and indivisible personality?' he asked in *Blast*. 'You must be a duet in everything' (B2, 91). But he also entertained double-thoughts about this doubleness. In books like *The Apes of God* (1930), for instance, he disparaged the 'Split-Man' and distanced himself from this torn figure through a series of racist stereotypes.

We may pale at the contradictions, but Lewis had clearly signed up to contradiction in principle and in practice ('Contradict yourself. In order to live, you must remain broken up').[12] Live the gospel he did, but it makes it difficult to decipher what Lewis ultimately believed or what we should believe of him. If '*reality* is in fact simply *belief*,' as he boldly announced in 1927 (TWM, 351), then it's probably impossible to say how much reality Lewis ever enjoyed or how much he could believe in belief. He certainly knew the dangers of having no beliefs: As we shall see, the hazards of a completely adoxastic state is a frightening motif of his fiction. He also attacked the idea that fiction itself was a belief-free zone, a mere assembly of pseudo-beliefs piggybacking on a series of pseudo-statements. Lewis attributed this '*Disbelief Theory*' to I. A. Richards and T. S. Eliot (MWA, 77), even though Eliot had publicly distanced himself from Richards's claim that the poet had produced 'a complete severance between his poetry and *all* beliefs.'[13] If Eliot doubted the viability and desirability of such a severance, Lewis insisted, nonetheless, on presenting the poet as a convinced 'pseudoist.' There was something insincere, Lewis felt, in Eliot's devotion to an impersonal poetry or 'the suppression of the personality and the creation of a privileged *play-boy alter ego*' (MWA, 88). Once again, Lewis seemed to toss rocks from a glasshouse:

12. Lewis, 'The Code of the Herdman,' 7.

13. Richards, *Poetry and Science*, 76. Eliot, moreover, had done the distancing in Lewis's own journal. See Eliot, 'A Note on Poetry and Belief.'

> If there is to be an 'insincerity,' I prefer it should occur in the opposite sense—namely that 'the man, the personality' should exaggerate, a little artificially perhaps, his beliefs—rather than leave a meaningless shell behind him, and go to hide in a volatilized hypostasization of his personal feelings. That may be more 'insincere' in the one sense, but for the extrovert activities it is more satisfactory: the man is thus 'most himself' (even if a little too much himself to be quite the perfect self, on occasion). (MWA, 91)

By defending a histrionics of conviction, Lewis also seemed to present himself as a devoted 'pseudoist,' someone who performs himself to the point of pantomime. The aim, as he once put it in *Blast*, is to become 'an amorphous imitation of yourself inside yourself' (B2, 91). This may be a Vorticist's guide to authenticity, but it is also the code of a fictionalist—a figure who pretends to believe that he really believes and always risks demonstrating to himself that he doesn't. As the Bailiff puts it in *The Childermass* (1928): 'To be human is to bluff.'[14] If we have largely lauded the fictive attitude throughout this book—its epistemic athleticism, its mix of flexibility and openness, its knack of double vision—then Lewis might give us pause and make us wonder about its limits. For he shows how this attitude can become disastrously overextended. This was the cautionary tale that Lewis drew of the romantic soul, a figure who could only play with reality or treat all life as fiction. The problem is brilliantly enacted in *Tarr*—Lewis's first and arguably finest novel and the work I will focus on here—though the issue is staged throughout his oeuvre. Lewis recognised the importance of being earnest, but as we can see from the theatre of conviction recommended above, he also found sincerity an ordeal. Commuting from his station in 'the Great Without,' he returned to human fictions with an insuppressible leer. This was a condition of irony—a response to and enactment of the 'Eternal Duet of Existence' (B2, 91). But Lewis helps us to see that irony has its toxic sides. He was clearly alert to the hazards, but this only seemed to make the sickness worse. His was a terminal case: humour without end.

14. Lewis, *The Human Age: Book 1: Childermass*, 337.

Blast the Romantic

If Lewis defined the 'romantic' as '*the opposite of the real,*' he spent much of his career pretending to be reality's bulldog (TWM, 5). He was, however, a pretty late combatant in this particular culture war. From Goethe to Hegel to Nietzsche in Germany, through to Lasserre and Maurras in France, and on to Hulme and Eliot in England, the moral and epistemic sicknesses of romanticism had been endlessly diagnosed, with several antidotes proposed (strong doses of classicism, for instance, were often deemed the best treatment method). Like many of his predecessors, Lewis identified romanticism with at least three interrelated vices: a sentimentalisation of nature,[15] a cult of emotion (the nature within oneself), and an exorbitant subjectivism or metaphysical inwardness. 'By definition,' he explained, 'romance is always inside and not outside. It is as we say subjective. It is the material of magic. It partakes of the action of a drug.'[16] Romantic inwardness appears as a type of psychosis in 'Franciscan Adventures' (1927). The tramp in this story—'a sickly figure of early republican romance'—literally wrestles with his own imagination, fighting fictitious antagonists and other phantoms of the mind while remaining ostentatiously unmoved by his real circumstances (WB, 131). Spellbound by his own inner music, he loses touch 'more and more with unlyricized reality' (WB, 121).[17]

Romanticism was easily satirised, but, as Lewis discovered, it was not so easily escaped. The problem stemmed in part from the elusiveness of what he was so keen to defend—raw reality—but the issue had also a more practical dimension, with Lewis locking horns with romantics over the nature of personhood and one of its defining attributes: freedom. The 'complexity of the problem of human freedom,'[18] for Lewis, and his

15. Lewis, *The Enemy*, 150. Irving Babbitt also identified romanticism with an 'emotional naturalism.' Babbitt, *Rousseau and Romanticism*, x.

16. Lewis, *Blasting and Bombadiering*, 121. All further references will appear in the text under the abbreviation 'BB.'

17. As Schelling explained, modern lyric poetry has 'a preponderance of reflection and subjectivity, since it lacks any objectivity in life.' See Schelling, *The Philosophy of Art*, 211.

18. Lewis, *The Mysterious Mr Bull*, 199.

devotion to that problem, are all too easily transcended by reports of Lewis's 'anti-individualism' or 'post-individualistic' outlook—a position in which the 'illusion of freedom' is allegedly systematically exposed.[19] In *The Art of Being Ruled,* Lewis certainly wondered if the concept of liberty was not dead for most people; as he paradoxically puts it, 'The enemy of the human race, "liberty," is dead—and men are free once more!'[20] It is difficult to tell if Lewis disparages the masses for turning their backs on liberty or for entertaining such illusions in the first place. 'We each possess a sort of bogus "free will,"' he insisted in 1939, thus seeming to confirm his deep-seated hostility to a naive voluntarism.[21] Yet freedom is only '*sort of* bogus.' If it is an illusion, then it is one that is constitutive of humanity: However unverifiable, this foundational 'as if' makes humans what they are. As he put it in 1927, 'The instinct for freedom' is something 'we all have' (TWM, 297). For all the talk of Lewis's 'antihumanism'[22]—and his own apparent quest for a 'non-human,' even 'inhuman,' outlook—he was reluctant to retire a normative conception of humanity in which freedom operated as a fundamental value. As he emphatically declared in 1934: '*Freedom* is certainly our human goal' (MWA, 116). Even his disastrous support for Hitler was cast, however opportunistically, as a fight 'for the sake of freedom.'[23]

But if a belief in freedom is a basic condition of humanity, it can never be properly shown to exist. This conundrum of liberty cuts across Lewis's entire oeuvre and is one of the generative problems of *Tarr*. Whatever way we interpret liberty (as independence or spontaneity or as a more demanding form of self-rule), it remains a highly ambiguous value in Lewis's first novel: Cherished as an ideal, it is also disparaged as an illusion, yielding an ambivalence that is never ultimately resolved. The

19. Peppis, 'Anti-Individualism and Fictions of National Character in Wyndham Lewis's *Tarr*'; Jameson, *Fables of Aggression*, 109; Levenson, *Modernism and the Fate of Individuality*, 130.

20. Lewis, *The Art of Being Ruled*, 132. All further references will appear in the text under the abbreviation 'ABR.'

21. Lewis, *The Hitler Cult*, 178.

22. Sherry, 'Anatomy of Folly,' 123; Sheehan, *Modernism, Narrative, and Humanism*, 103; Ophir, 'Toward a Pitiless Fiction.'

23. Lewis, *Hitler*, 202. Further references will appear in the text under the abbreviation 'H.'

irresolution is bound up with the novel's use of irony—an irony that is itself expressive of the problem of freedom. Irony distances individuals from their world, affording them some transcendence or liberty of assent over their circumstances, but the same ironic distance impedes individuals from becoming practical agents within the world: It is an impotent or practically inefficacious form of freedom. For Hegel, such irony was one of the hallmarks of the romantic. The same ironic impotence also explains why 'political romanticism' is virtually an oxymoron for Carl Schmitt: Irony precludes genuine decision and decisive action—in other words, it forfeits from the start the basic prerequisites of the political. Schmitt was an admirer of Lewis and wondered if they were not kindred souls.[24] Their mutual antipathy to romanticism—and indeed liberalism—might suggest that they were, but as we shall see, *Tarr* also critiques the idea of the groundless decision or decisive deed which was later championed by Schmitt as an alternative to romantic indecision and liberal paralysis. The modern 'romance of action'—as Lewis later identified it—was a surrender of freedom, not a bold assertion of agency (TWM, 20).

The case against romanticism in *Tarr* is largely advanced through the novel's eponymous hero. Modernists often asserted their antiromantic credentials through intemperate attacks on Rousseau,[25] and Frederick Tarr is no exception: He boasts, for instance, that his worldview is 'the exact opposite of Jean-Jacques" (T, 228)—and in Tarr's eyes, the gospel of Jean-Jacques is essentially an emotional naturalism. And yet Tarr remains a curiously Rousseauian figure. Like the author of the *Second Discourse* (1754), Tarr yearns for an unsullied independence and regards social life as a severe constraint ('we are all sicknesses for each other' [T, 63]). He believes the 'individual is rustic' and sometimes views nature as a pure space of freedom (T, 11). Indeed, the admiration is reciprocal: 'Nature,' we are told (in a narrative voice that often indulges the romanticism of its subject), 'loved the genius and liberty in him' (T, 47). Tarr insists that his rallying cry—'Back to the Earth!'—is

24. Schmitt, *Aufzeichnungen der Jahre 1947–1951*, 16.

25. See Dwan, 'Modernism and Rousseau.'

not a Rousseauian credo (T, 304). Rousseau 'poetized his wild nature' and sentimentalised its goodness, but nature, for Tarr, is an aggressive, even malign, energy (T, 228).

The ambiguity of this antiromanticism is clearly anticipated (if not inspired) by Nietzsche, even if Tarr tends to view himself as a vast improvement on the superman (T, 304). Nietzsche had mocked Rousseau's putative belief in the recoverability of naturalness; however, on other occasions he sponsored his own 'return to nature'—a return that would nonetheless lead him away from clichés of natural goodness towards a 'high, free, even terrible nature.'[26] Tarr also despairs of the conventional morality-tale that masquerades as nature, and wants to unleash a more authentic form of naturalness. He presents himself as a 'new animal'; in Anastasya's mocking eyes, however, he is merely Rousseau reborn (T, 304). Tarr, and perhaps Lewis himself, suspect that their sustained campaign against romanticism is another version of the same thing.[27] Tarr simply inverts its traditional content: 'He, instead of having conceived the world as more chivalrous and marvellous than it was, had conceived it as empty of all dignity, sense, and generousness.' These are 'inverse illusions'—no less fantastical than the romanticism they supplant (T, 236).

Tarr's ambiguous appraisal of nature is expressive of the problem of freedom. Total liberty, for Tarr, seems to imply an absence of social determination, which is why nature, when conceived, at least, as a presocial or asocial state, is sometimes cast as a site of freedom. Throughout the narrative he worries about the ways other people may connive against his independence. He regards love as a 'malady' (T, 62) that leads to a loss of self or a bad conquest of others, and he is similarly dismissive of friendship: There 'are no "friends" in this life' (T, 15). Ironically, much of Tarr's gospel of independence is elaborated in discussion with others; in fact, a 'great many of Frederick Tarr's resolutions came from his conversation' (T, 19). But embarrassed by this social dependence,

26. Nietzsche, *Will to Power*, 72, 73. Nietzsche, *The Anti-Christ, Ecce Homo, Twilight of the Idols and Other Writings*, 221.

27. Eliot, 'Contemporanea.'

Tarr chooses to present communication in a way that is trivially true but also deeply tendentious, as merely a public means of communing with himself. Thus, when he 'solicited advice, it was transparently a matter of form' (T, 21). Other people, he insists, are mere catalysts, never a real source of good counsel—a fact which interlocutors such as Butcher deeply resent.

The narrative voice provides a highly charitable interpretation of Tarr's spirit of independence (although here a form of free indirect discourse may be working to expose the full extent of his self-delusion): 'He was the kind of man who, if he ever should wish to influence the world, would do it so that he might touch himself more plastically through others' (T, 22). This masturbatory fantasy is merely given a little more frisson by the mediation of other people. If Carl Schmitt associated romanticism with a 'subjectified occasionalism'—an attitude that assumes that there are no genuine agents or causes outside of the ego itself—then elements of this self-absorption can be seen in Tarr.[28] Other people are a mere 'occasion' for Tarr's experience of himself. This is painfully evident in his break-up with Bertha Lunken: It is undertaken 'to test a funny mood'—a mood of '*complete indifference*' (T, 51–52). Bertha is simply a setting for Tarr's own psychological drama; paradoxically, his indifference is the only true object of interest.

Predictably, Tarr disparages the herd morality of others and gazes at them with 'autocratic scorn'—'autocracy,' literally self-government, seems to be his primary ambition (T, 11). Tarr sometimes implies, of course, that he has no self to govern or from which to govern. In a much-discussed passage, he presents himself as a series of painted mummy-cases, containing 'nothing but innumerable other painted cases inside, smaller and smaller ones.' At the bottom of this recursive series there is no 'live core,' only another painting like the rest: 'His kernel was a painting'—an entirely appropriate existential state, Tarr believes, for an artist (T, 46). But this seeming disavowal of the self's underlying essence is, potentially at least, a radicalisation of the idea of freedom as self-determination. Much depends, of course, on the authorship of the

28. Schmitt, *Political Romanticism*, 17–18.

painting and what (if anything) it depicts, whether it is expressive, mimetic, or a mixed kind of self-imitation that is also self-constituting. Tarr's inner painting raises the idea, at least, that the self is its own work of art. It points to a radical freedom in which the project of self-determination is not constrained in advance by an essential core. Here even the content of the self must be self-determined or self-authored if Tarr's autocratic ambitions are to be realised. Arguably, Nietzsche was an advocate of this radical form of self-creation, although the roots of the idea stretch back to Fichte's self-positing 'I.' As Fichte put it, 'It is the very nature of I-hood to determine itself unconditionally.'[29] But Tarr finds it difficult to secure his independence from any thing or value that is not rooted in himself. Indeed, he is 'bitterly ashamed of a slovenly, common portion of [his] life' steered by heteronomous norms and expressive of his sad dependency on others (T, 13). His desire for society and, in particular, his sexual interest in women, seduce him away from the project of total self-rule.

Tarr, as a consequence, has an almost Platonic distrust of the senses and believes that bodily desire connives against freedom. 'A man,' he declares, 'is the opposite of his appetite' (T, 7). Since the appetites of the body are sensible and are subject to the laws of physical necessity, they appear to be antithetical to genuine freedom. Like his fictional hero, Lewis repeatedly disparaged 'living for sensation' as a seductive type of thraldom (ABR, 136). And he championed in its stead a 'very rare freedom . . . possessed by the intellect alone.' This freedom 'is contingent on no physical circumstance' in a way that implies that the intellect is some noumenal entity transcending material forms of determination (ABR, 135). If absolute freedom, for Lewis, implies the sovereignty of the intellect, it also seems to involve a radical type of spontaneity—a form of agency or causal power that is not subject to other causes. The determination of appetite and even emotion do not meet these conditions: They are triggered in part by internal causes that are ultimately contingent on external factors. To make emotion or bodily desire criterial for one's action is to surrender to contingency and so to abdicate one's freedom.

29. Fichte, *Foundations of Transcendental Philosophy*, 315.

It is arguable whether anyone in *Tarr* is really free in this fully indeterminist sense, but the thraldom of the appetite is perhaps best captured in the risible figure of Otto Kreisler. He remains, throughout the narrative, a slave to his own passions, locked within the realm of physical necessity. Kreisler's subjection to the biochemical laws of his own nature is starkly depicted in the 1928 edition of *Tarr*. Note, for instance, the following description of Kreisler's gaze: 'How could it be expected to understand? It was an eye, and it stuck—it blinked—it trembled. It signalled: the gland shot a tear into it. It clouded. It was simple though: it was amazed and did not understand.'[30] This is a resolutely physical depiction, with Lewis's 'philosophy of the EYE,' routing the pretentions of the would-be 'I' (MWA, 118). So, the subject of perception here is simply a biological organ, the impersonal mechanics of which are emphasised through the repeated subject pronoun 'it,' while the syntactical chain—'it stuck—it blinked—it trembled. It signalled. . . . It clouded'—enacts a series of sensory inputs and outputs that never yield anything so spiritual as understanding. No one in Lewis is entirely exempt from this hyper-physical rendering—it is basic to his self-described 'externalist' method—but Kreisler, in particular, is ruthlessly reduced.[31] In the 1918 edition, Kreisler is already a profoundly heteronomous creature; he is 'a property of Nature, or a favourite slave' (T, 75). In the 1928 version of the novel, he becomes 'a thing, scarcely any longer a Mensch' (T2, 102).

Kreisler's enslavement to nature points to a fundamental ambiguity in *Tarr* and the rest of Lewis's work: Nature is at times a space of freedom outside social determination, but at other times it is a prison—a causal system in which everything is subject to mechanical laws. This is why romanticism is such a disaster for Lewis: The identification with nature that it sponsors as an ideal of freedom is, in fact, freedom's opposite. Consequently, many of Lewis's heroic figures turn their backs on nature. In the 1932 version of *The Enemy of the Stars*, for instance, Arghol

30. Lewis, *Tarr*, 103. Further references to the 2010 edition will be given in the text under the abbreviation 'T2.'

31. Lewis, *Creatures of Habit and Creatures of Change*, 201. All further references will appear in the text under the abbreviation 'CHCC.'

commands Hanp to return to 'bustling Mother Nature, and spit in her face.'[32] As the gendering of nature suggests, Lewis's anti-naturalism travels hand-in-hand with a fierce misogyny. Women, it would appear, are nature's mercenaries: In 'Cantleman's Spring-Mate'—one of Lewis's most rancid short stories—all women are 'contaminated with Nature's hostile power and might be treated as spies or enemies.' Tarr may regard sexual congress with a woman as a bad surrender to natural determination, but Cantleman is convinced that once it is engaged in with sufficient violence that he is 'outwitting Nature.'[33] Kreisler's rape of Bertha may express the same unhinged vindictiveness, but it ultimately confirms his unfreedom as much as it may protest against it: He had 'revenged himself as a machine might do' (T, 187). However, in the narrator's judgement, this mechanical vengeance is entirely apt as far as Bertha is concerned. She has sentimentalised mechanism by glorifying the passions; the unfreedom she exalts is finally visited upon her as the horror of rape. Such 'conclusive physical matters,' the narrator callously concludes, 'were a culmination of her romance' (T, 181). Women are thus the scapegoats as much as they are the advocates of incontinence in Lewis. 'The Feminine Conception of Freedom' (ABR, 239)—namely, the pathology of emotion and 'hostility to the intellect'—is Lewis's version of slavery (ABR, 244).

Lewis may cast women as symbols of unfreedom, but this misogyny brings small comfort to his male protagonists. Freedom remains a problem for everyone in Lewis's bleak universe, and it stems from two main factors: first, the social constitution of the self and, second, its embodied nature. These facts of selfhood preclude absolute independence and spontaneity—the prerequisites of freedom in an indeterminist sense. The relentless use of machine metaphors in his prose, and human automata in his painting, gives the lie to this model of freedom. Human beings often seem to inhabit an entirely determined cosmos: They are complex machines trapped within the larger mechanism of nature. Thus, Bertha is a 'contented machine' (T, 286), Anastasya is a 'larger

32. Lewis, *Collected Poems and Plays*, 176.

33. Lewis, 'Cantleman's Spring-Mate,' 13, 14.

machine of repressed, moping senses' (T, 203), Kreisler is a 'large rusty machine of a man' (T, 137), and Tarr is an unwieldy locomotive 'full of sinister piston-rods, organ-like shapes, heavy drills' (T, 4). In 1934, Lewis argued that romanticism was a desperate attempt to salvage freedom from mechanism: It attempted to step 'outside the machine' by invoking a purely personal emotion (CHCC, 225). However, by making emotion a constituent of freedom, the romantic libertarian merely capitulates to the mechanism they deplore. Perhaps so, but Lewis's own responses to mechanism were highly unstable. Anxious to resist romantic myths of escape, he often talked up, or even celebrated, humanity's subjection to mechanical laws. For instance, he claimed that the central tenet of Vorticism was that '"the inner world of the imagination" was not an asylum from the brutality of mechanical life.' Vorticism, as he put it, 'identified itself with that brutality.'[34] Yet Lewis also wished to dissociate humanity from mechanism as ardently as any so-called romantic. In fact, all art rested on the premise 'that, although helpless in the face of the material world, we are in some way superior to and independent of it.'[35] Irony was an expression of this superiority and independence for Lewis, though it turns out to be a very troubled attempt to escape the machine.

The Laughing Animal

Lewis's remarks on comedy provide us with an initial steer on the more general question of irony in his work.[36] Comedy, he claimed in 1927, arose from the disjunction between freedom and physical necessity. This incompatibility made human beings irreducibly ridiculous, 'for they are all *things*, or physical bodies, behaving as *persons*'—that is to say, as if they are free agents (WB, 158). As Lewis readily admits, his views about comedy ultimately rest on the dichotomy between mind and body; this is his enabling 'as if'—something he self-consciously

34. Lewis, *Wyndham Lewis On Art*, 341.

35. Lewis, *Tyro*, 1.2, 26.

36. Or as Lewis put it: '*Homo animal ridens*, that is it—that is our true description' (MWA, 288).

assumes without 'arguing for it' (WB, 156). On the basis of this metaphysical assumption, human beings seem to be intrinsically absurd, for they are ultimately inexplicable to themselves and to others: There is no way of squaring humanity's pretension to freedom with the mechanical laws of the physical universe. Thus the 'movement or intelligent behaviour of matter, any autonomous movement of matter, is essentially comic' (WB, 159).

According to Lewis, the absurdity of things behaving as persons is only dispelled when the concept of a 'person,' 'mind,' 'self'—or whatever ghost that traditionally resides in the machine—is retired. His use of irony is often read as such a proposal; it is a systematic attack on traditional superstitions of selfhood.[37] Thus Lewis purportedly inverts Henri Bergson's popular theories of laughter: If comedy, for Bergson, is a reprimand to humans for behaving as automata, Lewis ridicules them for ever courting the belief that they could be otherwise. But this interpretation seems at odds with both the sense and weighting of Lewis's claim that 'the state of . . . the human being is more desirable than the state of the automaton.'[38] And while Lewis clearly delights in exposing the hubris and self-delusion of much of humanity's pretensions to freedom, he also struggles to hide his own commitment to the principle. After all, human absurdity stems from the fact that a man is 'ridiculous *because he is a man,* instead of a thing' (WB, 159). Lewis thus makes the positive assertion that humans are distinct from or are more than material objects and, in doing so, he appears to preserve his faith in the category of the person. He also retains the mind-body dualisms that have often accompanied metaphysical accounts of personhood: He thus approves of a man who dissociates himself from the 'machine' he inhabits, emphatically endorsing his conviction that 'the man's body was not him' (WB, 160). This may, perhaps, be a simple ventriloquisation of a vain conceit, but the vanity is constitutive: It makes humans what they are. Unlike potatoes, lampposts, or stones (Lewis's examples), human beings pretend to be free agents. They are

37. Sherry, 'Anatomy of Folly,' 123–24; North, *Machine-Age Comedy*, 118.

38. Lewis, *Tyro*, 1.2, 26.

thus absurd, for such claims cannot be fully squared with their physical constitution.

Lewis was not the first to wrestle with this seeming absurdity. The apparent contradiction between freedom and physical determinism had led figures such as Kant, for instance, to distinguish between a phenomenal world governed by iron laws of physical necessity and a noumenal realm that was independent of space and time and in which freedom was, at least, a theoretical possibility. For Kant, freedom was a necessary postulate of practical life, but it could never really be known to exist, because freedom was spontaneous or unconditioned, while knowledge of any phenomenon—according to the second analogy of the 'First Critique'—involved relating phenomena to anterior conditions and causes.[39] So freedom as an uncaused cause could never be known.

One might argue that the 'unknowability' of freedom made any discussion of it fundamentally ironic—ironic, that is, in the sense sketched out by Friedrich Schlegel, according to whom the irresolvable conflict between the unconditioned and conditioned, or 'the absolute and the relative' is the constitutive feature of irony.[40] The ironist attempts to access the absolute while simultaneously conceding that any attempt to know the unconditioned would falsify it by reducing it to a determinate concept and making it seem conditioned or relative. Irony thus attests to both the impossibility and practical necessity of communication about unconditioned entities. If freedom is entirely unconditioned, it might be viewed as the ultimate object of irony in Schlegel's sense, but Schlegel himself did not make this connection, perhaps because he grew increasingly sceptical of Kant's indeterminist account of freedom and the dualisms that were used to sustain such an all-or-nothing liberty.[41] Yet, according to Hegel's uncharitable assessment, Schlegel's theory of irony was an extravagant commitment to freedom in this indeterminist sense: It was an attitude adopted by an ego that regarded every condition or determining ground for the self as inimical to its freedom.

39. Kant, *Critique of Pure Reason*, 304.

40. Schlegel, *Philosophical Fragments*, 13.

41. See Beiser, *The Romantic Imperative*, 149–52.

Schlegel had modelled his own conception of irony on the practice of Socrates: It was a principled scepticism operating in the service of absolute truth. But Hegel maintained that Schlegel's style of romantic irony was the exact opposite: It abandoned truth in the name of infinite scepticism, acknowledging no absolute apart from that great virtuoso of doubt—the ego itself. Romantic irony was thus a shallow subjectivism; here 'nothing is treated *in and for itself* and as valuable in itself, but only as produced by the subjectivity of the *ego*.'[42] In Hegel's eyes, this vanity was ultimately self-defeating; ascribing no intrinsic value to the world, the ego could not take itself seriously as an empirical agent within the world. Moreover, pledged to an infinity of possibilities, the ironist could never limit himself to any determinate conclusion, value, or project. Schlegel, in fact, condemned people for remaining in 'possible worlds' removed from any actual existence; he also stressed the 'value & divinity of self-restriction' in the face of infinite possibilities, but these remarks were either overlooked or ignored by Hegel.[43] Hegel simply continued to insist that romantic irony repudiated all restriction and limitation. It culminated in a form of paralysis that masqueraded as freedom.

Lewis ultimately produced a very similar indictment of irony while remaining addicted to the empty freedom of an ironic attitude. Despite what the Hegels and Schlegels of the world might profess, irony—or a particular subset of it called humour—is, for Lewis, a distinctly English trait, although he sometimes extends it into a British or Northern characteristic. It is a trait that Lewis also attributes to himself: 'You must not think that I dissociate myself from the humorous outlook. I am terribly English: I am always laughing.'[44] From the outset of his career he produced diametrically opposed visions of humour: 'BLAST HUMOUR Quack ENGLISH drug for stupidity and sleepiness' (B1, 17); 'BLESS ENGLISH HUMOUR it is the great barbarous weapon of the genius

42. Hegel, *Aesthetics*, 1.64.

43. Schlegel, *Philosophical Fragments*, 22, 4.

44. Lewis, *The Mysterious Mr Bull*, 95.

among races' (B1, 26); 'The English "Sense of Humour" is the Great Enemy of England' (B2, 11); 'BLESS ALL ENGLISH EYES that grow crows-feet with their FANCY and ENERGY' (B1, 26). These contradictions are expressive of the humour that they simultaneously evaluate; as Lewis announces, 'We set Humour at Humour's throat' (B1, 31). Schlegel maintained that paradox was the supreme form of irony, committed as the ironist is both to the need for, and to the impossibility of, communication about the unconditional.[45] Lewis equally revels in the infinite jest of paradox: 'We discharge ourselves on both sides. . . . We fight first on one side, then on the other, but always for the SAME cause, which is neither side or both sides and ours' (B1, 30).

This extreme contrariness might be viewed as Socratic irony or perhaps even, as he later proposed, Hegelian 'dialectic' (RA, 183)—contradiction in the service of the absolute or at least the reader's freedom to decide. But presumably Hegel would have been inclined to regard these blasts and blessings as a belated instance of romantic irony—one that treats logic itself as a constraint on freedom. Even the law of contradiction is one law too many for Lewis, and he performs his devotion to his own freedom in an ironic doubleness or a long series of boo-hurrahs. In *Blast*, humour is the guarantor of a fraught independence—operating as a 'hysterical WALL built around the EGO'—allowing the ironist an anxious distance from the limited and limiting perspectives he uses to define the world and that might define him. In this context, Lewis is prepared to bless the 'separating, ungregarious BRITISH GRIN.' He also praises the 'solitude of LAUGHTER' (B1, 26). But the same isolating properties of humour also mean that it risks degenerating into an extreme subjectivism and consequently becoming the 'Arch enemy' of reality (B1, 17). As Hegel maintained, romantic humour entails 'the perversion and derangement of everything objective and real by means of wit and the play of a subjective outlook.'[46] Lewis admitted to the practical hazards of this subjectivism in 'A Soldier of Humour.' The narrator here has an incurable case of the metaphysical giggles:

45. Schlegel, *Philosophical Fragments*, 6.
46. Hegel, *Aesthetics*, 1.576.

> I am *never* serious about anything. I simply cannot help converting everything into burlesque patterns. And I admit that I am disposed to forget that people are real—that they are, that is, not subjective patterns belonging specifically to me, in the course of this joke-life, which indeed has for its very principle a denial of the accepted actual. (WB, 6)

Tarr also worries about the solipsism of humour: 'Humour paralyses the sense for reality and wraps people in a phlegmatic and hysterical dream-world' (T, 27). He is resolved to escape these chimeras and declares a moratorium on irony, but he can never quite deliver on this resolve: 'The curse of humour was in him, anchoring him at one end of the see-saw whose movement and contradiction was life' (T, 236–37).

Tarr, it seems, is the romantic ironist par excellence—particularly as this figure is represented by Hegel and by Schmitt. He regards all social forms as a limit to his freedom; yet he also recognises that he cannot subsist without these forms. So, he submits to them ironically, approaching life not quite as a novel but as a farce—if not always a particularly amusing one. His relationship with Bertha is a 'weary farce' (T, 47) or 'silly joke' (T, 22). His dealings with Kreisler are a 'half-farce' (T, 233). Kreisler himself is 'a joke,' albeit a particularly dangerous one ('Jokes . . . were able to make you sweat' [T, 238]). Tarr is ultimately aware that his irony is self-undermining and that his 'contempt for everyone degraded him' (T, 236). In the 1928 version of the novel, Lewis presents this as 'the Cynic's dishonourable condition,' but it is also the romantic ironist's—a sceptical standpoint that yields an impaired type of agency (T2, 206). Despite his autocratic ambitions, Tarr is a curiously parasitic creature: His character lacks the power 'to initiate anything of its own accord' (T, 238)—true freedom in an indeterminist philosophical scheme is a capacity for an 'absolute beginning,' but Tarr is incapable of it.[47] We are told that he co-opts the events of other people's lives, making them elements of the drama of his own existence, and while he likes to assume directorship of operations, he is cruelly embarrassed when he finds himself a performer in someone else's show. 'Tarr liked his own farces,'

47. Kant, *Critique of Pure Reason*, 409; Fichte, *Foundations of Transcendental Philosophy*, 288.

Lewis wrote in 1928, 'but to be drawn into the service of one of Kreisler's was a humiliation' (T2, 216). The supreme ironist now finds himself to be the plaything of others.

Given the novel's ironic treatment of its central ironist, it is unclear where *Tarr* ultimately stands on the question of irony. The very phrasing of this problem may seem question-begging or contradictory, since both the possibility and desirability of an ultimate stand about anything seems to be disputed by the presence of irony in the first place. The 'irony of irony,' Schlegel had noted in 1800, was that it rebounded upon itself and threatened to run wild, making its meaning or function impossible to recover.[48] The only way out of this problem, Schlegel maintained, was through a higher irony, one that subsumed all other ironies—although it is difficult to see how this supposedly transcendent irony would not trigger yet another ironic regress. Perhaps *Tarr* represents the higher irony that Schlegel had been waiting for: By ironising romantic irony, the novel potentially wins some purchase upon this condition and its attendant vices—subjectivism, scepticism, and moral paralysis. Schmitt proposed that romantics would have escaped the dead end of irony if they had been able to ironise themselves, but, unfortunately, they were incapable of this self-criticism.[49] Tarr, at least, is able to 'laugh at himself' and arguably the whole novel is a testament to Lewis's own capacity for self-ridicule (T, 236). Yet the danger remains that self-irony is merely a repetition of the ironic position it ridicules. So, while Tarr insists that 'the giving up of play . . . had to take the form of play,' this may be more a surrender to the problem of irony than an escape from it (T, 29). On another level, the novel's 'modernist' irony may be a simple amplification of the romantic gamesmanship condemned by Hegel, Schmitt, and Lewis himself.

The comedic features of *Tarr* are, perhaps, an expression of satire rather than mere humour, at least as Lewis later distinguished these terms. Humour, he argued in 1938, was a tame, morally circumscribed practice that baulks from 'laughing at *everything*' (CHCC, 280). In

48. Bernstein, *Classic and Romantic German Aesthetics*, 304.

49. Schmitt, *Political Romanticism*, 72–73.

satire, on the hand, the joke becomes absolute—it has 'no Queensberry Rules' or moral limits (CHCC, 282). If *Tarr* recognises no moral boundaries to the mechanics of its own wit, this may be because the novel has no moral foundations at all, the only certainty being its doubt about everything; it thus embodies the extreme form of scepticism that Hegel attributed to romantic irony. The novel's generic instability may be expressive of this scepticism—lurching between comedy and tragedy, it resists the ethical content that is arguably latent in both genres. Of course, the coherence of such all-encompassing scepticism may ultimately be disputed: Something needs to be believed, perhaps, for even doubt to be possible.[50] Absolute irony, therefore, is arguably a mood at odds with itself, for even irony would seem to require us to be serious about something. That said, it is difficult to determine what *Tarr* is ultimately serious about.

Resistance to a final standpoint or ultimate reckoning is clearly a 'romantic' attitude—at least in Lewis's mind. In the 'Song of the Militant Romance,' for instance, the romantic mantra 'never completion' reflects a desire for life to remain an absolute possibility or infinite 'promise' (CCP, 33). From this 'romantic' perspective, closure of any kind is a problem, for it represents a sad restriction of possibilities. The question haunts the ending of *Tarr*. The novel ostensibly ends with a marriage: Tarr marries Bertha who is pregnant with Kreisler's child. Tarr initially finds it hard to explain why he has 'gone through this form' (T, 314). His apparent concession to social form is also the novel's settlement upon a determinate aesthetic form—*Tarr* now appears to close like a conventional comedy of manners. But the novel circles back on its own conventionalism, debating the significance of its now no longer final marriage-act. In the ensuing debate between Tarr and Anastasya, the marriage is cast as an execution of a duty; the rhetoric of duty is construed in turn as a species of sentimentalism; sentimentality is subsequently presented (in a strained attempt to out-Nietzsche Nietzsche) as a '*privilege*' of the strong (T, 316). And so forth. The debate is never resolved; it is simply abandoned.

50. See Wittgenstein, *On Certainty*, 125.

Marriage may represent, for Tarr, a rare moment of decision, but the event has no binding qualities: He insists that things remain 'exactly the same as before,' allowing him to continue his affair with Anastasya (T, 314). True to his own subjectivism, Tarr's deed has only as much meaning as he is prepared to give it—in this instance, very little. In a final passage, effectively an epilogue, we learn that Tarr gets divorced: His marriage was only a pseudo-ending and is not allowed to close the narrative of his life. Indeed, the hero will go on to enjoy a long series of romantic trysts, involving a whole matrushka set of new partners from Rose Fawcett to Prism Dirkes. The structure of *Tarr* is thus complicit with the irony of its central protagonist, emphasising, as it does, the provisionality of all attachments. Superficially, the novel's open-ended ending appears to promote a 'romantic' conception of freedom—an absolute absence of closure in the name of infinite possibility. Yet, despite the novel's efforts to keep all options open, Tarr ultimately says goodbye to the autocracy that he had once envisioned for himself. Caught in the eternal swing of the 'pendulum' of sexual desire he becomes a symbol of the incontinence and mechanistic behaviour he once disparaged (T, 318). The great autocrat has become appetite's slave, in what might be read as the novel's final irony.

If the notion of a final irony again sounds like a contradiction, it's not clear that Lewis would be particularly cowed by this incoherence. It is thus impossible to determine whether irony in *Tarr* is 'ultimately' an attempt to discredit a bad type of freedom or whether it is a capitulation to that freedom, or whether it amounts to an attack on the idea of freedom *tout court*. In the end, the problem of irony is always liable to be reexperienced as a hermeneutic issue: The irresolution and indecision that plagued the ironist is now transferred to the reader (as Lewis later claimed, the synthesizer of his dance of opposites was supposed to be you and me). One response may be to *decide* or to *resolve* upon a definitive or final interpretation for the novel, despite or perhaps because of the absence of grounds for such a surely definitive reading. However, the practical and conceptual hazards of such 'decisionism' were well known to Lewis and they, too, find powerful expression in *Tarr*. Once again it involves a very 'romantic' paradox: an abdication of freedom in the very pursuit of it.

Acting Free

In *Left Wings Over Europe* (1936), Lewis complained that the 'words "freedom" and "democracy" are mere habits—word-habits—with the British Democracy.'[51] Modern Britons had no understanding of the '*rigours of true freedom*' (LW, 295). They had forgotten that freedom was 'not merely a passive affair' (LW, 296–97). To put the matter in more technical terms, liberty was not a mere 'opportunity-concept'—guaranteeing abstract possibilities for action—but an 'exercise-concept' demanding a strenuous practice of something.[52] 'True freedom,' Lewis explained, 'involves the full activity of the free human agent, man or woman: it requires a great deal of discipline and hard work: it entails a very great deal of discomfort and hard knocks' (LW, 295). But this demanding conception of liberty was lost on most people: The 'majority of men have to be persuaded or coerced into freedom.' Indeed, they usually viewed freedom as an absence of constraint or immunity from obligation. '*Freedom* and *irresponsibility*,' Lewis, complained, 'are commutative terms, where the average man is concerned' (LW, 294).

How well Lewis lived up to his own strictures on freedom is a debatable matter, but his protagonist Frederick Tarr is hopelessly ill-equipped to assume the burden of freedom in an active sense. He is the quintessential romantic, as Schmitt would present this figure in 1919: a man incapable of relinquishing his 'superior irony' in a way that would allow him to take a definitive stand on anything.[53] 'To be free,' Lewis argued, 'you must learn *not* to smile' (LW, 296). Unfortunately, Tarr cannot cease smiling. His passivity is a perverse expression of his love of freedom: Any action would mean a forfeiture of other possibilities and Tarr conflates freedom with possibility. Liberty for him is a limitless opportunity-concept, which means that no opportunity can be truly seized. Tarr, moreover, has a profound 'dislike for action' because he can never be sure that his actions are fully his own: Their social situatedness

51. Lewis, *Left Wings Over Europe*, 294. Further references are given in the text under the abbreviation 'LW.'

52. Taylor, *Philosophy and the Human Sciences*, 213.

53. Schmitt, *Political Romanticism*, 100.

and ultimately their physical character mean that actions are always liable to be determined by others or by the brute world (T, 235). He thus prefers to be a passive spectator rather than a deluded pseudo-agent. It is a passivity to which Lewis was sympathetic. 'We are not born to be *absolute observers*,' he admitted; human beings were designed to be participants as much as spectators. And yet for all his commitment to active freedom, he remained convinced that without the detachment of the spectator attitude 'men sink to the level of insects' (WB, 158). For that reason, he was highly dubious of an ethos that recommended action for the sake of action. He called this the 'romance of action' and claimed that it had wreaked havoc on the modern world. Once the detachment of the rational spectator was abandoned for the simple fact of acting, you have a species of 'undiluted sensationalism'—a surrender of autonomy only masquerading as the expression of freedom (TWM, 20).

He traced modernity's cult of action to Georges Sorel: 'of all the apostles of dangerous living, pure action, "heroism," blood and iron, Georges Sorel was the worst—the most shrewd and irresponsible' (RA, 37). Lewis was clearly drawn to Sorel's celebration of the warrior virtues, and his own reflections on violence could sometimes be blood-curdling.[54] Unlike Sorel, whose advocacy of martial valour can occasionally read like fond nostalgia for Machiavellian *virtù*, Lewis's pugilism often seemed to be removed from any broader political objective, the pleasure of violence becoming a kind of end in itself ('Killing somebody must be the greatest pleasure in existence' [B1, 133]). Lewis attacked the 'romance of war' while also admitting to being '*half* a romantic' in his susceptibility to its charms (BB, 193). He gradually managed to distance himself from this romanticisation of violence and of action. Indeed, his objections to the 'romance of action' were already to be seen in *Tarr*. They are incarnated in the figure of Otto Kreisler—a man who hurls himself into violent deeds, raping and murdering largely because 'the rusty machine had a thirst for action' (T, 137). Kreisler's deeds may be decisive, but they are not particularly free: In their total submission to mechanical impulse, they are forms of servitude.

54. On his interest in Sorel, see Mengham, 'From Georges Sorel to *Blast*.'

The homicidal Kreisler is a grotesque embodiment of where the 'romance of action' may end up. Given Schmitt's sense of identification with Lewis, it is also worth noting that Kreisler's fate operates as a proleptic criticism of the kind of decisionism that Schmitt would promote as an alternative to liberal jurisprudence and politicking. Liberals, in Schmit's eyes, had a shallow, even romantic, confidence in the powers of rational discussion. Naively committed to peace as the *telos* of politics and to discussion as its ultimate form, they endlessly talked shop and thus avoided the essence of the political: 'the exacting moral decision.'[55] But dictators can at least stop talking and make decisions.[56] That rulers might make bad decisions did not seem to worry Schmitt so much; 'as far as the most essential issues are concerned, making a decision is more important than how a decision is made.'[57] In fact, there is nothing in Schmitt's account of matters to pronounce an 'absolute' decision bad; this deed of the mind is 'independent of argumentative substantiation.'[58] The decision is utterly spontaneous and makes no appeal to prior norms or antecedent conditions for its content or legitimacy. If Schmitt denounced romantics for their denial of causality, his theory of the decision is an ambiguous assertion of the same principle: Ostensibly the cause of everything, the decision itself has no cause. It is 'created out of nothingness.'[59]

It is easy to understand why Schmitt believed he and Lewis were kindred spirits: Both dwelt on the existential value of enmity; both were deeply hostile to romanticism; both decried liberalism and parliamentary democracy;[60] both were drawn to dictatorship, believing

55. Schmitt, *Political Theology*, 65. Indeed, in their impotent chatter, liberals were little different to political romantics—figures who also stood aside from every serious 'decision.' Schmitt, *Political Romanticism*, 124.

56. The great virtue of dictatorship, for Schmitt, therefore, was that it was 'the opposite of discussion.' Schmitt, *Political Theology*, 63. Lewis, on the other hand, emphasised the importance of rational discussion. 'Debate is of the essence of a true democracy. And we get far too little of it.' See Lewis, *Count Your Dead*, 28.

57. Schmitt, *Political Theology*, 55–56.

58. Schmitt, *Political Theology*, 31.

59. Schmitt, *Political Theology*, 66.

60. As Lewis confidently declared in 1926, 'Parliamentary rule is finished' (ABR, 70).

that it reinstated the concept of the person into public life;[61] both had grim trysts with Hitler. And yet much of Lewis's writing stands apart from and even parodies Schmitt's brand of decisionism. In *Tarr*, for instance, the enmity Kreisler feels for the man he ultimately kills might be read as an anticipation and rebuttal of Schmitt's friend-enemy distinction—the constitutive moment of political life in Schmitt's universe.[62] Of course, Schmitt distinguished between public and private animosity, so in one respect the analogy fails; however, the capricious nature of Kreisler's rancour points to a more general problem with decisionism: its conflation of arbitrariness with agency. The most disturbing feature of Kreisler's hatred for Soltyk, for instance, is its random character: Sexual jealousy might be invoked as its cause, but this seems to be a weak pretext for a virtually groundless enmity. Indeed, the collective decision to embark on a murderous duel is 'a whim,' 'a caprice'—even if it is pursued 'with a dogged persistency, with which our whims are often served' (T, 260).

The whimsical nature of the murderous duel may be a symbolic commentary on the way many of Lewis's contemporaries embarked on war ('as though, for instance, they had woken up in the early morning and decided to go fishing' [T, 260]), but it also emphasises the moral arbitrariness of Sorel's 'romance of action' as well as Schmitt's subsequent decisionism. The groundlessness of Kreisler's violence or the decision to embark on a duel may feel like freedom. Kreisler notes how the 'obstinacy of a caprice' awakens his will and distinguishes him from everything that is 'prearranged and unavoidable' (T, 262). His will appears to be free in that it is seemingly spontaneous, acknowledging no prior conditions or independent justification. But this merely suggests that spontaneity is an insufficient criterion of freedom; at best, it describes the 'negative' face of liberty—a necessary absence of determining

61. Schmitt tried to model his conception of political agency on the individual subject, ruing the fact that the 'personal and decisionistic element in the concept of sovereignty was lost.' Schmitt, *Political Theology*, 48. Lewis was worried that 'the very concept of *the person* is a thing of the past, in public life,' but he also suggested that modern authoritarianism was restoring personality to politics. Lewis, *The Enemy* 3, p. 78.

62. Schmitt, *The Concept of the Political*, 26.

causes. This seems to miss out on what some might call freedom's 'positive' features, namely, the ability to act on the basis of reasons, which—qua reasons—are defensible to oneself and to others. Bereft of grounds for his actions, or of principles for his existence as a whole, he moves through life like 'a sleeper' (T, 258), or as someone who is 'practically dead' (T, 257). He is a sadly impaired agent.

Kreisler thus exposes the unfreedom of 'the romance of action.' It marks either a surrender to impulse and thus to mechanism, or it pretends to escape causal determinism by glorifying arbitrariness (of course, the latter may be less of an escape from causality than a simple ignorance of its mechanics). Either way it marks the abdication of rational agency, which is repeatedly figured by Lewis as a type of death. The arbitrariness of Kreisler as a man of action may bring into relief the virtues of inaction, and Tarr's type of irony. But their differences should not be exaggerated. Both are extreme egotists: Kreisler is a 'self-centred city' (T, 75); Tarr worships the 'fetish within' (T, 3). Both find it difficult to attribute meaning to the world around them; both, as a consequence, struggle to invest their own actions in the world with significance. Irony, as we have seen, is an expression of this scepticism, but so, too, is the 'romance of action': There is no authoritative principle for one's actions, the only principle is action itself. This may seem like an escape from meaninglessness, but it is arguably a surrender to it.

Throughout the 1920s and beyond Lewis continued to attack the 'romance of action' for its denigration of the intellect (TWM, 20). 'The life of the intelligence,' he insisted, 'is the very incarnation of freedom' (ABR, 374). But he sometimes struggled to show how this freedom would operate as a practical force in the world. Given his demanding strictures about freedom—as something distinct from 'physical circumstances,' removed from the mob of the senses and the pathology of emotion—it is difficult to see how freedom might act whilst remaining itself (ABR, 135). Indeed, the distinction between an agential attitude and a reflective attitude in Lewis was extraordinarily strong ('you simply cannot *act* and *think* at one and the same time' [RA, 76]). This can make the very idea of rational action—or practical freedom—look elusive.

Nor was it easy to gauge how freedom, for Lewis, could be politically embodied. In fact, by often construing freedom as an absence of social determination, Lewis intimated that the very idea of 'a society of "free men"' was a contradiction in terms (ABR, 151). Thus Lewis's 'politics of the intellect' (ABR, 373) appeared to imply a freedom from politics as such, even if he increasingly doubted the possibility of this independence.[63] 'Do not play with political notions,' he insisted in 1917, 'for that is a compromise with the herd'—a rule that arguably breaks its own injunction against politics in its antipopulist commitments.[64] The demand not to 'play' at politicking might be read, of course, as a plea to take it seriously and as time went on Lewis certainly seemed to do so. According to his own assessment, he 'became a politician' after the futile brutalities of World War I (BB, 185).

And yet one might well wonder if Lewis ever succeeded in doing more than playing with politics—no matter how much he might have mugged up on Machiavelli or locked horns with Rousseau—since he always appeared to approach the business with an ironic reserve. His political life may be read as an attempt to escape his own romantic irony—or as an alarming instantiation in it. In 1929, he maintained, for instance, that his views were 'partly communist and partly fascist, with a distinct streak of monarchism in [his] marxism, but at bottom anarchist with a healthy passion for order.'[65] Adopting the ironist's art of paradox, Lewis arguably attempts to forestall commitment to any position. Even his bolder moves, like his atrocious decision to serve as an 'exponent' of the 'austrian house-painter' and 'inspired *german peasant*,' Adolf Hitler, can read like a strangely tongue-in-cheek exercise (H, 143, 7, 176). It is hard to know how serious he was when he described Hitler as a 'Man of Peace' (H, 44). Still, the issue may be that he never took Hitler—or anything else—seriously enough. Schmitt called this type

63. In Lewis's 'Bill of Rights,' he defended the right 'to act and to think non-politically in everything in complete detachment from all the intolerant watchwords and formulas by which we are beset.' Lewis, *The Enemy*, no. 3, p. 27.

64. Lewis, *The Little Review* 4, no. 3, p. 7.

65. Lewis, *The Enemy*, no. 3, p. 70.

of unseriousness 'political romanticism,' but it was also a demonstration of a dangerously fictive approach to key questions of life.

This book has often talked up the cognitive and practical benefits of a fictive attitude: the pleasures that can be gleaned from what Lewis might have called 'the Great Between'—between an agent's attitude and a spectator's, between total belief and scepticism—and the virtues to be found in halfway houses, not least a spirit of openness, provisionality, and a resistance to judgement. But Lewis also reveals the limits of openness and life lived as fiction. If he condemned the romantic for exceeding those limits, he never seemed able to respect them himself. He, too, emphasised the value of operating 'as if' and showed how we are often compelled 'to lay more stress upon what is pragmatical and *useful*, and less upon what is perhaps eternally true' (H, 129). The fact that this argument was deployed in defence of Hitler's ludicrous views on race shows the dark places to which our 'as ifs' can bring us. He retained an open mind on all the wrong questions. The title of his would-be critique of antisemitism (not least his own) says it all: *The Jews: Are They Human?* The joke may have been derived from G. J. Renier's book *The English: Are They Human?* (1931), but it was another moment where the ironist had lost the run of himself.[66] Richard Rorty liked to present irony as a liberal virtue, but Lewis demonstrates that the laughing animal can serve almost any cause.[67] Irony may allow us to live amphibiously—scuttling between the 'Great Within' and the 'Great Without'—but it should also allow us to remain human. Lewis proudly reported that he had been called a 'Rogue Elephant, a Cannibal Shark, and a crocodile' (BB, 12). Eliot declared him an 'orang-outang of genius.'[68] Lewis was more inclined to think of himself as 'a caged, and rather sardonic, lion, in a particularly contemptible and ill-run Zoo' (BB, 12). Hee-hee to all that, yet it's hard not to feel that at some point something human in himself had died laughing.

66. On this point, see Waddell, 'Lewis and Fascism,' 87–88.

67. Richard Rorty, *Contingency Irony and Solidarity*. Rorty later felt that this devotion to irony was 'misguided.' See Rorty, 'Reply to J. B. Schneewind,' 506.

68. Eliot, 'Contemporanea,' 84.

7

Theories—Murdoch

IRIS MURDOCH could feel 'ambivalent about ambivalence' and often acknowledged the limits of irony.[1] In this sense, she was a little like Wyndham Lewis, although on most other levels the two writers could not be more antithetical. Much of life had a comic aspect to Murdoch—and she regarded 'the funny as central to the human pilgrimage'—but she was also a woman who could stop smiling and get serious for a moment, not least about the gravity of moral life.[2] 'Moral seriousness,' she insisted, is required of us all.[3] She admitted to feeling scared of discovering that morality is hollow and that it doesn't really matter how you behave, but she also scotched this thought by stressing 'the impossibility' of ever fully finding this out.[4] If Lewis's search for an objective vision of the world often brought him to the 'Great Without'—a space outside ethics and many of the values we might call 'human'—Murdoch presented morality as the most objective thing there is. She, too, wanted to find Reality with a capital 'R,' but her intuitions about this ultimate place were very different to Lewis's. As she insisted, 'morality, goodness, is realism'—not that anyone finds this reality business easy (EM, 347).

1. Murdoch, *Living on Paper*, 523. All further references are given in the text under the abbreviation, 'L.'

2. Murdoch, *Existentialists and Mystics*, 450. All further references are given in the text under the abbreviation 'EM.'

3. Murdoch, *Metaphysics as a Guide to Morals*, 333. All further references are given in the text under the abbreviation 'MGM.'

4. Dooley, *From a Tiny Corner in the House of Fiction*, 133.

Our addiction to dream-worlds, our frenzied responsibilities to our castles in Spain, all our tangos with our own shadows in the cave, are Murdoch's great comic themes, though they also yield a kind of horror and nausea that would match the best of Sartre or Lewis. 'Man is a suffering animal,' we are told in one of her novels, and Murdoch takes no small delight in watching him grimace.[5] Love is tough, and truth is sore, in these life lessons.

The way that fiction delivers its lessons is my focus here. Murdoch never seemed to lose confidence in the cognitive and didactic value of art: It was 'truth-seeking' and 'truth-revealing' (EM, 11), a 'fundamental method of explanation' (EM, 492)—'the most educational thing we have' (EM, 461). She had no time for noncognitive and nonassertoric views of art ('a novel clearly tells us something . . . , art is a kind of statement' [EM, 245]). Though art could make statements, she also recognised that many of them could be false. Art's ability to mislead is reflected in the critical vocabulary we apply to it ('Words such as "sentimental," "pretentious," "self-indulgent," "trivial,"' she insisted, 'impute some kind of falsehood' [EM, 11]). Art, she also admitted, often spent too much time cheering us up and could concede too much to our yearning for form. Here the aesthetic risked becoming 'magic' or 'fantasy'—Murdoch's terms for the false imagination, the neverland in which most of us live. But the measure of good art was the way it 'breaks the grip of our own dull fantasy life and stirs us to the effort of true vision' (EM, 14). Art helps us to get real. In this regard, it might seem to resemble philosophy—another would-be truth-teller—yet the ancient quarrel between these two disciplines would also be restaged across Murdoch's writing.[6]

5. Murdoch, *The Black Prince*, 348. All further references are given in the text under the abbreviation 'BP.'

6. Murdoch had a deep respect for the rigour of philosophy, but she also worried that this same virtue had made it overspecialised. As she complained, 'Philosophy has left us without a way of envisaging the whole person and has even popularised a very partial view' (EM 280). For this reason, literature had 'taken over' some of the tasks of philosophy (EM, 294), committed, as it was, to delivering a more holistic view of life. Art, she insisted, was more in contact with ordinary forms of thought than philosophy and partly for this reason it '*proves* more than philosophy can' (EM, 458).

In *Art and Eros* she dramatised the old enmity in the form of a Platonic dialogue, emphasising the literariness of Plato's method while also rehearsing some of his charges against art: that all art was lies; that it was a distraction from reality; that it indulged the lower parts of the soul; that it was a corrupt shortcut to truth, abandoning as it did the discipline and virtues of method; that it was ultimately rhetoric, entertaining—at best—a purely opportunistic relationship to truth. Yet Murdoch also boxed well for art, strongly reasserting its realist vocation: 'Art is about the pilgrimage from appearance to reality (the subject of every good play and novel) and exemplifies in spite of Plato what his philosophy teaches concerning the therapy of the soul' (EM, 456). But since art and philosophy have the same goal—truth, reality, the good—both might easily seem to be vulnerably substitutable in Murdoch's universe. Indeed, if they were commensurate with reference to their ultimate end, one of these practices could look like an inferior version of the other. The danger of Murdoch's or indeed any cognitive approach to art, is that it risks making the aesthetic purely instrumental to the end of cognition. The hazards of this instrumentalism were epitomised, for Murdoch, by the 'philosophical novel,' a mean halfway house that she never wanted to reside in,[7] though many of the charges that she made against this form—that it *said* what it should have *showed*, that it reduced characters to thesis-bears, that it betrayed an impatience with the brute 'stuff' of the world that was untranslatable into concepts—would resurface in criticisms of her own work.[8]

Kant, at least, had secured the autonomy of art by stressing its epistemic impotence (aesthetic judgement 'does not belong to the faculty of cognition at all'), but Murdoch resisted this scorched earth defence.[9]

7. 'I'm not a philosophical novelist,' Murdoch declared in 1976. Or as she put it earlier in the same interview: 'I certainly don't want to mix philosophy and fiction—they're totally different disciplines.' Dooley, *From a Tiny Corner*, 42, 36.

8. Murdoch's objections to the philosophical novel were often directed at Sartre and indeed de Beauvoir. See Murdoch, *Sartre*. For her criticisms of de Beauvoir, see Dooley, *From a Tiny Corner*, 36. On the different ways in which Murdoch might think philosophically through fiction, see Forsberg, *Language Lost and Found*. See also Leeson, *Iris Murdoch*.

9. Kant, *Critique of the Power of Judgment*, 26.

Art, she insisted, is 'cognition in another mode' (EM, 11). Or, as Acastos puts it in *Art and Eros*: 'Art is *thinking*' (EM, 472). But how exactly does literature think and how does this thought remain specific to itself? In *The Fire and the Sun*, Murdoch claimed that art combined two distinctive forms of thought. 'Art undoes the work of philosophy,' she maintained, 'by deliberately fusing knowledge by acquaintance and knowledge by description' (EM, 414). So, like philosophy, art deals in statements about or representations of some particular 'X,' but it also tries to 'acquaint' us with that 'X'—recovering what it's like to be that 'X' or what's it like to be a 'Y' trying to understand that 'X.' Many of Murdoch's philosophical contemporaries would query the very concept of 'knowledge by acquaintance'—stressing its ungrammatical uses of the word 'know' and its apparent commitment to elusive inward states—but this would-be knowledge at least accounts for the distinctiveness of art's cognitive vocation. It seeks to combine the descriptive and the experiential in the same thought or, to put it differently, to fuse objective and subjective viewpoints.[10] The difficulty of such mergers has been studied throughout this book and the problem shapes the basic form of Murdoch's fiction.

The problematic factor is the very subjectivity that Murdoch wants to express and celebrate in art. Murdoch is often unsure what ontological status, epistemic power, or indeed moral value to give to this order of experience (here again there are strange symmetries with Lewis). Subjectivity may be our defining quality, and the place we all live in, but it is also, for Murdoch, an endless source of illusion. Egoism, in her work, is an epistemic disease as much as it is a moral vice—just as it was for George Eliot. We are repeatedly 'blinded by self' (EM 382), and perfect objectivity seems to require

10. Agan, this was very much Lukács's sense of art. 'The goal of all great art is to provide a picture of reality in which the contradiction between appearance and reality, the particular and the general, the immediate and the conceptual, etc., is so resolved that the two converge into a spontaneous integrity in the direct impression of the work of art and provide an impression of an inseparable integrity.' Lukács, *Writer and Critic and Other Essays*, 35.

a radical 'unselfing.'[11] Other people's egos, however, remain an object of respect and concern for Murdoch—indeed, full recognition of the selfhood of another is a key objective of moral thought. Yet the problem of thinking our way into another—indeed, whether the self is thinkable either from within or from without—remains a key issue in Murdoch. The difficulty was clearly animated for her by contemporary philosophical debates about the metaphysics of mind, or what Wittgenstein sometimes called the 'delusion' of the inner.[12] Wittgenstein may have been a philosophical hero for Murdoch—'To say I am interested in Wittgenstein puts it too mildly. I am Wittgenstein' (L, 420)—but she had mixed feelings about his efforts to talk us out of our devotion to a metaphysical privacy or secret cabinet of the self. As she admitted in her journal in 1948, Wittgenstein's assault on certain psychological and phenomenological accounts of inwardness went against 'all [her] instincts.' Instead, Murdoch was inclined to believe that inwardness was one of the most basic and precious things about us and she worried about its retirement from philosophical thought. Here she was determined to 'Fight Witt. at every step!'[13] Her novels, however, paint a more ambivalent picture. If, like many novels, they often supply an inside view of human experience, they also nurse doubts about the intelligibility or even the desirability of recovering the life within. Indeed, 'inwardness' in Murdoch's fiction is often the darkest of those caves that shut us out from the sun.

The tension between the subjective and the objective explored throughout this book thus reaches a certain apogee in Murdoch. The

11. Like Eliot, Murdoch repeatedly presents egoism as an epistemic problem as much as it is a moral one. As someone says in *The Fire and the Sun*: 'To overcome egoism in its protean forms of fantasy and illusion . . . is automatically to become more moral' (EM, 425).

12. 'The inner is a delusion. That is: the whole complex of ideas alluded to by this word is like a painted curtain drawn in front of the scene of the actual word use.' Wittgenstein, *Last Writings on the Philosophy of Psychology*, 2.84.

13. Journal of Iris Murdoch (6.23), 24 February 1948, as quoted in Chumhaill and Wiseman, *Metaphysical Animals*, 206.

difficulty of integrating these perspectives, she suggests, is 'the problem of truth' and consequently a problem of art (MGM, 295). Murdoch's own fiction is repeatedly torn between standpoints—between particular and general perspectives, between situated and detached positions, between inner and outer viewpoints. While it might be hoped that these different perspectives might ultimately tell a complete and unified story—this was also George Eliot's dream—it never quite does so in Murdoch. One of the other great themes of her writing, after all, is the limits of the thinkable and the resistance the world poses to our conceptual schemes—a point she often makes at philosophy's expense. 'Good art,' she maintains, 'accepts and celebrates and meditates upon the defeat of the discursive intellect by the world' and we see these happy defeats throughout her fiction (MGM, 88). Unlike much philosophising, art has the wisdom to remain confused.

Ancient Quarrels

'I don't think philosophy influences my work as a novelist,' Murdoch declared in an interview in 1976.[14] However, in her letters she sometimes took a different view: 'My novels are full of philosophy' (L, 319). Evidence for the second position can be found throughout her fiction: Her novels abound with philosophical quotations, philosophical statements, and philosophical arguments. Moreover, philosophy generates some of the more strained moments of wit in her work ('Love laughs at locksmiths and also at Locke').[15] Funny folk in *An Accidental Man* give the name 'Kierkegaard' to their motorcar, presumably on homophonic grounds, but also, perhaps, because driven at sufficient speed the machine induces fear and trembling. Philosophy also shapes much of Murdoch's symbolism: Caves are seldom mere holes in a rock but repeatedly hark back to Plato's parable. The sound of a fountain in a deserted

14. Bellamy and Murdoch, 'An Interview with Iris Murdoch,' 131.

15. Murdoch, *An Accidental Man*, 332. All further references are given in the text under the abbreviation 'AM.'

garden is not just a sound; its seeming mind-independence is a 'gentle refutation of Berkeley'—or so we are told.[16]

Murdoch proclaimed herself unenthused by the philosophical *longeurs* of Thomas Mann's characters,[17] but her own creations don't hold back: 'I suspect you of being a crypto-Platonist'; 'I always thought the ontological proof was based on a gross logical fallacy';[18] 'But you see, the basis of all being is mental.'[19] Some characters take issue with their own high-flying chatter—'You and I always talk metaphysics. But all metaphysics is devilish, *devilish*.'[20] These ironically remain quite philosophical criticisms, though what counts as philosophy is also a point of dispute: 'Philosophy? Do you mean popular science or the trivial contraptions of vulgar empiricism?'[21] The point of these arguments may be to reveal the limits of philosophical argument—or indeed argument as such. They tend to be sloppily conducted and are often means of evasion ('But you're trying to force me to have is an argument which isn't *the* argument of the situation').[22] Moreover, they are repeatedly routed by the sheer facticity of others ('In her presence, in the overwhelming atmosphere of her personality, his arguments simply did not begin to exist').[23] Arguments generally fail as means of persuasion in Murdoch—often something more vigorous is required—blackmail, say, or kidnapping, or blows.

Yet philosophy retains its lure for a large posse of Murdoch's characters. Many of them are professional academics or enthusiastic

16. Murdoch, *Under the Net*, 234. All further references are given in the text under the abbreviation 'UN.'

17. Meyers, *Remembering Iris Murdoch*, 94.

18. Murdoch, *The Unicorn*, 100. All further references are given in the text under the abbreviation 'U.'

19. Murdoch, *A Word Child*, 46. All further references are given in the text under the abbreviation 'WC.'

20. Murdoch, *The Nice and the Good*, 123. All further references are given in the text under the abbreviation 'NG.'

21. Murdoch, *Message to the Planet*, 89.

22. Murdoch, *The Sea, The Sea*, 361. All further references are given in the text under the abbreviation 'SS.'

23. Murdoch, *The Sandcastle*, 147.

amateurs wedded to grand projects. Marcus in *The Time of the Angels* has embarked on a book provisionally entitled *Morality in a World Without God*;[24] Rupert in *A Fairly Honourable Defeat* is engaged on an ambitious treatise on love; Benet in *Jackson's Dilemma* labours over a project on Heidegger. Characters who are not committed to a treatise still make ample allusion to philosophy ('How right Plato was to think that, embracing a lovely boy, he was on the road to the Good' [BP, 210]; 'I think I'm a bit of an existentialist';[25] '*Homo homini lupus,* Willy, *homo homini lupus*' [NG, 125]). Wittgenstein seems to be the real rock star. *Nuns and Soldiers* begins with the invocation of his name, initiating a deathbed conversation on his relative merits, while Nigel wanders through *Bruno's Dream* reciting some of the more famous lines of the *Tractatus*. Elsewhere we learn about the philosopher's dietary views,[26] his famous hypothesis about talking lions,[27] and his thoughts on the impossibility of hypocrisy in dogs.[28] His claims that love is testable also feature and might seem to vindicate Murdoch's many novelistic love-tests.[29]

Wittgenstein often presented philosophy as a specialised practice that alienates itself from ordinary language in its doomed attempts to provide foundations for it, but the talk of Murdoch's characters seems to attest to the ordinariness of philosophy. They indicate that it is perfectly natural to wonder about our epistemic access to the world or to other minds. It may even be normal to lie on one's deathbed and feel that 'death refutes induction' (as the great man said, the ordinary does

24. Murdoch, *The Time of the Angels*, 67. All further references are given in the text under the abbreviation 'TA.'

25. Murdoch, *Henry and Cato*, 286. All further references are given in the text under the abbreviation 'HC.'

26. Murdoch, *A Word Child*, 86.

27. Murdoch, *A Fairly Honourable Defeat*, 39.

28. Murdoch, *The Philosopher's Pupil*, 87. All further references are given in the text under the abbreviation 'PP.' According to Wittgenstein's notes from the 1940s: 'A dog could not pretend to be in pain because its life is too simple for that. It does not have the joints necessary for such movements.' Wittgenstein, *Last Writings on the Philosophy of Psychology*, 1.111.

29. As she puts it in *Under the Net*: 'Love is not a feeling. It can be tested. Love is action' (UN, 45).

not 'always make the *impression* of ordinariness').[30] But the price of such ordinariness is a certain social exclusivity. Her characters can usually rely on substantial educational capital—much of it acquired at Oxbridge—to service their philosophical musings. The domestic servant Pattie, on the other hand, literally stumbles over a copy of *Sein und Zeit.* When she later peruses some of its contents, it means 'absolutely nothing to her' (TA, 150).

The joke, of course, may be against Heidegger—for all Murdoch's admiration of his work, she also felt he lacked 'an essential connection between ordinary people and ordinary life'—or it may be a rebuke to philosophy in general.[31] Though it may be fun to quote Plato or to make a hobby of Heidegger, philosophy potentially represents a corrupt holiday from the everyday, a bad abdication of our ordinary grasp of the world. There is a Platonic strain in Murdoch where ordinariness takes place in a cave and 'ordinary human consciousness is a tissue of illusion' (HC, 169). Nonetheless, yearning for a lost ordinariness is a leitmotif of her fiction and it often issues from the mouths of philosophers. Take Rozanov, for instance: 'He longed to live with ordinariness and see it simply with clear calm eyes' (PP, 135). But Rozanov, like philosophy, isn't very good at this.

So, while philosophy may be ubiquitous in Murdoch's fiction, it is also repeatedly disparaged. It is 'a mug's game' (PP, 133); it is 'the prattling of a child' (TA, 170); it is a form of 'empty thinking by ignorant conceited men who think they can digest without eating';[32] it is 'the worst lie of all' (AM, 90). Academic philosophers repeatedly encourage those who will listen not to take up philosophy. It may be little more than an attempt to advertise his Wittgensteinian credentials, but the aim of the philosopher Dave is 'to dissuade the young from philosophy' (UN, 25). Instead, he urges people to become orderlies in hospitals (as Wittgenstein had once been). Murdoch draws attention to the dangers

30. Murdoch, *Bruno's Dream*, 7. All further references are given in the text under the abbreviation 'BD.' Wittgenstein, *Philosophical Investigations*, 156.

31. Murdoch, 'Manuscript on Heidegger,' as cited in Browning, *Why Iris Murdoch Matters*, 46.

32. Murdoch, *The Book and the Brotherhood*, 22.

and even cruelty of such advice: George in *The Philosopher's Pupil* feels his life has been ruined by his mentor's insistence that he give up philosophy. The great anti-teacher does not follow his own advice, but he does believe that philosophers operate under 'a curse' (PP, 274). His death in the end is attributed to an idea—a terrible recognition of the 'futility of philosophy' and presumably of his own life's work (PP, 553).

There may be an element of self-parody in these accounts of a doomed discipline. The description of Rozanov's initial career (he was 'a sceptic, a reductionist, a linguistic analyst . . . of the most austerely anti-metaphysical school') is a far cry from Murdoch's philosophical enterprise. But his later ventures—it was 'said that he had become a neo-Platonist' and a 'metaphysical moralist'—have a much more Murdochian aspect. Murdoch stokes the affinities by making Rozanov the author of a 'seminal work, *Nostalgia for the Particular*' (the title of Murdoch's first philosophical publication [PP, 83]). Even more self-referential, or self-immolating, is Rupert's gospel of goodness in *A Fairly Honourable Defeat*. Or consider Marcus's ambitions in *The Time of the Angels*: He intends 'to rescue the idea of an Absolute in morals by showing it to be implied in the unavoidable human activity of moral evaluation at its most unsophisticated level' (TA, 68). Such moral hope is lampooned by other characters, and when pressed to offer verbal defences of their work both Rupert and Marcus stammer. The amateurishness of these efforts—Rupert concedes that he is not 'a proper philosopher'—may reflect Murdoch's worries about the untechnical quality of her own philosophical work (arguably one of its most attractive features). But the irony she extends to these well-meaning ventures is also a noble refusal to exempt her own moral theory from the indictment of philosophy within her fiction.

In Defence of Particulars

The case against philosophy, as we have seen, has a distinctly Wittgensteinian aspect: Philosophy alienates itself from our ordinary use of concepts in an attempt to recover the deep structure of reality or of our practices. But as Murdoch argued in her early philosophical work,

'There may be no deep structure' (EM, 74). Her fictional philosopher Rozamov is adamant that there is no such structure (PP, 193), while Hilary in *A Word Child* is balder still: 'There's nothing behind ordinary life' (WC, 87). Murdoch's Platonists, those cave dwellers who dream of the sun, may find Hilary too defeatist; nonetheless, metaphysics is repeatedly taken to task in her novels as a doomed attempt to exceed the limits of our language. In *Bruno's Dream*, Nigel recites the relevant lines from the *Tractatus*: 'Whereof we cannot speak. Thereof we must be silent' (BD, 83).

Murdoch also draws upon Wittgenstein to make a further charge against philosophy: It disregards particulars in its search for an overarching theory. As Annadine, the metafictional mouthpiece of the character Hugo Belfounder in *Under the Net* declares: 'All theorizing is flight. We must be ruled by the situation itself and this is unutterably particular' (UN, 98). Commentators have noted the rich links between Hugo and Wittgenstein, the great scourge of 'theory.' In fact, Hugo is too Wittgensteinian even to enlist the word 'theory': Presumably, important differences—between description, explanation, and various forms of justification—can be lost within this capacious concept. Nonetheless, Hugo is convinced that the aspiration to generality that is often to be found in theories distorts the richness of our practices. 'We defend ourselves by descriptions and tame the world by generalizing,' Bradley Pearson declares in *The Black Prince* (BP, 82). There is an obvious self-referential problem—or joke—here and it suggests that it may be unwise to generalise about generality; after all, we encounter very different forms of it in everyday life. According to R. M. Hare, we should also distinguish between generality and universality, for many universal rules can be highly specific and self-qualifying.[33] Murdoch, however, took issue with Hare's emphasis on universal rules. It was a mistake, she insisted, to believe that morality was codifiable; it was equally tendentious to present universality as a necessary or sufficient criterion of right (EM, 76–98). To put ourselves in everyone's shoes is often to betray our distinctiveness as agents and the particularity of the situations we face.

33. Hare, 'Universalisability.'

As Randall complains of the dutiful Ann in *An Unofficial Rose*: 'Ann lives by rules and her acts don't have places, they don't belong anywhere.'[34] True virtue is attentive to context and is shaped by the situations in which it lives.

Murdoch repeatedly called for a thinking that would be more attuned to the world's particularity. She wondered if philosophy might learn to think without theories (and used Wittgenstein as evidence to suggest that it could), but she explicitly championed art as a forum for this kind of thought. So, the *Notebook of Particulars*—the sketchbook that Miles keeps in *Bruno's Dream*—is in a sense the paradigm for all art (BD, 51). Miles may prioritise poetry as a form, yet Murdoch often argued that the novel was the supreme host of the particular: It embraced 'the invincible variety, contingency and scarcely communicable frightfulness of life'—often with a smile on its face (MGM, 96). How well her own novels live up to this billing can certainly be queried, but the importance of attending to specifics is a recurrent theme of her fiction, where it functions as a kind of therapy, ethical task, and spiritual vocation. As Hugo declares in *Under the Net*, 'God is detail' (UN, 292). Hugo duly alerts Jake to his impoverished vision of things—not simply by precept but by lived example:

> But it was as if his very mode of being revealed to me how hopelessly my own vision of the world was blurred by generality. I felt like a man who, having vaguely thought that flowers are all much the same, goes for a walk with a botanist. Only this simile doesn't fit Hugo either, for a botanist not only notices details but classifies. Hugo only noticed details. He never classified. It was as if his vision were sharpened to the point where even classification was impossible, for each thing was seen as absolutely unique. (UN, 72)

Language here is under strain and similes fail to do justice to the particularities they seek to identify. Indeed, Hugo feels that 'language is a machine for making falsehoods' (UN, 71). The 'unutterably particular' is precisely that: unutterable.

34. Murdoch, *An Unofficial Rose*, 102.

The ineffability of the real is a leitmotif in Murdoch's work, where it functions as a limit not only to philosophy but to literature itself. Both are arguably taken to task when Jake writes up his conversations with Hugo as a series of Platonic dialogues. *The Silencer*, as the book is called, is not silent enough. It is a work in deep contradiction with itself—an abstract defence of the particular, a theory about the limits of theories, a verbose defence of the ineffable. It is, we are told, 'a travesty and falsification'—indeed, 'a betrayal of everything' (UN, 73–74).

So, while critics have taken Murdoch to task for her insensitivity to particulars, they have often overlooked how these criticisms are produced within her own fiction. *Under the Net* is a novel of ideas about the tyranny of ideas. It is a self-indicting form of art which suggests that all stories are 'lies' (UN, 98). The novel itself may represent something more complex—it speaks the truth about its own deceit—but it is acutely aware of the ways art may fail to accommodate the texture of the world. Ventriloquising Plato, Murdoch notes how art often 'undermines our sense of reality' (EM, 422). This is partly because artworks are beholden to their own form—to principles of unity, closure, or basic intelligibility—and falsely impute such form to reality. This is where art becomes a kind of magic for Murdoch—a form of wish fulfilment that does an injustice to particulars. She may have hoped to do away with magic in her work, but her novels often seem to draw attention to their own conjuring. When Harriet—a stubborn particular standing in the way of the resolution of plot—is dispatched by a hail of bullets at a German airport in *The Sacred and Profane Love Machine*, the novel seems to advertise the violence within its own conception of order. 'Oddly enough the world *could* be set in order. . . . Harriet had gone. . . . she had been thoroughly and forever mopped up and tidied away.'[35] These are the ruminations of Harriet's egomaniacal husband, but the use of free indirect discourse also has a way of making them the narrator's. Structurally, at least, the novel colludes with Blaise's sense of tidiness. In *The Unicorn* characters seem to comment on the extreme neatness of the

35. Murdoch, *The Sacred and Profane Love Machine*, 302. All further references are given in the text under the abbreviation 'SPLM.'

novel's plotting: 'It was like a comedy by Shakespeare. All the ends of the story were being bound up in a good way.' Others find the trickery rather dull ('You both feel you are sitting out the end of some rather tedious film, don't you, where you already know what's going to happen?' [U, 209]).

These are novels of ideation and know themselves as so. Precisely because art has a cognitive dimension, for Murdoch, it can also be deeply false. Here literature supplies more order or intelligibility to the world than it possesses, encouraging us 'to believe in the omnipotence of thought' (EM, 422). This is a particular hazard in the 'novel of ideas' or the 'philosophical novel'—it can foster a corrupt confidence that the world is adequate or reducible to our conceptual schemes. Murdoch, therefore, repeatedly sets out to disturb such confidence in her fiction. The grandiose abstractions about love or goodness that are championed by her protagonists, for instance, are repeatedly exposed by the basic mechanics of plot. In *A Fairly Honourable Defeat*, for instance, Rupert dramatically falls short of his own love-theorising and it yields a grim kind of bathos. According to Murdoch, bathos 'is the revenge of the fragmentary world upon a pretentious pseudo-unity' (MGM, 98). Rupert's treatise on love is one of these pseudo-unities and the world has its revenge; it is torn to shreds by the novel's end. Muddle, in Murdoch, is irreducible, and the particular will not be suborned by the concepts that would hold it in thrall.

But this defence of the particular is not without its own metaphysical burden. As Nicholas quips to his sister Annette when she eulogises about '*le concret*' in *The Flight from the Enchanter*: '*Le concret! C'est ce qu'il y a de plus abstrait*.'[36] Motivating the search for the mute particular, we may feel, is a problematic confidence in the brute 'given' or 'thing-in-itself'—a fantasy that the world will make itself available to us without the intercession of ideas. Murdoch conceded that the case for particulars could be overstated—so much so that it would lead to a taboo against concepts (EM, 152). She may have celebrated a form of 'thinking without theories' (L, 439)—and viewed literature as an ideal space for

36. Murdoch, *Flight from the Enchanter*, 59.

this kind of thought—yet as her own fiction attests, 'all expression is weighted with theory' (UN, 99). This may amount to an injunction against speech, or it may be a call to relinquish the kind of particularism that would render all speech inadequate. If she often invoked Wittgenstein's reflections about the limits of language in her chastisement of philosophy, she also took seriously his point that efforts to exceed those limits are liable to produce nonsense. Some might argue that Murdoch is never nonsensical enough: that her fictional worlds are too sane or sanitised by concepts and theories (even her dogs seem to think in full sentences).[37] However, Bradley Pearson rightly resents the presumption that 'truth ceases to be when it is not stammered' (BP, 81). We are, after all, sense-making creatures or, as Jake puts it, 'theory-making animals' (UN, 97). And though we should attend to the particularities of situations, Jake makes the point that many of the situations we confront owe their very being to theories.

This is borne out by many of the love trysts in the novels. These situations are repeatedly constituted by the various theories that are brought to bear on them, and there are countless instances of these—'Love is the only justice,' (NG, 305); 'Love is persecution' (UN, 45); 'Love is knowledge' (BP, 366); 'Love is concerned with possession and vindication of self' (BP, 410); '[L]ove brings . . . a vision of selflessness' (BP, 210)—to take some of the pithier aphorisms from these elaborate love-machines. Ironically, love is often theorised as a state of sense-certainty that has no need of interpretation: 'Love doesn't rely on "evidence" and "induction." Love *knows*' (SS, 362). In other words, love is the myth of the given in its most seductive form: It has no need of concepts and is 'its own absolute justification' (WC, 125). 'Extreme love,' we are told, 'has the stamp of the indubitable' and love is seldom less than extreme in Murdoch.[38] These theories tend to jar with their own content—should something so certain of itself require so much interpretation?—and often advertise the shortcomings of those who profess them. Or the generalities ironically vindicate another view of love that can be found

37. See Zed's thinking in Murdoch, *Philosopher's Pupil*, 248.

38. Murdoch, *A Severed Head*, 125.

across Murdoch's oeuvre: Love is an attentiveness to particulars—a solicitude that is often lost to solipsistic certainties or noisy love-theorising. Of course, this too is a theory and may not do full justice to what love involves. But the fantasy of doing without theories would seem to be another romanticism. Those who profess to have 'no theories' in Murdoch are usually self-deceived (BP, 19).

Adorno's utopia of cognition may also have been Murdoch's—'to unseal the nonconceptual' without denying its ontological independence—yet, like Adorno, she also recognised that this could not be done without the use of concepts and theories.[39] All novels are condemned to be novels of ideas on some basic level. Although we continue to fetishize the novel as 'the genre of the particular,' this description may not be particular or capacious enough.[40] For one thing, it overlooks the role of generality within the novel form—from its use of generic conventions to its enlistment of typologies of symbolism or character, to its deployment of general concepts such as love, goodness, or evil. As we have seen, the particularities of Murdoch's novels may expose the inadequacy of such concepts, but the fraught theorising of her protagonists can also be viewed in a much more idealistic vein: It suggests that our various *conceptions* (of love or beauty, for instance) can never exhaust the richness of the overarching *concept*. This is a point she repeatedly makes about goodness—it exceeds definition—and the enactment of this in her fiction can give a very Platonic character to Murdoch's novels of ideas.

'Good art,' Murdoch concluded, 'is both very general and very particular,' a double life that is attributable to the fact that art is essentially a form of thought or 'organised vision' (EM, 15). Fundamental to the life of thought, for Murdoch, is an ability to see differences and to separate things (this was, she suggested, 'a definition of rationality' [L, 430]), but she also stressed the importance of synthesising judgement. 'Intellect,' she declared, 'is naturally one-making' (MGM, 1). Of course, her novels repeatedly resist the false unities of the synthetic intellect—not

39. Adorno, *Negative Dialectics*, 10.

40. Mazzoni, *Theory of the Novel*, 344.

least when it is the individual ego that is doing the synthesising. Bradley Pearson, for instance, 'has a way of seeing everything in his own way and making it all fit together in his own picture' (BP, 393)—and Murdoch's novels often seek to punish this egotistical symmetry by destroying such pictures. The human subject is the great source of pattern within the world and the great flaw within it. The reality and dignity of the subjective is repeatedly acknowledged in Murdoch. The human mind, we are told, is 'the most particular and individual of all natural things,' even if the same qualities can make it difficult to grasp both the reality and particularity of other minds (EM, 215). Yet this remains the key moral and epistemic task across Murdoch's writing. It is also built into one of her more famous love definitions—'love is the perception of individuals' (EM, 215). The fragility of this love is expressed in the very fabric of her own art.

Losing Our Minds

'The unconscious mind,' Murdoch liked to say, 'is not a philosopher' (EM, 21), though she also noted how philosophy was raising increasingly sceptical questions about mind—not least versions of it that we can't in principle or, by definition, know. Indeed, Murdoch felt she was witnessing the philosophical 'disappearance of mind' (EM, 61). Gilbert Ryle's attacks on dualistic accounts—ghosts lingering in machines—combined with Wittgenstein's doubts about the intelligibility of certain constructions of 'inner experience' had led, she believed, to a thorough vitiation of the concept. The famous claim of the *Philosophical Investigations*—that 'an "inner process" stands in need of outer criteria'—risked banishing, she believed, a whole series of vague feelings, inchoate thoughts, and impressions from the republic of meaning (MGM, 271).[41] Such resistance to the mess inside ultimately lends itself to a crude verificationism—if not in Wittgenstein, then in many of his followers—where only those events and entities that are publicly verifiable have a right to our

41. Wittgenstein, *Philosophical Investigations*, 153. Murdoch would find his insistence on these outward criteria 'unbearably narrow' (MGM, 275).

attention. In her famous tale of 'M' and 'D' in *The Sovereignty of Good,* Murdoch took issue with this reductive outlook. Here a mother ('M') undergoes a sea change in her attitude to her daughter-in-law ('D'): What had once appeared vulgar and coarse in 'D' now functions as generous, open, and spontaneous (EM, 312–15). According to Murdoch, the dominant forms of contemporary moral philosophy cannot account for this shift, since it involves no 'outward' or behavioural change ('M,' it seems, is a well-bred Englishwoman and has remained meticulously polite in all her dealings with 'D'). Moreover, the internal reflections that drive and follow such change would seem to be ruled out from the start in certain behaviouralist and crudely verificationist approaches to ethics—the view that 'only the "outer" is real' (MGM, 157).

The accuracy and fairness of Murdoch's account of philosophical trends can certainly be questioned—alongside her conviction that the inner life needed to be defended from those who did not possess any (L, 217). Nonetheless, it helps to account for the cognitive function she accords to literature: It is one of the most powerful devices we possess for studying the inner life and the phenomenology of moral experience. Inwardness is clearly a major theme of her fiction—'We are such inward secret creatures, that inwardness is the most amazing thing about us, even more amazing than our reason' (though it's also worth stressing that this eulogy comes from a pathological egotist [SS, 189]). It's not, of course, always sunny inside. Murdoch's people are often lost to 'a tempestuous inferno of private thoughts' (BD, 218). Or we find characters trapped behind their own faces: 'How strange that behind a smiling chattering mask one may rehearse in the utmost detail pictures and conversations which constitute torture, that behind that mask one may weep, one may howl' (WC, 97). This is how Hilary Burde feels in *A Word Child,* though it might as easily capture the initial feelings of Murdoch's 'M' as she surveys the little vulgarian who has married her son. Nonetheless, a devotion to some kind of inner experience shapes the form of Murdoch's novels and it helps to explain why she regarded the invention of character to be one of the most important and difficult aspects of the novelist's craft: making inwardness publicly available while also suggesting that mind is not reducible to its public expressions.

The creation of character, for Murdoch, is as much a moral achievement as it is an aesthetic one, for it reflects a deep respect for the distinctness, complexity, and value of others. 'A great novelist,' she maintained, 'displays a real apprehension of persons other than the author as having a right to exist and to have a separate mode of being which is important and interesting to themselves' (EM, 271). This rendering of character may seem naive, not least because it seems to conflate fictional entities with real persons.[42] When her own creations make this mistake we are invited to laugh (recall the protests of Charles Arrowby: 'I don't despise women. I was in love with all of Shakespeare's heroines before I was twelve' [SS, 176]). According to R. M. Hare, 'No work of fiction can be about a concrete individual,' and he used Murdoch's own work as evidence of the fact.[43] Jake in *Under the Net,* he believed, is not a specific person, but *a type* of individual, though he shares this fate with all literary characters. The value of casting characters as types can certainly be questioned, but it is an outlook that Murdoch's fiction seems to invite. Note, for instance, how the titles of her novels repeatedly advertise the typological role of the personalities that will feature (*The Flight from the Enchanter, The Good Apprentice,* or *The Philosopher's Pupil,* to name but a few). Moreover, various personality types reoccur in her work—the dangerous sorcerer, the artist, the quasi-saint—and the recirculation of traffic would be noted by Murdoch herself ('I wish I could create more different kinds of character. There are certain recognisable types in my novels, perhaps five people who tend to recur').[44]

Critics have had fun with this. In Murdochland, according to Martin Amis, characters are often substitutable: 'The men have all names like Hilary and Julian. The women all have names like Julian and Hilary.'[45]

42. On the defensibility of treating characters *as if* they are real people, see Cavell, *Must We Mean What We Say?*, 246–49. Also Anderson, Moi, and Felski, *Character.*

43. Hare, 'Universalisability,' 310.

44. Bellamy and Murdoch, 'An Interview with Iris Murdoch,' 139.

45. Amis, *The War Against Cliché*, 91.

Too many of them are called Hugo, in Colin Burrow's eyes. Murdoch, he concludes, is an 'anti-novelist' because she 'is not very good at particularising people.'[46] This conclusion, however, reflects a rather constrained conception of the novel. It doesn't give much quarter, at least, to Lukács's emphasis on the typical within the novelistic: his conviction (derived from Engels) that each literary character 'is simultaneously a type and a particular individual.'[47] The object of character, we might argue, then, is not *simply* to particularise or to flood the world with unique kinds. As recent criticism suggests, its proper function may be to gather examples of general kinds under a proper noun.[48] The method invites us to conclude that people are less particular than they like to think. If Charles Arrowby, Bradley Pearson, or Hilary Burde are exemplifications of 'egotism,' then they invite us to reflect on the ways that we too participate in the type. These figures, we might say, are concrete universals, embodying and dramatizing traits that we all share. This might allow Murdoch to aspire to what she identified in great art: its powerful fusion of the general and the particular.

But the problem of characterisation in Murdoch cannot be so easily explained away—not least because it reveals fundamental tensions in the way she thinks about people and thinks about thinking. The issue can be seen if we return to her description-cum-rule—'love is the perception of individuals'—and dwell on the different genitive functions of the preposition 'of.' The individual nature of perception can make the perception of individuals quite difficult. This might make perception more irregular than it is, but Murdoch often implies that our thoughts about others are constrained by the subjective character of our own thought, and she often wants us to cultivate a wider or more objective vision. Yet this raises questions about how we should attend to another person or, indeed, to ourselves. To what extent does another's subjectivity or first-person perspective need to be built into or limit a third-person assessment of them? The issue even arises when we attempt to

46. Burrow, 'I Am a Severed Head.' Burrow's quota on Hugos is rather tough, since the name appears in only two of her twenty-six novels.

47. Lukács, *Writer and Critic and Other Essays*, 35.

48. See, for instance, Kunin, *Character as Form*.

look at ourselves and note the often painful gap between a third-person perspective of who and what we are and our first-person sense of ourselves. For ethical and epistemic reasons, Murdoch is attracted to the Wittgensteinian thought: 'What is valid for the third person is . . . valid, however queer this may sound, for the first person too.'[49] But she repeatedly shows how the first person often wants things the other way round, craving general assent to its own sense of what's valid. The result can be nonsense and narcissism: something that the third-person perspective cannot credit either for moral or epistemic reasons. And yet the mewling ego may refuse to back down. The question is whether this resistance is always wrong, whether something deep and valuable would be lost if first-person perspectives were always routed by a third-person outlook. The issue is a representational problem as much as it is an ethical or epistemic one and affects how characters are presented and judged throughout her writing.

'Can one know what is going on in another person in the way he himself knows it?' Wittgenstein suggests that this may be a false question: that it sets the wrong test for the third-person knower, since it is not clear that the first person ever 'knows' her own thought.[50] She expresses it or is 'certain' of it, but the grammar of 'knowing' is more public, testable, or verifiable ('One can only *know* . . . where there are clear rules of evidence').[51] Inner states have outward criteria which make them knowable to a third person—in this sense people aren't as mysterious as we might like to think. We don't need to locate a person's inner face; we can usually determine what their outer one is saying. Of course, people can lie to us with their faces—as Bradley Pearson notes, 'Feigning is essential in the lives of us imperfect beings' (BK,186)—but, as Wittgenstein maintained, even feigning affirms that there are public criteria for inward states. People can see through us, and we see

49. Wittgenstein, *Remarks on the Philosophy of Psychology*, 1.175.

50. Wittgenstein tends to deflate these doubts: '"But the fact is that a human being knows only his *own* thoughts" ("But the fact is that only I know of my own thinking.") "And I don't either," one might say.' See Wittgenstein, *Remarks on the Philosophy of Psychology*, 1.107.

51. Wittgenstein, *Last Writings on the Philosophy of Psychology*, 2.49. On the differences between knowledge and certainty, see Wittgenstein, *On Certainty*.

ourselves through others. And yet the obscurity of others remains a lived problem in Murdoch: 'What are you thinking? She had cried. Oh how it maddens me not to know' (SPLM, 23).

The question of self-knowledge might seem to be a little more straightforward. However, Murdoch also shows how difficult this can be, split as we often are between first-person and third-person perspectives on ourselves:

> There is . . . an eternal discrepancy between the self-knowledge which we gain by observing ourselves objectively and the self-awareness which we have of ourselves subjectively: a discrepancy which probably makes it impossible for us ever to arrive at the truth. Our self-knowledge is too abstract, our self-awareness is too intimate and swoony and dazed. (BP, 189–90)

Here, at least, Murdoch is reluctant to accept that the inner is entirely reducible to the outer, even for the ego itself. But the passage also makes us wonder about the extent to which inwardness can be a viable object of representation. The problem, again, is sometimes registered in her own form. It can often feel as if we could do with a bit more swooniness and less external judgement within her narrative voice ('Danby was fundamentally a very absurd person, a contingent person' [BD, 57]; 'Jessica had never developed . . . the faculty which is sometimes called moral sense' [NG, 81]; 'The sad truth was that Mary simply did not love him enough to see him clearly' [NG, 88]). Here knowledge by description, even a certain kind of theory-making, has superseded knowledge by acquaintance. This may be because the Wittgenstein within her (she *was* Wittgenstein, remember) was always reluctant to conceive of 'acquaintance,' or the phenomenology of inward states, with knowledge. Nonetheless, it can feel as if the narrator's knowledge in Murdoch is all too external or serenely descriptive at key points in the game.

Murdoch, admittedly, deploys free indirect style in an attempt to make things more inward-leaning: 'Was it giddiness she was feeling now, a dazzled sensation of spinning drunkenness, or was it something else, disgust, fear, horror as at some dreadfulness, some unspeakable filth of the universe?' (FHD, 178). Here inwardness struggles to know itself and exceeds the characters' and narrator's attempts to describe its contents. Murdoch's first-person narratives—*Under the Net, The Black Prince, The Sea, The Sea,* and *A Word Child*—are equally soaked in inwardness, a quality that sometimes risks overwhelming the world. Take Bradley Pearson's moment of nausea in *The Black Prince*: 'Out in the street some blackness boiled in my eyes. Sun, filtered through hazy cloud, dazzled me. People loomed in front of me in bulky shadowy shapes and passed me like ghosts, like trees walking' (BP, 114). Yet the stream of consciousness in Murdoch is never a flood.[52] She sympathised with Lukács's critique of the prioritisation of interiority under modernism: his sense that it led beyond the intelligible.[53] The criticisms also chimed with Wittgenstein's interrogation of metaphysical privacy—an inner music that no one (even its lonely player) could possibly hear. Murdoch's representational methods often tacitly concede to the impossibility of a private language—even her most manic characters tend to think in publicly accessible phrases. It is a style that sometimes suggests that 'the inner is the outer, the outer is the inner,' at least where meaning is concerned (PP, 552).

And yet the inner is never quite the outer in her fiction—though this again returns us to Murdoch's fundamental ambivalence about the knowability and even value of inward states. Charles Arrowby is deeply committed to his 'secret vital busy inwardness' (SS, 518), even if this metaphysical privacy can also make him unfathomable to others and to himself. 'Oh everything's *inside*,' Pearson complains, 'that's the trouble' (BP, 307). This is the condition of a solipsist who has relinquished—indeed, seemingly eaten—the world. Pearson is conflicted about the inwardness he simultaneously cultivates. If it secures a precious independence from others, it can also make other people entirely unfathomable ('Oh the tormenting strangeness of our ignorance of other minds, the privileged comfort of the secrecy of our own!' [BP, 239]). Bradley feels he knows his own secrets, but the metaphysical privacy he

52. For her comments on the stream of consciousness (its reality but also its representational limits), see Murdoch, *Metaphysics as a Guide to Morals*, 172–73; 258–59.

53. See her use of Lukács in Murdoch, *Sartre*, 82–83.

invests in can also render the ego a secret to itself. After all, we can only guess what our inner faces look like. The same issue leaves Charles Arrowby feeling despondent: 'Most of what we think we know about our minds is pseudo-knowledge' (SS, 189). Know thyself may be an ancient precept for living, but Murdoch often seems to doubt the possibility or value of this kind of wisdom—at least if it's interpreted as a carte blanche to infinite introspection. As she declares in *The Sovereignty of Good*: '"Self-knowledge," in the sense of a minute understanding of one's own machinery, seems to me, except at a fairly simple level, usually a delusion' (EM, 355). The introspective gaze, moreover, tends to make us face in the wrong direction in our search for meaning or value, towards the ever-retreating horizon of the 'inner me' and not towards reality proper.[54]

And yet for all of her criticisms of self-absorption and self-obsession, Murdoch also wants to insist on the reality and value of this inner me. Narcissists as they are, Bradley Pearson and Charles Arrowby have a point when they stress its importance and irreducibility. This, at least, is the position Murdoch explicitly takes up in her philosophy and it is tacitly honoured in her fiction. As she insists: 'The concept of the individual as it has been developed and exhibited in the west since Homer *requires* the idea of consciousness, inwardness, privacy, separate worlds' (MGM, 294). The shadowlands of the inner self may be hard to access or to chart, but some consultation of our fuzzy feelings and messy intuitions is an essential prerequisite for moral inquiry, and a more general attunement to value: for an evaluative take on the world is often supplied to us through these sentiments.[55] Murdoch is hostile to any philosophical programme that would seek to dismiss or bypass them: 'The

54. Again, this reflects mixed responses to Wittgenstein. 'Do not try to analyse your inner experience,' Wittgenstein counselled, in the *Philosophical Investigations*. But Murdoch was often inclined to ask 'Why not?' (MGM, 270) and felt that Wittgenstein had overcommitted himself on this point. And yet her own scepticism about the desirability and value of self-analysis is also clear.

55. 'I want to assert and indicate the importance and omnipresence of a reflective experiential background to moral decision and action, and with this the omnipresence of value . . . in human activity' (MGM, 259).

individual "inner life" presents itself as something not to be analysed away' (MGM, 278).

She repeatedly worried, therefore, about the ways that Wittgenstein 'excludes inner life' (MGM, 77), though this may have overstated his resistance to inwardness. Wittgenstein readily conceded that much of ordinary life includes the inner, but he was keen to insist that it is less mysterious than we think. In daily affairs, as he suggests, the inner finds its ground in the outer and is always posited when we interact with one another. He put the matter most vividly in a late note:

> It's always presupposed that the person who smiles *is* a human being, and not just what smiles is a human body. Certain circumstances and the connection with other forms of behaviour are also presupposed. But when all that has been presupposed, someone else's smile is pleasing to me.
>
> If I ask someone on the street for directions then I prefer a friendly answer to an unfriendly one. I react immediately to someone else's behaviour. I presuppose the *inner* insofar as I presuppose the *human*.[56]

So, it is a measure of my humanity and yours that we attribute inwardness to each other. And yet Murdoch is keen to show that these attributions are more contingent and variable than we think and depend very much on perspective. We can, after all, look at the world with a cold eye in ways that might bring us to the outer limits of the inner or the human in ourselves and in others. This, we may remember, was the basic orientation of Lewis's 'inhuman' or 'external' gaze and it is significant that we often find people attempting a similarly distanced vision in Murdoch, even practicing this outlook upon themselves. The results can be both powerful and depressing.

Consider Danby's confrontation with the reflection of himself in *Bruno's Dream*: 'He was an obese elderly man with white hair and a face coarsened by drink' (BD, 182). Think, too, of Harriet's moment of self-alienation through a mirror: 'The calm face she had known all these years was gone and a strange woman stared back, big eyes and

56. Wittgenstein, *Last Writings on the Philosophy of Psychology*, 2.84.

distraught, her mouth ugly with grief' (SPLM, 125). Or take Bradley Pearson's moment of self-transcendence in the bedroom of a would-be lover:

> I looked down and regarded her body, which was plump, fleshy. I drew my hand down over her stomach which contracted under my fingers. I felt excited, stunned, but this was not quite desire. I seemed to be outside, seeing myself as in a picture, a fully dressed elderly man in a dark suit and a blue tie lying beside a pink naked pear-shaped lady. (BP, 158)

This external vision is not without its cruelty, whether it is extended to oneself or to pear-shaped others. To objectify others—as Bradley repeatedly does—is not to see them objectively or at least comprehensively; the fact of their inwardness needs to be built into any adequate account of what they are. And yet Bradley repeatedly fails to acknowledge this dimension of others. Take his comically inept attempts to comfort his distraught sister: 'I sat for a time patting her with the awkward ineffectual gesture of a small child trying to pat an animal' (BP, 78). Here and elsewhere, Bradley struggles to fathom other humans—or doesn't struggle enough. If Murdoch often glorifies a condition of detachment in her ethics, Pearson can seem pathologically detached from the sister he observes: 'I could see Priscilla wearing my red and white striped pyjamas, flopped in a deliberately uncomfortable position, her arms spread wide like a puppet, still steadily crying. The horror of the world seen without charm' (BP, 85). This reveals the horror of a way of seeing as much as the charmlessness of an object seen. Priscilla may be a clown—she is certainly dressed as one—but the portrait advertises the dangers of a thoroughly disenchanted or 'external' perspective.[57] It marks a radical failure of empathy—a total refusal to engage with the inwardness of another being.

57. As Murdoch suggests elsewhere, the 'exercise of *detachment* is difficult and valuable whether the thing contemplated is a human being or the root of a tree or the vibration of a colour or a sound' (EM, 353).

Bradley may be incapable of empathy because he is too trapped within his own inwardness and thus remains 'outside' ordinary human values and relationships (here perhaps the language of the inner and the outer begins to break down just as Wittgenstein maintained it always would). Bradley is an extreme case, but he is not unique. Most of us live life from the inside and may struggle to harmonise our subjective viewpoint with a broader vision. When Monty tells Blaise that matters which loom large within his own consciousness are trivial from a cosmic point of view, Blaise makes a valid protest: 'But I live in my consciousness' (SPLM, 112). However, Murdoch often wants us to reside elsewhere: away from the 'fat relentless ego' (EM, 342), and at some hygienic remove from the 'filth' of one's own consciousness (WC, 26). 'Where can I live?' Bruno asks Lisa. Lisa's answer is simple: 'Outside' (BD, 167). But outside is a big place. How far we have to go in order to encounter reality—beyond a personal viewpoint, beyond a human one, beyond any contingent perspective whatsoever?—is far from clear. Many parts of this outward journey can leave us and other people looking or feeling diminished. From an external perspective the self can appear as 'an agitating puppet'—a predictable machine steered by physical laws (BD, 167). Regarded from loftier heights the self might even seem to disappear.

This may, of course, be the point, though it might make us wonder why Murdoch worried so much about salvaging the inner and taking issue with any programme that would seek to liquidate it. Her own moral programme can often seem just as drastic. Murdoch was keen to insist in conversation that the moral task is not the total extermination of the ego: 'What is to be "destroyed" is one's egoism, not oneself.'[58] Yet the call to unselfing in Murdoch is often accompanied by a strange rhetorical extremism. 'Ultimately we are nothing,' she declares, in *Metaphysics as a Guide to Morals* (MGM, 501). The same view repeatedly circulates in her fiction (when Cato complains, 'I feel I'm nobody, nothing' he receives the therapeutic response: 'It's what we all are' [HC,

58. Dooley, *From a Tiny Corner*, 200.

388]). When the illusoriness of the self is conceded, our troubles might seem to fade away: 'Things can't matter very much, she thought, because one isn't anything' (BD, 293). If things no longer matter so much, it may be because all mattering has been left behind. This radical devaluation would be a deeply ironic result, because the journey into the great outside is intended to reveal how 'every little thing matters' (SPLM, 322). Perhaps everything does, but the flight from the ego in Murdoch might appear to lead beyond all value.

Much depends, of course, on what a value is, in Murdoch—whether it is ontologically subjective and observer-relative or whether it is some intrinsic feature of the universe. We have seen how she often talks of 'the good' as something deeply objective and ontologically independent—as real if not more real than things and humans, but reducible to neither. To access this 'transcendent reality,' as she calls it, we must abandon the palace of illusion—namely our private ego (EM, 376). Here moral objectivity presupposes 'a kind of intellectual ability to perceive what is true, which is automatically at the same time a suppression of self' (EM, 353).[59] However, value in Murdoch is also a texture or colour we give to reality. It is activated by real features of others and the world, but it is constituted in part by our consciousness. As she declares: 'The concept of consciousness and the concept of value "must" be internally linked' (MGM, 256). Here things acquire significance by the way we attend to them. The human being in this context is 'a value-bearer or value-donor' (MGM, 256). If there are moral facts in the world, 'the "facts" are set up by human (that is moral) agents' (MGM, 26).

Murdoch is sometimes prepared to admit that moral life is partly a 'fabrication,' but she also wants us to preserve many of our realist intuitions about this constructed world. As in the case of colour, value may involve a particular way of seeing but it is not something we simply elect to see.[60] We can still use the language of discovery rather than invention

59. 'Forsake thyself'—the credo that Maggie found so attractive in *The Mill on the Floss*—clearly has its attractions for Murdoch. Eliot, *Mill on the Floss*, 209.

60. Murdoch, in these contexts, can sound like a moral anti-realist, even a fictionalist: 'We have already partly willed our world when we come to look at it; and we must admit moral responsibility for this "fabricated" world, however difficult it may be to control the process of

when we encounter it and retain our sense of responsibility to 'a reality which is beyond us' (MGM, 214). Yet it remains ontologically subjective or observer-relative, requiring something from us or within us to bring it into being. As Murdoch once put it: 'It is into ourselves that we must look. . . . The proof that every little thing matters is to be found there' (MGM, 495). But we might well ask, then, if the radical unselfing she advocates would also be value-denying, a destruction of the good in the name of the good. It can certainly make the differences between the nihilist and the saint in Murdoch appear vanishingly thin. How much self survives the project of unselfing is, of course, a key question—whether it culminates in a thin self or a dead self.[61] We might also ask how this purified soul goes about the business of loving. The practice, after all, was supposed to involve the perception of individuals. However, the 'impersonal love' that is often eulogised in Murdoch's philosophy and fiction risks reducing love to a pure abstraction (BD, 265). The object may be to see another as an end-in-itself, but this also seems to demand the end of the self that sees. A lover so impersonal, we may feel, is no longer a person, and may struggle to see others as such.[62]

Perhaps Murdoch regarded her own creations with an impersonal love, though this has led some to believe that she did not like them very much.[63] Her characters usually take themselves very seriously; yet, observed from the outside—as they so often are—they frequently come across as absurd.[64] 'Every man is tiny and comic to his neighbour,' Bradley Pearson insists, and the external perspective is a rich source of irony in her fiction (BP, 390). Here perspective puts values to the test.

---

fabrication' (EM, 201). Though Murdoch presents the will as a constitutive force here, she is generally keen to downplay the role given to particular kinds of willing and choosing in ethics.

61. Murdoch often suggests that some self but not much self is left behind after goodness has done its work ('the good self is very small indeed' [EM, 355]).

62. Murdoch seems to acknowledge the catastrophic sides of such love in *The Nice and the Good*: 'Love did not move toward life, it moved toward death, toward the roaring sea-caves of annihilation' (NG, 109). But again, perhaps annihilation is the point.

63. See Nussbaum, 'Love and Vision,' 48.

64. 'I'm not mocking my characters,' Murdoch insisted, going on to add: 'The comedy is very deep in the form.' Dooley, *From a Tiny Corner*, 200.

What is valid for the third person may be valid for the first, but Murdoch also shows how we renege on this sentiment both for good and bad reasons. Much of 'the weirdness of being human' (MGM, 257) stems from the fact that we can take general and particular, detached and committed perspectives on the world and ourselves, without knowing for sure what the right perspective is. Murdoch may have been ambivalent about ambivalence, but it features in the very bones of her work, radiating the feeling that this may be our most natural condition. This is not a cause of gloom for Murdoch. Our doubleness, she believes, is celebrated in the novel and this explains why, for all its painful ironies, it is a comic—even a happy—form.

Epilogue

ETHICAL CRITICISM NOW

IN *THE AWKWARD AGE* a mother asks her daughter a question that parents don't often ask their children: 'What's the use of being good?'[1] The question might appear to assume too much by making usefulness the ultimate criterion of value; it also supposes too little by suggesting that morality is in need of some justification. A mind so unconvinced is arguably already corrupt; by asking her question—not least of all to her child—the mother possibly reveals that she is already one of the damned. But fiction, I have argued, often brings us to this troubling meta-ethical space, asking us to consider the practical significance of morality within our lives. Or perhaps it settles the question rather quickly—and shows how we have already begged it by tucking up with a book.

In the very act of reading a novel, we might seem to live out an answer to how much morality matters: not very much, or not as much as some moralists think. The bookish, yes, have long stressed the moral significance of books—their importance as self-care, as boot camp for the soul, as clever engines for imagining others—and I have made a qualified case for each of these features of fiction throughout this study. But I have also maintained that morality does not exhaust our sense of value. Nor is it the prism for every good thought. Iris Murdoch liked to claim

1. James, *The Awkward Age*, in *Novels, 1896–1899*, 858.

that 'consciousness itself is a form of moral activity: what we attend to, how we attend, whether we attend.'[2] But this risks making morality either vanishingly broad or oppressively ubiquitous—a demand that obtains, as Murdoch insists, 'every single second.'[3] The moral of many novels—even perhaps Murdoch's own—is that we can only cope with so much morality—at least its more demanding and ambitious versions.[4] If Murdoch is right, and we 'are almost always morally active,' then we might well feel that art allows us a holiday from the good and supplies a relatively safe space for our 'irresponsible' sides.[5] Assuming some moral virtues remain operative in aesthetic play, we might be tempted to say that the game prioritises honesty over decency, allowing us to come clean to each other about our uglier or more unmanageable feelings. For this reason, art has long been viewed as a purge or form of therapy.[6] Nelson Goodman was only half-joking when he suggested that 'theatres and museums function as adjuncts to the Departments of Public Health.'[7] If art supplies this therapeutic function, it may be unethical to require it to be good.[8]

A viable ethical criticism, I have argued, must recognise its limits—not least the limits of the moral itself—if it is to do justice to its object and, indeed, the world. Novels may be, as Murdoch put it, 'amazingly moral,' but they are also amazed by the moral—its complexity, its compelling power, and its strange elusiveness, how hard it is to make good on our claims about the good.[9] The job is made harder, of course, by

2. Murdoch, *Metaphysics as a Guide to Morals*, 167.

3. Murdoch, *Metaphysics as a Guide to Morals*, 495.

4. This is one way of reading the ending of *Middlemarch*, the settling for good with a small 'g' rather than a big one.

5. James Wood, *The Irresponsible Self*.

6. Or as Collingwood put it: 'Art is the community's medicine for the worst disease of mind.' Collingwood, *The Principles of Art*, 336. For a discussion of the therapeutic value of literature, see Aubry and Travis, *Rethinking Therapeutic Culture*.

7. Goodman, *The Languages of Art*, 248.

8. Collingwood also took the view that art allowed us to discharge dangerous emotions in make-believe situations, making it 'less likely that they will discharge themselves in practical life.' Collingwood, *The Principles of Art*, 86.

9. Murdoch, *Metaphysics as a Guide to Morals*, 97.

the need to align morality with other kinds of thinking and valuing. Murdoch may be right—'almost all our language is value language'—but not all of our value language is moral.[10] One of the virtues of the novel is the way it exposes the richness of the normative, the heterogeneous pulls and repulsions that can cluster around a single symbol—a dove, a golden bowl, a lighthouse, a bell. We are drawn to different goods—moral, aesthetic, epistemic, political—and if our values cross-pollinate, they also clash. Life is usually a business of managing the din. The conflicts between moral and aesthetic values can certainly be softened by the cultivation of a broad sense of normativity that we have sometimes called 'ethics'—an inclusive sense of value that can see the worth of self-regarding acts from navel-gazing to novel-writing, and acknowledges the importance of the aesthetic to any concept of the 'good' life.[11] But this capaciousness won't defuse all tensions, and some books seem designed to cause trouble. Take Nabokov's portrait of an eloquent paedophile[12] or some of the flowers of evil that we have encountered in this book—not least the sack of mental ferrets that is Wyndham Lewis's *Tarr*.[13]

Books of this kind may lead us to think that there are basic threshold conditions—of a moral sort—that have to be met before artworks can be enjoyed. The limit will always be tested by the next de Sade or *American Psycho*, but because of the diversity of the normative even sick books might have their singular virtues. Hume had a point, of course, when he proposed that we tend to have an imaginative resistance to material we find deeply offensive: 'Whatever indulgence we may give to the writer on account of his prejudices, we cannot prevail on ourselves to enter into his sentiments, or bear an affection to characters,

10. Murdoch, *Sartre*, 32.

11. See Williams, *Ethics and the Limits of Philosophy*.

12. For a defence of the moral complexity of *Lolita*, see Gaut, *Art, Emotion and Ethics*, 194–202. See also Phelan, *Living to Tell About It*, 98–131. For a discussion of the novel's aesthetic significance, see also Aubry, *Guilty Aesthetic Pleasures*, 140–66.

13. Lewis's 'non-moral' satire was aimed at the 'self-elected officials of the Good Life,' though he was convinced, of course, that these were, in fact, votaries of 'the Bad Life.' Lewis, *Men Without Art*, 129.

which we plainly discover to be blameable.'[14] Nabokov clearly wants to trouble this conviction, though Humbert Humbert might also appear to prove Hume right. Hume largely presented his case as an empirical description of how our minds work—the disgust-response is basic and not necessarily under our control. Nonetheless, Hume also proposed that if we are convinced of the rectitude of our moral norms then we are entirely within our rights to remain unmoved by an artwork. The good judge, he concludes, is jealous of his standards and will 'not pervert the sentiments of his heart for a moment, in complaisance to any writer whatsoever.'[15]

Today, human beings have never been more Humean—at least in their resistance to writerly perversion, and their devotion to their own standards of rectitude.[16] The critique of certain authors and certain tastes—and its often aggressive counter-critique—may indicate that ethical criticism is alive and well, or that it has entered some fevered state. Both on and off campuses (and our communicative infrastructure has blurred the boundary line) debate about moral harms is often vituperative. It was noted long ago that questions concerning 'the just and the unjust, the noble and the shameful, the good and the bad' are always liable to cause 'hatred and anger'—not least because these notions are both fundamental and contestable.[17] Nonetheless, it can still seem as if our standards of civility in argument—if argument remains the right term—have declined, while the moral demands we make on each other have never been higher. Or it can feel as if a cartoonish moralism has supplanted the labour of real virtue, including any sense that there may be different kinds—moral, aesthetic, or epistemic. It can be hard for anyone to navigate this space with integrity. If moral life has always involved a certain amount of theatre—as I have argued throughout this book—then the theatre appears to have fallen on bad times, and no one

14. See Hume, 'On the Standard of Taste,' 195.

15. Hume, 'On the Standard of Taste,' 195.

16. Garth Greenwell has recently claimed: 'Within the small world of people who care about literature and art, the culture is as moralistic as it has ever been in my lifetime.' Greenwell, 'A Moral Education.'

17. Plato, *Euthyphro*, 7 b-d. See Plato, *Complete Works*, 6–7.

likes their role in the pantomime.[18] Which isn't to say that we can all pretend to stop pretending, though we may all wish for more interesting lines.

It's always easy to believe that one inhabits an 'Age of Indignation'—as Arthur Danto clearly did—and to feel a little indignant about this fact.[19] Concerns about a marauding moralism are nothing new—such worries, we've seen, are a central feature of James's fiction—and they have produced a long tradition of meta-moralising.[20] Lionel Trilling produced a thoughtful version of this at the end of the 1940s. Ruing the narrow righteousness of his times, he also intimated that there was something perennial about the problem. History provided vivid illustration of the fact that 'the moral passions are even more wilful and imperious and impatient than the self-seeking passions.'[21] However, Trilling deemed literature an important palliative: It helped to restore some 'moral realism' to intellectual life. By 'realism' he did not mean a revived sense of the objectivity of the good, but more a sense of its complexity and its limits—indeed an understanding of the 'dangers of the moral life itself.'[22] Here we would learn to face the ugly side of our most generous wishes: the presumption of our pity, say, or the coercive element of our altruism. In Trilling's eyes, the best space to acquire this schooling in realism was the novel:

> For our time the most effective agent of the moral imagination has been the novel of the last two hundred years. It was never, either aesthetically or morally, a perfect form and its faults and failures can be quickly enumerated. But its greatness and its practical usefulness lay in its unremitting work of involving the reader himself in the moral life, inviting him to put his own motives under examination, suggesting

18. Zadie Smith suggests that a certain performativity has encroached on the way we now read (or don't): 'We've gotten into the habit of not experiencing the private, risky act of reading so much as performing our response to what we read.' Smith, 'Fascinated to Presume,' 83.

19. See Danto, 'Beauty and Morality,' 375.

20. For the critique of moralism in James, for instance, see Diamond, 'Henry James, Moral Philosophers, Moralism.'

21. Trilling, 'Manners, Morals, and the Novel,' 26.

22. Trilling, 'Manners, Morals, and the Novel,' 25.

> that reality is not as he sees it. It taught us, as no other genre ever did, the extent of human variety and the value of variety. It was the literary form to which the emotions of understanding and forgiveness were indigenous, as if by the definition of the form itself. At the moment its impulse does not seem strong, for there never was a time when the virtues of its greatness were so likely to be thought of as weaknesses. Yet there never was a time when its particular activity was so much needed, was of so much practical, political and social use—so much so that if its impulse does not respond to the need, we can be sad not only over a waning form of art but also over a waning freedom.[23]

The aptness of many of these reflections today may underline the eternal nature of the problem and the fragility of Trilling's solution. Trilling offers a committed defence of the novel's powers, but perhaps readers have never lived up to the levels of self-scrutiny or suspension of self-belief that he envisions for the form.[24] A totally open mind, we may feel, is neither feasible nor desirable, and asks for a suspension of certainties that are a basic condition of understanding. We need our 'moral prejudices'—or we might prefer to call them our principles—to see anything morally.[25] Trilling, at any rate, was fairly realistic about the prospects of 'moral realism' and the limits life imposed on our appetite for doubt or complexity: 'Life presses us so hard, time is so short, the suffering of the world is so huge, simple, unendurable—anything that complicates our moral fervor in dealing with reality as we immediately see it and wish to drive headlong upon it, must be regarded with some impatience.'[26] None of us has the time to fantasise at length about that mark on the wall, or to nurse doubt by the fire in our dressing gowns.

Like Trilling, I still see the novel as a school of uncertainty in ever more strident and harried times, though I have also tried to

23. Trilling, 'Manners, Morals, and the Novel,' 27.

24. Rita Felski, for instance, prioritises an attachment to attachment over a critical method of 'unbinding and unravelling.' See Felski, *Hooked*, 3.

25. See Hume, 'Of Moral Prejudices,' in *Essays: Moral, Political, and Literary*, 1.7–10. Hume insisted, nonetheless, on the necessity of overruling at least some prejudices as a condition of reception of a work.

26. Hume, 'Of Moral Prejudices,' in *Essays: Moral, Political, and Literary*, 26.

acknowledge the epistemic limits of doubt and the moral hazards of all forms of wonder. The hazards were both acknowledged and romanticised by Martha Nussbaum when she turned her sights to 'ethical criticism' in the 1980s. Nussbaum was drawn to the Jamesian metaphor of 'adventure' to describe the moral and epistemic journeys that novels condition.[27] However, they are not much of an adventure if we always know the moral outcome in advance—namely, that it will make Aristotelians of us all—or are already acquainted with the better person we will be by the time we finish a book.[28] As Cora Diamond argued, we should resist 'the idea of possibilities as fixed in advance' both in literature and in life.[29] Diamond herself is an admirable defender and practitioner of openness; nonetheless, her own confidence in literature's moral powers is itself possibility-limiting. If novels give us 'a sense of life as lived in a world of wonderful possibilities,' as Diamond contended, there is some risk here of pre-judging the epistemic and existential prospects by conceiving them all as 'wonderful' (unless the adjective in this context is evaluatively neutral, indicating a very literal invitation to wonder).[30] James's own sense of the 'horribly possible' says it all.[31]

Nussbaum liked to claim that 'the novel is itself a moral achievement' but this can feel like a historically provincial confidence.[32] One reason I started out with the Victorian novel is that it is often uncertain about its own moral status—or must make the case for itself to an often sceptical or suspicious audience. Perhaps we increasingly resemble our Victorian forebears in our willingness to challenge the moral propriety of what we read. This may be no bad thing, but it makes Nussbaum's investment in the goodness of literature increasingly hard to replicate. It was never easy to limp out of a Wyndham Lewis novel convinced that

27. See, in particular, Nussbaum, *Love's Knowledge*, 142–43, 179–81. For a critique of the sentimentalisation of adventure, see Maher, 'Making Good on Henry James,' chap. 3.

28. On adventure, see Diamond, 'Missing the Adventure,' in *The Realistic Spirit*.

29. Diamond, *The Realistic Spirit*, 312.

30. Diamond, *The Realistic Spirit*, 313.

31. James, *The Golden Bowl*, 468.

32. Nussbaum, *Love's Knowledge*, 46.

'the novel as a genre, in its basic structure and aspiration is . . . a defender of the Enlightenment ideal of the equality and dignity of all human life.'[33] This was fantastical in 1995, but it is even more implausible now. Nussbaum's guiding principle that the 'artist's task *is* a moral task' still sustains much of our criticism—indeed, the principle is more widely entrenched than ever—but readers are a lot more alert to the ways artists fail in the task.[34] The iconoclasm that this produces is often energising, though it can make the kind of friendship with books advocated by Proust or critics like Booth appear a little too fond.[35] Or perhaps the partisanship communicated in the metaphor of friendship remains very much in place. The only difference is that we are more willing to draw the corollary and treat some texts as enemies.

Reading may still be an adventure, but we are clearly more attuned now to its moral risks. Indeed, since the 1980s—when Nussbaum and Diamond launched their critical ships—there has been a clear moralisation of risk itself in cultural encounters. If Trilling highlighted the dangers of the moral, we increasingly moralise about dangers. The language of safety may not be quite the force it was when a pandemic raged, but it still does significant normative work in our culture. Moreover, it has thickened our sense of the harms books can do and the ways they can make us feel unsafe. It is all too easy to dismiss this as hyperbole and to present the manoeuvre as an infantilising inflation of the harm principle or safety demand.[36] Safety clearly *is* a human good and its unequal distribution *is* a moral and political problem.[37] But the same inequality can make certain professions of unsafety in relatively secure educational environments appear insensitive or even decadent—an entitled form of campus fiction.

33. Nussbaum, *Poetic Justice*, 46.

34. Nussbaum, *Love's Knowledge*, 163.

35. See Proust, 'On Reading,' 122–23. See also Booth, *The Company We Keep*.

36. On a related point Stefan Collini is emphatic: 'We should resist any temptation to equate offence with harm'—and harm, he suggests, is largely a matter of law ('Offending someone's beliefs, no matter how central they think those beliefs are to their identity, does not constitute the kind of harm the law can rightly be used to prevent'). See Collini, *That's Offensive!*, 55.

37. Srinivasan, 'The Politics of Safety.'

An attendant and ever more prevalent irony, however, is that arbitrary attempts by governments to police safety—and consequently speech—on campuses effectively make universities unsafe for all.

No doubt safety of some kind is a condition of aesthetic experience. As Dewey noted: 'A man who finds himself in a field with an angry bull has but one desire and thought: to attain a place of safety. Once in security, he may enjoy the spectacle of untamed power.'[38] Our security, of course, can have its meannesses—the feeling of it being enhanced by the sight of another's vulnerability or even pain, be it, say, the bull's or the matador's.[39] We pity the eyeless Oedipus or the broken Lear, but, as Rousseau observed, our compassion can be a sublimated form of gloating ('Pity is sweet, because, when we put ourselves in the place of one who suffers, we are aware nevertheless, of the pleasure of not suffering).'[40] Art may also indulge a dubious desire to feel invincible. In Freud's eyes, for instance, our romances and adventures draw on a wish to feel absolutely secure. Through all the trials that we undergo with the adventuring hero, we are nonetheless told: 'Nothing can happen to you!'[41] Yet it's worth reiterating that some adventures end rather badly, even perhaps for the reader. The bad luck of Conrad's Jim, for instance, may expose the terrible contingency of our own good fortune, leaving us feeling a little less safe on our sofas. Indeed, some books seem to whisper: 'Anything can happen to you!'

Stories, then, get under our skin. There may even be some complacency in Wilde's contention that 'art does not hurt us' (*The Picture of*

38. Dewey, *Art as Experience*, 259.

39. Lucretius noted long ago how the spectator on the shore draws pleasure from the sight of those in danger at sea—not that we revel in 'any man's distress,' but we are sensitised to the sweetness of our own safety. See Lucretius, *On the Nature of the Universe*, 36. On the aesthetic and ethical implications of such spectatorship, see Blumenberg, *Shipwreck with Spectator*. I'm grateful to Joe Moshenska for introducing me to Blumenberg.

40. Rousseau, *Émile*, 221. Many of us might prefer to travel with Burke on this point: Security is a condition of our enjoyment of a tragedy, but it is not the reason for or intentional object of our pleasure. See Burke, *A Philosophical Enquiry*, 41.

41. Freud, 'Creative Writers and Daydreaming,' 30. On these points, I am indebted to Bevis, *Wordsworth's Fun*, 194.

Dorian Gray, after all, would seem to paint a different picture).[42] Not only does art offend with instances of violence, racism, and sexism—often endowed with the strange glamour of the aesthetic—it repeatedly raises troubling questions about the very concept of the moral: its objectivity, its motivations, its function, or its value. It marks a serious failure of imagination—both moral and aesthetic—not to appreciate how artworks upset and unfix us. We can strive to manage the risks, issuing cautions and content warnings, but we can't insulate ourselves from all hazard, not least because risk, as Dewey noted, is an irreducible feature of thinking itself.[43] As I have shown, not all reflection is good for us, if the 'good' is understood in instrumental or practical terms. The object of thought may be to arrive at some truth, but we are all liable to feel a little like Madame de Sabran at times ('I don't rejoice as you do in the discovery of *truth*. I am afraid it will hurt me').[44] Hence the value of fiction as a veil or deflection from reflection, but also its power to disturb when it confronts us with truth or the what's-it-likeness of dark and dangerous states. We should not, of course, sensationalise the risks.[45] It is clear that there are much swifter routes to corruption or meltdown than a novel. Yet 'the risk of wrongness' of various kinds is basic to aesthetic experience.[46] It can't and shouldn't be entirely safe.

It isn't easy to say why it's all worth the risk or what exactly art is supposed to *do* for us on a practical level. Countless theories have been proposed, none of them discrete and certainly none of them definitive:

42. Wilde, *The Critic as Artist*, in *Complete Works*, 1135. This, admittedly is Gilbert's view—not necessarily Wilde's.

43. Dewey made the point about 'perception' in general. Dewey, *Art as Experience*, 276.

44. James, *Literary Criticism*, 2.656.

45. Obviously very different views have been solicited on the comfort of books: They were, for Pater, at least, 'a sort of cloistral refuge, from the vulgarities of the actual world.' Pater, *Appreciations*, 14. In D. A. Miller's eyes, such refuge is also a form of bad faith: If it presupposes the freedom of the reader from 'the surveillance, suspicion, reading, and rape of others,' it also indulges 'the freedom to read about characters who oversee, suspect, read, and rape one another.' See Miller, *The Novel and the Police*, 162.

46. Smith, 'Fascinated to Presume,' 86. Bromwich also maintains that the 'work of art . . . matters because it brings its audience close to a scene of risk.' See Bromwich, 'How Moral Is Taste,' in *Skeptical Music*, 234.

Some see art as a simulation room or mental gym that trains us up for life.[47] Some view it as a school of sentiment in which feelings are modelled and learned.[48] Some conceive of art in purely expressive terms: It is a trusted laxative for the soul. Some stress its communicative function and solidarity-building role ('Art,' Dewey argued, 'renders men aware of their union with one another in origin and destiny').[49] Others approach art in more individual terms, as a forum for self-creation, self-perfection, or less taxing kinds of self-pleasure.[50] Nelson Goodman acknowledged all of these public and private uses, but he felt they failed to cater sufficiently to what he saw as art's primary end: 'Cognition in and for itself.'[51] Pragmatists—indeed anyone—might struggle to determine what knowing in and for itself amounts to, while Kantians might worry that this traffic with knowledge makes art impure and stops it from being truly in and for itself.

There is no ultimate way of deciding between each of these rival theories—many of them being an elaboration of one dimension of art. However, I have tried to stake out a nervous middle between literature's cognitive role—the way it attunes us to certain truths about ourselves—and the more therapeutic sides of the fictive (not least in the way it can sometimes help us to bypass truth or to reconstitute it). While I have often dwelt on the different ways that literature can help us to know, I've also tried to acknowledge (in a Kantian spirit) its incompleteness as a form of knowledge—the way it resists full conceptualisation or a simple trade in propositions. This is partly because art's object for much of the time is opaque—an elusive inwardness that we share and constitute between us and which commits us to a series of 'as if' or 'what's-it-like' descriptions whose truth-status might seem impossible to vouchsafe. But the elusiveness of this truth also stems from the fact that art's role isn't

47. See, for instance, Landy, *How to Do Things with Fictions*.

48. See Collingwood on this point, *The Principles of Art*.

49. Dewey, *Art as Experience*, 275.

50. This is very much part of the *Bildung* tradition *or* what Bentham and Mill called 'self-culture.' One of the most influential recent defenders of perfectionism has been Stanley Cavell. See, in particular, Cavell, *Conditions Handsome and Unhandsome*.

51. Goodman, *The Languages of Art*, 258.

simply descriptive, it is also inaugural and often helps to invent the inwardness that it sets out to describe. As Murdoch noted: 'Man is a creature who makes pictures of himself and then comes to resemble the picture.'[52] The way art colludes in the invention of our selves may again reinforce its ethical responsibilities both for its producers and its consumers alike. My teenage attempts to become Stephen Dedalus didn't work out so well for me or for others. No one should ever try to be Tarr or, perhaps, any of Iris Murdoch's characters. But, again, the modelling function of art is only one model.

Art has many sides, but probably no essential core. Its meaning is its use, and its uses are rich and multiple. However, we have seen how art also troubles the logic of use. Wilde on this point was characteristically categorical—'All art is quite useless'—though many have derived a perverse utility (moral and cognitive) from this uselessness.[53] It seems obvious, nonetheless, that the moralisation of art is bound up with a certain embarrassment about its questionable use-value. It doesn't feel entirely coincidental that 'ethical criticism' began to flourish at a time when the prestige of the humanities in the United States and elsewhere was in decline. If the decline has continued precipitously ever since, the reasons for this are not due to the failure of ethical criticism to make the case for the personal and social benefits of art. That case has been relentlessly made.[54] And yet all the case-making risks selling art short by downplaying its intrinsic worth or by assigning an instrumental role to the values that it plays host to, not least 'cognition in and for itself.' We may still find this a rather gnomic formulation, but it's fairly clear that knowledge is something we are drawn to, though it doesn't necessarily make us happier or more virtuous. Ever since we ate that apple, the value of knowing seems to be intrinsic and art is organised around its primitive draw. Art brings us to some dark places, but it also caters to this basic cognitive need.

52. Murdoch, 'Metaphysics and Ethics,' in *Existentialists and Mystics*, 67, 70, or 71.

53. Wilde, 'Preface,' *The Picture of Dorian Gray*, in *Complete Works*, 17. For a qualified defence of this position see Lamarque, *The Uselessness of Art*.

54. See, in particular, Nussbaum, *Not for Profit*. For another defence, see Small, *The Value of the Humanities*.

If ethical criticism sometimes sells out on what it defends, it also risks overselling art's social and political benefits. I have never been convinced that judges would judge better if they read fiction.[55] Nor am I confident that a mass outbreak of novel-reading would lead to a more compassionate form of citizenship.[56] Even if there were new surges of compassion in public life, I am not sure that this would make us all more just.[57] Broader political realities, moreover, should not be ignored: If literature educates, it also requires some education, and this is a resource to which we have unequal access. Indeed, as Michael Sandel has argued, education both reflects and foments inequalities, often giving a meritocratic benediction to huge asymmetries of status and income.[58] It can feed a narcissistic confidence that the lucky are the deserving and the deserving are the smart, while all the time repressing the social and economic conditions that determine what smartness is and how it is distributed. Since the smugness of this inequality has been a source of huge resentment, it would be unfortunate if a little novel-reading convinced the smart that they were also the most compassionate. It has long been noted, after all, that art can pander to a bad confidence in our own sensitivity. This is the charge Rousseau famously made against the theatre: We are impressed with ourselves when we give our tears to fictions; yet we are often inured to suffering when we encounter it in real life.[59]

The idea that fiction might make moral spectators of us all while undermining us as moral agents lies at the heart of Hegel's critique of the 'beautiful soul' and survives even in William James—a man deeply receptive to art in all its forms.[60] James summoned up a very specific vision to make a general point: 'The weeping of a Russian lady over the

55. This is one of Nussbaum's claims in *Poetic Justice*.

56. For the view that the arts can foster civic compassion, see, in particular, Nussbaum, *Political Emotions*.

57. On the limits of compassion or pity as a political good, see, for instance, Boyd, 'Pity's Pathologies Portrayed.'

58. Sandel, *The Tyranny of Merit*.

59. Rousseau, *Politics and the Arts*.

60. As Hegel put it, the beautiful soul 'lives in dread of besmirching the splendour of its inner being by action and an existence; and, in order to preserve the purity of its heart, it flees from contact with the actual world.' Hegel, *Phenomenology of Spirit*, 400.

fictitious personages in the play, while her coachman is freezing to death on his seat outside, is the sort of thing that everywhere happens on a less glaring scale.'[61] Presumably, the play wasn't one of Henry's (no one should freeze to death for one of those); however, the vision of the coachman was enough to convince William that 'the habit of excessive novel-reading and theatre-going will produce true monsters'—at least if moral feeling is not cashed in for moral action.[62] His brother's novels certainly complicated the distinction between acting and watching, but they hardly dismantled the charge that books can pander to moral voyeurism. *The Sacred Fount*, after all, seems to invite us to become second-order voyeurs—and it is hard to know if this is to savour or to admonish the first-order kind. Thankfully, there is little empirical evidence to suggest that novels turn us into monsters of indolence or self-satisfaction. Despite his ethical fears, William James remained an avid reader of fiction. He even suggested that literature might ultimately be the best moral teacher—precisely because of its tentative and nondogmatic character.[63] There is a lot to be said for this view—indeed, it is the position tacitly assumed throughout this book—but I also think the moral case for literature can undermine what it ostensibly celebrates: moral and epistemic humility or the pleasures that might be found in our uncertainty when confronted by art.

Moral overreach in literary criticism has led to understandable attempts to sharpen its objectives, delimit its areas of expertise, and to clarify the normativity that should inform its judgements. And it has produced bold efforts to stress the difference, indeed 'incompatibility,' between an aesthetic education and a moral one.[64] As Michael Clune argues: 'The very openness to values that is a hallmark of expert artistic

61. James, *The Principles of Psychology*, 1.129.

62. Newman made a similar point and claimed that 'the *danger* of an elegant and polite education is, that it separates feeling and acting; it teaches us to think, speak, and be affected aright, without forcing us to practise what is right.' He singled out novel-reading as an example of this. Newman, 'The Danger of Accomplishments (Sermon 30),' 371.

63. William James, 'The Moral Philosopher and the Moral Life,' in *The Will to Believe*, 159.

64. As Michael Clune put it: 'I side with Plato on the ultimate incompatibility of aesthetic and moral education.' Clune also sides with Plato on the idea that equality can undermine normative judgement. See Clune, *A Defense of Judgment*, 186.

judgment offers a challenge to the project of moral education.'[65] I am not sure one needs much expertise to be open to value (the reverse is often the case), though I share Clune's sense of the disruptive power of openness.[66] The same receptivity, however, makes it impossible to exclude moral values or their discussion from a literary education, not least because they are a constitutive element of the aesthetic phenomenon itself. Clune, it appears, has no interest in such exclusions—indeed, he hopes to restore evaluative and cognitive breadth to the discipline[67]—but this also indicates that his resistance to moral education is something of a straw man, at least when it is reduced to 'the practice of using literary works to illustrate and propagate positive moral attitudes.'[68] Ethical criticism—Soviet-style, De-Santis-style or liberal—has always had its crude moments and always will, but it is usually more Socratic or questioning than this. What I have tried to emphasise throughout this book is that art can provide a moral education without it being a moralistic one. The difficulty of drawing the line doesn't indicate that the distinction is redundant.

Faced with a crude moralism, some defenders of the aesthetic have been inclined to raise the drawbridge and to insist on an absolute divide between moral and aesthetic values.[69] Yet, as James noted, this overlooks blended virtues and risks hollowing out the basic content of art: It is, after all, deeply interested in the world and all its moral aspects. The same point was later made by Adorno in a characteristically paradoxical vein:

> Take a look at the widespread inclination (which to this day has not been mitigated by education) to perceive art in terms of extra-aesthetic

65. Clune, *A Defense of Judgment*, 186.

66. On the value of openness, see also Hartman, *Getting It Right*, 52–58.

67. As Clune argues, 'Literature's concerns have never been confined to the boundaries of any academic discipline.' *A Defense of Judgment*, 104.

68. Clune, *A Defense of Judgment*, 186.

69. Henry James was impressed by Turgenev's strong sense of the differences—'the conviction that art and morality are two perfectly different things, and that the former has no more to do with the latter than it has with astronomy or embryology'—but couldn't quite share this conviction himself. See James, *Literary Criticism*, 2.1014.

> or pre-aesthetic criteria. This tendency is, on the one hand, a mark of atrocious backwardness or of the regressive consciousness of many people. On the other hand, there is no denying that that tendency is promoted by something in art itself. If art is perceived strictly in aesthetic terms, then it cannot be properly perceived in aesthetic terms.[70]

The 'conscience of taste'—to reinvoke James's phrase—often dictates that art must not be subordinated to morality, but it also indicates that there is a normativity that is internal to art—values that can thicken into something ethical: say, attentiveness in James or Murdoch, self-questioning in Trilling, or 'openness' in Clune.[71] Here the divide between a cognitive virtue and a moral one is vanishingly thin. It was precisely because of these ambiguous goods that Kant deemed art to be a 'symbol' of morality—a symbol, moreover, that appears to participate in what it describes—even though he argued vigorously for art's independence from moral constraints.[72] The argument for independence itself was an indication of a spiritual bond between the two spheres of value: Since freedom was the common good that conditioned both art and morality, to impose moral conditions on art was to undermine that freedom. However, the exercise of the mind's freedom in the judgement of the beautiful—or imagination's pursuit of its own law in art—was, for Kant, a symbol of the will's power to determine itself by moral laws. Art also provides a schooling in 'disinterestedness' or impartial judgement that is, for Kant, an essential element of moral experience. This disinterestedness is not indifference or *apatheia* and can remain supremely interested in the world and in others.[73]

It can seem, nonetheless, as if the world has lost interest in disinterest as a principle of art or life. It was long thought—or hoped—that art could talk us out of our more grasping desires or narrow service to

70. Adorno, *Aesthetic Theory*, 9.

71. James, *Literary Criticism*, 2.888.

72. Kant, *Critique of the Power of Judgement*, 225.

73. 'A judgement on an object of pleasure can be entirely *disinterested* yet still very *interesting*, i.e. it is not grounded on any interest but it produces an interest; all pure moral judgements are like this.' Kant, *Critique of the Power of Judgement*, 91. For a good discussion of the interestingness and interestedness of disinterest, see Chaouli, *Thinking with Kant's Critique of Judgement*.

ourselves by allowing us to get lost in thought or to deliver ourselves to feelings that belong to or inhere in no one but almost function as a property of the artwork itself. For Adorno, this experience of 'self-negation' was a necessary condition of aesthetic experience.[74] But it has also been proposed that disinterestedness is neither possible nor desirable in art or anywhere else.[75] The fantasy of self-transcendence, we may conclude, is precisely that—a fantasy—and one that risks evacuating the very thing that draws us to art and is nourished by it: interest. Even Adorno felt that Kantian disinterest—or a desire without desire—yielded little more than a 'castrated hedonism.'[76] This sounds rather sore, but it is also perhaps a little dangerous. If art switches off key parts of ourselves—as a condition of aesthetic experience—we may also need those parts to be up and running for the rest of moral life. It also shows the dangers of transporting aesthetic attitudes into our practical worlds. The kind of detachment demanded from some of the classic defences of the aesthetic can seem to involve a kind of impartiality that is morally insane. Take Ruskin's counsel: 'Does a man die at your feet—your business is not to help him, but to note the colour of his lips.'[77] Beauty's true scientists don't do CPR.

Disinterestedness, then, can seem morally questionable, epistemologically naive—as William James proclaimed, 'There is *no* "truth" without *some* interest'—and pointlessly ascetic.[78] It can feed, moreover, the same dubious self-benediction that we have already observed, allowing beautiful souls to add impartiality to their list of attributes. There is no denying that art is expressive of interests, but I do think that absorption in a work is a

74. Adorno, *Aesthetic Theory*, 375. Or as he put it earlier in the same book: 'Today the consumer is allowed to project his impulses and mimetic residues on to anything he pleases, including art, whereas in the past the individual was expected to forget himself, lose himself in art in the process of viewing, listening and reading. Ideally, the individual effected his identification with art not by assimilating the work of art to himself, but by assimilating himself to the work.' *Aesthetic Theory*, 25.

75. Nietzsche, for instance, was highly suspicious of Kant's interest in disinterest. See Nietzsche, *Genealogy of Morality*, 78–80.

76. Adorno, *Aesthetic Theory*, 16.

77. Ruskin, *Modern Painters*, vol. II, appendix, 13.

78. James, *Selected Letters*, 240.

phenomenological reality and constitutes a pleasurable form of self-forgetting.[79] As Woolf shows in *To the Lighthouse,* the reading of a novel makes even egotists like Mr. Ramsay calm down and find some escape from their own will. The experience provides only temporary respite—and Mr. Ramsay soon returns to being an irritant to himself and others—but the reprieve it depicts is real enough. A novel, of course, also confirms how we are all interested perceivers—by getting us to see through the motivated viewpoints of others—but in order to perceive even this we must lend ourselves to the grammar of the work.[80] If characters are beside themselves in free indirect discourse—partly themselves, partly their narrators—readers are beside themselves, too, lending their bodies to the voices and thoughts of others. Here we are not quite ourselves.

This form of possession by a text can feel like self-expansion, allowing us the sense of living another life, but it is also a kind of self-transcendence or disinterest. The moral properties of such transports should not be exaggerated: We may forget ourselves in the theatre or in a novel, but we may also forget the coachman shivering in the snow, not to mention the colour of his lips. At best, perhaps, the experience makes us sociable. So, we leave the theatre or the novel convinced that our pleasure in the artwork is shareable—indeed, that other people can feel, even should feel, the same way as we do.[81] This conviction has the potential to make us insufferable, but it might also bring us to a different kind of disinterestedness—the principle activated by our attempts to persuade others about the value of an artwork or the legitimacy of our feelings within the space of reasons. The disinterestedness may never be achieved—not least because the criteria upon which it draws are always imperfect: incomplete, historically contingent, and geographically provincial—and is best seen as a regulative ideal or enabling fiction. But

79. 'Take me out of myself,' Conrad suggests, is the demand all readers make from a novel. Conrad, *Notes on Life and Letters,* 16.

80. As Wittgenstein put it: 'A work of art forces us—as one might say—to see it in the right perspective.' Wittgenstein, *Culture and Value,* 4e. According to Adorno: 'The viewer enters into a contract with the art work so as to make it speak.' Adorno, *Aesthetic Theory,* 375.

81. Kant claims that when we experience aesthetic pleasure, we 'have grounds for expecting a similar pleasure of everyone.' Kant, *Critique of the Power of Judgement,* 97.

it is a mistake to dwell on the simple fraudulence of that fiction, for it sells short our experience of artworks and the conversations we may have with each other by our shared belief in that principle.

Perhaps this is what someone with a professional stake in the illusion of disinterested judgement would inevitably say. The deep interests lying behind disinterestedness have long been the focus of Pierre Bourdieu's analyses of both the academy and the art world—a method that exposes if not the hypocrisy, then the naiveté of those who choose to trade in this value.[82] The same, of course, might be said of all aspects of intellectual and moral life. Indeed, a genealogical or functionalist method in which values are ultimately reducible to 'interests'—usually of an economic or political kind—can leave very little of our ordinary moral picture intact. Fredric Jameson couldn't have expressed this scorched earth policy more crisply than he did in 1981: 'It is ethics itself which is the ideological vehicle and the legitimation of concrete structures of power and domination.'[83] This is one way of silencing the moralisers, but it does raise questions about where the normativity is to be derived for one's own moralising. For the moralising doesn't really stop, though it may continue in another key and with different words.[84]

An ethical criticism that ignores structural injustice is clearly deficient, but so is a criticism that reduces all moral meaning to structures of domination. This is another way of missing the richness and heterogeneity of the normative. Jameson's assumption that 'everything in "the last analysis" is political' is in a sense trivially true—most of the goods we have up and running in life require the protection of a state or some form of power—but it also risks depriving both ethics and art of their relative autonomy and intrinsic value.[85] The reductivism is abetted by the

82. As Bourdieu put it: 'Intellectuals and artists are so situated in social space that they have a particular interest in disinterestedness.' See Bourdieu, *Distinction*, 317.

83. Jameson, *The Political Unconscious*, 114. Jameson here is ventriloquising Nietzsche in ways that make it hard to decide what his own meta-ethical position is. I am grateful to Damian Maher for homing in on this sentence in Jameson. See Maher, 'Making Good on Henry James,' 28.

84. The classic critiques of morality, therefore—that it is the resentment of the weak or might pretending to be right—have always faced the problem of self-reference, though they also attune us to the impotence and vainglory of much moralising criticism.

85. Jameson, *The Political Unconscious*, 20.

banalisation of a genealogical and functionalist method. So, the meaning of a speech-act performed by 'x' is often reduced to the social origins of 'x' or the social effects of the speech-act (and the effects are sometimes predicted by profiling the origins). The method possesses persuasive power (which partly explains its success), but sometimes we may be interested in the actual content of what 'x' says and may feel that its meaning is not entirely determined by either its causes or its social effects.[86] The vulgarisation of functionalist critique was evident across the 1930s in the various polemics about 'bourgeois' thought. It even appears in Wittgenstein's withering assessment of the mathematician and philosopher Frank Ramsey: 'a bourgeois thinker. I.e. he thought with the aim of clearing up the affairs of some particular community.'[87] These days the bourgeois get less of a hard time and the superficial and the morally complacent are usually called something else. Or we invoke different identities and forms of groupthink organised around concepts of race or gender. But it can still feed a sad diminishment or bad inflation of persons when they are seen as either tokens or spokespersons for 'some particular community.'[88]

In a world where social fictions of race and gender do such real work—and sexism and racism make painful inroads into people's freedom—it might seem wishful or insensitive (another instance of 'moralising criticism') to expect people to moralise differently or to conduct our business in a less identitarian vein.[89] But it can appear, in the meantime, that we moralise in bad faith because everyone, it seems, is always already *parti pris*. It yields a familiar set of ironies: Dismissive of disinterestedness, we condemn the interestedness of others; we moralise in the knowledge that morality is politics by other means; we continue to engage with art, aware that it is merely the aestheticisation of our interests (with interest often narrowly conceived). This, obviously, is a caricature, which I hope we will never wholly live out, but it can show how

86. The best defence of this critical method is found in Geuss, *The Idea of Critical Theory*.

87. Wittgenstein, *Culture and Value*, 17e.

88. For an inside view of the constraints this puts on a writer, see Younge, *Pigeonholed*.

89. On the erroneousness of these fictions and their compelling power, see Appiah, *The Lies That Bind*.

far we have travelled from the idea of disinterestedness in art—the sense that we could momentarily forget who we are and slough off our prescribed identities in the face of an artwork. Equally fantastical, perhaps, was the idea that a person could transcend their socially determined role and assume the anonymity of the universal when they entered the public sphere or the republic of letters as an author or a critic.[90] We know that this was always, in part, a fiction, and that access to the space of reasons is itself unequal, making even reason itself appear a guilty party.[91] But intellectual life still needs such fictions, as does moral life. Kant was right to suggest that morality involved some great 'as ifs'—a freedom we can never entirely know and a disinterestedness we can never be sure of. We can never be certain, for instance, that we are acting out of a genuine respect for the moral law or out of mere self-interest.[92] If disinterestedness cannot be guaranteed, we can still hold fast to our uncertainty—a modest virtue in certain times. For the foreseeable future, at least, the task of ethical criticism may be to keep a little bit of unknowingness alive.

90. This is the position taken up by Kant in his celebrated essay 'What Is Enlightenment?' See Kant, *Practical Philosophy*, 11–22.

91. On unequal access to expression and interpretation, see Fricker, *Epistemic Injustice*.

92. As he declares in *The Metaphysics of Morals*, 'We cannot show with certainty in any example that the will is . . . determined merely through the law, without any other incentive.' See Kant, *Practical Philosophy*, 72.

BIBLIOGRAPHY

Abell, Catherine. *Fiction: A Philosophical Analysis*. Oxford University Press, 2020.

Acheraïou, Amar. *Joseph Conrad and the Reader: Questioning Modern Theories of Narrative and Readership*. Palgrave Macmillan, 2009.

Adorno, Theodor. *Aesthetic Theory*. Translated by C. Lenhardt. Edited by Gretel Adorno and Rolf Tiedemann. Routledge and Kegan Paul, 1984.

———. *Negative Dialectics*. Translated by E. B. Ashton. Routledge, 1973.

Albrecht, Thomas. 'Sympathy and Alterity: The Ethical Sublime in Romola.' In *Antipodean George Eliot*, edited by Margaret Harris and Matthew Sussman. Routledge, 2023.

———. *The Ethical Vision of George Eliot*. Routledge, 2020.

Alexander, Melissa. *Conversation Pieces: Virginia Woolf and Object Philosophy*. Oxford University Press, 2026.

Altes, Liesbeth Korthals. 'Ethical Turn.' In *Routledge Encyclopedia of Narrative Theory*, edited by D. Herman, Manfred Jahn, and Marie Laure Ryan. Routledge, Taylor and Francis Group, 2005.

Amis, Martin. *The War Against Cliché: Essays and Reviews 1971–2000*. Vintage, 2001.

Anderson, Amanda. *The Powers of Distance: Cosmopolitanism and the Cultivation of Detachment*. Princeton University Press, 2001.

Anderson, Amanda, Toril Moi, and Rita Felski. *Character: Three Inquiries in Literary Studies*. University of Chicago Press, 2019.

Anscombe, G. E. M. *Intention*. 2nd ed. Harvard University Press, 1963.

Appiah, Anthony. *As If: Idealization and Ideals*. Harvard University Press, 2017.

———. *The Lies That Bind: Rethinking Identity*. Profile Books, 2018.

Aristotle. *Nicomachean Ethics*. Edited and translated by Roger Crisp. Cambridge University Press, 2000.

Armstrong, Isobel. 'George Eliot, Hegel, and Middlemarch.' *19: Interdisciplinary Studies in the Long Nineteenth Century*, no. 29 (2020).

Armstrong, Paul B. *The Challenge of Bewilderment: Understanding and Representation in James, Conrad, and Ford*. Cornell University Press, 1987.

Aubry, Timothy. *Guilty Aesthetic Pleasures*. Harvard University Press, 2018.

Aubry, Timothy, and Trysh Travis, eds. *Rethinking Therapeutic Culture*. University of Chicago Press, 2015.

Augustine. *Treatises on Various Subjects*. Edited by Roy J. Deferrari. Vol. 16. Catholic University of America Press, 1952.

Austin, J. L. *How to Do Things with Words*. Edited by M. Sbisà and J. O. Urmson. Harvard University Press, 1962.

Babbitt, Irving. *Rousseau and Romanticism*. Houghton Mifflin, 1919.

Bagehot, Walter. 'Charles Dickens.' In *Charles Dickens: The Critical Heritage*, edited by Philip Collins. Routledge and Kegan Paul, 1971.

Ballard, J. G. *Crash*. Vintage, 1995.

Banfield, Ann. *The Phantom Table: Woolf, Fry, Russell, and the Epistemology of Modernism*. Cambridge University Press, 2000.

Beardsley, Monroe C. *Aesthetics: Problems in the Philosophy of Criticism*. Harcourt Brace, 1958.

Beer, Gillian. 'Hume, Stephen, and Elegy in *To the Lighthouse*.' In *Virginia Woolf: The Common Ground*. Edinburgh University Press, 1996.

Beiser, Frederick C. *The Romantic Imperative: The Concept of Early German Romanticism*. Cambridge University Press, 2003.

Bell, Vanessa. *Selected Letters of Vanessa Bell*. Edited by Regina Marler. Bloomsbury, 1993.

Bellamy, Michael O., and Iris Murdoch. 'An Interview with Iris Murdoch.' *Contemporary Literature* 18, no. 2 (1977): 129–40.

Bentham, Jeremy. *The Works of Jeremy Bentham*. Edited by John Bowring. 11 vols. Edinburgh; London: W. Tait; Simkin, Marshall, and Co., 1843.

Berkeley, George. *Principles of Human Knowledge and Three Dialogues*. Edited by Howard Robinson. Oxford University Press, 1996.

Berman, Russell A. *Fiction Sets You Free: Literature, Liberty, and Western Culture*. University of Iowa Press, 2007

Bernstein, J. M., ed. *Classic and Romantic German Aesthetics*. Cambridge University Press, 2003.

Bersani, Leo. 'The Jamesian Lie.' In *A Future for Astyanax: Character and Desire in Literature*. Little, Brown and Co., 1969.

Best, Stephen, and Sharon Marcus. 'Surface Reading: An Introduction.' *Representations* 108, no. 1 (2009): 1–21.

Bevis, Matthew. *Wordsworth's Fun*. University of Chicago Press, 2019.

Bewes, Timothy. *Free Indirect: The Novel in a Postfictional Age*. Columbia University Press, 2022.

Bicchieri, Cristina. *The Grammar of Society: The Nature and Dynamics of Social Norms*. Cambridge University Press, 2006.

Blackburn, Simon. *Essays in Quasi-Realism*. Oxford University Press, 1993.

———. 'Perspectives, Fictions, Errors, Play.' In *Nietzsche and Morality*, edited by Neil Sinhababu and Brian Leiter. Oxford University Press, 2007.

Blake, Kathleen. *The Pleasures of Benthamism*. Oxford University Press, 2009.

Blumenberg, Hans. *Shipwreck With Spectator: Paradigm of a Metaphor For Existence*. Translated by Steven Rendall. MIT Press, 1997.

Booth, Wayne. *A Rhetoric of Irony*. University of Chicago Press, 1974.

———. *The Company We Keep: An Ethics of Fiction*. University of California Press, 1988.

Bourdieu, Pierre. *Distinction: A Social Critique of the Judgement of Taste*. Translated by Richard Nice. Harvard University Press, 1984.

Boyd, Richard. 'Pity's Pathologies Portrayed: Rousseau and the Limits of Democratic Compassion.' *Political Theory* 32, no. 4 (2004): 519–46.

Boxall, Peter. *The Value of the Novel*. Cambridge, 2015.
Bridges, Robert. *The Spirit of Man, an Anthology in English & French from the Philosophers & Poets*. Longmans, Green and Co., 1916.
Bromwich, David. *Skeptical Music: Essays on Modern Poetry*. University of Chicago Press, 2001.
Browning, Gary. *Why Iris Murdoch Matters*. Bloomsbury, 2018.
Brudney, Daniel. 'Lord Jim and Moral Judgment: Literature and Moral Philosophy.' *Journal of Aesthetics and Art Criticism* 56, no. 3 (1998): 265–81.
Burke, Edmund. *A Philosophical Enquiry into the Origin of Our Ideas of the Sublime and the Beautiful*. Edited by Paul Guyer. Oxford University Press, 2015.
Burrow, Colin. 'I Am a Severed Head.' *London Review of Books* 38, no. 16 (11 August 2016).
———. 'Just Say It, Henry.' *London Review of Books* 46, no. 16 (14 August 2024).
Butler, Samuel. *Luck, or Cunning as the Main Means of Organic Modification*. London: Jonathan Cape, 1887.
Callard, Agnes. *Open Socrates: The Case for Philosophical Life*. Allen Lane, 2025.
Carlisle, Clare. *The Marriage Question: George Eliot's Double Life*. Allen Lane, 2023.
Carlisle, Janice M. '*Little Dorrit*: Necessary Fictions.' *Studies in the Novel* 7, no. 2 (1975): 195–214.
Carroll, David J. *George Eliot: The Critical Heritage*. Vikas, 1971.
Carroll, Lewis. *Alice's Adventures in Wonderland; and, Through the Looking Glass and What Alice Found There*. Edited by Peter Hunt. Oxford University Press, 2009.
Caserio, Robert L. *Plot, Story, and the Novel: From Dickens and Poe to the Modern Period*. Princeton University Press, 1979.
Cavell, Stanley. *Conditions Handsome and Unhandsome: The Constitution of Emersonian Perfectionism*. University of Chicago Press, 1990.
———. *Must We Mean What We Say?: A Book of Essays*. Cambridge University Press, 1976.
———. *The Claim of Reason: Wittgenstein, Skepticism, Morality and Tragedy*. Oxford University Press, 2023.
Chaouli, Michel. *Thinking with Kant's Critique of Judgment*. Harvard University Press, 2017.
Chesterton, G. K. *Charles Dickens: A Critical Study*. Dodd, Mead and Co., 1906.
Chumhaill, Clare Mac, and Rachel Wiseman. *Metaphysical Animals: How Four Women Brought Philosophy Back to Life*. Chatto and Windus, 2022.
Church, Ian M., and Robert J. Hartman, eds. *The Routledge Handbook of the Philosophy and Psychology of Luck*. Routledge, 2019.
Climacus, Johannes [Søren Kierkegaard]. *Concluding Unscientific Postscript to Philosophical Fragments*. Translated by Edna H. Hong and Howard V. Hong. Princeton University Press, 1992.
Clune, Michael W. *A Defense of Judgment*. University of Chicago Press, 2021.
Coetzee, J. M. *Elizabeth Costello*. Vintage, 2004.
Cohen, Ted. *Thinking of Others: On the Talent for Metaphor*. Princeton University Press, 2008.
Cohn, Dorrit. *The Distinction of Fiction*. Johns Hopkins University Press, 1999.
———. *Transparent Minds: Narrative Modes for Presenting Consciousness in Fiction*. Princeton University Press, 1978.
Coleridge, Samuel Taylor. *Biographia Literaria, or, Biographical Sketches of My Literary Life and Opinions*. Edited by Walter Jackson Bate and James Engell. 2 vols. Princeton University Press, 1983.

———. *Lectures on Shakespeare*. Edinburgh University Press, 2022.

Collingwood, R. G. *Speculum Mentis: or, the Map of Knowledge*. Clarendon Press, 1924.

———. *The Principles of Art*. Oxford University Press, 1958, [1938].

Collini, Stefan. *Public Moralists: Political Thought and Intellectual Life in Britain 1850–1930*. Clarendon Press, 1991.

———. *That's Offensive!: Criticism, Identity, Respect*. Seagull Books, 2010.

Collins, Philip, ed. *Charles Dickens: The Critical Heritage*. Routledge and Kegan Paul, 1971.

Collits, Terry. *Postcolonial Conrad: Paradoxes of Empire*. Routledge, 2005.

Colvin, Sidney, and John Morley. 'Daniel Deronda.' *Fortnightly Review* 26 (November 1876): 601–16.

Comte, Auguste. *System of Positive Polity, or Treatise on Sociology Instituting the Religion of Humanity*. Translated by Richard Congreve and Henry Dix Hutton. Edited by Samuel Lobb and Fredric Harrison. 4 vols. London: Longmans, Green and Co., 1875–77.

Conrad, Joseph. *A Personal Record*. Edited by Zdzisław Najder and J. H. Stape. Cambridge University Press, 2008.

———. *Chance: A Tale in Two Parts*. Edited by Martin Ray. Oxford University Press, 2002.

———. *Heart of Darkness*. Edited by Timothy S. Hayes. Penguin, 2012.

———. *Lord Jim*. Edited by Cedric Watts. Roadview Press, 2001.

———. *Notes on Life and Letters*. Edited by J. H. Stape. Cambridge University Press, 2004.

———. *Suspense*. Edited by Gene M. Moore. Cambridge University Press, 2011.

———. *The Letters of Joseph Conrad*. Edited by Frederick R. Karl and Laurence Davies. 9 vols. Cambridge University Press, 1983–2007.

———. *'Twixt Land and Sea: Tales*. Edited by Jacques Berthoud, Laura L. Davis, and S. W. Reid. Cambridge University Press, 2008.

———. *Under Western Eyes*. Edited by Jeremy Hawthorn. Oxford University Press, 2003.

———. *Youth, Heart of Darkness, The End of the Tether*. Edited by Owen Knowles. Cambridge University Press, 2010.

Conrad, Peter. *Dickens the Enchanter: Inside the Explosive Imagination of the Great Story-Teller*. Bloomsbury, 2025.

Cox, C. B. 'Joseph Conrad and the Question of Suicide.' *Bulletin of the John Rylands Library (2014)* 55, no. 1 (1972): 285–99.

Cusk, Rachel. *Outline*. Faber and Faber, 2014.

Dahmane, Razak. '"A Mere Question of Figures": Measures, Mystery and Metaphor in *Hard Times*.' *Dickens Studies Annual* 23 (1994): 137.

Danto, Arthur C. 'Beauty and Morality.' In *Embodied Meanings: Critical Essays and Aesthetic Meditations*. Farrar, Straus Giroux, 1994.

Darwall, Stephen L. *The Second-Person Standpoint: Morality, Respect, and Accountability*. Harvard University Press, 2006.

Darwin, Charles. *On the Origin of Species*. Edited by William Bynum. Penguin, 2009.

Daston, Lorraine. *Objectivity*. Princeton University Press, 2007.

Davidson, Donald. 'What Metaphors Mean.' In *On Metaphor*, edited by Sheldon Sacks. University of Chicago Press, 1978.

da Vinci, Leonardo. *Notebooks*. Translated by Thereza Wells. Edited by Irma A. Richter and Thereza Wells. Oxford University Press, 2008.

Davis, Todd F., and Kenneth Womack. *Mapping the Ethical Turn: A Reader in Ethics, Culture, and Literary Theory*. University Press of Virginia, 2001.

Day, Jon. *Novel Sensations: Modernist Fiction and the Problem of Qualia*. Edinburgh University Press, 2020.

Dennett, Daniel. *Consciousness Explained*. Penguin, 1993.

———. *Intuition Pumps and Other Tools for Thinking*. Penguin, 2013.

———. 'Why Everyone Is a Novelist.' *Times Literary Supplement* (September 1988): 16–22.

Dewey, John. *Art as Experience: The Collected Works of John Dewey*. Edited by Jo Ann Boydston et. al. Vol. 10. Southern Illinois Press, 1987.

Diamond, Cora. 'Henry James, Moral Philosophers, Moralism.' *Henry James Review* 18, no. 3 (1997): 243–57.

———. 'Losing Your Concepts.' *Ethics* 98, no. 2 (1988): 255–77.

———. 'Missing the Adventure: Reply to Martha Nussbaum.' In *The Realistic Spirit: Wittgenstein, Philosophy, and the Mind*. MIT Press, 1991.

———. 'The Difficulty of Reality and the Difficulty of Philosophy.' In *Philosophy and Animal Life*, edited by Stanley Cavell et al. Columbia University Press, 2008.

———. *The Realistic Spirit: Wittgenstein, Philosophy, and the Mind*. MIT Press, 1991.

Dickens, Charles. *Bleak House*. Edited by Nicola Bradbury. Penguin, 1996.

———. *David Copperfield*. Edited by Nina Burgis and Andrew Sanders. Oxford University Press, 2009.

———. *Hard Times*. 3rd ed. Edited by Fred Kaplan and Sylvère Monod. W. W. Norton and Co., 2001.

———. *Little Dorrit*. Edited by Harvey Peter Sucksmith. Oxford University Press, 2008.

———. *Selected Journalism, 1850–1870*. Edited by David Pascoe. Penguin Books, 1997.

———. *Sketches by Boz*. Edited by Dennis Walder. Penguin, 1995.

———. *The Letters of Charles Dickens: 1820–1870*. Edited by Madeline House, Graham Storey, and Kathleen Tillotson. 12 vols. Oxford University Press, 1965–2002.

———. *The Pickwick Papers*. Edited by James Kinsley. Clarendon Press, 1986.

Dickens, Charles, ed. 'The Spirit of Fiction.' *All the Year Round*, no. 18 (27 July 1867).

Diogenes Laertius. *Lives of Eminent Philosophers*. Translated by R. D. Hicks. Heinemann, 1925.

Dixon, Thomas. *The Invention of Altruism: Making Moral Meanings in Victorian Britain*. Oxford University Press/British Academy, 2008.

Dolin, Tim. 'The Grounds of Exception: Liberal Sympathy and Its Limits in Daniel Deronda and C. H. Pearson's National Life and Character.' In *Antipodean George Eliot*, edited by Margaret Harris and Matthew Sussman. Routledge, 2023.

Dooley, Gillian, ed. *From a Tiny Corner in the House of Fiction: Conversations with Iris Murdoch*. South Carolina Press, 2003.

Durnan, Kailana. 'Getting Bored with Hard Times.' *Dickens Studies Annual* 49, no. 2 (2018): 402–28.

Dwan, David. 'Modernism and Rousseau.' *Textual Practice* 27, no. 4 (2013): 537–63.

Edel, Leon, and Gordon N. Ray, eds. *Henry James and H. G. Wells: A Record of Their Friendship, Their Debate on the Art of Fiction, and Their Quarrel*. Rupert Hart-Davis, 1959.

Eliot, George. *Adam Bede*. Edited by Carol A. Martin. Oxford University Press, 2008.

———. 'Belles Lettres and Art.' *Westminster Review* 66 (July 1856): 257–78.

———. *Daniel Deronda*. Edited by Graham Handley. Clarendon Press, 1984.

———. *Essays of George Eliot*. Edited by Thomas Pinney. Routledge, 1963.

———. *Felix Holt, the Radical*. Edited by Lynda Mugglestone. Penguin, 1995.

———. *Impressions of Theophrastus Such*. 2nd ed. Edinburgh: Blackwood and Sons, 1879.

———. *Middlemarch*. Edited by David Carroll. Oxford University Press, 1998.

———. *Romola*. Edited by Dorothea Barrett. Penguin, 2005.

———. *Scenes of Clerical Life*. Edited by David Lodge. Penguin, 1985.

———. *Some George Eliot Notebooks: An Edition of the Carl H. Pforzheimer Library's George Eliot Holograph Notebooks, Mss 707, 708, 709, 710, 711*. Edited by William Baker. University Press Salzburg, 1976.

———. *The George Eliot Letters*. Edited by Gordon S. Haight and Gordon Sherman. 9 vols. Oxford University Press, 1954–78.

———. *The Lifted Veil and Brother Jacob*. Edited by Helen Small. Oxford University Press, 1999.

———. *The Mill on the Floss*. Edited by Gordon Sherman Haight and Juliette Atkinson. Oxford University Press, 2015.

———. *The Spanish Gypsy*. Edinburgh: Blackwood and Sons, 1879.

Eliot, George, trans. *Spinoza's Ethics*. Edited by Clare Carlisle. Princeton University Press, 2020.

Eliot, T. S. 'A Note on Poetry and Belief.' *The Enemy* 1 (1927): 15–17.

———. 'Contemporanea.' *The Egoist* 5, no. 6 (1918): 84.

———. *The Complete Prose of T. S. Eliot: The Critical Edition*. Edited by Ronald Schuchard and Jewel Spears Brooker. 8 vols. Vol. 1, *Apprentice Years, 1905–1918*. Johns Hopkins University Press, 2015.

Evans, Marian. *The Essence of Christianity*. London: Kegan Paul, Trench, Trübner, and Co., 1890 [1854].

Farina, Jonathan. '"Dickens's as If": Analogy and Victorian Virtual Reality.' *Victorian Studies* 53, no. 3 (2011): 427–36.

Felski, Rita. *Hooked: Art and Attachment*. University of Chicago Press, 2020.

———. *The Limits of Critique*. University of Chicago Press, 2015.

Fessenbecker, Patrick. 'The Fragility of Rationality: George Eliot on Akrasia and the Law of Consequences.' *British Journal for the History of Philosophy* 29, no. 2 (2021): 275–91.

———. 'Sympathy, Vocation, and Moral Deliberation in George Eliot.' *ELH* 85, no. 2 (2018): 501–32

Fichte, Johann Gottlieb. *Foundations of Transcendental Philosophy (1796/99)*. Edited and Translated by Daniel Breazeale. Cornell University Press, 1992.

Fields, Annie. *Memories of a Hostess: A Chronicle of Eminent Friendships, Drawn Chiefly from the Diaries of Mrs. James T. Fields*. Edited by Mark Antony De Wolfe Howe. Atlantic Monthly Press, 1922.

Fields, James T. 'Some Memories of Charles Dickens.' *Atlantic Monthly*, 26 (1 August 1870).

Flaubert, Gustave. *Madame Bovary*. Translated by Geoffrey Wall. Penguin, 2003.

Fogelin, Robert J. 'Hume and the Missing Shade of Blue.' *Philosophy and Phenomenological Research* 45, no. 2 (1984): 263–71.

———. *Hume's Skepticism in the Treatise of Human Nature*. Routledge and Kegan Paul, 1985.

Forsberg, Niklas. *Language Lost and Found: On Iris Murdoch and the Limits of Philosophical Discourse*. Bloomsbury, 2013.

Forster, E. M. *Aspects of the Novel*. Edited by Oliver Stallybrass. Penguin Books, 2005.

Frankfurt, Harry G. 'Identification and Wholeheartedness.' In *The Importance of What We Care About*. Cambridge University Press, 1988.

———. 'On Bullshit.' In *The Importance of What We Care About*. Cambridge University Press, 1998.

Freud, Sigmund. 'Creative Writers and Daydreaming.' In *The Uncanny*, translated by David McLintock. Penguin, 2003.

Fricker, Miranda. *Epistemic Injustice: Power and the Ethics of Knowing*. Oxford University Press, 2007.

Friend, Stacie. 'The Real Foundations of Fictional Worlds.' *Australian Journal of Philosophy* 95, no. 1 (2017): 29–42.

Frye, Northrop. *The Anatomy of Criticism*. Princeton University Press, 1957.

Gaita, Raimond. *Good and Evil: An Absolute Conception*. Routledge, 2004.

Gallagher, Catherine. 'The Rise of Fictionality.' In *The Novel*, Vol. 1, *History, Geography and Culture*, edited by Franco Moretti. Princeton University Press, 2006.

Garber, Marjorie, Beatrice Hanssen, and Rebecca L. Walkowitz, eds. *The Turn to Ethics*. Routledge, 2000.

Gass, William H. *Fiction and the Figures of Life*. Nonpareil Books, 1979.

Gatens, Moira. 'A Roar of Sound: George Eliot on Sympathy and the Problem of Other Minds.' In *Antipodean George Eliot*, edited by Margaret Harris and Matthew Sussman. Routledge, 2023.

Gaut, Berys. *Art, Emotion and Ethics*. Oxford University Press, 2007.

Gekoski, R. A. *Conrad: The Moral World of the Novelist*. Elek, 1978.

Gettelman, Debra. *Imagining Otherwise: How Readers Help to Write Nineteenth-Century Novels*. Princeton University Press, 2024.

Geuss, Raymond. *The Idea of a Critical Theory: Habermas and the Frankfurt School*. Cambridge University Press, 1981.

Ghent, Dorothy Van. 'Lord Jim.' In *The English Novel: Form and Function*. Rinehart and Co., 1953.

Goldberg, S. L. *Agents and Lives: Moral Thinking in Literature*. Cambridge University Press, 1993.

Goldie, Peter. *The Mess Inside: Narrative, Emotion, and the Mind*. Oxford University Press, 2012.

Goodman, Nelson. *The Languages of Art: An Approach to the Theory of Symbols*. Hackett, 1976.

Greaney, Michael. *Conrad, Language, and Narrative*. Cambridge University Press, 2001.

Greenwell, Garth. 'A Moral Education.' *Yale Review* 111, no. 1 (2023): 12–37.

Greer, Erin Elizabeth. *Fiction, Philosophy and the Ideal of Conversation*. Edinburgh University Press, 2024.

Greiner, Rae. *Sympathetic Realism in Nineteenth-Century British Fiction*. Johns Hopkins University Press, 2012.

Hacker, P. M. S. 'Is There Anything It Is Like to Be a Bat?' *Philosophy* 77, no. 2 (2002): 157–74.
Hale, Dorothy J. *The Novel and the New Ethics*. Stanford University Press, 2020.
Hämäläinen, Nora. *Literature and Moral Theory*. Bloomsbury Academic, 2016.
Hamburger, Käte. *The Logic of Literature*. Translated by Marilynn Rose. Indiana University Press, 1973.
Hampson, Robert. *Joseph Conrad: Betrayal and Identity*. Macmillan, 1992.
Hanna, Nathan. 'Moral Luck Defended.' *Noûs* 48, no. 4 (2014): 683–98.
Hardy, Barbara. 'The Moment of Disenchantment in George Eliot's Novels.' *Review of English Studies* 5, no. 19 (1954): 256–64.
Hare, R. M. 'Universalisability.' *Proceedings of the Aristotelian Society* 55 (1955): 295.
Harpham, Geoffrey Galt. *Getting It Right: Language, Literature, and Ethics*. University of Chicago Press, 1992.
Harris, Margaret, and Matthew Sussman, eds. *Antipodean George Eliot*. Routledge, 2023.
Hartman, Robert J. *In Defense of Moral Luck: Why Luck Often Affects Praiseworthiness and Blameworthiness*. Routledge, 2017.
Hegel, Georg Wilhelm Friedrich. *Aesthetics: Lectures on Fine Art*. Edited by T. M. Knox. 2 vols. Oxford University Press, 1975.
———. *Elements of the Philosophy of Right*. Translated by H. B. Nisbet. Edited by Allen W. Wood. Cambridge University Press, 1991.
———. *The Phenomenology of Spirit*. Translated by Arnold V. Miller. Oxford University Press, 1977.
Hertz, Neil. *George Eliot's Pulse*. Stanford University Press, 2003.
Hintikka, Jaakko. 'Virginia Woolf and Our Knowledge of the External World.' *Journal of Aesthetics and Art Criticism* 38, no. 1 (1979): 5.
Hume, David. *An Enquiry Concerning Human Understanding*. Oxford University Press, 2001.
———. *An Enquiry Concerning the Principles of Morals*. Edited by Tom L. Beauchamp. Oxford University Press, 1998.
———. *A Treatise of Human Nature*. Edited by David Fate Norton and Mary J. Norton. Oxford University Press, 2000.
———. 'Of Moral Prejudices.' In *Essays: Moral, Political, and Literary*, edited by Tom L. Beauchamp. Oxford University Press, 1985.
———. 'On the Standard of Taste.' In *Essays: Moral, Political, and Literary*, edited by Tom L. Beauchamp. Oxford University Press, 1985.
Hunter, Allan. *Joseph Conrad and the Ethics of Darwinism: The Challenges of Science*. Routledge, 1983.
Hutto, Daniel D., ed. *Narrative and Understanding Persons*. Cambridge University Press, 2007.
James, Henry. *Collected Stories*. Edited by John Bayley. 2 vols. Everyman, 1999.
———. *Collected Travel Writings*. Library of America, 1993.
———. *Daisy Miller*. Edited by David Lodge. Penguin, 2007.
———. *Henry James: Letters*. Edited by Leon Edel. 4 vols. Belknap, 1974–84.
———. 'Is There a Life After Death?' In *The James Family: A Group Biography*, edited by F. O. Matthiessen. Knopf, 1961.
———. *Literary Criticism*. 2 vols. Library of America, 1984.

———. *Novels, 1896–1899*. Library of America, 2003.

———. *Novels, 1901–1902*. Edited by Leo Bersani. Library of America, 2006.

———. *The Ambassadors*. Edited by Christopher Butler. Oxford University Press, 2008.

———. *The Complete Notebooks of Henry James*. Edited by Leon Edel and Lyall H. Powers. Oxford University Press, 1987.

———. *The Golden Bowl*. Edited by Virginia Llewellyn Smith. Oxford University Press, 2009.

———. *The Letters of Henry James*. Edited by Percy Lubbock. 2 vols. Charles Scribner, 1920.

———. *The Letters of Henry James*, Vol. 4, *1895–1916*. Edited by Leon Edel. Belknap, 1984.

———. *The Portrait of a Lady*. Edited by Roger Luckhurst. Oxford University Press, 2009.

———. *The Spoils of Poynton*. Edited by Bernard Arthur Richards. Oxford University Press, 2000.

———. *The Tragic Muse*. Edited by Philip Horne. Penguin, 1995.

———. *The Wings of the Dove*. Edited by Millicent Bell. Penguin, 2008.

James, William. *Pragmatism*. Harvard University Press, 1975.

———. *Selected Letters*. Edited by Elizabeth Hardwick. Doubleday, 1980.

———. *Talks to Teachers on Psychology, and to Students on Some of Life's Ideals*. Harvard University Press, 1983.

———. *The Principles of Psychology*. Edited by Fredson Bowers, Frederick Burkhardt and Kęstutis Skrupskelis. 2 vols. Harvard University Press, 1981.

———. *The Will to Believe and Other Essays in Popular Philosophy*. Harvard University Press, 1979.

———. *Writings, 1878–1899*. Library of America, 1992.

Jameson, Fredric. *Fables of Aggression: Wyndham Lewis, the Modernist as Fascist*. Verso, 2008.

———. *The Political Unconscious: Narrative as a Socially Symbolic Act*. Routledge, 2002 [1981].

Joyce, Richard. *The Myth of Morality*. Cambridge University Press, 2001.

Kafka, Franz. *Letters to Friends, Family, and Editors*. Translated by Richard Winston and Clara Winston. Edited by Max Brod. Schocken, 1978.

Kalderon, Mark Eli. *Moral Fictionalism*. Clarendon Press, 2005.

Kant, Immanuel. *Anthropology, History, and Education*. Edited by Robert B. Louden and Günter Zöller. Cambridge University Press, 2013.

———. *Critique of Pure Reason*. Edited by Paul Guyer and Allen W. Wood. Cambridge University Press, 1998.

———. *Critique of the Power of Judgment*. Translated by Eric Matthews. Edited by Paul Guyer. Cambridge University Press, 2000.

———. *Lectures on Anthropology*. Translated by Robert R. Clewis and G. Felicitas Munzel. Edited by Robert B. Louden and Allen W. Wood. Cambridge University Press, 2013.

———. *Practical Philosophy*. Translated by Mary J. Gregor. Edited by Mary J. Gregor and Allen W. Wood. Cambridge University Press, 1996.

Keable, Ian. *Charles Dickens Magician: Conjuring in Life, Letters and Literature*. Ian Keable, 2014.

Keynes, J. M. 'My Early Beliefs.' In *Essays in Biography: Collected Writings of J. M. Keynes*. Edited by D. Moggridge. Macmillan, 1972.

Kunin, Aaron. *Character as Form*. Bloomsbury, 2019.

Lackey, Michael. 'Modernist Anti-Philosophicalism and Virginia Woolf's Critique of Philosophy.' *Journal of Modern Literature* 29, no. 4 (2006): 76–98.

Lamarque, Peter. 'How Can We Fear and Pity Fictions?' *British Journal of Aesthetics* 21, no. 4 (1981): 291–304.

———. *The Uselessness of Art: Essays in the Philosophy of Art and Literature*. Sussex Academic Press, 2020.

Lamarque, Peter, and Stein Haugom Olsen. *Truth, Fiction, and Literature: A Philosophical Perspective*. Clarendon Press, 1994.

Land, Stephen K. *Conrad and the Paradox of Plot*. Macmillan, 1984.

Landy, Joshua. *How to Do Things with Fictions*. Oxford University Press, 2012.

Langton, Rae. *Sexual Solipsism: Philosophical Essays on Pornography and Objectification*. Oxford University Press, 2009.

Latham, Sean. *'Am I a Snob?': Modernism and the Novel*. Cornell University Press, 2003.

Latus, Andrew. 'Moral and Epistemic Luck.' *Journal of Philosophical Research* 25 (2000): 149–72.

Lear, Jonathan. *A Case for Irony*. Harvard University Press, 2011.

Leavis, F. R. *The Great Tradition: George Eliot, Henry James, Joseph Conrad*. Faber and Faber, 2008.

Leeson, Miles. *Iris Murdoch: Philosophical Novelist*. Bloomsbury, 2010.

Levenson, Michael H. *Modernism and the Fate of Individuality: Character and Novelistic Form from Conrad to Woolf*. Cambridge University Press, 1991.

Levy, Neil. *Hard Luck: How Luck Undermines Free Will and Moral Responsibility*. Oxford University Press, 2011.

Lewes, George Henry. *Comte's Philosophy of the Sciences*. London: G. H. Bohn, 1853.

———. 'Dickens in Relation to Criticism.' *Fortnightly Review* 11 (1872): 141.

———. *Problems of Life and Mind*. 3 vols. London: Trübner and Co., 1874–79.

Lewis, Wyndham. *Apes of God*. Black Sparrow Press, 1981.

———. *Blasting and Bombadiering*. Eyre and Spottiswoode, 1937.

———. *Collected Poems and Plays*. Edited by Alan Munton. Cancarnet, 1979.

———. *Count Your Dead: They Are Alive!* Lovat Dickson Ltd., 1937.

———. *Creatures of Habit and Creatures of Change: Essays on Art, Literature and Society, 1914–15*. Edited by Paul Edwards. Black Sparrow Press, 1989.

———. *Hitler*. Chatto and Windus, 1931.

———. *Left Wings Over Europe, or, How to Make a War About Nothin*. Jonathan Cape, 1936.

———. *Men Without Art*. Cassell and Co., 1934.

———. *Rude Assignment*. Edited by Toby Foshay. Black Sparrow Press, 1984.

———. *Tarr*. Egoist Press, 1918.

———. *Tarr*. Edited by Scott W. Klein. Oxford University Press, 2010.

———. *The Art of Being Ruled*. Edited by Reed Way Dasenbrock. Black Sparrow Press, 1989.

———. 'The Code of the Herdman.' *The Little Review* 4, no. 3 (1917).

———. *The Correspondence of Ezra Pound and Wyndham Lewis*. Edited by Timothy Materer. New Directions, 1985.

———. *The Enemy* 1 (1927).

———. *The Enemy* 3 (1929).

———. *The Hitler Cult*. Dent, 1939.

———. *The Letters of Wyndham Lewis*. Edited by W. K. Rose. Menthuen, 1963.
———. 'Cantlelman's Spring-Mate.' In *The Little Review* 4, no. 6 (October 1917) 8–14.
———. *The Human Age: Book 1: Childermass*. Calder Press, 2000.
———. *The Mysterious Mr Bull*. Robert Hale, 1938.
———. *The Wild Body: A Soldier of Humour and Other Stories*. Penguin, 2004.
———. *Time and Western Man*. Edited by Paul Edwards. Black Sparrow Press, 1994.
———. *Tyro* 1, no. 2 (1922).
———. *Wyndham Lewis on Art*. Edited by Michel Fox and C. J. Fox. Thames and Hudson, 1969.
Lewis, Wyndham, ed. *Blast* 1 (1914).
———. *Blast* 2 (1915).
Light, Alison. *Mrs. Woolf and the Servants: The Hidden Heart of Domestic Service*. Fig Tree, 2007.
Linton, E. Lynn. *My Literary Life: Reminiscences of Dickens, Thackeray, George Eliot, Etc.* London: Hodder and Stoughton, 1899.
Locke, John. *An Essay Concerning Human Understanding*. Edited by R. S. Woolhouse. Penguin Books, 2004.
Long, William F. '"It Is Said That Dickens Is Insane": Documenting a Rumor.' *Dickens Quarterly* 38, no. 4 (2021): 452–66.
Lucretius. *On the Nature of the Universe*. Translated by Ronald Melville. Oxford University Press, 1999.
Lukács, Georg. *The Theory of the Novel*. Translated by Anna Bostock. Merlin Press, 1971.
———. *Writer and Critic and Other Essays*. Edited by Arthur D. Kahn. The Universal Library, 1971.
Mackie, J. L. *Ethics: Inventing Right and Wrong*. Penguin, 1977.
Mackin, Timothy. 'Private Worlds, Public Minds: Woolf, Russell, and Photographic Vision.' *Journal of Modern Literature* 33, no. 3 (2010): 112–30.
Maher, Damian. 'Making Good on Henry James: Moral Philosophers on Aesthetic Education's Imperfections.' DPhil diss., University of Oxford, 2024.
Mandel, David R., Denis J. Hilton, and Patrizia Catellani, eds. *The Psychology of Counterfactual Thinking*. Routledge, 2014.
Mann, Thomas. *Reflections of a Non-Political Man*. Translated by Walter D. Morris. Ungar, 1987.
Markovits, Stefanie. 'George Eliot's Problem with Action.' *Studies in English Literature, 1500–1900* 41, no. 4 (2001): 785–803.
Marx, Karl. *Capital: A Critique of Political Economy*. Translated by Ben Fowkes. Penguin Books, 1976.
Marx, Karl, and Friedrich Engels. *Collected Works*. 50 vols. Lawrence and Wishart, 1975–2000.
Mazzoni, Guido. *Theory of the Novel*. Translated by Zakiya Hanafi. Harvard University Press, 2017.
McGinn, Colin. *Mindsight: Image, Dream, Meaning*. Harvard University Press, 2004.
———. *The Subjective View: Secondary Qualities and Indexical Thoughts*. Clarendon Press, 1983.
Mengham, Rod. 'From Georges Sorel to *Blast*.' In *The Violent Muse: Violence and the Artistic Imagination in Europe, 1910–1939*, edited by Jana Howlett and Rod Mengham. Manchester University Press, 1994.
Meyers, Jeffrey. *Remembering Iris Murdoch: Letters and Interviews*. Palgrave Macmillan, 2013.

Mill, J. S. *Collected Works*. Edited by J. M Robson et al. 33 vols. University of Toronto Press, 1963–91.
———. *Utilitarianism*. Edited by Roger Crisp. Oxford University Press, 1998.
Miller, Andrew H. *On Not Being Someone Else: Tales of Our Unled Lives*. Harvard University Press, 2020.
Miller, D. A. *Jane Austen, or, the Secret of Style*. Princeton University Press, 2003.
———. *The Novel and the Police*. University of California Press, 1988.
Miller, Eric Randolph. 'Is Literature Self-Referential?' *Philosophy and Literature* 20, no. 2 (1996): 475–86.
Miller, J. Hillis. *Literature as Conduct: Speech Acts in Henry James*. Fordham University Press, 2005.
Moi, Toril. *Revolution of the Ordinary: Literary Studies After Wittgenstein, Austin, and Cavell*. University of Chicago Press, 2017.
Monk, Ray. *Ludwig Wittgenstein: The Duty of Genius*. Vintage, 1991.
Montaigne, Michel de. *An Apology for Raymond Sebond*. Translated by M. A. Screech. Penguin, 1993.
Moore, Gene M. 'Slavery and Racism in Joseph Conrad's Eastern World.' *Journal of Modern Literature* 30, no. 4 (2007): 20–38.
Moser, Thomas C. *Joseph Conrad: Achievement and Decline*. Archon Books, 1966.
Mullan, John. *The Artful Dickens: The Tricks and Ploys of the Great Novelist*. Bloomsbury, 2020.
Murdoch, Iris. *A Fairly Honourable Defeat*. Vintage, 2001 [1970].
———. *A Severed Head*. Vintage, 2001 [1961].
———. *A Word Child*. Vintage, 2002 [1975].
———. *An Accidental Man*. Vintage, 2003 [1971].
———. *An Unofficial Rose*. Vintage, 2008 [1962].
———. *Bruno's Dream*. Chatto and Windus, 1969.
———. *Henry and Cato*. Open Road, 1976.
———. *Existentialists and Mystics: Writings on Philosophy and Literature*. Edited by Peter J. Conradi. Chatto and Windus, 1999 [1997].
———. *Flight from the Enchanter*. Vintage, 2000 [1956].
———. *Living on Paper: Letters from Iris Murdoch, 1934–1995*. Edited by Avril Horner and Anne Rowe. Chatto and Windus, 2015.
———. *Message to the Planet*. Vintage, 2000 [1989].
———. *Metaphysics as a Guide to Morals*. Vintage, 1992.
———. *Sartre: Romantic Rationalist*. Vintage, 1999 [1953].
———. *The Black Prince*. Vintage, 2013 [1973].
———. *The Book and the Brotherhood*. Vintage, 2003 [1987].
———. *The Nice and the Good*. Vintage, 2000 [1968].
———. *The Philosopher's Pupil*. Vintage, 2000 [1983].
———. *The Sacred and Profane Love Machine*. Vintage, 2003 [1974].
———. *The Sandcastle*. Vintage, 2003 [1957].
———. *The Sea, The Sea*. Vintage, 1999 [1978].
———. *The Time of the Angels*. Vintage, 2002 [1966].

———. *The Unicorn*. Vintage, 2000 [1963].
———. *Under the Net*. Vintage, 2002 [1954].
Murphy, Ruth. '"Let Me Look Again": The Moral Philosophy and Literature Debate at 40.' *New Literary History* 55, no. 1 (2024): 21–46.
Nagel, Thomas. *Mortal Questions*. Cambridge University Press, 1979.
———. *The View from Nowhere*. Oxford University Press, 1986.
Najder, Zdzisław. *Joseph Conrad: A Chronicle*. Rutgers University Press, 1984.
Newman, John Henry. 'The Danger of Accomplishments (Sermon 30).' In *Parochial and Plain Sermons*. Vol. 2, Longman, Green and Co., 1908.
Newsom, Robert. *A Likely Story: Probability and Play in Fiction*. Rutgers University Press, 1988.
Newton, Adam Zachary. *Narrative Ethics*. Harvard University Press, 1995.
Nietzsche, Friedrich. *On the Genealogy of Morality*. Edited by Keith Ansell-Pearson. Cambridge University Press, 1994.
———. *The Anti-Christ, Ecce Homo, Twilight of the Idols and Other Writings*. Translated by Judith Norman. Edited by Aaron Ridley and Judith Norman. Cambridge University Press, 2005.
———. *The Birth of Tragedy and Other Writings*. Translated by Ronald Speirs. Edited by Raymond Geuss and Ronald Speirs. Cambridge University Press, 1999.
———. *Twilight of the Idols and the Anti-Christ*. Translated by R. J. Hollingdale. Penguin, 1990.
———. *Twilight of the Idols, or, How to Philosophize with a Hammer*. Edited by Duncan Large. Oxford University Press, 1998.
———. *Will to Power*. Edited by R. J. Hollingdale and Walter Kaufmann. Vintage Books, 1968.
———.*The Gay Science: With a Prelude in German Rhymes and an Appendix of Songs*. Translated by Josefine Nauckhoff and Adrian Del Caro. Edited by Bernard Williams. Cambridge University Press, 2001.
North, Michael. *Machine-Age Comedy*. Oxford University Press, 2009.
Novalis. *Philosophical Writings*. Edited and Translated by Margaret Mahony Stoljar. State University of New York Press, 1997.
Nussbaum, Martha. *Cultivating Humanity: A Classical Defense of Reform in Liberal Education*. Harvard University Press, 2003.
———. 'Love and Vision: Iris Murdoch on Eros and the Individual.' In *Iris Murdoch and the Search for Human Goodness*, edited by W. Schweiker and M. Antonaccio. University of Chicago Press, 1996.
———. *Love's Knowledge: Essays on Philosophy and Literature*. Oxford University Press, 1990.
———. *Not for Profit: Why Democracy Needs the Humanities*. Princeton University Press, 2010.
———. 'Objectification.' *Philosophy & Public Affairs* 24, no. 4 (1995): 249–91.
———. *Poetic Justice: The Literary Imagination and Public Life*. Beacon Press, 1997.
———. *Political Emotions: Why Love Matters for Justice*. Belknap Press, 2013.
———. *The Fragility of Goodness: Luck and Ethics in Greek Tragedy and Philosophy*. Cambridge University Press, 2001.
O'Hara, Kieron. *Joseph Conrad Today*. Societas, 2007.
Ogden, C. K. *Bentham's Theory of Fictions*. Kegan Paul, Trench, Trübner and Co., 1932.

Ong, Yi-Ping. *The Art of Being: Poetics of the Novel and Existentialist Philosophy*. Harvard University Press, 2018.

Ophir, Ella Zohar. 'Toward a Pitiless Fiction: Abstraction, Comedy, and Modernist Antihumanism.' *Modern Fiction Studies* 52, no. 1 (2006): 92–120.

Ortega y Gasset, José. *The Dehumanization of Art; and Other Essays on Art, Culture and Literature*. Translated by Helene Weyl. Princeton University Press, 1968.

Orwell, George. *Essays*. Penguin, 1971.

Palmer, Frank. *Literature and Moral Understanding: A Philosophical Essay on Ethics, Aesthetics, Education, and Culture*. Clarendon Press, 1992.

Parker, David. *Ethics, Theory, and the Novel*. Cambridge University Press, 1994.

Pater, Walter. *Appreciations: With an Essay on Style*. London: Macmillan, 1895.

Peirce, Charles S. *The Essential Peirce: Selected Philosophical Writings*. Edited by Nathan Houser and Christian J. W. Kloesel. Indiana University Press, 1992.

Peppis, Paul. 'Anti-Individualism and the Fictions of National Character in Wyndham Lewis's Tarr.' *Twentieth Century Literature* 40, no. 2 (1994): 226–55.

Perlowski, Jan. 'On Conrad and Kipling.' Translated by Halina Carroll-Najder. In *Under Familial Eyes*, edited by Zdzislaw Najder. Cambridge University Press, 1983.

Phelan, James. *Living to Tell About It: A Rhetoric and Ethics of Character Narration*. Cornell University Press, 2005.

Phillips, Adam. *Missing Out: In Praise of the Unlived Life*. Hamish Hamilton, 2012.

Pinion, F. B., ed. *A George Eliot Miscellany: A Supplement to Her Novels*. Macmillan Press, 1982.

Pippin, Robert B. *Henry James and Modern Moral Life*. Cambridge University Press, 2000.

Plato. *Complete Works*. Edited by John M. Cooper and D. S. Hutchinson. Hackett, 1997.

———. *Euthyphro*. Translated by G. M. A. Grube. In *Five Dialogues: Euthyphro, Apology, Crito, Meno, Phaedo*. Hackett, 2009.

Posner, Richard A. 'Against Ethical Criticism.' *Philosophy and Literature* 21, no. 1 (1997): 1–27.

———. 'Against Ethical Criticism, Part 2.' *Philosophy and Literature*. 22, no. 2 (1998): 394–412.

Pritchard, Duncan. 'Moral and Epistemic Luck.' *Metaphilosophy* 37, no. 1 (2006): 1–25.

Proust, Marcel. 'On Reading.' In *On Reading Ruskin*. Yale University Press, 1987.

Quigley, Megan. *Modernist Fiction and Vagueness: Philosophy, Form, and Language*. Cambridge University Press, 2015.

———. 'Reading Virginia Woolf Logically: Resolute Approaches to the Voyage Out and Wittgenstein's Tractatus.' *Poetics Today* 41, no. 1 (2020): 101–16.

Radford, Colin. 'Tears and Fiction.' *Philosophy* 52, no. 200 (1977): 208–13.

Radford, Colin, and Michael Weston. 'How Can We Be Moved by the Fate of Anna Karenina?' *Aristotelian Society* 49, no. 1 (1975): 67–93.

Raz, Joseph. *The Practice of Value*. Edited by R. Jay Wallace. Clarendon Press, 2003.

Rescher, Nicholas. 'Moral Luck.' In *Moral Luck*, edited by Daniel Statman. SUNY Press, 1993.

Richards, I. A. *Poetry and Science*. Norton, 1926.

———. *Principles of Literary Criticism*. Routledge, 2001.

Rorty, Amelie Oksenberg. 'User-Friendly Self-Deception.' *Philosophy* 69, no. 268 (1994): 211–28.

Rorty, Richard. *Contingency Irony and Solidarity*. Cambridge University Press, 1989.

———. 'Reply to J. B. Schneewind.' In *The Philosophy of Richard Rorty*, edited by Randall E. Auxier and Lewis Edwin Hahn. Open Court, 2010.

Rosenbaum, S. P. 'The Philosophical Realism of Virginia Woolf.' In *English Literature and British Philosophy*, edited by S. P. Rosenbaum. University of Chicago Press, 1971.

Rosenthal, Jesse. *Good Form: The Ethical Experience of the Victorian Novel*. Princeton University Press, 2017.

Rousseau, Jean-Jacques. *Émile*. Translated by Allan Bloom. Penguin, 1991.

———. *Politics and the Arts: Letter to M. D'Alembert on the Theatre*. Translated by Allan Bloom. Cornell University Press, 1968.

———. *The Discourses and Other Early Political Writings*. Edited by Victor Gourevitch. Cambridge University Press, 1997.

Rowe, M. W. 'Lamarque and Olsen on Literature and Truth.' *Philosophical Quarterly* 47, no. 188 (1997): 322–41.

Rudd, Anthony. *Self, Value, and Narrative: A Kierkegaardian Approach*. Oxford University Press, 2012.

Ruskin, John. *Modern Painters*. E. P. Dutton, 1906.

———. *The Works of John Ruskin*. 39 vols. George Allen, 1909.

Russell, Bertrand. *An Inquiry into Meaning and Truth: The William James Lectures for 1940, Delivered at Harvard University*. Penguin, 1962.

———. *Sceptical Essays*. Routledge, 2004.

Russell, David. *Tact: Aesthetic Liberalism and the Essay Form in Nineteenth-Century Britain*. Princeton University Press, 2017.

Ryle, Gilbert. *The Concept of Mind*. Penguin, 1990 [1949].

Saint-Beuve, C. A. *Les Cahiers de Saint-Beuve*. Paris: Alphonse Lemerre, 1876.

Sandel, Michael J. *The Tyranny of Merit: What's Become of the Common Good?* Penguin, 2020.

Sartre, Jean-Paul. *Literary Essays*. Translated by Annette Michelson. Philosophical Library, 1957.

———. *Nausea*. Edited by Robert Baldick. Penguin, 1964.

———. *The Imaginary: A Phenomenological Psychology of the Imagination*. Edited by Arlette Elkaim-Sartre. Routledge, 2004.

Schelling, Friedrich Wilhelm Joseph von. *The Philosophy of Art*. Edited and Translated by Douglas W. Stott. University of Minnesota Press, 1989.

Schlegel, Friedrich. *Philosophical Fragments*. Translated by Peter Firchow. Minnesota University Press, 1991.

Schmitt, Carl. *Aufzeichnungen Der Jahre 1947–1951*. Edited by Eberhard Freiherr von Medem. Duncker and Humbolt, 1991.

———. *Political Romanticism*. Translated by Guy Oakes. Transaction Publishers, 2011.

———. *Political Theology: Four Chapters on the Concept of Sovereignty*. Translated by George Schwab. University of Chicago Press, 2005.

———. *The Concept of the Political*. Translated by George Schwab. University of Chicago Press, 1996.

Schnauder, Ludwig. *Free Will and Determinism in Joseph Conrad's Major Novels*. Rodopi, 2009.

Scruton, Roger. *Art and Imagination: A Study in the Philosophy of Mind*. Methuen, 1974.

Searle, John R. *Expression and Meaning: Studies in the Theory of Speech Acts*. Cambridge University Press, 1979.

———. *The Construction of Social Reality*. Penguin, 1995.

Sellars, Wilfrid. *Empiricism and the Philosophy of Mind*. Edited by Robert Brandom. Harvard University Press, 1997.

Shakespeare, William. *Hamlet*. Edited by T. J. B. Spencer. Penguin Books, 2015.

Shanafelt, Carrie. 'Jeremy Bentham and the Pleasures of Fiction.' *Revue d'études benthamiennes* 20, no. 20 (2021).

Sheehan, Paul. *Modernism, Narrative and Humanism*. Cambridge University Press, 2002.

Sherry, Norman. *Conrad's Eastern World*. Cambridge University Press, 1966.

Sherry, Vincent B. 'An Anatomy of Folly: Wyndham Lewis, the Body Politic, and Comedy.' *Modernism/Modernity* 4, no. 2 (1997): 121–38.

Sidgwick, Henry. *The Methods of Ethics*. 7th ed. Hackett, 1981.

Siebers, Tobin. *Morals & Stories*. Columbia University Press, 1992.

———. *The Ethics of Criticism*. Cornell University Press, 1988.

Simmons, Allan. *Joseph Conrad*. Palgrave, 2006.

Small, Helen. *The Value of the Humanities*. Oxford University Press, 2013.

Smith, Adam. *The Theory of Moral Sentiments*. Edited by Knud Haakonssen. Cambridge University Press, 2002.

Smith, Zadie. 'Fascinated to Presume: In Defence of Fiction.' In *Dead and Alive: Essays*. Penguin, 2025.

Spencer, Herbert. *The Principles of Biology*. Williams and Norgate, 1864.

Spinoza, Benedictus de. *Spinoza's Ethics*. Edited by Clare Carlisle. Princeton University Press, 2020.

Srinivasan, Amia. 'The Politics of Safety.' *Financial Times*, 13 August 2021.

Statman, Daniel. 'Moral and Epistemic Luck.' *Ratio* 4, no. 2 (1991): 146–56.

Steinberg, Erwin R. 'G. E. Moore's Table and Chair in *To the Lighthouse*.' *Journal of Modern Literature* 15, no. 1 (1988): 161–68.

Stephen, Leslie. *English Thought in the Eighteenth Century*. 2 vols. London: Smith, Elder and Co., 1876.

Stephen, Leslie, ed. *Dictionary of National Biography*. Oxford University Press, 1973.

Stevens, Wallace. *Opus Posthumous*. Edited by S. F. Morse. Faber and Faber, 1959.

Stevenson, Robert Louis. 'A Humble Remonstrance.' *Longman's Magazine* 5, no. 26 (1884): 139–47.

———. *Essays in the Art of Writing*. Chatto and Windus, 1905.

Stolzenberg, Nomi Maya. 'Bentham's Theory of Fictions. A "Curious Double Language."' *Cardozo Studies in Law and Literature* 11, no. 2 (1999): 223–61.

Stone, Marjorie. 'Dickens, Bentham, and the Fictions of the Law: A Victorian Controversy and Its Consequences.' *Victorian Studies* 29, no. 1 (1985): 125–54.

Strawson, Galen. 'Against Narrativity.' *Ratio* 17, no. 4 (2004): 428–52.

Strawson, Peter. *Freedom and Resentment, and Other Essays*. Routledge, 2008.

Sully, James. 'George Eliot's Art.' *Mind* 6, no. 23 (1881): 378–94.

Sussman, Matthew. *Stylistic Virtue and Victorian Fiction: Form, Ethics, and the Novel*. Cambridge University Press, 2021.

Taine, Hippolyte. *A History of English Literature*. Translated by H. Van Laun. 4 vols. Chatto and Windus, 1907.
Takashima, Kazuya. 'Bentham's Theory of Language: Its Structure, Originality, and Significance to His Political Radicalism.' *Revue d'études benthamiennes* 16, no. 16 (2019).
Tate, Gregory. *The Poet's Mind: The Psychology of Victorian Poetry 1830–1870*. Oxford University Press, 2012.
Taylor, Charles. *Philosophy and the Human Sciences: Philosophical Papers 2*. Cambridge University Press, 1985.
Thackeray, William Makepeace. *The Letters and Private Papers of William Makepeace Thackeray*. Edited by Gordon N. Ray. 4 vols. Oxford University Press, 1945.
Tredy, Denis, Annick Dupperay, and Adrian Harding. *Henry James and the Poetics of Duplicity*. Cambridge Scholars Publishing, 2013.
Trilling, Lionel. 'Manners, Morals, and the Novel.' *Kenyon Review* 10, no. 1 (1948): 11–27.
Tsutsui, Mizuki. 'The Morality of Fiction-Making in *Our Mutual Friend*.' *Dickens Quarterly* 39, no. 2 (2022): 159–75.
Vaihinger, Hans. *The Philosophy of 'As If': A System of the Theoretical, Practical and Religious Fictions of Mankind*. Translated by C. K. Ogden. Harcourt, Brace and Co., 1924.
Waddell, Nathan. 'Lewis and Fascism.' In *The Cambridge Companion to Wyndham Lewis*, edited by Tyrus Miller. Cambridge University Press, 2015.
Walker, Margaret Urban. 'Moral Luck and the Virtues of Impure Agency.' *Metaphilosophy* 22, no. 1–2 (1991): 14–27.
Walton, Kendall L. 'Fearing Fictions.' *Journal of Philosophy* 75, no. 1 (1978): 5–27.
———. 'How Remote Are Fictional Worlds from the Real World?' *Journal of Aesthetics and Art Criticism* 37, no. 1 (1978): 11.
———. *Mimesis as Make-Believe: On the Foundations of the Representational Arts*. Harvard University Press, 1990.
Watt, Ian. *Conrad in the Nineteenth Century*. Chatto and Windus, 1980.
———. *Essays on Conrad*. Edited by Frank Kermode. Cambridge University Press, 2009.
White, Andrea. *Joseph Conrad and the Adventure Tradition: Constructing and Deconstructing the Imperial Subject*. Cambridge University Press, 1993.
Wiggins, David. *Needs, Values, Truth: Essays in the Philosophy of Value*. Blackwell, 1987.
Wilde, Oscar. *Complete Works of Oscar Wilde*. Harper Collins, 1999.
———. *Essays and Lectures*. Methuen, 1908.
Williams, Bernard. *Ethics and the Limits of Philosophy*. Harvard University Press, 1985.
———. *Moral Luck: Philosophical Papers, 1973–1980*. Cambridge University Press, 1981.
———. *Problems of the Self: Philosophical Papers, 1956–1972*. Cambridge University Press, 1973.
———. *Shame and Necessity*. University of California Press, 1993.
———. 'The Human Prejudice.' In *Philosophy as a Humanistic Discipline*. Cambridge University Press, 2000.
———. *Truth and Truthfulness: An Essay in Genealogy*. Princeton University Press, 2002.
Williams, Carolyn. 'Melodrama and the Realist Novel.' In *The Cambridge Companion to English Melodrama*, edited by Carolyn Williams. Cambridge University Press, 2018.

Williams, Daniel. *The Art of Uncertainty: Probable Realism and the Victorian Novel*. Cambridge University Press, 2024.

Williams, Michael. *Unnatural Doubts: Epistemological Realism and the Basis of Scepticism*. Princeton University Press, 1996.

Wilson, Catherine. 'Literature and Knowledge.' *Philosophy* 58, no. 226 (1983): 489–96.

Wittgenstein, Ludwig. *Culture and Value*. Translated by Peter Winch. Edited by G. H. von Wright and Heikki Nyman. University of Chicago Press, 1980.

———. *Last Writings on the Philosophy of Psychology*. Translated by C. G. Luckhardt and Maximilian A. E. Aue. Edited by G. H. von Wright and Heikki Nyman. 2 vols. Blackwell, 1982–92.

———. *Notebooks 1914–16*. Translated by G. E. M. Anscombe. Edited by G. H. von Wright and G. E. M. Anscombe. Harper, 1961.

———. *On Certainty*. Edited by G. E. M. Anscombe and G. H. von Wright. Harper Collins, 1972.

———. *Philosophical Investigations*. Edited by G. E. M. Blackwell, 1953.

———. *Remarks on the Philosophy of Psychology*. Translated by G. E. M. Anscombe. Edited by G. E. M. Anscombe and G. H. von Wright. 2 vols. University of Chicago Press, 1980.

———. *Tractatus Logico-Philosophicus*. Translated by D. F. Pears and B. F. McGuinness. Routledge, 2001.

Wollaeger, Mark A. *Joseph Conrad and the Fictions of Skepticism*. Stanford University Press, 1990.

Wood, James. *The Irresponsible Self: On Laughter and the Novel*. Pimlico, 2005.

Wood, Joanne A. 'Lighthouse Bodies: The Neutral Monism of Virginia Woolf and Bertrand Russell.' *Journal of the History of Ideas* 55, no. 3 (1994): 483–502.

Wood, Michael. 'What Henry Knew.' In *Literature and the Taste of Knowledge*. Cambridge University Press, 2005.

Woolf, Virginia. *A Haunted House: The Complete Shorter Fiction*. Vintage, 2003.

———. *Collected Essays*. Edited by Andrew McNeillie. 6 vols. Hogarth Press, 1988.

———. *Diary of Virginia Woolf*, Vol. 2, *1920–1924*. Edited by Anne Olivier Bell and Andrew McNeillie. Penguin, 1981.

———. *Diary of Virginia Woolf*, Vol. 3, *1925–1930*. Edited by Anne Olivier Bell and Andrew McNeillie. Penguin, 1982.

———. *Jacob's Room*. Edited by Sue Roe. Penguin, 1992.

———. *Letters of Virginia Woolf*, Vol. 2, *1912–1922*. Hogarth, 1976.

———. *Letters of Virginia Woolf*, Vol. 3, *1923–1928*. Hogarth, 1977.

———. *Moments of Being*. Edited by Jeanne Schulkind and Hermione Lee. Pimlico, 2002.

———. *Mrs Dalloway*. Edited by Elaine Showalter and Stella McNichol. Penguin, 1992.

———. *Night and Day*. Vintage, 2000.

———. *Orlando: A Biography*. Edited by Brenda Lyons and Sandra M. Gilbert. Penguin, 1993.

———. Reading Notebooks. Berg Collection. New York Public Library.

———. *The Diary of Virginia Woolf. Volume 1: 1915–1919*. Edited by Anne Olivier Bell and Matthew Holliday. Granta Publications, 2023.

———. *The Waves*. Edited by Kate Flint. Penguin, 1992.

———. *To the Lighthouse*. Edited by Stella McNichol and Hermione Lee. Penguin, 1992.

Wordsworth, William. *The Poetical Works of William Wordsworth*. Edited by William Angus Knight. 8 vols. Macmillan, 1896.
Yanal, Robert J. *Paradoxes of Emotion and Fiction*. Pennsylvania State University Press, 1999.
Younge, Gary. *Pigeonholed: Creative Freedom as an Act of Resistance*. Faber, 2025.
Yousef, Nancy. *The Aesthetic Commonplace: Wordsworth, Eliot, Wittgenstein, and the Language of Every Day*. Oxford University Press, 2022.
Zhang, Dora. *Strange Likeness: Description and the Modernist Novel*. University of Chicago Press, 2020.
Zimmerman, Michael. 'Luck and Moral Responsibility.' *Ethics* 97, no. 2 (1987): 374–86.
Zumhagen-Yekplé, Karen. *A Different Order of Difficulty: Literature After Wittgenstein*. University of Chicago Press, 2020.

INDEX

A NOTE ON THE TYPE

This book has been composed in Arno, an Old-style serif typeface in the classic Venetian tradition, designed by Robert Slimbach at Adobe.